Through the Looking Glass

Observations in the Early Childhood Classroom

D0691015

Through the Looking Glass

Observations in the Early Childhood Classroom

THIRD EDITION

SHERYL NICOLSON
Saddleback College

SUSAN G. SHIPSTEAD
California State University, Fullerton

Upper Saddle River, New Jersey
Columbus, Ohio

Library of Congress Cataloging-in-Publication Data

Nicolson, Sheryl.
    Through the looking glass : observations in the early childhood classroom / Sheryl
Nicolson, Susan G. Shipstead.—3rd ed.
      p. cm.
    Includes bibliographical references and index.
    ISBN 0-13-042080-8
    1. Observation (Educational method) 2. Early childhood education. 3. Child
development. I. Shipstead, Susan G. II. Title.
    LB1027.28.N53 2002
372.21—dc21

                    2001032864

Vice President and Publisher: Jeffery W. Johnston
Executive Editor: Ann Castel Davis
Associate Editor: Christina M. Kalisch
Editorial Assistant: Keli Gemrich
Production Editor: Linda Hillis Bayma
Production Coordination: Carlisle Publishers Services
Photo Coordinator: Carol Sykes
Design Coordinator: Diane C. Lorenzo
Cover Designer: Jason Moore
Cover Photo: Susan G. Shipstead
Production Manager: Laura Messerly
Director of Marketing: Kevin Flanagan
Marketing Manager: Amy June
Marketing Services Coordinator: Barbara Koontz

This book was set in Palatino by Carlisle Communications, Ltd. It was printed and bound by Maple Vail.
The cover was printed by Phoenix Color Corp.

Photo Credits: Brian Cummings, p. 24; Sheryl Nicolson, pp. 80, 134; Susan Shipstead, pp. 2, 11, 16, 21, 27,
32, 40, 42, 49, 53, 73, 76, 79, 87, 99, 105, 112, 120, 122, 128, 140, 148, 152, 158, 162, 168, 171, 173, 178, 183, 186,
188, 200, 206, 214, 222, 228, 234, 242, 244, 254, 262, 271, 278, 285, 287, 298, 304, 307, 323, 328, 331, 346, 351,
357, 364, 369.

Pearson Education Ltd., *London*
Pearson Education Australia Pty. Limited, *Sydney*
Pearson Education Singapore Pte. Ltd.
Pearson Education North Asia Ltd., *Hong Kong*
Pearson Education Canada, Ltd., *Toronto*
Pearson Educación de Mexico, S.A. de C.V.
Pearson Education–Japan, *Tokyo*
Pearson Education Malaysia Pte. Ltd.
Pearson Education, *Upper Saddle River, New Jersey*

10 9 8 7 6 5 4 3 2 1
ISBN 0-13-042080-8

For my husband Norm, whose gentle love and constant support made this book and so much more possible. For my Mom and Dad, each with special gifts that I've woven into my life. And for all children, especially those who are close to me—Christopher, Ryan, and Garrett. May your lives be enriched by teachers who see clearly through the looking glass.

—S.N.

In my life I am blessed with a great love, Patrick;
Two treasured children, Matthew and Maggie;
And the rich memories of my parents.
To you five, I dedicate this work.

—S. G. S.

Preface

In the fall of 1988, we taught a course on observation in the early childhood classroom, and therein we sowed the seeds of the first edition of *Through the Looking Glass.* The third edition you hold in your hands is the product of our continued commitment to write a book on observation that unites solid methodological instruction with a broad understanding of children's development. We have found that learning *how* to observe while also paying close attention to *what* to observe encourages educational practitioners to use their skills to full potential. This book maintains a close relationship between observing, understanding what one observes, and improving the educational curriculum and environment.

NEW TO THIS EDITION

Because our goal in *Through the Looking Glass* is to integrate observation and child development within a professional context, we have included several helpful features in the text. As the material we wanted to include in Chapter 1 grew, we decided to develop it into two chapters for more manageable digestion. We are excited about the information about professional development in Chapter 1, including the reader's responsibilities and an introduction to professional organizations, developmentally appropriate practice, and ethical conduct in early childhood education. The second chapter turns to the more nuts-and-bolts issues of finding the time to observe, learning the basics of observation, and minimizing subjectivity. All our chapters now end with two reflections: one personal and one ethical. We hope these reflections will help our readers integrate information into their personal storehouses of knowledge and connect their daily work with our professional values as early childhood educators. Chapters 3 and 4, describing highlights of development during the preschool and primary grade years, have been updated and serve to establish a common ground of information for both knowledgeable and novice readers in the field of child development. Our "Growth Indicators" of child development from these two chapters are concrete guides to *what* to observe and are reprinted in Appendix A for easy access. In each chapter presenting an observational method, we offer two detailed examples, one preschool and one primary grade, to model how educators effectively study issues in classrooms, interpret the data, and initiate follow-through plans. Brief vignettes at the beginning of each chapter ask the reader to ponder a question or problem that anticipates the chapter's content. "Practice Activities" and "Off on Your Own" provide abundant opportunities to add to the reader's expertise in the observational process, and our new "Quick Reviews" at the ends of most chapters serve to underscore the major points.

On completion of the original manuscript, we flipped a coin to determine the first author's name. We hope our readers remember that the order was set by chance and is a fair reflection of the teamwork that produced *Through the Looking Glass.*

Special Acknowledgments

This work builds on many years of memorable and invaluable experiences in the field of early childhood education. From my beginning college days and continuing into the present, my life has been touched by numerous caring and committed professionals. I especially want to thank the Cooperative Urban Teacher Education Program sponsored by the University of Missouri at Kansas City for teaching me to recognize, respect, and appreciate varied cultural perspectives; Janece Kline for facilitating my transition from elementary to preschool teaching; Jonathan Knaupp at Arizona State University for excellent mentoring; Nancy Claxton, Pat Gardner, and Louise Dean-Wheelock for their professional leadership, wise counsel, and treasured friendship; Susan Shipstead, co-author, for her incredible ability to always be her best; and the many children and college students I have had the privilege of working with—they have been my true teachers!

—*Sheryl Nicolson*

Many of my contributions to *Through the Looking Glass* have direct threads running to significant people from my past. I send global appreciation to the many children, teachers, directors, and students with whom I have had the good fortune to work. I am indebted to Courtney Cazden for a masterful class on observation at Harvard. My work at High/Scope Educational Research Foundation was enhanced by experiences with Dave Weikart, Clay Shouse, Carole Thomson, Joanna Phinney, Mary Hohmann, Linda Rogers, and Bernie Banet; I salute one and all. I was forever changed by the exemplary instruction, guidance, and fine human nature of my Stanford heroes, John Flavell and Dick Snow; I thank John and remember Dick with warmth in my heart. My final thanks go to Judy Ramirez and Diana Guerin whose professional and wise leadership has graced my 15 years at CSUF in the Child and Adolescent Studies department.

Each edition of this book has been marked by life changes as time inexorably moves forward. My children were still in elementary school when Sherry and I began the first edition, but now my son, who has had his eyes to the sky since he was 2 years old, has graduated from the United States Air Force Academy and is living his dream in pilot school. My daughter, who has been a remarkable writer since early childhood, now begins her college years at Harvard, far from her California home. Both have stories sprinkled throughout these pages, and until they are parents, I suspect they will not comprehend the joy I feel in being their mother.

—*Susan G. Shipstead*

COLLECTIVE ACKNOWLEDGMENTS

We wish to thank our students, friends, and colleagues who offered valuable suggestions for our third edition, especially the students in observation classes at Saddleback College and students in child development practicums at California State University, Fullerton. We send our gratitude to the many friends and educators who contributed ideas or welcomed us into their schools and classrooms: Ingrid Andrews, Sheri Bentley, Stephanie Crilly, Pauline Dinger, Heather Eazell, Lucy Groetsch, Zoila Hamidi, Jim Lee, Jerri Tait, Georgie Tiernan, and Star Walkingstick. The writing of this revision was assisted by the helpful research done by Veronica Fuhs and Carole Raylin.

The library staffs at Saddleback College and California State University, Fullerton offered time-saving help, and they, too, have our thanks.

Revision of the manuscript for the third edition is only half of the tremendous task of creating a new book. We would like to express our appreciation to those who carried out the publishing half, the fine staff at Merrill. In particular we thank Ann Davis, Editor; Christina Kalisch, Associate Editor; Linda Bayma, Production Editor; Carol Sykes, Photo Editor; and Kevin Flanagan, Marketing Manager. Our book moved smoothly through production thanks to Debbie Stone, Copy Editor, and Lea Baranowski at Carlisle Publishers Services.

The reviewers of our third edition offered important suggestions, insights, and information. Their various regional perspectives, backgrounds, and experiences were beneficial to us as we worked to make revisions that meet the needs of all observers. Your contributions were most helpful, and we thank you! Our reviewers included Phyllis Cuevas, McNeese State University; Berta Harris, San Diego City College; Lisa Monroe, University of Oklahoma; and Jillian Oxtoby, Borough of Manhattan Community College.

Discover the Companion Website Accompanying This Book

THE PRENTICE HALL COMPANION WEBSITE:
A VIRTUAL LEARNING ENVIRONMENT

Technology is a constantly growing and changing aspect of our field that is creating a need for content and resources. To address this emerging need, Prentice Hall has developed an online learning environment for students and professors alike—Companion Websites—to support our textbooks.

In creating a Companion Website, our goal is to build on and enhance what the textbook already offers. For this reason, the content for each user-friendly website is organized by topic and provides the professor and student with a variety of meaningful resources. Common features of a Companion Website include:

For the Professor—

Every Companion Website integrates **Syllabus Manager**™, an online syllabus creation and management utility.

- **Syllabus Manager**™ provides you, the instructor, with an easy, step-by-step process to create and revise syllabi, with direct links into the Companion Website and other online content without having to learn HTML.

- Students may log on to your syllabus during any study session. All they need to know is the web address for the Companion Website and the password you've assigned to your syllabus.

- After you have created a syllabus using **Syllabus Manager**™, students may enter the syllabus for their course section from any point in the Companion Website.

- Clicking on a date, the student is shown the list of activities for the assignment. The activities for each assignment are linked directly to actual content, saving time for students.

- Adding assignments consists of clicking on the desired due date, then filling in the details of the assignment—name of the assignment, instructions, and whether it is a one-time or repeating assignment.

- In addition, links to other activities can be created easily. If the activity is online, a URL can be entered in the space provided, and it will be linked automatically in the final syllabus.
- Your completed syllabus is hosted on our servers, allowing convenient updates from any computer on the Internet. Changes you make to your syllabus are immediately available to your students at their next logon.

For the Student—

- **Topic Overviews**—outline key concepts in topic areas
- **Web Links**—general websites related to topic areas as well as associations and professional organizations
- **Read About It**—timely articles that enable you to become more aware of important issues in early childhood education
- **Learn by Doing**—put concepts into action, participate in activities, complete lesson plans, examine strategies, and more
- **For Teachers**—access information that you will need to know as an in-service teacher, including information on materials, activities, lessons, curriculum, and state standards
- **Visit a School**—visit a school's website to see concepts, theories, and strategies in action
- **Electronic Bluebook**—send homework or essays directly to your instructor's email with this paperless form
- **Message Board**—serves as a virtual bulletin board to post—or respond to—questions or comments to/from a national audience
- **Chat**—real-time chat with anyone who is using the text anywhere in the country—ideal for discussion and study groups, class projects, etc.

To take advantage of these and other resources, please visit the *Through the Looking Glass: Observations in the Early Childhood Classroom,* Third Edition, Companion Website at

www.prenhall.com/nicolson

Contents

PART I	PREPARING THE LOOKING GLASS	1

Chapter 1   The Educated Observer   2

Ambitions and Organization of This Book   4
Professional Development   6
   Take Charge of Your Education: Active Reading and Active Learning   6
   Learn About Professional Organizations   7
   Developmentally Appropriate Practice   8
   Ethical Conduct in Early Childhood Education   9
The Educated Observer   10
   Commitment to All Children   10
   Reasons for Observing   12
   Authentic Assessment   12
Quick Review   13
Take a Moment to Reflect   14
   Personal Reflection   14
   Ethical Reflection   14

Chapter 2   On the Road to Sound Observations   16

Taking the First Steps   18
   The Teacher's Role in Observation   18
   Observational Topics   20
Moving Down the Path   23
   Guidelines for Observation   23
   Observer Subjectivity   25
Quick Review   29
Take a Moment to Reflect   31
   Personal Reflection   31
   Ethical Reflection   31

Chapter 3   Highlights of Development During the Preschool Years   32

Selected Highlights of Physical Development   34
   Body Growth   34

Brain Development   34
Motor Development   35
Gross Motor Skills   37
Fine Motor Skills   40
Selected Highlights of Cognitive Development   44
Representational Abilities   45
Language   47
Reasoning   50
Social Cognition   51
Classification   53
Seriation   54
Number Development   55
Memory   56
Selected Highlights of Psychosocial Development   58
Expanding Relationships with Adults and Peers   58
Self-Concept   59
Play   61
Fears   62
Aggression   63
Impulse Control   65
Selected Highlights of Creative Development   67
Quick Review   75
Take a Moment to Reflect   75
Personal Reflection   75
Ethical Reflection   75

Chapter 4   **Highlights of Development During the Primary Grades Years   76**

Selected Highlights of Physical Development   78
Body Growth   78
Motor Development   78
Gross Motor Skills   79
Fine Motor Skills   81
Elements Affecting Motor Development   83
Selected Highlights of Cognitive Development   85
Representational Abilities   85
Language   86
Logical Thought   89
Metacognition   91
Classification   92
Number Development   92
Memory   94
Selected Highlights of Psychosocial Development   96
Self-Concept and Self-Esteem   96
Advances in Play   97

Moral Reasoning and Prosocial Behavior   98
Relationships with Peers   101
Managing Stress   103
Selected Highlights of Creative Development   104
Quick Review   109
Take a Moment to Reflect   110
Personal Reflection   110
Ethical Reflection   110

PART II   OBSERVING INDIVIDUAL CHILDREN   111

**Chapter 5   Observing the Development of Individual Children by Using
                  Running Records   112**

Overview of Observing Using Running Records   114
Description   114
Purpose   115
Guidelines for Writing Running Records   115
Integration of Developmental Theory and Observation   122
Preschool Example   122
Primary Grade Example   126
Applications   129
Strengths and Limitations   129
Quick Review   131
Take a Moment to Reflect   132
Personal Reflection   132
Ethical Reflection   133

**Chapter 6   Observing the Development of Individual Children by Using
                  Anecdotal Records   134**

Overview of Observing Using Anecdotal Records   136
Description   136
Purpose   138
Guidelines for Writing Anecdotes   140
Integration of Developmental Theory and Observation   144
Preschool Example   145
Primary Grade Example   147
Anecdotes and Other Forms of Recording   150
Applications   151
Strengths and Limitations   151
Quick Review   155
Take a Moment to Reflect   156
Personal Reflection   156
Ethical Reflection   157

Chapter 7   **Observing the Development of Individual Children by Using Checklists   158**

Overview of Observing Using Checklists   160
  Description   160
  Purpose   161
  Guidelines for Constructing a Checklist   163
Integration of Developmental Theory and Observation   165
  Preschool Example   165
  Primary Grade Example   169
Applications   172
  Strengths and Limitations   172
Quick Review   174
Take a Moment to Reflect   176
  Personal Reflection   176
  Ethical Reflection   176

Chapter 8   **Observing the Development of Individual Children by Using Rating Scales   178**

Overview of Observing Using Rating Scales   180
  Description   180
  Purpose   185
  Guidelines for Constructing Rating Scales   185
Integration of Developmental Theory and Observation   186
  Preschool Example   186
  Primary Grade Example   190
Applications   194
  Strengths and Limitations   194
Quick Review   196
Take a Moment to Reflect   198
  Personal Reflection   198
  Ethical Reflection   198

Chapter 9   **Observing the Development of Individual Children by Using ABC Narrative Event Sampling   200**

Overview of Observing Using ABC Narrative Event Sampling   202
  Sampling   202
  Description   203
  Purpose   205
  Guidelines for ABC Narrative Event Sampling   205
Integration of Developmental Theory and Observation   207
  Preschool Example   207
  Primary Grade Example   211

Applications   216
    Strengths and Limitations   217
Quick Review   218
Take a Moment to Reflect   220
    Personal Reflection   220
    Ethical Reflection   221

Chapter 10   Classroom Portfolios and Parent Conferences   222

Overview of Child Portfolios   224
    Portfolio System Description   225
    Storage Choices for Teachers' Observations   226
    Storage Choices for Children's Work   232
    Guidelines for Designing a Portfolio System   234
Overview of Parent Conferences   235
    Conference Preparation and Content   235
    Getting Started   238
    Supporting Documentation   240
    Guidelines for Parent Conferences   241
    Guidelines for Using Videotapes During Parent Conferences   243
Applications   243
Quick Review   250
Take a Moment to Reflect   252
    Personal Reflection   252
    Ethical Reflection   252

**PART III   OBSERVING CHILDREN, TEACHERS, INTERACTIONS,
              AND ENVIRONMENTS   253**

**Chapter 11   Observing Children and Teachers at Work by Using
              Tally Event Sampling   254**

Overview of Observing Using Tally Event Sampling   256
    Description   256
    Purpose   259
    Recording Time   259
    Guidelines for Constructing Tally Event Sampling Instruments   260
Integration of Classroom Situations and Observation   260
    Preschool Example   260
    Primary Grade Example   270
Applications   273
    Strengths and Limitations   273
Quick Review   275
Take a Moment to Reflect   276

Personal Reflection   276
Ethical Reflection   277

Chapter 12   Observing Children and Teachers at Work by Using Time Sampling   278

Overview of Observing Using Time Sampling   280
Description   280
Purpose   281
Guidelines for Constructing Time Sampling Instruments   281
Integration of Classroom Situations and Observation   286
Preschool Example   286
Primary Grade Example   292
Applications   299
Strengths and Limitations   299
Quick Review   302
Take a Moment to Reflect   303
Personal Reflection   303
Ethical Reflection   303

Chapter 13   Designing Observational Instruments to Use in the Early Childhood Classroom   304

Select an Appropriate Topic, and Formulate an Observational Question   306
Classroom Example   307
Select an Appropriate Method of Observation   308
Classroom Example   308
Research the Topic in Libraries and Classrooms   309
Classroom Example   309
Identify Clear, Distinct Categories   309
Classroom Example   309
Design a Recording Form   310
Classroom Example   311
Pilot Test the Instrument   311
Classroom Example   311
Establish Inter-Rater Reliability   311
Classroom Example   313
Collect Data   315
Classroom Example   315
Analyze and Present the Data   317
Frequencies   317
Classroom Example   317
Percentages   317
Classroom Example   318
Visual Presentations   320
Classroom Example   320
Conclusion   321

Interpret the Data   321
    Classroom Example   321
Formulate Follow-Through Plans   323
    Classroom Example   324
Quick Review   325
Take a Moment to Reflect   326
    Personal Reflection   326
    Ethical Reflection   327

Chapter 14   Selecting Methods to Observe, Plan, and Enrich the Physical Environment   328

Indoor Environments   330
    Room Arrangement   332
    Lighting   339
    Visual Appeal   341
Outdoor Environments   347
    Developmental Benefits   347
    Outdoor Design Factors   348
    Teacher's Role   350
    Outdoor Materials and Equipment Selection   350
Observing the Physical Environment   353
    Classroom Example   354
Quick Review   360
Take a Moment to Reflect   361
    Personal Reflection   361
    Ethical Reflection   361

PART IV   OBSERVING CLEARLY   363

Chapter 15   Through the Looking Glass   364

The Teacher's Commitment to Observation   368
The Benefits of Observation in the Early Childhood Classroom   369
Take a Moment to Reflect   370
    Personal Reflection   370
    Ethical Reflection   371

Appendix A   Growth Indicators   372

Appendix B   Quick Review Answers   376

Glossary   379

References   384

Index   394

I

Preparing the Looking Glass

Chapter 1   The Educated Observer

Chapter 2   On the Road to Sound Observations

Chapter 3   Highlights of Development During the
Preschool Years

Chapter 4   Highlights of Development During the
Primary Grade Years

1 The Educated Observer

Imagine you are an early childhood educator in a preschool classroom. This morning, you are standing outside near the swings. As you turn your head, you catch a glimpse of Annie whisking the red tractor away from Tajima.

- What are your initial thoughts?
- What details do your senses absorb?
- Do you smell the first hints of lunch about to be served, which might have reminded the youngster of a fleeting opportunity to get the treasured toy?
- What do you see the child do?
- What do you hear the child say?
- Did the child have the toy first and simply reclaim it?
- Had the child been wandering around the play yard when she grabbed the toy in an unprovoked act?

Even in an ordinary situation such as this, you may accurately or inaccurately appraise the situation and respond appropriately or inappropriately. Your skills as an observer make a difference in your guidance and education of this young child.

Continuing on this flight of fantasy, consider what you might know about the child and this behavior.

- Is this the first time you have seen this child grab a toy from another, or has this deed been a frequent classroom concern?
- Have you noticed a pattern of preceding events that predictably prompt this act, such as rejection by other children?
- What circumstances or expectations outside of school might have promoted this seizure? For example, is the child dreadfully lonely now that a beloved sibling has gone off to college? Or has grabbing become the child's common strategy to procure a desired object since it's ignored in the home?

Stop for a moment and think about what else you want to know about this child and the episode before you decide how to respond. What major piece of this puzzle is not yet in place? What information is crucial to your thoughtful and appropriate response?

Your understanding of the child's developmental level is essential to the selection of a supportive response. If the child is a 2½-year-old whose energies have advanced her gross motor skills more than her language skills, you would evaluate the event and respond differently than if the child is a 5-year-old with well-developed language skills. One of your jobs as an educator of young children is to understand child development in enough detail that your responses are individually based and ensure future growth.

For those who have studied child development and early childhood programs and who can employ a variety of observational methods, the classroom provides countless opportunities to apply useful information for the benefit of individual children. Such educators enter the field of early childhood education equipped with the ability to plan activities, experiences, and environments that enhance children's growth, and with experience, they can select materials that challenge individual children at opportune moments. They can suggest and organize activities that encourage children to think differently about familiar experiences. They can respond to problem behaviors with flexible strategies. They can view children's similarities and differences with a broad perspective. They can improve their own teaching effectiveness. They can guide children's social growth. The list goes on and on.

Set your sights high. You can be a remarkable teacher if you understand child development within a broad context *and* are able to provide materials and experiences that optimize each child's total development. The keys are knowledge and observation.

AMBITIONS AND ORGANIZATION OF THIS BOOK

Knowledge and observation—this book tackles both. As authors, we are committed to a book on observation that unites solid methodological instruction with a broad understanding of children's development. We have found that learning *how* to observe while also paying close attention to *what* to observe encourages educational practitioners to use their skills to their full potential. This book maintains a close relationship between observing, understanding what one observes, and improving the educational curriculum and environment for each child.

Following an introduction to professional development in this chapter and observational concerns in Chapter 2, the first knowledge key—how children grow and develop—is supported by Chapters 3 and 4. There is a wealth of information to cover, and even in condensed form, two chapters are needed to cover it. Recognize, however, that development is gradual and individual differences abound.

The break between the preschool (Chapter 3) and primary grade (Chapter 4) years is not abrupt; for example, a 4-year-old in preschool may be more advanced in some areas than a 5-year-old in kindergarten. Also realize that *seeing* a child's behavior is not necessarily the same as *understanding* it. An observer might see a child stacking blocks, but unless the observer understands block building within the context of child development, he or she has limited resources to plan appropriate and supportive interactions and activities. Therefore, in order to establish a common ground of information for both knowledgeable and novice readers in the field of child development, Chapters 3 and 4 describe highlights of development during the preschool and primary grade years. As you study what to observe in these two chapters, "Growth Indicators" will summarize the key points and provide specific reminders. When a strong child development foundation is united with a clear awareness of the educational experiences that optimize learning and development, early childhood professionals will be prepared to use to full advantage the observational skills learned from this book.

The second key to becoming a remarkable teacher is learning to observe children, teachers, and programs; *Through the Looking Glass* presents seven observational methods:

1. Running records
2. Anecdotal records
3. Checklists
4. Rating scales
5. ABC narrative event sampling
6. Tally event sampling
7. Time sampling

One chapter is devoted to each of these methods. In addition to explaining how to use the method, each chapter offers two detailed examples, one from preschool and one from the primary grades, to show how educators effectively use the observational method, interpret the data, and initiate follow-through plans. Readers may pause at several points in each chapter to engage in active learning activities, quick reviews, and reflections. These methodology chapters (5, 6, 7, 8, 9, 11, and 12) are arranged to build on the reader's expanding understanding of observation.

The classroom observations of early childhood educators feed directly into their record-keeping and conferencing practices, investigations of unique questions and problems, and evaluations of the classroom environment. Chapter 10 shows how to systematically organize observations in portfolios and efficiently communicate the results through dynamic parent conferences that enhance family–school partnerships. Chapter 13 describes and illustrates the process for constructing instruments used to answer specific classroom questions; the process is illustrated through a classroom example in which teachers observe children's separations from their parents and use the data to plan supportive strategies. And finally, Chapter 14 examines the characteristics of indoor and outdoor environments and suggests appropriate observational choices. Whether designing a new facility, setting up a classroom for the first time, or reorganizing throughout the year, this chapter shows how information gleaned from environmental observations can help teachers provide optimal learning conditions for children.

There you have the plan of *Through the Looking Glass:* sequentially arranged chapters committed to your expanding professional growth, knowledge about children, and observational skills.

PROFESSIONAL DEVELOPMENT

Take Charge of Your Education: Active Reading and Active Learning

In the beginning of this chapter, you imagined a preschool vignette and gave thoughtful consideration to why a child might have grabbed a toy away from another. This exercise demonstrates that learning is not passive; you did not simply receive the significance of the discussion. One of your jobs as a reader is to stop and think about the points, examples, and questions raised in this book. Make the information your own by thinking about how it relates to your unique store of knowledge and experience. Expect to answer questions in the book and raise more of your own. To enhance this process, each chapter begins with a vignette and ends with an invitation to reflect on pertinent topics.

Beyond working as an active reader, you will be asked to participate in practice activities and apply what you have learned in each chapter. Search for additional opportunities to explore topics and ideas new to you. Look, listen, and watch the young children around you—in grocery stores, in shopping malls, and in your own and your friends' homes. Plan field trips to observe model early childhood education centers. Integrate your new knowledge with your own experience. How does it fit? What questions do you have? Are there inconsistencies? What else do you need to know? How can you further your own education? Actively explore these ideas.

>>

OFF ON YOUR OWN 1.1

Visitation of an Exemplary Early Childhood Program

Draw on the experiences of your instructor, classmates, and other colleagues to generate a list of excellent early childhood educational programs in your area. Select one, and schedule a visit. Make a list of what you liked about the program. Be sure to include:

- three materials you saw children enjoying inside the classroom,
- three pieces of equipment or materials you saw children enjoying outside,
- three interesting activities,

- three questions teachers asked or comments they made to children that elicited thoughtful replies, and
- notes about what one child did for 10 minutes during a free choice time.

Share your impressions during your next class session.

>>>

Learn About Professional Organizations

Professional organizations offer camaraderie, publications, conferences, position statements, advocacy opportunities, and sponsored events to support and guide early childhood educators at all points in their careers. You will find plenty of company in your commitment to children. The following organizations are two of the largest.

Founded in 1926, membership in the National Association for the Education of Young Children (NAEYC) was over 103,000 in 2000. "NAEYC exists for the purpose of leading and consolidating the efforts of individuals and groups working to achieve healthy development and constructive education for all young children. Primary attention is devoted to assuring the provision of high quality early childhood programs for young children" (NAEYC, 2000).

The Association for Childhood Education International (ACEI) was founded in 1892 "to promote and support in the global community the optimal education and development of children, from birth through early adolescence, and to influence the professional growth of educators and the efforts of others who are committed to the needs of children in a changing society" (ACEI, 2000). Begin by learning more about one of these professional organizations in Off on Your Own exercise 1.2.

>>>

OFF ON YOUR OWN 1.2

Professional Organization Exercise

Choose one of the following:

1. Visit the website for the National Association for the Education of Young Children (http://www.naeyc.org) to obtain an overview of the information available. You may want to divide the work with others for reporting back on the following links:

   - Parents
   - Professional Development
   - Conferences
   - Accreditation

- Public Policy Issues
- Week of the Young Child
- Membership Information
- About NAEYC
- Young Children International

Summarize the content. What are the major topics included? When was the information last updated on this website?

or

2. Visit the website of the Association for Childhood Education International (http://www.acei.org) to investigate the position paper on "Preparation of Early Childhood Education Teachers." Summarize and report back about the preparation areas that interest you:

- General Education
- Foundations of Early Childhood Education
- Child Development
- Learning and Teaching process
- Professional Laboratory Experiences

>>

Developmentally Appropriate Practice

Professional early childhood educators are committed to **developmentally appropriate** practice that

> draws on at least three critical, interrelated bodies of knowledge: (1) what teachers know about how children develop and learn; (2) what teachers know about the individual children in their group; and (3) knowledge of the social and cultural context in which those children live and learn. (Bredekamp & Copple, 1997, p. vii)

Let's think for a moment about what each of these points means. Knowledge about how children develop and learn guides teachers as they plan experiences, activities, and interactions. For example, a 10-minute lecture on the color wheel is an inappropriate activity for preschool children because it is in conflict with the active nature of their learning. In contrast, experiences that encourage children to discover the combinatory principles of colors are developmentally appropriate (e.g., explorations with red, yellow, and blue fingerpaints in the art area or red, yellow, and blue food coloring with ice cube trays at the water table). "A developmentally appropriate framework of education uses knowledge about child development and learning to set achievable but challenging goals for all children" (Bredekamp & Copple, 1997, p. 38). Teachers savvy about child development are likely to provide activities that are interesting and stimulating to children at their own developmental levels.

The second element of developmentally appropriate practice requires that early childhood educators respond to children as individuals and respect their diversity. For example, although teachers provide blocks as developmentally appropriate materials for all young children, they tailor specific activities and interactions to the individual needs and interests of the particular children in their classes. Observing a novice builder stacking square blocks, a supportive teacher, over the course of the next week, might start a rectangle stack next to his square stack, offer cylinders for stacking, and suggest stringing beads in the manipulative area or gluing wood chips in a stack in the construction area. The same teacher, observing an experienced builder interested in constructing elaborate freeway systems might add some photos of freeways to the block area, thereby encouraging the child to consider alternative supports for elevated roads. Instead of always using blocks, the photos might suggest trying upside-down cups or small tinkertoy structures. You have probably already noted that observation is key to the fulfillment of this second element. Teachers cannot respond to children on an individual basis unless they are aware of what they are doing, talking about, and finding interesting.

Teachers' choices of developmentally appropriate materials, experiences, and interactions also reflect their understanding of the societal and cultural influences on the children in their groups; their choices demonstrate their respect for the diversity these children bring to the classroom. Children cannot be taught in isolation from the society and culture in which they are growing up. For example, young children's interactions with adults, choices of activities, favorite toys, selections of pleasure books, and views of money may all have cultural components that are not immediately apparent to even the sensitive teacher. In Chapter 5 we will see how some behaviors of one child are bewildering to her kindergarten teacher because of cultural differences between the two. Developmentally appropriate practice implies that early childhood educators teach whole children by responding to their developmental levels, individuality, and cultural connections.

Ethical Conduct in Early Childhood Education

The daily work of early childhood educators often involves ethical issues. Typically, however, there is little candid discussion about the underlying values that can guide educators in ethical decision making. For example, educators are obligated "to develop relationships of mutual trust with the families we serve" (Feeney & Kipnis, 1992, p. 6), but what does this mean in practical terms? How is this ideal translated into action? Think about how teachers can encourage open communication between home and school, send home frequent notes about children's achievements and interests, prepare periodic newsletters to keep parents informed, welcome parent volunteers into the classroom, and plan for substantive, interactive parent conferences. As people who work with children both directly (e.g., teachers) and indirectly (e.g., administrators) chart their way through often muddy ethical waters, they appreciate the guidance from NAEYC's Code of Ethical Conduct. The core values are as follows:

- Appreciating childhood as a unique and valuable stage of the human life-cycle
- Basing our work with children on knowledge of child development
- Appreciating and supporting the close ties between the child and family
- Recognizing that children are best understood and supported in the context of family, culture, community, and society
- Respecting the dignity, worth, and uniqueness of each individual (child, family member, and colleague)
- Helping children and adults achieve their full potential in the context of relationships that are based on trust, respect, and positive regard (Feeney & Kipnis, 1992, p. 2)

At the end of each chapter, in a section entitled "Take a Moment to Reflect," you will have an opportunity to consider one of the Code's elements. In the meantime, familiarize yourself with the Code's content and organization by completing Off on Your Own 1.3 exercise.

>>

OFF ON YOUR OWN 1.3

Code of Ethical Conduct Exercise

Use the NAEYC website to locate and read through the Code of Ethical Conduct (http://www.naeyc.org; click on "About NAEYC," then "Position Statements," then "Code of Ethical Conduct and Statement of Commitment"). Answer the following questions:

- What are the headings of the four sections?
- What is the difference between ideals and principles? Give an example of each.
- Identify I-2.3. Provide an example of the support of this ideal in an early childhood educational program.

>>

THE EDUCATED OBSERVER

Commitment to All Children

During your study of observation, you will serve children well if you continue to advance your knowledge about children and serve as an advocate for children in your community. Joining a professional organization is a good start. Think about early childhood education from a broad perspective for a moment by reading words of wisdom from Marion Wright Edelman, President of the Children's Defense Fund:

> Like parenting, teaching is a mission, not just a task or a job . . . How sad and unfair that the children who come into the world with the least—whose parents are the least able to provide them with health care, good nutrition, shelter, and stimulation—are also the children who are least likely to have access to quality developmental early childhood education. Children who are the least likely to be read to and sung to at home by their mothers, or by their fathers, whom some too seldom see or know, are the most likely to attend schools with the least qualified teachers, the poorest equipment and supplies, and the fewest counselors. They are least likely to have access to school nurses and art and music programs and computers and to have opportunities for after-school and summer enrichment programs that affluent parents can pay for. And they are likely to live in neighborhoods with fewer safe playgrounds and greater violence and drug trafficking. (Edelman, 1999, pp. 22–23)

There is work to be done in your particular community, in your particular educational program, and with your particular children. Communities, programs, and children vary tremendously across our land, but all will be supported by teachers who understand child development, respect and embrace the diversity in our children and families, observe children, plan developmentally appropriate experiences, and are committed to the full potential of each and every child.

Observation helps each child receive an optimal education.

Reasons for Observing

"Rather than marching students through the curriculum in lock step, teachers should modify their instruction to meet students' varying readiness levels, learning preferences, and interests" (Willis & Mann, 2000, p. 1); such a teaching philosophy is called **differentiated instruction.** When teachers plan daily activities for the entire class and never stop to evaluate how they were interpreted and experienced by individual children, there is no hope for each child to receive an optimal education. Such hope is plentiful, however, when teachers know the details of each child's physical, cognitive, psychosocial, and creative development and use this knowledge to plan supportive and challenging experiences. Box 1.1 lists eight critical reasons for classroom observation.

Authentic Assessment

There is a crucial need for good descriptions . . . of children in settings where they spend substantial portions of their time. Descriptions of this sort are useful in a number of ways. They should provide bases for programs for children and families. (Pellegrini, 1996, p. 5)

No doubt you have already begun to imagine observing children in early childhood educational settings. Look carefully at those visions. Do you see yourself, for example, placing 10 wooden beads in front of 3-year-olds, one at a time, and asking them to count as many beads as they can? Do you imagine yourself holding a notepad to document how many objects each child can enumerate? Or do you imagine yourself

---

Box 1.1

Reasons for Observing in the Early Childhood Classroom

- Chart developmental growth (physical, cognitive, psychosocial, and creative) for each child.
- Evaluate each child's strengths and limitations from a realistic perspective.
- Analyze specific problems.
- Plan appropriate curriculum, materials, responses, strategies, and interactions based on individual needs.
- Plan responsive environments indoors and outdoors.
- Maintain records for study teams, conferences, and ongoing feedback to parents.
- Arrive at a comprehensive understanding of each child or a teacher through the application of several observational methods.
- Appraise teacher practices, and design staff development.

on the floor with a 3-year-old who has intently been stringing wooden beads and then exclaims, "Look, I have a ho-ho bunch!" You imagine saying, "You're right; there are a whole bunch of beads on your string. I wonder how many you have." The child asserts, "I can count them," and proceeds to do so. You pull a small notepad out of your pocket and make a note of this child's current number skills.

The difference between the two imaginary visions is the difference between inauthentic and **authentic assessments.** In the first vision, you had concocted a test of counting, but even with limited experience with young children, you suspect they are not very interested in performing under contrived conditions. An accurate understanding of children's strengths and limitations can be gained only by genuinely working with them. The admonitions from professional organizations and researchers are quite clear:

> The methods of assessment are appropriate to the age and experiences of young children. Therefore, assessment of young children relies heavily on the results of observations of children's development, descriptive data, collections of representative work by children, and demonstrated performance during authentic, not contrived, activities. (Bredekamp & Copple, 1997, p. 21)

> Observational methods are useful for evaluation of children and teachers to the extent that they do not put them in anxiety-producing situations; thus, we have a higher likelihood of getting a truer measure of their competence. (Pellegrini, 1996, p. 7)

Thus, the educated observer practices authentic assessment in the early childhood program.

> QUICK REVIEW <

1. Each chapter opens with a _____ (a short story or scenario) to stimulate your active reading and active learning.

2. If an activity is developmentally appropriate, it takes into account knowledge about child development, individual children, and their social and cultural environments.

   ❑   True

   ❑   False

3. Following a review of child development through the preschool and primary grade years, seven methods of observation are presented in *Through the Looking Glass.* The authors are committed to studying not only *how* to observe but also *what* to observe.

   ❑   True

   ❑   False

4. What does NAEYC stand for?

5. What does ACEI stand for?

6. Describe one core value of NAEYC's Code of Ethical Conduct.

7. According to Marion Wright Edelman, we are fortunate that children who come from families with few resources have access to the best early childhood educational programs.

    ❑   True

    ❑   False

8. When teachers try to adapt their instruction to children's individual needs, abilities, and interests, they are following the teaching philosophy of

    _____.

9. Describe two reasons to observe in the early childhood program.

10. Authentic assessment results from

    a. scores on standardized tests

    b. report cards with letter grades

    c. pass/fail tests of physical, cognitive, psychosocial, and creative development

    d. observation of naturally occurring activities

TAKE A MOMENT TO REFLECT

Personal Reflection

Most likely you are reading this book because you have a strong affection for and interest in children. Reflect on the way these feelings and interests came about and how they were nourished over the years.

1. Describe a memorable incident with a child or children that clarified how much you care about children.

2. Recall an incident with a child in which you know your presence was helpful. You may have offered security or comfort, supported a complex problem-solving process, explained a troublesome concept, brought fun into learning, or praised significant efforts. The list does not stop here.

Ethical Reflection

NAEYC Ideal I–4.1 is "to provide the community with high-quality (age and individually appropriate, and culturally and socially sensitive) education/care programs and services" (Feeney & Kipnis, 1992, p. 10). Gonzalez-Mena (1997) wrote:

When things work well, children in a bicultural or multicultural program grow up to be highly competent people—able to move freely and comfortably with or away from their own people. They feel good about themselves. They fit, and when they find themselves in a situation where they don't fit, they have a better chance of adapting without giving up anything of themselves or their culture. (p. 98)

Who do you know that might meet this description? What early childhood programs have you observed that demonstrate the preceding NAEYC ideal?

2

On the Road to Sound Observations

Yorum and Dion, students in a child development class, visit a nearby preschool classroom to complete their first observation assignment: observe for 30 minutes in an early childhood setting. As they leave the school, Yorum exclaims with glee, "Mrs. Beatty has personality plus. Isn't she a great teacher? She has the children doing so many exciting things; in fact, if we could put a plaid cotton dress on her, she could have been the preschool teacher I had 16 years ago. I remember making those exact same penguins. I loved preschool. Isn't it amazing that these children are doing the same play activities I did?"

Dion is quiet for a few moments and then responds, "I understand how familiar activities can be fun to see, but I didn't have the same reaction. I didn't really see what you saw. I'm not sure what activities were going on as I was so distressed that she rewards the children with stickers when they are quiet, lines them up to go outside or go to the bathroom, and tells them they are wrong if they don't have the answer she is looking for. Isn't it funny that we were in the same class and came away with such different impressions?"

As Yorum and Dion begin the journey to sound observations, the focus of this chapter, they reflect on their first classroom observation and come face to face with a fundamental question that troubles all students of observation. They ask, "How can we prepare ourselves for successful observations and see what's happening with as much clarity as possible?" This chapter answers that question by first developing a foundation for the observational process through examination of the teacher's role and exploration of suitable topics for classroom study. Building on that foundation, the guidelines for effective and unobtrusive observation in the early childhood classroom are examined next. Finally, minimizing subjectivity in observation and gaining practice in developing observational skills that are more objective than subjective are introduced. Let us begin.

TAKING THE FIRST STEPS

The Teacher's Role in Observation

In the vibrant classroom, the teacher frequently has a pen and pad in hand to write observational notes using a variety of methods. "Constant observational monitoring provides teachers with the information necessary to judge the current competencies of children and the extent to which teacher assistance is warranted" (Katz & McClellan, 1997, p. 59); the process occurs daily and is the foundation for rich teaching and learning experiences.

On a daily basis, teachers document children's small developmental steps and plan supportive experiences. Weekly, they supplement the curriculum and learning environment according to the appraised needs of individual children. They also use their observational skills to choose appropriate responses to behavioral difficulties, such as a preschool child grabbing a toy from another child or a primary grade child using fists to solve a playground problem. Teachers use the well-drawn details gleaned from classroom observation to measure and record each child's developmental growth over the entire year in an individual **portfolio** (a collection of observational records and work samples for one child that reflect developmental growth, usually kept for a period of 1 year). This wealth of information is used to communicate with parents during conferences or, on some occasions, study teams of specialists.

Framer (1994) emphasized the importance of the teacher's role in the process of observing:

> Good teachers are keen observers. Crucial to teaching is the ability to observe and listen to children. It is through this process that teachers can discover students' skills, interests, and needs. Good teachers are able to use the information they gather to augment the learning environment so that it can both nourish children and grow from them. (p. 31)

From daily to weekly to monthly to yearly, teachers participate in the observational process for individual children through a cycle of recording, evaluating, planning, and communicating that is repeated over and over (see diagram on page 19). In the diagram note that the base of the triangle inside the circle represents shared family–teacher support for the center of the observation process, which is the child.

Be aware that although the child is usually the focus of observation, on occasion, observations may be used to evaluate a teacher's proficiency or classroom environments (see Chapters 11 to 14). In those cases the teacher's role in the observational cycle remains the same (observing, recording, planning, evaluating, communicating); however, the focus of the center triangle (e.g., teachers, teacher–children, environment, teaching strategies) changes to reflect the purpose of the observation.

Finding the Time

Inexperienced teachers often ask, "Where do classroom teachers find the time to complete written observations? Isn't the observational process terribly time-consuming?"

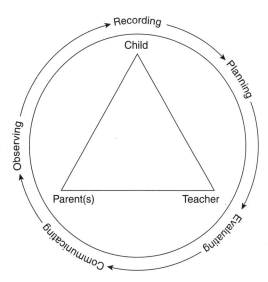

Do not be thrown off by initial perceptions. A careful look at a program may reveal time-saving modifications and identify moments that can be used for the observational process. Moving away from curricula that rely heavily on preparing product art frees the time needed to write observations and make plans based on emerging individual needs. Teachers are also freed up in class when product art gives way to creative art; teachers do not have to spend time ensuring that children correctly duplicate the product. Many K–3 teachers report that when less time is devoted to direct teaching and more is devoted to experiential learning (employing developmentally appropriate curricula), observational/recording intervals are plentiful. In addition, many preschool programs compensate their teachers for an additional planning hour each day so that they can record, file, and plan; teachers working at child-care centers can use nap time for these activities. Primary grade teachers have planning time built into their contracts. And don't forget, we live in the age of technology. A voice-activated computer may eventually become the recording system of choice because it will write, file, and organize, thus saving valuable time.

Flexibility and commitment are the cornerstones of effective daily observations. Teachers rely on their own rhythm and class happenings when gathering observations on children's growth in the areas of physical, cognitive, psychosocial, and creative development. From day to day new observational opportunities surge, rarely at the same time each day. Well-honed skills and the use of several methods of observation enable teachers to tune in to the unique ebb and flow within their classrooms while documenting each child's development clearly and comprehensively.

Novice teachers, however, may need to establish a daily rhythm. To avoid the "I tried it once and it didn't work" syndrome, consider an observational routine using a specific area of concentration.

Times to Observe	Times to Record and File
As children first arrive (see Jeffrey's and Thienkim's running records in Chapter 5, Lin's ABC event sampling in Chapter 9)	As children arrive
During center time, free choice time, or independent work time (see Taki's running record in Chapter 5, anecdotes in Chapter 6, Rachel's ABC event sampling in Chapter 9)	During center time, free choice, or independent work time if others are present to assist the children.
At snack time and lunch time (especially good for psychosocial anecdotes)	During lunchtime
During outdoor time (see Evan's running record in Chapter 6)	While children are at recess
When trained parent helpers are in the classroom (see Rosey's rating scale in Chapter 8)	After children depart

Figure 2.1
Examples of observing and recording/filing opportunities.

> We realize the process may seem a bit overwhelming to busy caregivers at first; but by beginning with spontaneous observations and gradually introducing regular planned observations, by focusing observations on only a few children at a time, and by scheduling time to interpret the observations, the assessment process can be manageable. (Leavitt & Eheart, 1991, p. 9)

Figure 2.1 describes specific observational and recording times that teachers have reported as successful. These examples are offered as possibilities, not rigid schedules.

Teachers set themselves up for success by talking with their administrators to establish time to observe, record, file, plan, and reflect. Staffs work cooperatively to determine the most useful time for these recordings within the teaching/learning environment. Class size, program content, daily schedules, school philosophy, and teacher–child ratios all play a part in customizing observational time management.

Observational Topics

In the chapter-opening vignette, Yorum and Dion ended up observing whether they liked or did not like the classroom activities and teacher strategies. Their understanding of the assignment was vague and lacked a common reason for observing; therefore, they left the school with different observational outcomes. Knowing what to observe provides a perimeter and sharpens our clarity.

The early childhood classroom provides diverse and abundant opportunities for observation.

What do you see when you look at the two photos above of preschool and primary grade children involved in active learning? Concentrate on what the children are doing. What materials or equipment are they using? What activities are in progress? What developmental characteristics can be identified? How are the children interacting? Reflect for a moment on your answers.

Now stop and write down topics that might be observed from looking at these photos; list the topics in Practice Activity 2.1. You may want to add other ideas not suggested by the photos. Think about examples of children's developmental growth, environmental influences, developmentally appropriate practices, family concerns, children with special needs, cultural awareness, and teaching strategies.

PRACTICE ACTIVITY 2.1

Topics of Observation

List topics to observe in an early childhood setting. Topics may be from the photographs or from your own experiences.

Examples:

- Children's motor skills
- Types of roles enacted in the dramatic play area
- Frequency of on-task behaviors

(continued)

1.

2.

3.

4.

5.

6.

The following is a typical list of observational topics brainstormed by teachers-in-training interested in preschool and primary grade classrooms. Their list may differ from yours; it is based on their own experiences.

Topics of Observation

1. Block building
2. Aggressive behavior on the playground
3. Classification skills
4. Personality
5. Listening and learning
6. Types of teacher questions
7. Clarity of speech
8. Children's separation from family
9. Maturity
10. Phonological awareness
11. Active role of teacher
12. Frequency and context of family involvement in school
13. Evidence of anti-bias curriculum
14. Organization of materials and equipment

Look at Practice Activity 2.1, and compare your ideas with the preceding list. Are there similarities? Did you think of items not on this list? Now study both lists carefully while thinking about how each topic could be observed in a classroom.

All the items on the "Topics of Observation" list are concerns teachers may have, but not all are directly observable. Some are too general and some too vague; being specific and knowing what area of a large topic we want to observe is crucial. Observation is most useful when we can pinpoint exactly what it is we are looking for and what it is we want to see. For example, "Aggressive behavior on the playground" could be categorized and accurately observed, but "Listening and learning" is too complex to specify exactly what behaviors we would be looking for. Thus, "Listening and learning" is too general and too vague. Narrowing the topic to state a specific act of listening, such as listening during story time, suggests distinct behaviors that could be observed and is thus a manageable focus for the teacher.

Let's try one more. How would you classify the topic "Personality"? Can you see that it is also too vague and general? "Personality" is multifaceted, making it difficult, if not impossible, to observe it as a whole. With some work, you may be able to break down topics that are complex, such as personality, and observe one aspect (e.g., dimensions of temperament). Now turn your attention to Practice Activity 2.2 to evaluate topics to observe.

PRACTICE ACTIVITY 2.2

Evaluation of Topics of Observation

Using your list from Practice Activity 2.1 and the Topics of Observation list, consider each item carefully, and determine if it is an appropriate topic of observation or if it is too general and vague. Place each item in the proper column below.

Appropriate Topic   Too General/Too Vague

(Example: Aggressive behavior   (Example: Listening and learning)
on the playground)

You are on the road to sound observation when you can identify topics that are specific and observable. If you found that in Practice Activity 2.1 you listed some vague or general items, see if you can now revise them to be more explicit, or delete them if they are not workable. As a teacher, you will conduct a variety of observations on many different topics. Continue to practice selecting appropriate behaviors to observe.

MOVING DOWN THE PATH

Guidelines for Observation

In learning to become a competent observer, you will be spending time in classrooms practicing various methods. Reasonable preparations for a classroom observation will help you get off to a good start and maximize the amount of information you will be able to gather. The following helpful suggestions apply to any observational method you select and may also be used in your own classroom with some modifications.

- Clarify the purpose of your observation. Spend time before the observation to examine its purpose. What is the assignment? Do you understand the method you plan to use? Concentrate on the "big picture" of your observation.

- Schedule your visit if you are observing in a classroom other than your own. No teacher will appreciate being surprised by your arrival. Phone about a week ahead to obtain permission and arrange the date, time, and length of your observation. Explain in general the purpose of your observation; for example, you might say that you will observe teacher-child interactions. If you describe your observation question in minute detail (e.g., What are the types and frequencies of the questions teachers ask children?), you risk prompting atypical behavior. Leave your phone number in case the teacher needs to contact you before your visit.

- Come equipped with the necessary materials and a warm smile. For most assignments you will need paper or your observation form, pencils or pens, and something firm to write on. Check in and show identification to the person at the front desk. Once inside the classroom, some normal anxiety about being observed can be alleviated by being friendly and greeting each adult individually.

- Select a position from which to observe. Look around the classroom to note your options. You want to be as inconspicuous as possible; thus, you should sit down and keep to the outskirts of activities in progress. You will increase your viewing range if you sit with your back to the wall. You want to find the fine

Observations may be collected inside and outside the classroom or, as this student is doing, through a one-way glass.

line that will allow you to hear and see what's going on without interfering in or detracting from the activity.

- Note "the lay of the land." If you are not acquainted with the classroom, spend about 10 minutes becoming familiar with the layout of the classroom, the materials accessible to the children, and what is going on. During this time you want to satisfy your curiosity about general matters so you can then turn your attention to the specifics of your observation. Drawing a rough map of the room will help you remember many details.

- Check your own biases and emotional responses to the children, teachers, and classroom. Acknowledge them and then try to clear away any judgments that may cloud your focus, such as the labeling of a child (e.g., spoiled, bossy, or stressed).

- Respond in a natural way to children's inquiries about your presence. If a child asks why you are there or what you are doing, respond with "I'm just visiting to see what preschool (or first grade or whatever) is like." This is usually enough to satisfy and reassure the child as you continue to observe.

- Fill in the appropriate heading for the observational method you are using.

Observer Subjectivity

Reflect, again, on the chapter-opening vignette. If Yorum had had a different preschool experience or had not attended preschool at all, would her looking glass have a different focus? If Dion had not been aware of developmentally appropriate practices, would he still have been distressed by the teacher's behaviors? As observers we cannot see with total clarity. What we observe is influenced by our experiences, biases, emotions, and even cultural and social norms. Observation cannot be free of subjectivity. How, then, do observers learn to recognize this possible hindrance and continue on the path to sound observation? Read on.

The material that follows provides recommendations for minimizing subjectivity, one of the most troublesome skills in observation. Consider this scenario. Two observers visit a kindergarten playground to describe an individual child's activity for 3 minutes. Unlike Yorum and Dion, these two observers have the same observational purpose and focus. They watch the same boy, Cyd, who is 5 years, 1 month old (5;1).

Observer A wrote:

The boy I am observing (Cyd, 5;1) is playing all alone with a dinosaur in the sand. He doesn't seem to have any friends. He plays with just one dinosaur all by himself for awhile. Then he gets bored and goes to get some other dinosaurs at the end of the sand area. He demands the teacher's attention, probably the only person who will listen to him. He tells her that the biggest dinosaur is the boss, probably what he wants to be all the time. No wonder he is playing alone.

Observer B wrote:

The boy (Cyd, 5;1) sits cross-legged in the middle of the sand area, reaches into the toy bin, and grasps a small plastic dinosaur in his right hand. He moves the dinosaur from side to side in the sand using a 5-inch hopping up-and-down motion. He leans on his left hand and pushes with his right leg, extends his body forward and upward to a standing position. Holding the dinosaur, he walks at an even pace to the edge of the sand area and places the dinosaur to the left of two other plastic dinosaurs lined up on the wood outlining the sand area. In a loud voice he exclaims, "Now you're all here." He spins around to the teacher and announces as he points to them in lined order, "Tyrannosaurus is the boss 'cause he's the biggest. The stegosaurus is the next boss 'cause he's the next biggest. The dimetrodon is the baby. He's not very big."

Both observers watched the same child, at the same time, engaging in the same activity. Yet the accounts are very different. Go back and study the two paragraphs. What are the specific elements that differentiate the two passages?

Observer A tried to explain many of Cyd's actions by drawing on personal impressions or feelings (e.g., "he gets bored," "probably the only person who will listen to him"). Consequently, Observer A has recorded an observation that is influenced by biases, assumptions, and emotional responses. This observation is filled with obvious examples of *subjectivity.*

In comparison, Observer B recorded more facts and visible behaviors. By recording accurately what was said and done with nothing added or omitted, this observer cautiously avoided evaluations, judgments, impressions, and personal speculations and was as objective as possible. This observation is not as much of a personal interpretation as Observer A's report. Therefore, Observer B's report is more *objective* than Observer A's report. Review Observer B's exact descriptions (e.g., "leans on his left hand," "pushes with his right leg"). Observations like these based on true behaviors are useful in keeping accurate records of the child's developmental abilities. The competent teacher would not miss the opportunity to note and record Cyd's display of seriation.

To test whether the observer has been objective to a reasonable degree, ask, "Would another observer concur with the description?" Learning to minimize subjectivity when observing is an ongoing challenge, and Bergen (1997) reminded us that it is impossible to be completely objective all the time.

> The goal of most observational techniques is to record observations without making judgments and to make inferences that are based on the factual data recorded, not on pre-existing opinion, emotions, or biases. However, postmodern thinkers assert that subjectivity is inevitable because there is no objective truth 'out there' that can be perceived . . . the best that observers can do is to be aware of their subjective reality and to acknowledge it as a part of their evaluation process. (pp. 116–117)

As reminded in the guidelines for observation on pages 23–25, observers should check their subjectivity by remembering the purpose of the observation and by asking themselves the following questions before they begin the observation itself. This step is so crucial to sound observation that some instructors of observation assign their students to clear their minds by writing down the answers to these questions.

• What is my first impression?

• Am I positively identifying with this experience based on my past? How might that influence what I see?

- Am I negatively identifying with this experience based on my past? How might that influence what I see?
- Am I annoyed or distracted by any particular behaviors that the children are exhibiting? How might that influence what I see?
- Am I annoyed or distracted by any particular teaching strategy that the teacher is exhibiting? How might that influence what I see?
- Am I annoyed or distracted by any particular environmental condition in the classroom? How might that influence what I see?
- Is there any social or cultural practice exhibited in this classroom that is not comfortable to me? How might that influence what I see?
- What judgments am I making?

Continue on the path to sound observation by completing the exercise in Practice Activity 2.3 to sharpen your objective eye.

PRACTICE ACTIVITY 2.3

Observation Descriptions

Examine the photo. Then list four statements describing what you see. Give attention to minimizing subjectivity.

(continued)

Example:
The enclosure on the right contains all the tigers.

1.

2.

3.

4.

Practicing objectivity (to the best of one's ability) is necessary to travel on the road to sound observation. While looking at the photo and completing Practice Activity 2.3, one observer wrote: "The children made a few enclosures." Is that an objective sentence? How many are "a few"? Can you see how our past experiences could influence what "a few" represents to different observers? A more objective statement would specify the number of enclosures. Another observer wrote: "The girls used many animals." "Many times" is also subjective. Look back to the statements you wrote in the Practice Activity. Were there instances when you noticed that certain adjectives or adverbs that describe given periods of time or the amount of something could determine whether the sentence was written as objectively as possible? Vague words that are used to describe time or amount can be referred to as red flag words—words that alert us to possible subjectivity. Practice Activity 2.4 provides an opportunity to identify such words.

PRACTICE ACTIVITY 2.4

Red Flag Words

Read the following sentences and underline all the words that indicate time or amount and that could be interpreted differently by separate observers.

1. There are a lot of children at the water table.
2. Toni twists her hair excessively.
3. Maithreyi has used some blocks to make a stack that is very tall.
4. Most of the children can count to 100.
5. Rhianna has many absences.
6. The children use the computer regularly.
7. At the writing center, Taynee and Phoebe exchange a few words.
8. Daisy frequently hits other children.

What other words could be considered red flag words?

The activity in Off on Your Own 2.1 offers an experience to apply all that you have learned in this chapter by observing in a classroom of your choice. Many people have been surprised to find how easily subjectivity can slip into their initial observations. You may find value in saving your initial observation and then comparing it to an observation made after studying this book. This comparison can be valuable feedback and a true measure of the distance you will have traveled.

>>

OFF ON YOUR OWN 2.1

Practice in Minimizing Observational Subjectivity

Following the general guidelines for observation, visit a preschool or primary school of your choice and record six statements (remembering to be aware of subjectivity) that accurately describe what you observe. The focus of your observation can be the children, teachers, environment, or interactions. Be sure to call ahead for permission, go prepared, and stay 15 to 20 minutes.

1.

2.

3.

4.

5.

6.

>>

> QUICK REVIEW <

1. Trained teachers observe on a daily basis and use the information gathered to plan appropriate programs.
   ❑ True
   ❑ False

2. The teacher's role in the cycle of observation is:

    a.

    b.

    c.

    d.

3. State the two cornerstones to effective daily observations.

    a.

    b.

4. A collection of observational records and work samples for one child, usually kept for a period of one year, is a _____.

5. Which topic below is not an appropriate topic to observe in the early childhood classroom?

    a. memory skills

    b. IQ

    c. empathy

    d. problem solving

6. Name two of the important guidelines to follow when practicing competent observation.

    a.

    b.

7. Minimizing subjectivity is one of the most troublesome skills in sound observation.

    ❑ True

    ❑ False

8. To check if an observer has been objective to a reasonable degree, one question to ask is:

    a. Would another observer concur with the description?

    b. Is it easy to understand what the observer saw?

    c. Has the observer recorded reasonable child behavior?

    d. Would the observer be likely to observe the same thing on another day?

9. Is the following statement an example of objective or subjective recording?

    The child is happy as she uses fluid hand-over-hand motions to cross the horizontal bars on the playground.

10. Which one of the following statements contains a red flag word and which word is it?

    a. There are 15 children in the class—7 girls and 8 boys.

    b. The child walked, scraping the toe of his right shoe for about 5 feet, until he reached the table with the puzzles.

c. The teacher rings a chime and warns the children that it is clean-up time in 5 more minutes.

d. The children squirm and talk to each other, seldom participating in the 45-minute circle time.

TAKE A MOMENT TO REFLECT

Personal Reflection

Think about your experiences with young children or observe a 2- or 3-year-old and then a 7- or 8-year-old. Reflect on how these children are developmentally similar or different.

1. Watch how they move and use their bodies. What kind of activities do they engage in both inside and outside the classroom?
2. Listen to their use of language. How long are their sentences? Is their grammar correct and articulation clear?
3. Study how the children solve problems. Are they self-resourceful? Do they work cooperatively together?
4. Observe their attention spans. Which activities capture their interest? How long can they attend in group situations? In individual situations?

Keep your ideas in mind as you read Chapters 3 and 4 that discuss, respectively, the characteristics of preschool and primary grade children.

Ethical Reflection

NAEYC Ideal I-3B.1 is "to assist the program in providing the highest quality of service" (Feeney & Kipnis, 1992, p. 6). Reflect on how sound observational practices lay the foundation for this ethical ideal.

3

Highlights of Development During the Preschool Years

Lupe (2;5) tightly grasps a purple jumbo crayon in her right fist, palm down, arm bent parallel to the table about 1 inch above it. She makes circular strokes of medium intensity. After completing four imperfect circles, she looks up at her teacher with delight and exclaims, "I make doughnuts!"

This carefully worded, detailed vignette records an observation of Lupe's coloring activity made by her teacher. Is the observer's job now complete? No. Once the observational information is collected, it needs to be thoughtfully analyzed and used. The results of this analysis, if applied by the teacher in the classroom, will enrich the curriculum and the activities planned for the child.

"Educators who are developmentally based in their instruction incorporate learning experiences that are appropriate not only for the chronological ages but also, and more importantly, for the developmental levels of the individuals being taught" (Gallahue & Ozmun, 1998, p. 3). If Lupe's teacher is cognizant of the development displayed by Lupe's coloring and the growth yet to come, then she or he has a developmental framework to guide activity planning. The following questions begin the process. What does Lupe's grasp indicate about her fine motor development? What does her assertion that the purple circles represent doughnuts demonstrate about her cognitive development? What does her ease in sharing her achievements with her teacher suggest about her psychosocial development? Understanding child development goes beyond appreciating children's current interests and skills or rejoicing in witnessing their achievements. Teachers need to know enough about child development and appropriate curriculum to make good judgments about what is age-appropriate and individually-appropriate for the children in their classrooms (Bredekamp & Rosegrant, 1992).

Chapters 3 and 4 make no attempt to supplant the wealth of information available in child-development textbooks. The purpose of these chapters is to highlight selected aspects of early childhood development (ages 2½ through 8) so the observer understands what growth looks like and what to watch for in the classroom. To further serve this purpose, the **growth indicators** of physical, cognitive, psychosocial, and creative development are identified in gray-shaded boxes, with each section giving examples of individual and cultural diversity. These are reproduced in Appendix A.

SELECTED HIGHLIGHTS OF PHYSICAL DEVELOPMENT

Body Growth

As toddlers add candles to their birthday cakes and move into their preschool years, their bodies lose that top-heavy look and appear slimmer as their torsos elongate (Santrock, 2001). This is why adults comment on how tall the preschooler is getting or that he or she appears to be all legs as his or her fifth birthday rolls around. By consulting growth charts, we see that the well-nourished preschool child in the United States typically increases in height by 2½ to 3 inches and gains about 4 to 6 lb per year (Berger, 2000). Individual growth rates are attributed to the genetic makeup of each child; therefore, the variation in height within an age group can be about 4 inches, and in weight about 10 lbs. It is clear that heredity is one of the major forces for physical individuality at this age.

Brain Development

Understanding how the brain functions and comprehending the controversial implications of brain development for classroom practices are currently hot topics for popular magazine articles, television specials, conferences, journals, new informative books, and research departments at major universities. "For a long time, scientists didn't understand the brain. . . Our skull hides a bewildering array of electrochemical activity, so our brain's awesome complexity is its own major barrier to understanding itself" (Sylwester, 1995, p. 1). It is through advances in brain imaging (e.g., CAT scans, MRIs, EEGs, SQUIDs, BEAMs, and PETs) that neuroscientists now have the tools to study brain activity, processes, and functions.

Examining Gardner's (1999) manageable list of the contributions of brain study to the field of education helps open the door to the mosaic of the mind and its important impact on learning. Study the list below and take time to relate your experiences to each point. As you read on in this chapter and explore other domains of development, come back to this list and rethink its applications.

1. *The tremendous importance of early experiences.* All experiences matter, but those in early life have particular importance for later life. Accordingly, education (in a general sense) should begin in the first months of life.

2. *The imperative "Use it or lose it."* The possession of brain tissue and potential connections is not enough. If that tissue is not stimulated by appropriate

sensory perception, and then used actively, it will eventually atrophy or be appropriated to other functions.

3. *The flexibility (more technically, the plasticity) of the early nervous system.* Young children can survive and thrive even if they are missing large portions of the nervous system. But as we age, our brain becomes far less flexible, and it becomes increasingly difficult to compensate for lost capacities and functions.

4. *The importance of action and activity.* The brain learns best and retains most when the organism is actively involved in exploring physical sites and materials and asking questions to which it actually craves answers. Merely passive experiences tend to attenuate and have little lasting impact.

5. *The specificity of human abilities and talents.* Far from being a generalized machine that works well or not so well, the human brain comprises numerous zones and neural networks, each geared to quite specific capacities. While nature is not entirely fair, and some individuals are blessed with more potentials and talents than others, abilities prove surprisingly independent of one another; a person can excel in one sphere while not faring well with others.

6. *The possible organizing role played in early childhood by music.* A number of intriguing studies suggest that learning a musical instrument in early life may yield positive consequences in other cognitive domains, including those valued in school. . . This novel research still requires extensive replication. However, it suggests that certain activities may assume privileged roles in the organization of subsequent experiences.

7. *The crucial role played by emotional coding.* The formative role of emotions in learning is being increasingly recognized. Experiences that have emotional consequences (and are registered as such) are likely to be retained and utilized subsequently. Individuals whose brains are impaired in ways that make it difficult for them to code experiences emotionally may also find it difficult to retain and make subsequent use of these experiences.*

Motor Development

"Oh I wish I had his energy!" remarked Clodine, as she watched her 4-year-old jetting around the play yard late in the day. Preschoolers often appear to be like little firecrackers, sparkling and bursting with fuel. These young children have mastered walking and have improved their balance and coordination through practice and maturation; they are now engaged in the motor skill adventures of running, jumping, hopping, galloping, skipping, climbing, balancing, kicking, catching, and throwing. "Skills vary by culture, of course; in certain nations, some 5-year-olds swim in waves or climb cliffs that few adults in other nations would attempt" (Berger, 2000, p. 249). Reflect on children's activities that you have seen, and watch young children in your neighborhood, at the park, or in the supermarket. They seem to seek out opportunities to exercise a variety of motor skills.

*From *The Disciplined Mind: What Students Should Understand* (pp. 81 and 82) by Howard Gardner, 1999. New York: Simon & Schuster. Copyright © 1999 by Simon & Schuster. Used by permission.

Axiom	Motor Development Example
Development occurs at individual maturational rates. Each child possesses his/her own genetic time clock.	In a group of 3-year olds, some jump by mustering all the energy they can harness for the task; other children jump with quick, easy movements.
Developmental areas (physical cognitive, psychosocial, and creative) and subsets within those areas overlap and are interdependent.	A child who is uncomfortable or shy around others may not participate in gross motor group activities, thus limiting opportunities for physical development.
	"Visual acuity, figure-ground perception, depth perception, and visual-motor coordination are important visual qualities that are developmentally based and that influence movement performance" (Gallahue & Ozmun, 1998, p. 298).
Motor development is generally predictable.	Children develop jumping abilities before hopping, and hopping before skipping.
Physical growth proceeds along a **cephalocaudal** (head to tail) pattern.	Babies can lift their heads before sitting. A young preschooler can more easily catch a ball than kick it.
Physical development advances in a **proximodistal** (from the center of the body to the outermost) pattern. Thus, children acquire gross motor control before fine motor control.	Young Morag scurries over to the riding trucks on the outside yard, smiling broadly as she plops herself down and powers the truck forward using her strong thighs.
	Four-year-old Tristin spends many happy preschool hours manipulating tiny houses and small wooden people on the "village floor map" made of fabric.
Perfecting motor skills is subject to individual interest, culture, maturation, instruction, and practice.	Some children cannot tie shoe laces because no one taught them, they didn't want to learn, or they have always worn shoes fastened with Velcro.

Figure 3.1
Developmental axioms.

Motor development is defined as "progressive change in movement behavior throughout the life cycle. Motor development involves continuous adaptation to changes in one's movement capabilities in the never-ending effort to achieve and maintain motor control and movement competence" (Gallahue, 1996, p. 24). Early childhood educators observe growth in this area by keeping records on children's **gross motor development** (maturity and capabilities of large muscles, such as arms and legs) and **fine motor development** (maturity and capabilities of small muscles, such as fingers). Motor development rests on basic developmental principles or **axioms** (Figure 3.1). Review these axioms, and take time to think about the implication of each axiom for motor development.

Gross Motor Skills

Identifying basic large motor skills and determining needed motor opportunities gear the teacher up for active observation. Begin the identification practice by studying the growth indicators in Box 3.1; they describe the key characteristics for gross motor development. "These fundamental locomotor skills can be thought of as the building blocks of the more specific skills developed later in childhood" [see Chapter 4] (Payne & Isaacs, 1999, p. 255). Because developmental axioms affect motor skill performance, development is denoted as a continuous process rather than chronological age expectations in Box 3.1.

Box 3.1

Preschool Growth Indicators of Gross Motor Development

Skill	Developing Characteristics
Increases competency in running	Running begins with a hurried walk that progresses to a flat-footed forward run then to a forward heel-to-toe pattern in which both feet briefly leave the ground at once. Child increasingly develops ability to run backward, to run on toes, and to run with greater speed. Child's initial inability to stop, start, and turn progresses to accomplished execution of starts, stops, and turns.
Increases competency in jumping	Jumping down begins with a low jump-down (about 2 ft) from a small crouch position landing with straight legs and arms waving in an uncontrolled manner. It progresses to jumping down from higher elevations in a knee-bent crouch start, with the child moving arms back to front to balance, and landing with knees bent at impact.
	Standing broad jump begins with jump distance of less than 1 ft and continues up to about 3 ft.
Increases competency in hopping	Hopping begins with 1 to 3 one-footed hops on one preferred foot accompanied by large arm movements. Hop progresses to a stiff-looking 7 to 9 hops, then to 10 or more hops (using either foot) executed with an easy bouncing action using ankles, knees, and hips.
	Hopping forward on two feet begins with feet together, semi-still legs, and arms waving up and down for two or three jumps. It progresses to rhythmic jumping with knees and arms bent in pogo-stick fashion.

(continued)

Skill	Developing Characteristics
Increases competency in galloping	Galloping begins with a variation on running. It progresses to a run-and-leap pattern, then to a step-together rhythmic gallop pattern with either foot leading.
Increases competency in skipping	Skipping begins with a hop on one foot and a walk on the other—it appears stiff, usually a flat-footed pattern accompanied by large arm movements. Skip progresses to a smooth rhythmic pattern, using alternate feet with arms bent at the elbow and swinging alternately with foot.
Increases competency in climbing	Climbing stairs begins with one foot followed by the other foot on the same stair (mark-time foot pattern) when climbing or descending stairs holding the support railing. Climbing progresses to using alternate feet when ascending and descending stairs; hand rails are eventually no longer used for support. As height of climb increases, equipment choice widens (e.g., trees, jungle gyms, ladders, ropes, and poles).
Increases competency in balancing	Balancing begins with standing on one foot with help and progresses to standing on one foot for about 10 seconds. In the final stage child can balance on one foot with his or her eyes shut.
	Balancing on a 3-inch-wide beam begins with a sideways step-together pattern. Child progresses to taking bigger steps, using an alternating foot pattern facing forward with arms extended for balance. In the final stage the child increases speed and uses an alternating-foot pattern with arms remaining at the child's side.
Increases competency in catching	Catching begins with extended arms straight in front of body with palms up to stop the ball and head turned away. It progresses to elbows bent with the lower arm perpendicular to sides of body, palms facing each other with thumbs up, eyes shut at impact—arms used to catch the ball. Child advances to using hands to embrace the ball and adjusting arms to speed and location of ball in a relaxed and appropriately timed manner.
Increases competency in one-hand throwing	Throwing begins with feet stationary facing the target and elbow bent, hand with ball about ear height, propelling the ball with the elbow in a forward and downward throwing motion. It progresses to an arm swing over shoulder and behind head; as the body turns to throwing side, ball is propelled with arm over head as the body weight moves

	forward. Child steps forward using the same-side leg as throwing arm. Child advances to using opposite raised elbow (hand bent downward) for balance as arm with ball is swung backward, elbow is bent, body turns to throwing side, and weight is on rear foot. When ball is propelled, the hips rotate toward target, the weight shifts forward, and child takes a step with opposite foot.
Increases competency in kicking	Kicking begins with using arms for balance and taking a short backward and forward stroke with limited bend in the leg. It progresses to one or more steps forward, with the stroke made with a bent knee on backstroke and follow-through. Child advances to running forward with quick steps, using the hip to propel the leg motion both backward and forward to maximum length with a high follow-through. The opposite leg bends at impact, and child lifts up on toe.

Note: Information in chart compiled from *Understanding Motor Development: Infants, Children, Adolescents, Adults* (4th ed.) by D. Gallahue & J. Ozmum, 1998, New York: McGraw-Hill; and *Developmental Physical Education for Today's Children* (4th ed.) by Gallahue, D. L. and Cleland, F., 2002, Champaign, IL: Human Kinetics. Adapted and reproduced by permission of the McGraw-Hill Companies.

It is important to observe and record not only that the child performed a specific motor skill but also how the child performed it. Adults may easily confirm that a child can run, but the trained observer uses developmental knowledge to ask detailed questions.

For example, does the child run with speed, control, smoothness, and endurance? Is the child's hopping balanced and performed with confidence using a spring-like action, or is it stiff and accompanied by large arm movements? When throwing a ball, does the child lead with the same foot or with the foot opposite the throwing arm? Observing detailed and numerous qualities offers a more complete picture of the child's gross motor abilities. Consider the following classroom anecdote for gross motor development. What can be said about how this child exhibits balancing skill?

2/6 Amy (4;11)   While standing up, Amy brought her left foot up under her left armpit, held it with her left hand, and balanced steadily on her right foot as she exclaimed, "Look, I'm hugging my foot."

In programs for preschoolers, children usually have daily outdoor opportunities to exercise their budding motor skills freely. Providing a sufficient number and variety of outdoor motor experiences will support children's development. Teachers can augment the fixed equipment by frequently adding assorted items (e.g., obstacle courses, wooden crawl-through shapes, parachute activities, ring-toss games, jump ropes, or different-sized balls). Movement activities assist in motor

Observation and recording of children's gross motor abilities lead to program planning based on individual needs.

development and can be carried out even during inclement weather; children often enjoy moving to recorded music with directions. Planned motor development programs with teacher assistance are necessary for optimal growth (Benelli & Yongue, 1995; Leppo, Davis, & Crim, 2000).

Fine Motor Skills

Throughout the early childhood years, children display various abilities in fine motor development. Some children put puzzles together with the greatest of ease, whereas others appear to be "all thumbs," especially when the pieces are small. In addition, fine motor tasks often require auxiliary capabilities. Picture the young child pouring juice from a small plastic pitcher during snack time. This child must have control over her or his fingers but also must have good concentration, visual acuity, and accurate judgment. It is a combination of practice and maturation that allows children to perform fine motor tasks with proficiency. The growth indicators listed in Box 3.2 provide the observational focus for these gradual developments.

Well-trained teachers are careful not to base evaluations of fine motor development on one task or on one occasion; observing the child in a natural setting and identifying the many fine motor tasks exhibited by the child over time will provide an accurate picture. To facilitate this expansive approach to assessment,

Box 3.2

Preschool Growth Indicators of Fine Motor Development

Growth Indicator	*Example*
Increases ability to grasp and control small objects	Outside, blowing bubbles, Lorna uses one hand to hold the skinny straw that is inserted into a hole on the side of the styrofoam cup. With her other hand she holds the cup, turns it upside down, and dips the rim into a soap mixture. Turning the cup right side up, she blows through the straw; multiple bubbles flow out the top of the cup.
Increases ability to fasten and unfasten	While playing Daddy in the housekeeping area, the child unbuttons and, for the first time, buttons the small fasteners on the coat of the 13-inch doll.
Increases ability to insert and remove small pieces	Prior to December, the puzzles in Maja's classroom contained a maximum of 10 pieces. Today the teacher introduces a 20-piece puzzle entitled "The City." Maja smiles triumphantly as she completes this puzzle on her first attempt.
Increases ability to string or lace	At the art table, several children are creating collages with pieces of beautiful junk. T. J. brings over a long piece of yarn, methodically wraps the ends with tape, and slowly and carefully (sometimes dropping pieces) strings 12 items to make a necklace. He asks the teacher to tie it around his neck.
Increases ability to cut with scissors	Moving from cutting play dough to cutting newspaper strips, the teacher reminds the child, "Cut from your belly button forward."

*Opportunities to exercise fine
motor skills help build
concentration, judgment, and
motor coordination.*

Figure 3.2 identifies many examples of fine motor tools available in different class-room areas. Not all the following tools will be found in every classroom; selections of specific tools are based on the children's developmental abilities, program goals, and teacher supervision. "Adults can certainly help [motor skill advance-ment] by offering tools, time, and encouragement" (Berger, 2000, p. 252).

A frequent observation in the area of fine motor development is the child's grasp of tools. The vignette in the beginning of this chapter reported, "Lupe (2;5) tightly grasps a purple jumbo crayon in her right fist, palm down, arm bent parallel to the table about 1 inch above it." To understand Lupe's development, consider the fol-lowing questions for observing advances in techniques using writing instruments (Cratty, 1986):

- Does the child hold the crayon using the supinate grasp ("all four fingers and the thumb wrapped around the pencil to form a fist" [Payne & Isaacs, 1999, p. 244]) with only the point touching the paper, controlling the movement from the shoulder and the elbow?

- Does she use a pincer grip using her hand and wrist as one unit while her lower arm is in the air (not touching the writing surface)? Pincer grip is also called the dynamic tripod, "a finger posture in which the thumb, middle finger, and index finger function as a tripod for the writing implement" (Payne & Isaacs, 1999, p. 243).

Area	Tools
Art	Paintbrushes, pencils, crayons, markers, scissors, paper punch, staplers, play dough and clay utensils, large needles for stitchery, wire, yarn, pipe cleaners.
Blocks	Small wooden people, small plastic animals, small cars and other small toy vehicles, small signs, small blocks, interlocking train tracks, writing tools/paper for making signs.
Cooking	Can opener, stirring and measuring spoons, forks, paring and spreading knives, spatula, rolling pin, strainer, cheese slicer, vegetable brush and peeler, colander, cookie cutters.
Dramatic Play	Eating utensils, small-handled cups and pouring utensils, dress-up clothes or doll clothes with fasteners (buttons, zippers, laces), clip earrings, paper play money, writing tools/paper for making grocery lists.
Language Arts	Felt tip pens; crayons; pencils of various sizes; flannel board pieces; typewriters; computers; hand and stick puppets; plastic magnetic and rubber stamp shapes, letters, and numbers.
Manipulatives and Math Aids	Pegs and peg boards of different sizes, Legos, puzzles, lacing boards, interlocking cubes, Tinkertoys, beads and strings, geoboards, parquetry blocks.
Music/ Movement	Hand castanets, xylophone, triangle, handbells, cymbals with small knobs, rainsticks, scarves, streamers.
Science	Magnifying glasses, magnets, toothbrushes for washing rocks, eye droppers, small items for balancing and classifying, funnels, gardening tools, prisms, timers, tongs.
Woodworking	Nails, hammers, screws with large heads, screwdrivers, vise, saw, small pieces of sanded wood, pencils, markers, rulers or straight edge, glue, Styrofoam squiggles for gluing, pliers, hole punch, string, washers, wire, sandpaper.

Figure 3.2
Preschool examples of fine motor tools.

- Does her hand rest anchored on the table as her fingers move together using the pincer grip in an adult fashion?

Children start to use the last technique between the ages of 5 and 7. Based on Cratty's sequences, the introductory chapter vignette shows that Lupe's "tool-grasping" development is in the beginning stage.

Some teachers of 4-year-olds worry about kindergarten readiness when children in their classrooms cannot competently perform writing and cutting tasks. A specific concern centers around appropriate pencil size in the preschool classroom.

Carlson and Cunningham's (1990) research on pencil size concluded "there was some evidence to support the existence of a positive relationship between management and performance. Therefore, the recommendation to early childhood educators is that both large and small diameter pencils be provided for school graphomotor activities" (p. 279).

In addition to choice of pencil size, prior to initial writing attempts, the child needs experience with writing tools that acquaints the child with the tools and aids in developing the needed fine motor control (Sovik, 1993). The teacher observes and notes whether children have shown an interest and whether they have had sufficient time and opportunities to practice—beginning with easy tasks, such as using scissors to cut play dough pieces or copying letters in their names using fluid marking pens on unlined paper.

Teachers also observe which hand children use more frequently to execute fine motor tasks. Developing a dominant hand (current research links this to heredity) is usually seen by age 3; for 9 of 10 people the right hand is dominant (Papalia, Olds, & Feldman, 1999). A few people, however, alternate their preferred hands for different tasks.

In summary of physical development, understanding the developmental axioms, observing growth indicators, describing performance qualities, and making adjustments for individual needs constitute a power switch that turns on teacher effectiveness. To more fully assimilate the information on physical development, become an avid informal observer of children. Keep up-to-date on the latest brain-development research. Key in to children's displays of motor skills. Discuss your expectations for children's gross and fine motor development with your peers. Check that your expectations are based on sound developmental information, and use your observations to build an experiential understanding.

SELECTED HIGHLIGHTS OF COGNITIVE DEVELOPMENT

The boundaries of the concept of cognition are far from clear-cut. Cognition is obviously involved when a child puts a puzzle together for the first time, but the mind is similarly at work when a child watches a friend spin around a playground bar and attempts to do the same. At the very least, both activities involve the coordinated efforts of noticing details, remembering, and making judgments. In this book cognition is viewed as a fertile and complex concept—even though it is not easily defined. It is enough to say, at this point, that cognitive development refers to the changing and expanding intellectual processes of human beings and that children, like all human beings, have individualized cognitive strengths and weaknesses (Gardner, 1999) and rely on a variety of strategies and ways of thinking to learn (Siegler, 2000).

The following highlights link children's growth to observable indicators. They offer the following selection of topics rather than an exhaustive accounting: representational abilities, language, reasoning, social cognition, classification, seriation, number development, and memory. Remember to view each child's development as steps along a continuum rather than as age-segmented skills.

Representational Abilities

Stop and recall your most recent car trip. Who drove? Where did you go? What route did you take? What did you pass along the way? Now analyze your memories of this trip. Did your thoughts contain mental images and/or words? Most readers will answer yes. Now let's consider infants. What is their thinking like? We know young infants do not rely on language and do not have the same abilities as young children to think about objects or experiences remote from the present. This is not to say infants do not think; their thinking is, however, somehow different. If a few 8-month-olds are asked to get their teddy bears, they can manage this trip even if it involves crawling through a room, down a hall, and into their bedrooms. These babies had something going on in their minds, but once they reach early childhood, the form of their thought processes will be altered.

The remarkable advancement in cognition from the infant to the young child hinges on the expanding ability to think representationally—that is, to involve "the use of words, gestures, pictures, or actions to represent [stand for] ideas, things, or behaviors" (Berger, 2000, p. 272). Infants demonstrate some symbolic thinking (e.g., they wave bye-bye and know someone will leave), but representational abilities explode during early childhood. Dolls can represent people, toy cars can be models of the vehicles children ride in daily, a scribbled circle can represent a doughnut, and an upright block stands for a high-rise apartment building. Words are symbols that stand for people, things, places, actions, and ideas, and numbers designate quantities of objects. Dramatic play often includes complex representations of how children interpret other people's actions (often with a little imagination thrown in).

As preschool children mature, they also learn how to interpret others' representations and are delighted when they recognize pictures of familiar scenes, a city skyline, or a famous landmark. With maturation, experience, interest, and guidance, most preschoolers learn to decode at least some written numbers and letters before they begin kindergarten. This achievement is notable because numbers and letters are abstract symbols, bearing no physical resemblance to the concepts represented.

Representational thought allows children to solve problems mentally. Rather than trying to force puzzle pieces into place, preschoolers are able to think of solutions; they may study the shape, color, and details of some pieces before trying to fit them in place. Once children develop representational thought, they are forever changed. Try to fathom thinking without being allowed to use words or mental images. Difficult? Impossible? The ability to think in symbols is, indeed, an integral part of human cognitive processes (see Box 3.3 for growth indicators of representational abilities), and one job of early childhood educators is to provide children with the materials, time, encouragement, and stimulation to represent in depth.

Box 3.3

Preschool Growth Indicators of Representational Abilities

Growth Indicator	*Example*
Forms mental images	Ayako says, "I want to work with the blue play dough like yesterday."
	Max asks how big the earth is. Parent tries to describe the immensity of our planet but knows the image is inaccurate when Max asks, "Is there a traffic cone at the end?"
Imitates	Josephyne uses fingers to try to represent a spider climbing up a water spout.
	Two children bark like their dogs and notice the differences.
	Justin pitches an imaginary ball, swings an imaginary bat, runs the imaginary bases, and waves to the imaginary crowd.
Uses language	Madeleine asks her caregiver if she can look in the drawer, and the caregiver says, "Sure." Maddy repeats "Sure" to herself, then proudly exclaims to another child, "Tom said yes!"
Pretends	A child pushes a toy car on the floor, saying "Vroom, vroom."
Role plays	In the house area, Jeffrey takes the role of a dad to three stuffed animals and cooks them breakfast.
Represents in two dimensions	
Represents in three dimensions	Using sand in a large sandbox, Weston constructs a model of the local shopping mall, decorating favorite stores with feathers.
	Hector peels back the outside edges of his string cheese and announces to his snack table companions, "Look, I'm eating a banana!"
Decodes others' representations	A child carefully studies a pumpkin patch photo to find details observed on a field trip.
	Marissa identifies the familiar "EXIT" sign in the adjoining classroom.

Language

The development of representational thought provides the means for children to understand that words can stand for people, objects, actions, places, feelings, and ideas. Children learn to understand and speak their language remarkably well within their social environments and without formal instruction. This competence is even more impressive when we bear in mind that the bulk of what they hear, comprehend, and speak is newly invented; speakers continually create new sentences. During the preschool years, most children become commendable participants in their native language as they unconsciously learn many rules of grammar. Furthermore, the number of words in their vocabularies explodes as children add new words to their mental maps of interconnected categories, sometimes after only one exposure (Golinkoff, Hirsh-Pasek, Bailey, & Wenger, 1992). This process is called **fast mapping.** Although fast mapping quickly builds vocabulary, children frequently acquire limited or erroneous understandings based on their limited experiences. Think about how the following 4-year-old fast mapped a new term in a very concrete manner, and evaluate his conclusion in the context of his particular store of words and grammar, previous experiences, and maturation:

> Gregory (4;3) was the prized ring bearer in a relative's wedding, but despite his mother's subtle attempts to quiet him, he persisted in making low growling sounds throughout the ceremony. Afterward, Gregory's mom complimented him on his steady walk up the aisle and careful support of the ring-pillow but asked him why he kept making those strange noises. Gregory drew a deep breath that puffed out his chest to proudly explain, "I was the ring bear!"

Achievement in language development goes beyond the obvious communication benefits because language is a vital connector to advancing cognition (Vygotsky, 1987). The growth indicators of language development in Box 3.4 provide a starting point for classroom observations.

Language development during early childhood has practical implications for the early childhood educator. To promote growth, adults talk with children about meaningful topics, take them to interesting places, engage them with other children, read to them, and model a rich and correct use of language—all activities that are part of a productive preschool. These activities guide children from their levels of independent functioning to more advanced levels that children can manage with the help of adults or more competent peers. Vygotsky's **zone of proximal development** describes "the hypothetical, dynamic region in which learning and development take place" (Berk & Winsler, 1995, p. 5):

> As children become more competent, adults place increasing demands on them, hold them to higher standards, and give them more difficult problems. The degree and kind of scaffolding and social support change as well, as parents and teachers implicitly target their interventions to the child's current zone of proximal development. (DeLoache, Miller, & Pierroutsakos, 1998, p. 842)

For example, children learn new words by actively listening to and talking with others; their social environments are keys to vocabulary development. So if *delicious*

Box 3.4

Preschool Growth Indicators of Language

Growth Indicator	*Example*
Advances, but does not complete, understanding of grammar	Skyler overgeneralizes some rules and says *foots* to indicate plural and *bited* to form past tense. Carlos learns some rule exceptions and uses *feet, sang, bit,* and *taught.* A grandmother coaches her young grandchild to record a message for her telephone answering machine. *Ellen:* Me and Grandma can't come to the phone right now. . . *Grandma:* Say, "Grandma and I." *Ellen:* OK. Me and Grandma can't come to the phone right now . . . The grandmother corrects twice more. The light seems to go on in the child's head, the grandmother pushes the record button, and the child confidently speaks. *Ellen:* Me and Grandma and I can't come to the phone right now!
Progresses in articulation, but limitations remain	A child explains, "The wight's too bright for the wabbit."
Expands vocabulary	Aaron studies sand stuck at the entrance to a clogged funnel and mutters, "Now this is a perdicament."
Constructs increasingly complex sentences (structure and length)	"This thumb is all right, but this thumb is not," declares Sarah Joy, clutching a sore thumb.
Converses with increasing competence with adults and peers	Steve sits chest-deep in wading pool. *Steve:* I don't need to go under. I'm too little to go under. I'll go under later. I'll go under on Tuesday. He cautiously puts face in water and gets out of pool "to think it over." *Adult:* Oh my! How brave you are! Are you going to think about how proud of yourself you are? *Steve:* No, I'm going to think about how it scared me.

Children's progress in the zone of proximal development is enhanced by involvement with adults and peers.

is in a child's vocabulary, then *scrumptious* is within her or his zone of proximal development (Genishi, McCarrier, & Nussbaum, 1988), and participation in a dynamic interchange with another may serve to add *scrumptious* to this child's vocabulary. This other person (adult or more competent peer) has provided an effective *scaffold,* or support, for the child's language advancement. However, Bloom (1998) cautions us, however, to remember and appreciate children's active roles in their own language learning:

> It is the child who initiates conversational exchanges most often when children and caregivers are engaged in free play and other activities of daily living. Thus, participation in early conversations is motivated by a child's own cognitive, social, and affective agenda to express something in mind and to direct the flow of the interaction in order to share the contents of mind. (p. 349)

Literacy experiences are essential to preschool children because "every child who participates in rich literacy experiences before entering school will be a child who is more likely to escape the fate of early failure in learning to read and of long-term difficulties with literacy learning" (Bishop, Yopp, & Yopp, 2000, pp. 4–5). These experiences include engaging in rich and frequent conversations, being read to regularly, visiting the local library, seeing adults valuing reading, receiving encouragement and motivation to read, and building vocabularies and knowledge. Language feeds directly into children's reading success: "The broader their vocabulary and the more sophisticated their sentence structure, the more likely they are to make sense of what they see in print" (p. 24).

Reasoning

Preschool children do not use adult logic to solve problems and usually do not do well on logic or abstract tasks. They manage quite well, however, in their own lives as they encounter objects and events of interest to them. Consider the following preschool examples:

- Jose studied a boat being repaired on land and commented, "You need a ladder to get into the boat when the boat is out of the water, and you don't need a ladder to get into the boat when the boat is in the water."
- Rebecca listened to a Berenstain Bear story that took place before Sister was born. "Is Brother really a brother?" she asked.
- "I know two kinds of *trip*," remarked Frank watching a plane fly by, "one when you go on an airplane and one when you fall down and hurt yourself."

All three examples illustrate thoughtful reasoning about a limited set of factors; see Box 3.5 for growth indicators of the development of reasoning in young children.

Although preschool children have limitations in their abilities to reason, they do not need to be changed. They do, however, need nourishment to develop their reasoning abilities. The nourishment teachers need to provide consists of diverse materials and experiences, time to explore and represent, and an interesting environment

---

Box 3.5

Preschool Growth Indicators of Reasoning

Growth Indicator	Example
Often reasons and problem-solves thoughtfully	A child stands behind a friend at the slide and notices, "I can see your back because I'm not you."
	When Umar's block structure tumbles down on the carpet for the second time, he reaches for a flat board and says, "I'm going to build it again on this."
Often reasons on the basis of perceptions (not logic)	Kelsey compares her broken cracker to her neighbor's whole one at snack time and complains, "Hey, Tillie got more."
Thinks in concrete or tangible terms	When the teacher reminds Jackson and Bobby to stick together on the walk around the block, Jackson looks at his hands and asks, "With what?"

in which their support of and participation in children's activities communicate their unwavering commitment. In short, teachers must engage children in their individual zones of proximal development. They do so both by responding to teachable moments as they arise in the classroom and by planning based on observation. Such nourishment is part of the early childhood educator's job.

Social Cognition

> Social cognition has as its objects humans and human affairs; it means cognition and knowledge about people and their doings. Machines, mathematics, and mental states are all objects of cognition, for example, but only people's knowledge about mental states would be regarded as a topic within *social* cognition. Social cognition bears on the strictly social and psychological world, not the physical and logico-mathematical ones, even though all three worlds obviously have people's fingerprints all over them. (Flavell & Miller, 1998, p. 851; emphasis in original)

As children mature developmentally and expand their social interactions within their communities, they learn more about themselves and others. **Social cognition** is not a single concept (Cutting & Dunn, 1999), and even preschool children know something about the topics of humans' desires, emotions, intentions, visual perspectives, and thinking. The bulk of recent research in social cognition has focused on children's developing **theory of mind,** which refers to "an understanding of mental processes, that is, of one's own or another's emotions, perceptions, and thoughts" (Berger & Thompson, 1995, p. 344) and which "is gradually acquired when children are between the ages of 2 and 5" (Jenkins & Astington, 2000, p. 216). Wellman & Hickling (1994) and Wellman, Hollander, & Schult (1996) provide evidence of young preschoolers' awareness that people have mental states different from their own. They therefore realize that a person may be angry even if they, themselves, are not. Furthermore, they understand that thought is not physical, that mental states can determine action (e.g., anger may lead to yelling), and that different people may have different thoughts about the same situation. If told that a person is trying to deceive, 3-year-olds reject that person's statements as truthful, thus demonstrating their awareness of the "intentional states of the speaker" (Lee & Cameron, 2000, p. 16). Several more years are required, however, before children view the mind as an independent and active entity constantly at work (Wellman & Hickling, 1994); for the time being, "young children tend to underestimate the amount of mental activity that *does* go on in a *conscious* mind . . . [and] overestimate the amount of (nondreaming) ideation that *can* go on in an *unconscious* mind" (Flavell, Green, Flavell, & Lin, 1999, p. 409; emphasis in original). The growth indicators in Box 3.6 summarize preschoolers' budding social cognition.

"Theory-of-mind research suggests that the understanding of mental states is central to social cognition" (Flavell & Miller, 1998, p. 883). Appropriate experiences for young children in the process of developing theories of mind are social interactions that stimulate their abilities to consider and respond to others' emotional, social, or cognitive points of view. For example, suppose a 4-year-old grabs a

Box 3.6

Preschool Growth Indicators of Social Cognition

Growth Indicator	*Example*
Understands that thinking is an internal, mental process	Roland sees a tipped-over trash can and says, "I wonder how that happened."
Understands that others have their own emotional, social, and cognitive points of view	Kurt accidentally spills a glass of juice and quickly looks at the teacher's face to gauge her reaction.
	Mayuko builds a block tunnel and calls to a friend to look at her through the opposite end.
Demonstrates limited interpretations of others' emotional, social, and cognitive points of view	Using a computer face-making program, Jessie makes a face and exclaims that her teacher, 15 ft across the room, should see it. Jessie leans to one side so she no longer blocks the teacher's view but does not understand that her teacher is too far away to discern the details of the face.

younger child's shovel in the sandbox. Should a teacher expect that the 4-year-old can consider the younger child's emotional perspective, at least well enough to imagine the other's feelings of hurt or anger or intimidation? The issue of preschoolers' understanding of others is central to many common interactions in and out of the classroom.

Fortunately, the preschool classroom offers a multitude of opportunities to stimulate and challenge children's evolving understanding of others' points of view. As children play collaboratively, they are stimulated to take the perspectives of others and be sure their communication is clear (Rogoff, 1998). Teachers can challenge children's social cognition as well. For example, a teacher, Ellie, calls up to Phung at the top of the jungle gym and asks what he sees from way up there.

"I see the pizza place across the street and the big tree and lots of cars driving past," he hollers down.

"What do you think I see from down here?" Ellie asks, interested to discover if the child recognizes that the wooden fence denies her the opportunity to see the pizza store, the cars, and the trunk of the big tree. If Phung's response indicates he understands that her perspective is different from his, she congratulates him for noticing that the fence blocks her view of the street. If, however, he assumes she sees what he sees, Ellie can cherish her next few moments as a teacher.

"I'll be right up," Ellie calls. "I want to admire your view." The teacher and child stand together on the jungle gym and talk about the tops of children's heads, the entire play yard, and the school roof, as well as the pizza store, big tree, and passing cars. Ellie notices Maria jumping next to the fence. "Look where Maria is. I wonder what she can see. Let's go take a look." She promotes Phung's active learning about others' perspectives through this teachable moment.

Let's return to the 4-year-old who grabbed the shovel. Is there reason to believe this child can take the other's feelings into consideration? Most likely, in the heat of the moment (the height of shovel desire), the 4-year-old never thought once, much less twice, about how the other child would feel when the shovel was grabbed away. If a teacher talked with the child after the act, however, some perspective-taking would probably emerge. Over time, as young children's natural impulsiveness declines with maturation and expanded communication skills and as people help them take notice of others' perspectives (emotional and otherwise), children build their theories of mind and become more aware of and responsive to others' points of view.

Classification

Children and adults rely on **classification** to deal logically with objects and ideas in their everyday lives. Objects in homes are classified in appropriate rooms; for example, you expect dishes to be in a kitchen. Classification also serves more detailed purposes. A third grader might sort a list of spelling words into groups of those mastered and those requiring study. A junior high student may have several

The availability of a variety of materials offers preschool children interesting cognitive experiences.

Box 3.7

Preschool Growth Indicators of Classification

Growth Indicator	Example
Explores diverse attributes of objects	Sophia turns several shells all around before choosing surfaces to press down into play dough during a printmaking activity.
Recognizes similarities and differences	Two 3-year-olds clean up the tinkertoys by matching colors in a labeled silverware tray.
	Dorine remarks that the two guinea pigs have the same kinds of wiggly noses and whiskers but different kinds of fur.
Sorts objects with increasing sophistication	An adult gives lettuce, carrot, parsley, and oatmeal to Hank, who is pretending to be a rabbit. After munching, he exclaims, "I ate all the vegetables and the oatmeal!"
	After a nature walk, Brady groups leaves of similar shape on a collage.

---

methods for sorting baseball cards. For ease of access, a gourmet cook organizes jars of spices, and an expert quilter sorts dozens of fabrics by color. When did this ability blossom? What classification behaviors can we expect to see in the early childhood classroom?

Early childhood classrooms offer abundant opportunities for children to classify objects. Using blocks, children might build enclosures to separate the wild from tame plastic animals, or they might construct a special road just for the trucks hauling supplies. To encourage children to notice similarities and differences and how things go together, the classroom environment may be organized so that children sort toys and supplies into labeled containers or onto labeled shelves and pegboards as they clean up. For example, shaking instruments and percussion instruments might be sorted when stored on the pegboard in the music area. Look for the growth indicators listed in Box 3.7 to evaluate classification skills in the preschool classroom.

Seriation

Seriation is arranging things or putting them in order according to one characteristic. It is another cognitive ability that progresses as children mature and gain experience with their world. Teachers often emphasize seriation by size (e.g., with blocks or sticks) and forget about the many other interesting attributes of objects

Box 3.8

Preschool Growth Indicators of Seriation

Growth Indicator	Example
Makes comparisons	At the sand table Teddy says, "Let's make this really soapy water be the ocean and this kinda soapy water be the lake."
Seriates a limited number of objects	Elke arranges three triangles by size and glues them on a flat piece of wood.

(e.g., textures of sandpaper in the construction area and color gradations of paint chips in the art area). Numerous objects available in the preschool classroom enable children to compare along various dimensions:

light to heavy	sweet to sour
short to long	light to dark
narrow to wide	clean to dirty
slow to fast	smooth to rough
high pitch to low pitch	young to old
loud to quiet	

In the preschool classroom, seriation begins with comparisons (Hohmann & Weikart, 1995). For example, before children can line up several sticks from short to long, they first need to compare a short and a long stick. Comparisons begin with two objects: for example, wet and dry hands, sweet and sour lemonade, high- and low-pitched singing, fast and slow dancing, light- and dark-green paper, and smooth and bumpy tree bark. These comparisons support the seriation skills to follow: seriating a few objects through trial and error to seriating many objects systematically (see Box 3.8 for growth indicators of seriation skills).

Number Development

Young children spontaneously and informally learn about numbers before formal schooling begins (Flavell, Miller, & Miller, 1993). Between the ages of 2 and 8, "children memorize the number words, come to understand that each word represents a different quantity, and develop their counting skills" (Geary, 1994, p. 34). Children seem to have informal knowledge that "adding makes more, subtracting yields less" (Ginsburg, Klein, & Starkey, 1998, p. 417) and that sharing involves dividing things up. Understanding, however, that all numbers represent specific quantities and learning to count many objects accurately are processes that develop gradually.

Box 3.9

Preschool Growth Indicators of Number Development

Growth Indicator	Example
Compares quantities of small sets	"Hey, she's got more!" complains a child with fewer apple slices than a neighbor.
Learns number names	Alvaro counts, "Threeteen fourteen, fiveteen."
	Children sing a counting song during circle time.
Understands numbers as representations of quantities	Josiah explains to teacher in the art area, "I need three pieces of paper to make roofs for those three office buildings."
Counts limited number of objects with one-to-one correspondence	On a rainy day, Chelsea counts nine umbrellas outside the door.

Young children first demonstrate their increasing understanding of numbers with small sets. For example, they can count three objects correctly before they master counting six objects. Although counting is conceptually grounded (Ginsburg, 1998), common counting errors include saying more than one number word for an object (e.g., counting five objects as [1, 2]−[3]−[4]−[5, 6]−[7]) and saying a number word without pointing to or counting an object (e.g., counting five objects as [1]−[2]−[3]−[4 in space]−[5]−[6]). The clear awareness that the end number (5, in this example) has to correspond to a specific quantity of objects requires some years of practice and maturation.

The preschool classroom can provide opportunities for children to learn number words, understand that each number represents a specific quantity, and develop counting skills. Over time, such activities will strengthen their understanding of number for use in practical contexts (see Box 3.9 for growth indicators of number development).

Memory

"Memory is at the center stage of cognition" (Schneider & Bjorklund, 1998, p. 467), and "the basic neurological architecture that supports memory development is established early in life" (Pressley & Schneider, 1997, p. 320). Preschoolers and adults thus share the same "basic hardware" because both **recognition** and **recall memory** are evident during early childhood. A 4-year-old child might hear a song at preschool and instantly recognize it from a visit to his cousin's 4 months earlier. Recall memory, on the other hand, builds on mental imagery or language; preschoolers, as we know, are capable of these representational skills. So when a

3-year-old retells her favorite story to a sibling, she demonstrates her recall memory. Although there are great advances from early childhood capacities, processing speeds, and abilities, the processes of recognition and recall memory are already in place. Beyond these general similarities, however, "different types of memory have different underlying neurological systems. Therefore, we should not expect that the various memory skills for any given child will be homogeneous. Just as there is great unevenness in general cognitive abilities . . . so too is there much heterogeneity of memory abilities" (Schneider & Bjorklund, 1998, p. 468).

"What the head knows has an enormous effect on what the head learns and remembers" (Flavell et al., 1993, p. 255). In other words, what a person knows has a powerful influence on what information that person can store from the environment and remember, and "it has been recognized for some time that memory performance is highly dependent on the developing knowledge base" (Pressley & Schneider, 1997, p. 32). For example, chess experts remembered gamelike chess arrangements better than nonexpert players, even when the experts were 10-year-olds and the nonexperts were adults (Chi, 1978). The experts' "heads" had more experience and skills with gamelike arrangements and thus were better prepared to remember them.

So it is with young children. Imagine a teacher reading a book about dinosaurs to a small group of children. Manuel listens attentively because he has been read to at home about dinosaurs, has visited museums of natural history to see dinosaur skeletons, and has played with plastic models of dinosaurs for hours on end. Tanya plays with dinosaurs at school and is also interested in the book, but Jeremy is content to sit in his teacher's lap as he casually glances from the illustrations to the ongoing classroom activities. After reading about the stegosaurus, the teacher turns the page and asks if anyone knows the name of the next dinosaur.

"Oh, I know, I know," exclaims Manuel, struggling to retrieve a name from his memory.

"This is an armored dinosaur," the teacher remarks as they admire the illustration. "Do you remember the name yet, Manuel?"

"No, but I know it," he groans.

"Ankylosaurus," says the teacher. "This dinosaur is an ankylosaurus."

"Yes, that's right. I know that. Ankylosaurus," pronounces Manuel easily.

The "heads" that Manuel, Tanya, and Jeremy brought to the story time were unique. Manuel's head already knew a lot about dinosaurs, and he was confidently able to recognize the ankylosaurus' name even though he could not recall it on his own (perhaps next time). Tanya knew less but probably learned something—perhaps that the ankylosaurus is an armored dinosaur. Time will tell. Jeremy might not have learned specific dinosaur facts from the conversation, but that's all right; he enjoyed the pleasant company and atmosphere at story time. Thus, even in preschool, children have different heads stemming from their developmental levels and past experiences (see Box 3.10 for growth indicators of memory); teachers cannot expect that everything they say goes into those heads in the same way.

Many interesting and important topics were not discussed in this section on cognitive development during the preschool years (e.g., young children's understanding of space and time and their expanding problem-solving abilities); readers may wish to study these topics independently. Also, although this section presented general trends in cognitive development, individual differences between children abound. These differences are normal and reflect human diversity.

SELECTED HIGHLIGHTS OF PSYCHOSOCIAL DEVELOPMENT

Human beings are social creatures, and who they become depends in large measure on the impact of their social worlds. **Psychosocial development** is the third developmental domain to be introduced. Although the domains of child development are categorized for practical study purposes, children are whole beings; their physical, cognitive, psychosocial, and creative developments are interrelated. For example, a preschool child's pumping skills on a swing set depend, in part, on large-muscle strength and coordination (physical development), understanding of when the legs go out and in (cognitive development), and encouragement from others (psychosocial development); once pumping is mastered, the child's creativity might stimulate the invention of new swinging skills. As in the other developmental domains, space and time considerations permit the review of only selected topics for the early childhood educator; this section discusses the child's expanding relationships with adults and peers, self-concept, play, fears, aggression, and impulse control.

Expanding Relationships with Adults and Peers

Young children depend on their parent(s), other family members, or guardians for comfort and as liaisons between their personal needs and desires and the larger world. Teachers of young children become sensitive to their own roles as new caregivers when they understand the resources inherent in and the intensity behind the child–family bond. For example, perceptive teachers may have a registration form to inquire about each child's routines, needs, interests, and skills so that they can make the environment welcoming and somewhat familiar. To reproduce a favorite home activity, dump trucks with pegs for filling and emptying are ready in the block area for one child's first day, and a special blanket is handy for rest time. Furthermore, alert teachers consciously look for opportunities to build their own relationships and styles of communication with each child. A teacher mixes colors and uses a pump next to a new child at the water table and, with a farewell hug, enthusiastically describes these activities to the parent at the end of the day.

To young children teachers are more than ships passing in the night. They are adults to whom young children reach out for security and companionship. To be effective, teachers establish their own positive and trusting relationships with each child in their care. Separation from parents will be less traumatic as children experience the emotional commitment from their teachers and thrive on the new variety of communication partners.

As young children venture away from their homes, they encounter peers in neighborhoods, play groups, preschools, child care, and social and recreational gatherings. The success of early friendships hinges "to a great extent on the child's ability to communicate and share a common frame of reference with their partner" (Ladd & Coleman, 1993, p. 72). The quantity and quality of friendships among young children vary considerably as parents control their access to one another. Hints that a friendship is in the making are that the children voluntarily spend time together and share a reciprocal, give-and-take relationship (Hartup, 1992). "By the third year of life, the tendency to prefer same-sex playmates is clearly established in girls, and is established in boys soon thereafter" (Maccoby, 1998, p. 19).

Expanding relationships with adults and peers can support young children's **prosocial behavior**—behavior that reflects concern for others. In general, prosocial behavior increases during the preschool years (Zahn-Waxler & Smith, 1992) as children become more aware of others' feelings and ideas. Empathy (the ability to feel *with* other people) generally increases but not always consistently. For example, if two preschoolers see the same child crying at the bottom of a slide, one may offer heartfelt help and the other may not. Researchers have found that children are more empathic when their parents "call strong attention to the distress their misbehavior caused someone else" (Goleman, 1995, p. 99). Teachers can do the same in their classrooms to encourage children to understand and appreciate others' emotions and to respond with a generous heart and actions. Box 3.11 relates growth indicators of expanding relationships with adults and peers.

Self-Concept

Humans are unique as a species in their capacity for self-consciousness. The sense of self is a psychological construct nourished by expanding cognitive and social maturity (see Box 3.12). During early childhood, children come to understand that

Box 3.11

Growth Indicators of Expanding Relationships with Adults and Peers

Growth Indicator	Example
Demonstrates strong attachment to parents and family	Cecilia asks for the fifth time in one hour, "When's my dad coming?"
Establishes emotional bonds to nonfamilial people	Stuart runs to his teacher to hug her good-bye at the end of the day.
Forms friendships	Upon arrival at child care, Maya asks her teacher, "Is Yvonne here yet? We're painting today."
Exhibits concern and empathy	Eddie looks up from a book in the story area and asks, "Who's crying? I'll go and check."
	"Oh my gosh, Farah," says her teacher in a concerned voice. "Look! Dougie's crying because you knocked his art project off the shelf with your coat. Let's go see how we can help." Farah, who accidentally caused this damage, willingly moves toward Dougie.

they have a physical self that takes up space and has unique physical attributes and a psychological self that is not visible from the outside. As discussed in the social cognition section, young children understand they have internal thoughts and emotions as part of this psychological self. Generally, preschoolers are quite pleased with themselves, and their self-evaluations tend to be positive and include overestimations of their abilities (Harter, 1998). Between the ages of 2 and 6, children hardly seem to notice their failures, but rather they tend to believe "they can win any race, skip perfectly, count accurately, and make up beautiful songs. Self-confidence is tied to competence, and competence demands repeated demonstration of mastery" (Berger, 2000, p. 306).

A critical part of children's conceptions of themselves is their **gender identity**—knowing whether they are a girl or boy. "Virtually all of human functioning has a gendered cast—appearance, mannerisms, communication, temperament, activities at home and outside, aspirations, and values" (Ruble & Martin, 1998, p. 933). Most 3-year-olds "are able to use gender labels to classify themselves and others" (Maccoby, 1998, p. 293); if they understand that genitalia determine one's gender, most also understand that gender is a permanent attribute (Bem, 1989).

In general, conformity to many gender-stereotyped roles and preferences is already evident in the preschool years. Perhaps because preschool children are only beginning to learn about the complex web of social conventions dealing with

---

Box 3.12

Growth Indicators of Self-Concept

Growth Indicator	Example
Understands the self has physical and psychological attributes	Colin sits with hands on his knees and declares, "I have hair on my legs like you, Dad."
	After a disagreement with an adult, child exclaims, "I get so mad at you!"
Aware of private, thinking self	"Hi, Sireena. What are you doing?" a teacher says to a child nestled in a beanbag chair. "Just dinkin'," Sireena replies.
Overestimates own abilities	After listening to a story that ends with, "No one's good at everything," child responds with self-confidence, "I am."
Correctly identifies own gender	Andreas points to self and a playmate and declares, "I'm a boy, and you're a girl."
Often rigidly applies gender roles	Jasmine says she wants to be a nurse when she grows up even though her mother is a doctor.

---

gender, they exaggerate their gender roles so as to get them cognitively clear. A young 3-year-old girl with short, baby-thin hair publicly reaffirms her gender every day by adamantly refusing to wear anything except dresses. As levels of moral reasoning advance and children distinguish between moral and social norms, they become less rigid about gender issues (Lobel & Menashri, 1993).

How individual children construe gender roles results from their unique blend of experiences within peer groups, social pressure, imitation and identification, biological influences, and their own self-regulation (Maccoby, 1980, 1990). Sometimes the strength of social pressure is evident as young children, having noticed the predominant gender of construction workers in their social environment, favor plastic models of men to represent these workers in the block area. Personal experiences, however, may help children form some nonstereotypic models. For example, a girl whose mother is a construction worker might well include a model of a woman in her block play or imitate the role herself.

Play

More than being a diversion to keep children busy, play serves a wide variety of functions during early childhood: fostering physical, intellectual, and social development; providing the medium for the expression of rich emotional values; and stimulating the creative aspect of children's personalities (Hendrick, 2001); the bonus is that play is distinctly fun (Maccoby, 1998). Although children do not set out to learn about concepts in their physical world when they play, that is often what happens. In preschool, an observer may be lucky enough to see children playing with materials and, incidentally, learning how to build a sturdy tower or combine effective amounts of sand and water to make a moldable mixture.

Often young children's play facilitates their social development. We are more watchful of young children's relationships with peers because they spend more time together in play groups, preschools, and child-care settings than in previous generations. As friendships evolve, children may play independently next to other children, engage in rough-and-tumble play, share common activities, or play cooperatively. Although the frequency of parallel play remains stable from 3 to 5, developing children increasingly use parallel play "as an entrée into more complex, cooperative play" (Rubin, Bukowski, & Parker, 1998, p. 635). Through endless hours of play graced with a multitude of playmates and adult support, young children learn a great deal about how to get along with others.

With increasing attention to and agreement on the roles, rules, and themes in their dramatic play, children reflect their growing capacity to understand the perspective of others; here we see children's theory of mind at work (Rubin et al., 1998). No one will scold children for being bossy if they are only pretending to be the neighborhood grouch. Or in the cloak of pretend roles, shy children can experiment with more assertive behaviors; they might find that the behaviors fit better than expected. Children also learn about their society through play, and they do so without personal risk. They might apply what they have learned about rules and punishments in a game of good guys/bad guys in which no one actually dies or goes to jail.

Play also serves the function of furthering physical development. Strength of large and small muscles, coordination, and flexibility are all advanced as young children play. The gross motor control of a 3-year-old is challenged by maneuvering a tricycle around traffic cones, and the fine motor skills of a 4-year-old are practiced by manipulating tools at the water table. The next section on creative development discusses the relationship between play and creativity.

Although some observers of play may focus on play with objects versus social play (e.g., Heidemann & Hewitt, 1992) and others may distinguish between functional, constructive, and dramatic/pretend play (Rubin et al., 1998), they all recognize the satisfaction that play gives to children. Even with our technological advances, "young children . . . still need to spend most of their time working with and constructing their own conceptions of forms, qualities, and objects through direct, multi-sensory experiences" (Elkind, 1998, p. 161); play serves this need. Although the amount and type of play vary across cultures, keep in mind the growth indicators listed in Box 3.13 for most American children.

Fears

"Fears are normal, and they help children solve developmental issues. They also call parents' attention to the child's struggle. They generate support from parents

---

Box 3.13

Growth Indicators of Play

Growth Indicator	*Example*
Explores materials on own	Lesley examines a toy trash truck and discovers one lever to raise the truck bed and one lever to open the back hatch.
Engages in physical play	Monty and Lee race for adjacent swings.
Expands social interactions	In the sandbox several children industriously dig with scoopers next to one another, speaking occasionally, while others cooperate to dig a moat around their "castle."
Engages in dramatic play with increasing attention to roles, rules, and themes	"Hurry up," one child prods another in the house area. "Hurry up an' get dressed, or we'll be late for work. You don't want your boss to get mad."

---

at a time when children need it" (Brazelton, 1992, p. 276). What are young and inexperienced children afraid of? First of all, they might be fearful of real objects, experiences, or people. Fears of this sort might come in the form of bathtub drains that make things disappear, loud noises, high places, people wearing masks, dogs, and strangers. Preschool children become increasingly able to think ahead and anticipate potential dangers. Depending on their culture, children might have a healthy fear of hot stoves, fast cars, rushing rivers, or galloping animals.

The origin of other fears might lie within as preschoolers' representational thought, which provides entry to a world of imagination, may feature frightening creatures or experiences. Children may fear what might happen; parents' divorce, fire, and abduction may lie in this category for some children.

Fortunately, "children can and do begin to take control of their fears" (Berger, 2000, p. 305). Adults may help children face their fears by listening to children talk about their fears, reassuring them, helping them find ways to handle fears, maintaining consistent controls on behavior, facilitating learning about the frightening objects, and assisting children in understanding and expressing fears (Brazelton, 1992). Above all, adults working with young children should view most fears (see Box 3.14 for growth indicators) as normal and indicative of developmental spurts or adjustments to stress.

Aggression

"In terms of frequency of aggressive acts, preschoolers are the most aggressive humans" (Coie & Dodge, 1998, p. 780). Fortunately, however, young children normally develop out of this stage. Toddlers and young preschoolers usually do not

---

Box 3.14

Growth Indicators of Fears

Growth Indicator	Example
Fears of real objects, people, and experiences	Margrit backs away from viewing a sea anemone, perceiving it as a sea "enemy."
	Garrett is suddenly fearful of the stenciled designs on his bedroom ceiling that now appear to him as large eyes.
Fears of the unknown or the imagined	After a nightmare Loren sticks close by his teacher for the morning and begins to cry when she goes into a dim closet for supplies.

---

mean to hurt others when they act aggressively; they are simply self-centered in their intent to get what they want. Their focus may be on a toy, a territory, or a privilege, such as being the first to ride a tricycle. This is descriptively called **instrumental aggression** because the intent is not to hurt. True **hostile aggression,** however, is not far behind and is evident when children focus their anger on another and their intent *is* to hurt or dominate the other either by physical or verbal means. Between the ages of 2 and 4, we see a decrease in physical aggression and an increase in verbal aggression that coincides with the development of children's language skills, impulse control, perspective-taking, empathy, and memory (Coie & Dodge, 1998). A general gender difference is noted: "indeed, direct aggression—both verbal and physical—is more common among boys than among girls" (Maccoby, 1998, p. 35), but for most boys, the frequency of rough play and fighting peaks at about the age of 4. Our social norms help to support low aggression levels for girls (Stormshak et al., 1999). Box 3.15 describes growth indicators of changes in aggression.

Children today seem to display more aggressive behavior than children did in previous generations.

> One reason is that postmodern youngsters have more to be upset and angry about. Many have parents who have separated or divorced, or who have such busy schedules that there is little time for sustained, enjoyable interactions. Also, some children may be upset—or influenced in other ways—by some of the violence and mayhem that is so endemic on TV. And they may be stressed by the long hours they have to spend away from their own homes. We cannot undo all these sources of anger and resentment, but we can recognize that this aggression is a reaction to life circumstances and not necessarily the expression of an angry personality. (Elkind, 1998, p. 84)

Teachers (and parents) may foster alternatives to aggressive behavior. Young children are rapidly developing their communicative abilities and, therefore, can be encouraged to substitute words for blows. The welfare of the victim, not the

---

Box 3.15

Growth Indicators of Changes in Aggression

Growth Indicator	Example
Instrumental aggression	Without making eye contact, Kendra grabs another's play dough.
Hostile aggression	"You big fat baby!" one child yells at another who won't relinquish the lemon-scented play dough.
Increasing reliance on communication to settle disputes	"Can I have the play dough now?" Enrique asks Mary Alice. "No," Mary Alice answers firmly. "Well, gimme *some* then," he counters.

---

aggressor, is the focus of the adult's first concern. Adults can also sensitize children to the feelings of others, for example, by involving the aggressor in the care of the victim; this strategy relates to an earlier discussion of theory of mind in which children are encouraged to understand and take into account others' points of view. Looking outward to society, adults may work to decrease the conspicuous and subtle violence in children's environments.

Impulse Control

Parents and teachers often put on blinders and deal with children's misdeeds as isolated events. Instead they would do well to remind themselves of where young children are in their development of **impulse control** and what can be done to foster it. Even though "preschool and kindergarten children are increasingly capable of voluntary control of their emotions, their interactions with others, and their problem-solving activities" (Bronson, 2000, p. 35), we know that they do not master self-regulation during this period. Young children typically act before they thoroughly think about consequences and respond immediately to interesting or exciting objects, people, and events. A brief study of impulse control enables you to see the forest of the development of impulse control rather than the trees of misdeeds.

What difference does impulse control make in children's lives? We know that "sustained attention and the ability to delay are positively related, and both develop over the preschool years" (Rothbart & Bates, 1998, p. 37). Indeed, we have known for a long time that self-control mechanisms allow children to develop a high quality of solitary play, attend to complex problems, anticipate dangers and guard their own safety, and sustain cooperative play with other children (Maccoby, 1980). Children "who had resisted temptation at four were now, as adolescents, more socially competent: personally effective, self-assertive, and better able to cope with the frustrations of life" (Goleman, 1995, p. 81). Further, "because moral and prosocial behaviors often require self-control and self-denial, it is logical that the ability to regulate one's own behavior is intimately involved in the development of prosocial behavior" (Eisenberg et al., 1999, p. 1369). There is also "strong evidence that inhibitory or effortful control contributes to conscience development in childhood" (Kochanska, Murray, & Coy, 1999, p. 274). Adults who want to foster the development of impulse control in children (see Box 3.16 for growth indicators) can profit from research finding maternal overcontrol associated with poor impulse control (Silverman & Ragusa, 1990) and from Maccoby's review of implications for child rearing:

- Provide children with a regular, predictable schedule in which novelty is regulated.
- Minimize the waiting time required of young children.
- Make the environment safe and childproof.
- Make appropriate decisions when children are too young to anticipate the consequences. Provide opportunities for age-appropriate decisions.
- Model self-control.
- Set clear limits and firm controls on children's behavior.
- Engage in joint activities with children.

The last strategy deserves a bit more attention, and here again we witness an application of Vygotsky's zone of proximal development. The hours teachers and

---

Box 3.16

Growth Indicators of Impulse Control

Growth Indicator	Example
Often acts before considering consequences	Upon awaking in the nap room where other children are still sleeping, Nicola calls loudly to teacher.
Has difficulty waiting	Like many of his classmates on their 3rd birthdays, Theodore blows out his candles before the song is over.
	Noticing problem behaviors every time preschoolers are lined up and asked to wait, the teacher abandons this procedure in favor of brief, direct transitions.
Makes choices at own developmental level	Kasumi studies two stacks of shirts in a drawer and calls down to parent, "Is it a short-sleeve day or a long-sleeve day?"
Benefits from joint activities with adults	Aynsley, who does not often exhibit self-sustained attention, on works intently on a sand city when a teacher is involved.

parents spend working and playing with children will encourage their self-control in the long run. Joint activities allow children to participate in a complex sequence of events that they are not yet able to manage on their own and to enjoy the rewards of delayed gratification. Consider a teacher making play dough with a small group of preschoolers. The children gain the experience of following several steps of an activity and produce a lovely product for their efforts. The teacher working alongside the children has the opportunity to model new ideas for children who are easily bored because they tend to work superficially with materials.

Preschool children's progress in learning about themselves and their social worlds is remarkable. "At the end of the preschool years, most children are ready to venture further out into the world and meet the expanded social demands of elementary school.

SELECTED HIGHLIGHTS OF CREATIVE DEVELOPMENT

Creativity is studied and explored from various perspectives and in many different ways (e.g., Csikszentmihalyi, 1996; Edwards, Gandini, & Forman, 1993; Feldman, 1999; Presbury, Benson, & Torrance, 1997). Definitions for creativity are also varied. For this chapter, the definition is linked to the early childhood classroom, in which the comparative basis for judging originality is the child herself/himself rather than adult standards, which mandate that the work be new to everyone (Schmirrmacher, 1998). During the preschool years, "creativity is a way of thinking and acting or making something that is original for the individual and valued by that person or others" (Mayesky, 1998, p. 4).

Feldman's work (1980) explored two approaches to creativity taken by psychologists. He labeled one approach the **trait approach** and the other the **process approach.** Feldman explained that the trait approach, fathered by J. P. Guilford, submits that creativity is innate and unfolds naturally; it is motivated from within to express itself and will do so, except under extreme conditions. This approach holds that each person is born with a certain measure of creativity.

On the other hand, the process approach "focuses on the interaction between the organism and the environment—the ongoing, ever changing construction of behavior" (Feldman, 1980, p. 90). Creativity is the result of having abilities and experiences that allow for practice and improvement. For example, interested family members and teachers can provide the necessary encouragement and opportunities for children to develop their abilities. "Environment appears to play a greater role than heredity in the development of creativity: identical twins reared apart show greater differences in creativity than in intellectual abilities" (Kagan & Gall, 1998, p. 186).

These two approaches, much akin to the nature-versus-nurture controversy, produce implications for the classroom. If we subscribed to the first approach—traits—teachers would need to do little. Today we find in the educational arena, however, the process approach is favored over the trait approach (Davis & Rimm, 1998).

Review the growth indicators in Box 3.17 (based on the creative skills identified by Gordon and Williams-Brown, 2000) to learn how creativity for young children is identified. Then read on to find out how to facilitate and cultivate creativity through the process approach.

Box 3.17

Preschool Growth Indicators of Creativity

Growth Indicator	Definition	Example
Expands flexibility and fluency	Sees alternatives, especially when one idea fails. Can change from one idea to another	While playing fire-fighter, one child uses the only hose. Another child (who usually seeks the teacher's assistance) rummages through the dramatic play materials and uses a vacuum cleaner attachment as a hose.
Expands sensitivity	Tunes in to senses and sees details in the surrounding environment	On a walk Effrin carefully observes an ant diligently dragging a bread crumb toward the ant hill and says, "Boy, he's working hard!"
Expands imagination	Composes and utilizes mental images of things not present	Chester, using a block as a microphone and standing on top of an outdoor play structure, sways back and forth as he signs, imitating a popular country western singer.
Expands risk-taking	Experiments with possibilities, being open to divergent thinking and acting on it	Olivia adds one more block to a precarious structure.
Expands self resourcefulness	Trusts one's own perceptions	A child uses the wheelbarrow to transport selected toys to the other side of the play yard.
Expands expressiveness and skills using creative materials	Develops necessary proficiency through practice and maturation (interrelated with fine motor and cognitive development)	A child's functional explorations and manipulations (stirring and mixing sand) become representational as cakes are created.

"In preschool children, this putting together of new ideas and products based on past experience is expressed primarily through the use of self-expressive materials, through imaginative pretend play, and through creative thought" (Hendrick, 1998, p. 290). Children of this age are involved with exploration, discovery, and new experiences. If observers slip quietly through the doors of quality preschools, they can see numerous examples of young children engaged in the creative process: constructing block structures and using accessory items; dressing up in high heels, wearing a waltz length silky nightie, and carrying around precious baby dolls; laboriously struggling to solve puzzle patterns; waving scarves and moving to the music of a favorite record; making mud pies with wet sand; building with nails and wood; drawing with crayons, markers, and chalk; and dictating original stories as an adult's hand races to capture every spoken word. In the famous child-care centers in Reggio Emilia, Italy, these abundant forms of creativity are considered languages, specifically referred to as the children's 100 languages (Rody, 1995).

Wise early childhood educators know that simply observing the emerging signs of creative growth listed in Box 3.17 is not enough to support creativity. By using the information obtained from observations of individual children, the teacher makes strategy decisions. The teacher may provide enticing classroom experiences based on a child's interests, offer encouragement related to the child's effort, co-construct a project through the child's lead, ask open-ended questions, arrange the environment to reflect a creative climate, and/or take field trips to appreciate creative expression in the community. Figure 3.3 offers suggestions for the teacher-in-training.

Let's take a closer look at two specific components of creativity—art and block play. When you are observing children engaged in these two activities, knowledge of typical growth is advantageous.

As children grow and develop at their own pace, so does their representational drawing. The individual growth rate is influenced by the child's cognitive development (e.g., representational thought), physical development (e.g., motor control), perceptual development (e.g., sensory awareness and space perception), and art experiences (e.g., opportunities to explore). Therefore, if the teacher understands and can identify the characteristics represented by a child's art work, an observational window opens.

While studying the growth indicators of children's drawing presented in Box 3.18, be aware of the developmental sequence from scribbling to the advancement of picture forms. The classroom teacher can collect a few samples of each child's drawings over time, dating each sample. Box 3.18 is a handy reference to use for interpretation of children's developmental growth in drawing.

Teachers can also observe and keep notes of the sequential development of three-dimensional art materials. When children are working with clay, the teacher can expect to see the following (Wolfgang & Wolfgang, 1992):

1. Random pounding
2. Controlled pounding
3. Rolling clay into snake-like rolls and later into circles
4. Adding pieces to the rolls and circles (facial features and body parts)
5. Combining products, such as people in cars or a boy on a horse (p. 31)

Condition	Examples of the Teacher's Role
Psychological safety	Provide "noncritical, nonevaluative and receptive atmosphere where fresh and even wild ideas may be safely proposed" (David & Rimm, 1998, p. 201).
	Develop an atmosphere of trust from the first day forth.
Real experiences	Provide experiences that develop the senses.
	Provide experiences with creative materials.
	Plan abundant field trips.
	Tune in to children's questions and interests on walks and field trips.
	Point out changes in nature.
Uninterrupted time blocks	Plan large time blocks for children to use materials of choice in ways that are congruent with their development.
	Permit important projects (e.g., block structures) to be left as is and worked on later.
Sufficient space	Provide space that is appropriate to selected activity (e.g., easel painting protected on the side, central space for overflow block structures, specified space for group activities, such as mural painting and dramatic play).
Open-ended materials	Use a help-yourself shelf in the child-directed art area. Provide a choice of tools to create with; items to draw, paint, paste on, or fold and tear, alternatives for fastening things together; and an assortment of ever-changing materials.
	Provide multiuse materials and equipment in all areas.
Accessible and organized materials	Minimize the child's need to hunt for materials and tendency to become distracted from selected activity by labeling and classifying materials within the areas.
	Define distinct areas of the room using low movable shelves or large area rugs of various colors.
Varied and abundant materials	Change the dramatic play area from time to time: include props for role-playing varied life experiences (e.g., pet store, hair salon, fire station).
	Survey the avenues for creative expression in the classroom. Observe and determine why some areas are more popular than others. Consider the materials and the activity choices. Are baskets of small plastic people or animals offered with the unit blocks? Are easel painting and another set-up activity (e.g., collages) offered as well as a help-yourself shelf in the art area?

Figure 3.3
Preschool classroom conditions affecting creative climate.

	Count the children. Are there enough items, or will children need to wait a long time to have a turn to express themselves?
Teacher's supportive attitude	Respect each child as unique and important, accept the child's level of expression, and use comments that enhance rather than stifle the creative process. Address the child's effort or the process rather than approve of the result. "Children's motivation and creativity can be destroyed if evaluation, reward, and competition are misused" (Amabile, 1989, p. 69).
Teacher's modeling	Exhibit curiosity, recognize curiosity in children, and encourage curiosity in daily experiences. Use your senses to explore with the children.
	Promote flexibility and sensitivity by asking open-ended questions rather than giving answers.
Aesthetic appreciation	Display art prints that have themes that correspond to various centers (e.g., science, books, blocks). Play a variety of musical selections during free choice time or nap time.
	Include children's books about artists, musicians, and writers in the book corner.
	Invite local artists, musicians, and writers to visit the class.

Figure 3.3 *(Continued)*
Preschool classroom conditions affecting creative climate.

When evaluating art experiences (two- or three-dimensional), consider the following warning: fostering creativity mandates art activities that are process-oriented (exploratory) rather than product-oriented (crafts). In November many classroom walls are filled with paper-plate turkeys that have strips of colored paper glued on to represent feathers. The head and feet are cut by the teacher and glued on by the children. All the turkeys look alike. Did the children express themselves creatively? No, they simply followed the teacher's directions.

> Most art experts in early childhood feel that children who are given predetermined crafts projects to follow are getting one message loud and clear—"Your art and crafts ideas aren't good enough. Follow this instead. The things you can buy, trace, or copy are always better than the things you can make." After many years of such messages, creativity begins to diminish. (Jalongo & Stamp, 1997, p. 39)

Art activities that duplicate a model or dictate a specific product stifle creative growth. Schirrmacher (1998) advised as follows: "Too many activities masquerade as creative art." Some of these include

- photocopied or mimeographed sheets
- cut-and-paste activities

Children's three-dimensional art develops in predictable sequences.

- tracing patterns
- coloring book pages
- dot-to-dot pages
- crafts
- holiday gifts
- seatwork or busywork." (p. 237)

Box 3.18

Preschool Growth Indicators of Drawing

Preschool (ages 2½–5)
- Scribbles, loops, zigzags, waves lines, makes jabs and arcs—often partially off the paper at first
- Produces chance forms or shapes
- Tries out different effects
- Finds meaning in the act itself, not in results or product
- Experiments with leaving a mark, using colors and motions to leave a sign or have an effect
- Makes separate lines, circlelike shapes; combines straight and curved lines
- Makes other basic forms and controlled marks; formulates first schema (personalized representational symbols), mandalalike shapes

Early primary (ages 4–6)
- Combines shapes into schemas; makes intentional image repetition of schemas; develops preferred schemas
- Begins drawing representations, often of people; letterlike forms; basic forms represented consistently—houses, flowers, boats, people, animals in profile
- Portrays meaning (subject matter) in an increasingly readable manner
- Repeats repertory or schemas, practices, and adds new elements
- Shows beginnings of individual style (e.g., typical way of drawing a house)
- Isolates figures, each discrete (no overlapping of whole or parts); shows no context or baseline and draws size and details according to perceived importance or interest (e.g., long arms)
- Present several figures on the page; begins representing events or narratives; places schematic figures in a larger concept, for example, knowing an elephant is a four-legged animal with a trunk, the child uses a well-established routine, or schema, for drawing animals—cats, dogs and so forth—and adds a trunk

Note: Adapted and reprinted with the permission of the National Association for the Education of Young Children. From *Considering Children's Art: Why and How to Value Their Works* by B. S. Engle. Copyright © 1995 by the National Association for the Education of Young Children.

Practitioners must be diligent not to cheat children out of the most obvious and basic creative experience by substituting product art for process art.

Another important pathway to creative expression that deserves extra attention is blocks. They are one of the most universal toys at home and school, and block play has been a part of early childhood education for over 75 years. The developmental values of block building are numerous. Blocks help children develop imagination; awareness of balance, form, and spatial relations; representation and classification abilities; patterning skills; size, shape, area, volume, and equivalency understandings; eye–hand coordination; and fine motor skills. Eventually blocks are used by children to set the scene for dramatic play, a rich source of language and cooperative play.

When first exposed to unit blocks, children need plenty of time to explore with them. Progressing at their own pace through sequential stages (see Box 3.19), children make new discoveries, including how to structure bridges, enclosures, or patterns; repetitions of these creations are commonly observed from day to day. Children who enter block play at older ages (4 through 6) pass quickly through all beginning stages, but they skip the first, elementary one (Hirsch, 1996). Making sketches or taking photos of children's expanding block development is an excellent observational aid.

Blocks seem to hold a magnetic attraction for young children. There can be times, however, when children ignore the block area. To rejuvenate enthusiasm, the teacher may add accessories reflecting the children's current interests (e.g., small plastic sea creatures), actively participate in block-building, or change the location of the block area. Strategies for teacher observation and interventions in block play are addressed in Chapter 12.

Box 3.19

Preschool Growth Indicators of Block Play

Stage 1	Child carries blocks around. Blocks not used for construction.
Stage 2	Child makes mostly rows, either horizontal (on the floor) or vertical (stacked). There is much repetition in this early building pattern.
Stage 3	Child makes bridges. Ⱳ Ⱳ
Stage 4	Child makes enclosures.
Stage 5	Child makes elaborate designs using pattern and balance.
Stage 6	Child names structures related to their functions (houses, boats, stairs).
Stage 7	Child reproduces or symbolizes familiar structures with buildings.

Note: From *The Block Book* (3rd ed.) (pp. 142–148) edited by Elisabeth S. Hirsch, 1996. Copyright © 1996 by the National Association for the Education of Young Children. Adapted and reprinted with permission from the National Association for the Education of Young Children.

> QUICK REVIEW <

This chapter gives a brief overview of the preschool child's multifaceted growth and development. Certainly no two children develop along the exact same course; individual children show different rates and strengths of physical, cognitive, psychosocial, and creative development. Yet development generally follows a predictable path. Understanding development and growth indicators along that path allows the teacher to identify each child's advances, missing neither the baby steps nor the giant leaps.

TAKE A MOMENT TO REFLECT

Personal Reflection

One of the developmental axioms (Figure 3.1) holds that each child develops at an individual maturational rate; each child possesses his/her own genetic time clock. Using information from your own or your child's preschool development, reflect on and answer the following questions (you may have to consult one of your parents):

1. What were your or your child's unique qualities?
2. Choose one of the four developmental domains and describe the significant strides you or your child made during the preschool years.
3. Discuss one example of how an adult (teacher, parent, or significant other) enhanced or hindered the developmental process.

Ethical Reflection

NAEYC Ideal I-1.2 is "to base program practices upon current knowledge in the field of child development and related disciplines and upon particular knowledge of each child" (Feeney & Kipnis, 1992, p. 4). Reflect upon how the process of understanding development and growth indicators enables the teacher to fulfill this ethical responsibility.

4 Highlights of Development During the Primary Grade Years

From *Life* magazine (Follmi, 1989) comes an article about a child from Tibet making a perilous journey from her remote and isolated village in the Himalayas to a school 100 miles away. In a small entourage, Diskit and her brother traveled single file on a frozen river following the leader, who, with a long stick, tapped the ice to test for strength. Stop and think for a moment how Diskit's secluded mountain life and unusual travel protocol might have shaped her perceptions of the physical world. Then read on.

> On the twelfth and final day, the landscape changes. The white of eternal ice gives way to the brown hills surrounding the valley of Ladakh. The exhausted travelers trade the frozen skin of the mighty river for a dirt road, and Lobsang and his children hitch a ride on a transport truck. Diskit cowers: The driver is a Sikh with a turban and a long moustache. She has never before seen an Indian who was not a Tibetan Buddhist. The vehicle overtakes a man on horseback. She tugs on her father's coat. "Abale," she asks, using the native word for father, "have you seen? Here the donkeys walk backward."

> "No," her father replies. "It's just that we're moving faster than it is." (p. 116)

Extraordinary, isn't it, from our Western, industrialized perspective that a primary grade child could perceive an object being overtaken as traveling backward? How can this be explained?

Diskit was a child with all her mental faculties intact. Her perceptual error of thinking that a man on a donkey was traveling backward as she overtook him on a truck was understandable in the context of her cultural experiences. Growing up in a small mountain village dedicated to growing barley in the summer and surviving frigid winters had not yet taught her about the traffic patterns she first observed, without understanding, in town. As she learned from new experiences, Diskit would doubtlessly become incredulous that she was ever capable of such a misinterpretation.

As you reflect on the development of preschool children as described in Chapter 3 and read about the development of primary grade children (K–3) in this chapter, think about how the various cultures familiar to you influence and moderate development. While reading, look for examples that answer the following question: In what ways can teachers be responsive to developmental needs that reflect cultural diversity? Selected highlights of physical, cognitive, psychosocial, and creative development are presented to document general growth trends; as in Chapter 3, however, remember that individual and cultural diversity is always evident.

SELECTED HIGHLIGHTS OF PHYSICAL DEVELOPMENT

Body Growth

As the active primary grade child's internal developmental timetable continues to unfold, the need for naps ceases, the first permanent teeth appear, the brain grows to about 90 percent of adult size, the "redundant synaptic connections between neurons continue to be pruned, increasing the organization of the brain" (Fabes & Martin, 2000, p. 307), and height and weight increase at a steady rate. Early childhood teachers, however, respect that "the range of normal development is quite broad" (Berger, 2000, p. 243). This range in physical appearance is illustrated in the photograph on p. 79. Each child possesses an individual genetic code and rate of maturation; therefore, differences in children's stature and body type (even within homogeneous age groups) are noticeable. Attention to this factor is necessary when observing and assessing a child.

In a room full of first- or second-graders, a general trend in physical growth development is evident, but individual differences can be easily spotted. Think back for a moment to your primary years. Were you an "average" child? If not, did you get dubbed with a nickname reflecting your physical development—half pint, peanut, lefty, freckle face, four eyes, tubby, or boney maroney? Maybe you knew someone who did. Do you think these individual growth deviations from the norm affect the primary age child? Consider how physical development may influence a child's self-esteem as you read the psychosocial development section in this chapter.

Motor Development

Motor development encompasses the changes in movement ability and body control. In this section, both gross motor development (the growth toward movement competence of arms, legs, and torso—large muscles of the body) and fine motor development (the growth toward efficient control of fingers, hands, and feet—small muscles of the body) are explored in an abbreviated form.

Surprisingly, they are all the same age!

Gross Motor Skills

During the primary grade years, children can be observed in three stages of gross motor development. In the first stage, some children are still engaged in perfecting the fundamental motor skills listed in Chapter 3's growth indicators of gross motor development (Box 3.1)—running, jumping, hopping, galloping, skipping, climbing, balancing, catching, throwing, and kicking. Other children move to the second and more complex stage of coordinating two or more skills to create a new skill, such as dribbling a ball. As motor-skill performance becomes more interwoven and specific, increased strength and judgment are required to carry out the task. Accomplishments in the second stage allow the child to move to the third stage and use these more specialized skills in a number of organized activities (Gallahue & Ozmun, 1998).

The complex process of motor development is enhanced by appropriate experiences, child interest, and support or encouragement from adults.

Did you participate in sports, dance, or recreational games that required movement skill? If so, when were you able to engage in combining motor skills in activities, such as basketball, skateboarding, ballet, tetherball, gymnastics, soccer, or volleyball? How did the process of learning the new activity unfold? What factors contributed to your success? Do you see any relationship between your gender, culture, family interests, or geographical location and the activities you pursued? What about your siblings or friends? Keep those answers in mind as we further explore the third stage of gross motor development.

"Movement skill learning . . . follows a predictable sequence progressing from the beginning, or "novice," level to intermediate, or "practice," level and finally to the advanced, or "fine tuning," level (Gallahue & Ozmun, 1998, p. 367). According to this concept, children who are beginners are building a mental framework for the movement activity, no matter at what stage their maturation is exhibited. They must focus intently on the details and may not yet have developed the body functions to execute the skills; therefore, they may appear awkward or uncoordinated.

As children's maturation develops and they gain skill experience, they move to the intermediate level and the awkwardness disappears. However, the performance still lacks the smoothness of the advanced level. The practice level allows children time to build kinesthetic confidence and focus on the goal of the movement activity rather than the fundamentals of the moves. In the final level, physical maturation is attained, and the movement is exhibited by smooth, coordinated movements that make the movement activity look easy.

If the primary grade child receives balanced nutritious meals and is given abundant practice opportunities both in and out of school, continuous muscle strength, balance, reaction time, endurance, and eye–hand coordination will develop. This growth facilitates gradual improvements in motor skill performance when coupled with a supportive environment of needed instruction or helpful encouragement. Other factors that may affect the degree of perfection in the performance of motor skills and movement activities are body size and inherited ability (Berger, 2000).

To avoid redundancy, growth indicators of motor development for Stage 1 are listed in Chapter 3, Box 3.1—fundamental motor skills: running, jumping, hopping, galloping, skipping, climbing, balancing, catching, throwing, and kicking. Be sure to review these and assess each child as an individual. The Stage 2 and 3 growth indicators for gross motor development are listed in Box 4.1. Using this chart will help guide ongoing observations and record-keeping. "Do not compare children's movement skills based on chronological age, as is usually done, but remember that many performer factors [e.g., heredity, culture, and environment] contribute to the development of each child's skills" (Burton, 1992, p. 4).

Fine Motor Skills

Most children approach the primary grade years having had a variety of experiences using tools controlled by the small muscles (e.g., puzzles, crayons, magnifying glasses, and clothing fasteners). As with gross motor skills, genetic makeup and maturation play key roles in the development of fine motor skills along with suitable experiences. As K–3 children gain increased small muscle control and eye–hand coordination, they can, with appropriate opportunities and practice, successfully engage in activities, such as coloring within chosen lines, cutting out intricate pictures, and using writing, drawing, and building tools.

During the primary grade years, observations of fine motor skills are often focused on the complex and advanced ability of handwriting. Keep in mind that proficiency with this process involves not only coordinated arm, wrist, hand, and finger movements but also honed perceptual skills, proper posture, appropriate instruction, and practice time (Kalverboer, Hopkins, & Geuze, 1993; Sovik, 1993). In kindergarten, handwriting begins with printing of unevenly formed letters and numbers from ½ to 2 inches in height and advances to effectively printing horizontally aligned letters and numbers about ¼ inch in height (Payne & Issacs, 1999). When a child reverses letters (e.g., prints the letter *b* instead of the letter *d*),

---

Box 4.1

Primary Grade Growth Indicators of Gross Motor Development

Growth Indicator	*Example*
Increases strength of legs and arms	Mandy's knuckles whiten as she gives an extra kick with her legs while reaching for the last rung on the overhead parallel bars. Today she finally makes it all the way across!
Increases speed	In the fourth game of neighborhood "hide and seek," whining complaints of the preschoolers echo in the streets, "Why do we always have to be *it?*" "Because you never catch us," laugh the older brothers and sisters, scampering off.
Increases coordination	Sheyenne dribbles the ball four times as she runs toward the basket, aims, and makes a successful jump shot to help her team win.
Increases agility	The boy begins to feel confident as he successfully dodges the ball again and again and again in the second grade game.
Increases endurance	Having just run eight laps around the track, Patrick smiles and heads for the water fountain, remembering that last year he could run only six laps.
Increases specialized skills in movement activities, such as sports, dance, and recreational games.	The child smoothly dribbles the soccer ball for seven yards before passing it to a teammate who is closer to the goal.

---

remember that the child's perceptual skills are still developing; reversals are not uncommon in children up to age 8 (Corbin, 1980). With this in mind, it is understandable that most children are not introduced to cursive writing until the second or third grade.

Optimal observations and recordings in the early childhood classroom (see Box 4.2 for fine motor growth indicators) are accomplished by viewing children as individuals who are developing at their own rate. These wise words exemplify that idea:

> One of the most well-established premises of human development is that there is a wide range of individual variation that is well within the range of "normal" and, of course, the inclusion of children with disabilities and special abilities further expands the range of individual differences in any one classroom. (Bredekamp, 1992, p. 31)

Box 4.2

Primary Growth Indicators of Fine Motor Development

Growth Indicator	*Example*
Increases ability to use writing tools, scissors, and small objects skillfully	The boy cuts an intricate snowflake out of folded paper, while his younger sister struggles to cut out a heart shape.
Increases ability to arrange numbers and letters uniformly	Five-year-old Kristen wrote: *1 2 3 4* Second grader Blake wrote: *1 2 3 4 5*
Increases eye–hand coordination	While playing Stak Attack, 8-year-old Sally carefully and slowly removes the bottom block from the stack, adding it to the top without toppling the 15-inch stack.

Elements Affecting Motor Development

Throughout this section on physical development, two major factors that influence the development of motor skills have been identified—maturation and environment. Figure 4.1 summarizes the main components of these factors. While reading them, think about the implications of these factors on observation and planning.

Developmentally appropriate curriculum planning based on observation keeps in mind the primary grade child's need for ample school opportunities to practice, exercise, and engage in physical play. In addition, special attention is paid to the following:

- Children who have poor diets and are overweight.
- Children who have long bus rides and then go directly into the classroom.
- Children who have not developed social skills and appear to withdraw or attach themselves to the teacher on the playground, seldom entering into physical activities.
- Children who continually use the outdoor play equipment for dramatic play rather than motor development.

Factors	Examples
Rate of body growth, increased strength, and maturity of the nervous system have an impact on physical development, delaying or advancing the process.	A tall kindergarten child has difficulty synchronizing the timing of the hop-and-step movement of the effective skipper. A child, frustrated because he cannot coordinate his eye–hand movements while playing jacks, doesn't get beyond the "threezes" for several months.
Ease in social participation and physical activities are mutually linked.	In a study on children's feelings of loneliness and their relationship to physical fitness, it was reported that "lonely children were less physically fit and physically active than were those who were not lonely" (Page, Frey, Talbert, & Falk, 1992, p. 211).
Encouragement, instruction, and opportunities to practice and influence the development of motor skills.	When learning to print letters, the child is taught to form the circles in letters *o, g, d,* and *q* by starting at the top and circling to the left, so the transition to writing those letters in cursive will be quicker and easier than trying to form new habits if the printed letters are learned with a motion of circling to the right.
Practice is often linked to interests, motivation, cultural expectations, family interests, and geographic location.	Children living in southern California may easily combine the fundamental motor skills into more complex skills through regularly riding a skateboard, playing soccer, or roller-blading. Children living in Vermont may perfect their skills through regularly skiing, ice-skating, or playing basketball.

Figure 4.1
Elements affecting motor development.

- Children who spend the majority of their out-of-school hours watching television or playing computer games, thus developing sedentary lifestyles.
- Children in city schools when Stage 3 smog alerts prohibit them from playing outdoors.
- Classroom schedules that do not allow for ample movement and rigorous activity during the day. Is one recess at 11:00 A.M. the best way to aid attention span?

Overall K–3 children are engulfed in a social environment in which motor skill performance is necessary for success in sports participation and other recreational activities. Fine motor skills are necessary for classroom success in writing, computer operation, and manipulation of art tools for creative expression. The knowledgeable teacher observes and understands maturational and cultural differences, provides practice opportunities, gives instruction and encouragement based on observations of individual interests, and maintains realistic expectations.

This chapter section on physical development is far from a comprehensive discussion of physical growth. To review the areas not covered (e.g., fundamental skill progressions, motor perception, and hand dominance), consult a child development book.

SELECTED HIGHLIGHTS OF COGNITIVE DEVELOPMENT

Representational Abilities

As children move from the preschool through the primary grade years, the complexity of their representational activities expands. (Recall from Chapter 3 that a representation is something that stands for—or represents—something else.) Children's role-plays, drawings, and models, for example, exhibit more details, concepts, and sophisticated designs than those produced a few years earlier. Furthermore, primary grade children are prepared to construct and decode abstract symbols. Older children can listen to a book with few picture aids and rely on their own mental imagery to augment the text. Their understanding of the meaning behind letters and numbers becomes more secure and skilled. Consider this example of growing familiarity with the representational meaning of numbers. A prekindergartner (4; 9) arranged magnets on the refrigerator in spite of missing a 3 and a 0.

The child explained that she used three sucker magnets because she didn't have a 3 and that a small round magnet was "almost like" a zero; clearly she understood the representations involved.

Because nothing about the symbol 3 suggests what it stands for, understanding numbers (and letters) as abstract representations is a critical cognitive step for primary grade children. This step results from maturing perceptual skills and from instruction. On the one hand, maturing perceptual skills allow children to make increasingly fine distinctions between symbols (e.g., between b and d). On the other hand, no amount of contemplation of an M or Σ will result in children's correct deciphering of the letter unless they have been taught its meaning. Elementary schools are responsible for teaching children the abstract representational systems of letters and numbers. Box 4.3 summarizes the growth indicators of young children's representational abilities to observe and support in primary grade classrooms.

Box 4.3

Primary Grade Growth Indicators of Representational Abilities

Growth Indicator	*Example*
Expands complexity of preschool growth indicators	Shonnie, Buddy, and Abdul engage in "school" dramatic play and sound remarkably like the people they represent!
• Forms mental images	A third-grader draws a person in profile.
• Imitates	Detlof constructs a personally designed car out of Legos
• Uses language	
• Pretends	A second grader competently reads *The Cat in the Hat* to a kindergartner during after-school care.
• Role-plays	
• Represents in two dimensions	
• Represents in three dimensions	
• Decodes others' representations	
Decodes and uses abstract symbols (letters and numbers)	

Language

A steady diet of television and video encounters does not promote language learning, and many of our children are suffering from a lack of stimulation. "Refinements of language, such as more complex grammar, vocabulary, and social usage, however, don't arrive so easily; they depend on the quality and quantity of interactions in both preschool and elementary years" (Healy, 1999, p. 89). Our current culture of rushing from one activity to the next and rarely engaging in quality conversations puts language learning, sustained attention, and problem-solving at risk (Healy, 1999). Providing a language-rich environment is of primary concern to adults who want to support children's development. To do so they engage in meaningful and frequent conversations, read books often and well, and write to communicate ideas and explore their thoughts.

The most far-reaching change in language during the primary grade years stems from children's growing understanding of language as a means of communication. Primary grade children become able to think about how they and others use language. Most children enjoy conversing with others and become aware of themselves and others as givers and receivers of messages. Further, by age 6 or 7, they are aware of their own inner speech, especially as they experience the common primary grade academic subjects (Flavell, Green, Flavell, & Grossman, 1997).

Primary grade children can construct complex representational models.

Primary grade children enter the exciting world of literacy. Children who enter kindergarten familiar with sounds, letters, and books are well prepared to learn to write and read (Adams, Treiman, & Pressley, 1998). These researchers remind us that "beyond the basics, the firmest prescription from research is that children should read as often, as broadly, and as thoughtfully as possible" (p. 336). Calkins (1997) agrees: "The secret to being a good reader is to read a lot" (p. 144), and she advises encouraging children to write in meaningful, rather than artificial, ways. Hopefully, teachers and parents of primary grade children provide encouragement as language skills develop in speaking, reading, and writing (see the growth indicators in Box 4.4).

Children need encouragement and a trusting environment in which to talk, write, and try out new words. Although more attention is paid to primary grade children's technical use of language (e.g., spelling and grammar) than to younger children's, continued emphasis on content before form reduces the risk of failure. Teachers want to encourage children to speak and write fluently, and that requires lots of practice, experience, and confidence. If children are continually under the critical eye of adults waiting to pounce on a misspoken or miswritten word, they are apt to pull back from language. On the other hand, engagement in their zones of proximal development (see Chapter 3) appropriately challenges children in a supportive environment.

A first grade teacher delighted in the content of a child's story and ignored the many errors and lack of a title. Try to figure out the words, and enjoy a chuckle.

Box 4.4

Primary Grade Growth Indicators of Language

Growth Indicator	Example
Expands vocabulary	Vinnie describes a new friend as "very considerate."
Understands there can be literal and figurative meanings of words	To describe her grandparents, Hannah sums up, "They're very old, and they can't talk very good; their voices *ruffle*."
	During a first grade story time, children laugh heartily as Amelia Bedelia literally follows directions to dust furniture, draw drapes, and dress chickens.
Discerns subtle differences among words	Tuong-Anh says, "Today the rain sounds sharp, not plunking like usual."
Uses and understands many grammatical rules and exceptions	A second grader is not confused by the passive sentence construction, "Trent was teased by Riley."
Becomes a proficient communicator with adults and peers	Nicholas contributes his viewpoints to the class discussion. "The color of the wind is whatever's behind it."
	To emphasize her anxiety before her first class play, a 6-year-old declares she has "monarchs" in her tummy.
Constructs and understands increasingly complex sentences (structure and length)	Carmela informs a friend, "My favorite dinner is barbecued ribs with extra sauce on the side, cole slaw, and creamy potatoes, and for dessert I like apples with cinnamon."
Learns to decode words and comprehend their meanings	A third grader reads a math word problem and easily ignores irrelevant information.
Writes with increasing proficiency	A second grader writes, "At first we did not noteice each other but then we grew to be firends. In a litte whie she came over to my hose."

Maggieodon is 67 pounds. It eats dog food with searup. And it 4 foot 2 inchs. My dinosaur is unusual becasa you can see rita trow its stmic. It is special becasa it has a long neke. It is all defrat cluers. It name mens Maggie tooth. It lives in water becasa if it din't it wold dri out and die.

At the beginning of third grade, this child was a prolific and able writer. Consider this short piece about a grandparent.

Gaga and the Raccoons

My grandma's name is Gaga. She died when she was 70 that was 3 years ago. Gaga's real name is Marge Gaede. She taught first, second, and third grade before she retired. After she retired gaga worked at the hands on museum in ann arbor. Gaga loved raccoons very much and to her great joy discovered that many raccoons lived in the forest behind her house. Every night Gaga would make peanut butter samwitchs and then she would throw them all over her yard. My family, Gaga and her husband Gampa and I all sit on the porch and wait and watch. Soon the raccoons began to come they ate and ate and ate. When the raccoons were full they slowly began to leave and I went to bed. When Gaga was still teaching her stutents gave her a shirt that said Fuzzies and Raccoons go togather. Fuzzies are little balls of thered with eyes that Gaga loved to make. When I was at Gaga's feunroll all I could think was Raccoons and Gagas go togather.

This child's language development flourished in an environment that encouraged talking about a wide range of interesting topics, reading books regularly, seeing adults read, and writing as a method of communication about personally meaningful subjects.

Logical Thought

A major cognitive advancement during the primary grades is children's increasing ability to reason logically and flexibly about problems with real objects. Indeed, "children aged 6 years have some understanding of logical consistency" (Ruffman, 1999, p. 883), and they "typically use a variety of strategies and ways of thinking, rather than just a single one, to solve a given problem" (Siegler, 2000, p. 28). Primary grade children's experiences and expanded mental flexibility allow them to understand logical operations, such as addition and subtraction. First graders who are beginning to learn math facts often treat $3 + 4 = 7$ and $7 - 3 = 4$ as two independent problems. Before the year is out, most will understand the logical connection between the two.

Primary grade children's logical thought may be demonstrated by asking them questions about conservation (the concept that something remains the same if nothing is added or taken away). In a conservation-of-length problem, two rulers are aligned and then one is simply moved over in full view of the child. If a young primary grade child asserts that the two rulers remain the same after the rearrangement and is asked why, the child is likely to justify this conclusion with a statement that focuses on the maintained identity of the objects; "It's the same stick" or "You just moved it over."

Given a variety of conservation problems, a primary grade child (particularly a 5- or 6-year-old) typically answers some correctly and some incorrectly. For example, the child who was right about the preceding conservation-of-length question might answer incorrectly on questions about conservation of matter and liquid 2 minutes later. This inconsistency is a bit perplexing. One would think that once a child understands that something remains the same if nothing is added or taken

Box 4.5

Primary Growth Indicators of Logical Thought

Growth Indicator	Example
Often reasons flexibly and logically about tangible problems	A child studies the groups of math manipulatives and exclaims, "Oh, I get it! A remainder is like leftover stuff. There's not enough to make another whole group."
Continues to demonstrate concrete thinking	Cassie looks at a photo book of Amish families with a parent who describes their religion and simple life. To exemplify the connection between beliefs and daily life, the parent explains the Amish reliance on hooks and eyes rather than modern zippers to fasten clothing. After attentive listening, Cassie asks thoughtfully, "Do they believe in elastic?"

away, this reasoning could be applied across the board on a variety of tasks. If the child said that two rulers are the same if one is moved over, why wouldn't the child also say that two equal globs of play dough remain equal if one is reshaped and two amounts of juice are the same if one is poured into a differently shaped container? Children do not become logical thinkers all at once. Although the basic concept of conservation is the same across tasks, some tasks are more difficult than others, even when they theoretically draw on the same cognitive concept. In addition, children have had varying experiences and have varying cognitive strengths. Adults should expect to see primary grade children draw on logical thought sometimes (but not always) and to observe individual differences among children. Box 4.5 describes growth indicators of logical thought.

The thinking of primary grade children remains concrete, based in the tangible world, so they reason best about the here and now. For example, an 8-year-old listened to an older child tell a joke about two friends, Joe and Casey, who loved baseball. The friends agreed that whoever died first would try to return to earth and let the other know if baseball is played in heaven. Joe died first, and one day Casey returned home to find him sitting in his living room. The 10-year-old delivered the punch line:

10-YEAR-OLD:	So Joe said, "I've got some good news and some bad news. The good news is there is baseball in heaven. The bad news is you're scheduled to pitch tomorrow."
8-YEAR-OLD:	I don't get it.
10-YEAR-OLD:	Well, see, for Casey to pitch in heaven, he's gotta die first.

8-YEAR-OLD: [No laughter but a moment of thought] So what did
                         Casey die of?

The joke bombed! Concrete thought simply did not allow the 8-year-old to discern the hidden agenda.

Metacognition

Building on preschool children's theories of mind, primary grade children gain specific knowledge about thinking—their own and that of other people. Metacognition is knowledge about cognition, and "metacognitive knowledge can be roughly subdivided into knowledge about *persons, tasks,* and *strategies*" (Flavell et al., 1993, p. 150). Metacognition is at work when you monitor your own understanding of information, take a list of growth indicators on an index card with you during an observational session, and adjust your study procedures for an essay versus multiple-choice exam. Similarly, children increasingly understand and make judgments about what thinking is like and how people are similar and different as thinkers. They learn about the varying requirements of cognitive tasks and how they and others can best approach them. School-age children become more acquainted with their minds in part through the process of inner speech, talking with themselves in the privacy of their own minds. "It is reasonable to think that experiences in elementary school would foster awareness of inner speech. Reading, writing, and arithmetic—the basic staples of primary grade education—all require considerable

Box 4.6

Primary Grade Growth Indicators of Metacognition

Growth Indicator	*Example*
Demonstrates increasing knowledge about people as cognitive processors	"I only need to work on these four spelling words 'cause I already know the others," the third grader explains. "Ask Rob Allen; he knows where everything is," suggests his brother.
Demonstrates increasing knowledge about cognitive requirements of tasks	A first grader glances at the instruction booklet of a new game and says, "You read it, Dad, and tell me how to play. I can't read all that, you know."
Demonstrates increasing knowledge about cognitive strategies	Annika rehearses spelling words by writing them down while Dekker practices them orally.

private speech on the part of the learner" (Flavell et al., 1997, p. 46). The growth indicators in Box 4.6 introduce metacognitive knowledge of primary grade children.

Classification

Classification skills undergo substantial development during the primary grade years. Although preschool children are generally content to sort a limited number of objects once, primary grade children can be challenged to sort and re-sort a larger number of objects. Thus, their greater mental flexibility enables them to select classifying attributes that guide their sorting and then abandon these attributes and begin again. Re-sorting is a notable achievement and one that they enjoy immensely; appreciate the collections and hobbies of school-age children that involve sorting and re-sorting.

A first grader sorts and re-sorts a collection of leaves into the following piles and then says no more groupings are possible:

1. Big leaves
   Little leaves

2. Green leaves
   Brown leaves
   Yellow leaves

3. Pointy leaves
   Roundish leaves

This child sorted real leaves on the basis of some physical similarities and differences. First, size differences guided the child's groupings, then color, then shape. This was a fine demonstration of sorting and re-sorting for a first grader.

As children's thinking becomes increasingly flexible (see Box 4.7 for growth indicators of classification abilities), they can sort and re-sort objects according to various concrete attributes. Young primary grade children, like the first grader who sorted the leaves, tend to select physical attributes of the objects themselves as the basis of classification and produce a limited number of groupings. As they mature and gain knowledge about the objects being sorted, children produce more abundant groupings but remain predominantly concrete in their approach to classification tasks. (They do not, for example, sort people on the basis of their political persuasions.) They may, however, begin to draw on their personal stores of knowledge and, for example, sort leaves into an evergreen pile and a deciduous pile; thus they are no longer tied to the objects' observable physical attributes.

Number Development

Children entering elementary school build on their number knowledge and counting skills as they begin to deal successfully with increasingly large sets of objects and numbers (Geary, 1994). During the primary years, they understand that the last number counted in a set represents its total number of objects (the cardinal

Box 4.7

Primary Grade Growth Indicators of Classification

Growth Indicator	*Example*

Sorts and re-sorts objects flexibly and usually by physical attributes	Amanda sorts model horses:
	1. Bays Grays
	   Chestnuts Blacks
	   Paints Whites
	
	2. Black mane
	   Brown mane
	   Gray or white mane
	
	3. Albino hooves
	   Brown hooves
	   Black hooves
	   Gray hooves
	
	4. Face markings
	   No face markings
	
	5. Famous or related to famous horses
	   Unknown horses
	
	(*Note:* Grouping 5 stems from Amanda's own knowledge about horses rather than physical features of the models.)

Compares whole class with parts with increasing accuracy	"Here's my stack of left-handed pitchers and here's the right handers, but look at how many pitchers I have all together," exclaims Donnie while sorting his baseball cards.

principle). Given a "tricky" conservation of number task with 12 marbles heaped in a pile compared to 12 arranged in a line, 8-year-olds are not tempted by their perceptual information to erroneously conclude that the sets are not equal; their correct judgments are based on numerical reasoning rather than perceptual cues.

Primary grade children also understand that numbers are serially ordered and, further, that any given number is made up of a group of smaller numbers (Geary, 1994). This concept enables them to understand that 10 is composed of 1 and 9, or 2 and 8, or 3 and 7, and is vital to their grasp of addition and subtraction. Suppose children were given a set of 3 objects and a set of 5 objects to add together. Over the first 2 or 3 years in school, "children progress from a *counting-all* strategy to *counting-on-from-first number* and then to *counting-on-from-larger number*" (Ginsburg, Klein, & Starkey, 1998, p. 417). Skill comparing relative quantities and employing measurement strategies to assess length, volume, weight, and the like also improves. Children's early success in arithmetic is based on the number concepts and fundamental skills outlined in Box 4.8.

Box 4.8

Primary Grade Growth Indicators of Number Development

Growth Indicator	*Example*
Counts increasingly large sets of objects	Before boarding a bus for a field trip, Lydia counts her 19 classmates, herself, and her teacher.
Understands cardinality	A kindergartner counts the lunch boxes and mentions to his friend that there are 13.
Develops measurement strategies	A second grader uses a ruler to measure the perimeter of the art table.
Adds and subtracts objects and numbers; begins to multiply and divide	Yohana studies six cup hooks, four of which are empty, and says, "I know what 6 take away 4 is." Rowley practices his addition flash cards with a parent.
	Given responsibility for distributing the after-school snack, a third grader equally divides four packages containing three peanut-butter crackers among his two siblings and himself.

Memory

Although preschool and primary grade children share the same basic memory processes (recognition and recall), memory skills become honed during the elementary years. Processing speed increases, and "a number of memory strategies emerge and develop" (Pressley & Schneider, 1997, p. 113). "The knowledge base continues to develop and greatly facilitates learning of content that is related to knowledge already possessed by children" (Schneider & Pressley, 1989, p. 320). Most notable during the primary grades are the strategies of rehearsal (repeating items to be remembered either mentally or aloud) and organization (clustering similar items to facilitate remembering).

During the primary grade years, children begin to use rehearsal and organization spontaneously. First graders faced with the task of learning their very first set of spelling words simply do not realize that rehearsal would be an appropriate study strategy, but they can rehearse when taught to do so (Schneider & Pressley, 1997). By the third grade, however, most children can effectively use rehearsal on their own. The same is true of organization.

The development of metamemory—knowledge about memory and a component of metacognition discussed earlier—makes the deliberate selection of memory strategies possible. Even during the primary grade years, children know some-

Box 4.9

Primary Grade Growth Indicators of Memory

Growth Indicator	*Example*
Increasingly uses memory strategies spontaneously and deliberately	"I'm going to write that word five more times without peeking; it's still kinda blurry," reports Paula, preparing for a spelling test.
Exhibits early development of metamemory, including knowledge about people as rememberers, varying task difficulty, and appropriate memory strategies	Samyr writes homework assignments in his notebook to avoid having to remember them.
	Children discuss pros and cons of stage plays versus radio plays and remark that the latter require less memorization.
	A third grader practices flash cards to study for a math test and reviews the chapter self-quiz to prepare for a social studies test.
Benefits from increased knowledge base	On a trip to the local museum to see the traveling exhibit of ancient Egyptian treasures, Joaquin can easily explain the relative ages of mummies because he understands the conventions of B.C. dating.

thing about memory. In an early metamemory study, for example, when kindergarten and first-, third-, and fifth-grade children were asked if it would be easier to learn the names of birds in town for the first or second time, many of the children (even the kindergartners) knew intuitively that the relearner would have the advantage (Kreutzer, Leonard, & Flavell, 1975). Ideas about memory (and the mind) gain clarity as 8- and 9-year-olds begin to distinguish between what they understand and what they have merely memorized (Lovett & Flavell, 1990). Furthermore, not only do primary grade children have some knowledge about memory as a cognitive process, but they also become more aware of when they must put out some effort to store or retrieve information; think about the growth indicators of memory presented in Box 4.9 in this light.

The cognitive development highlights presented in this section are not comprehensive. You may be interested in reading about problem-solving, reading comprehension, spatial relations, additional math concepts, and so forth. Although this section describes general trends in cognitive development, individual differences are always apparent. These differences are normal and reflect the beauty and complexity of human diversity.

SELECTED HIGHLIGHTS OF PSYCHOSOCIAL DEVELOPMENT

Self-Concept and Self-Esteem

In Chapter 3, we left the preschool child with a beginning understanding of the self as both a physical object and a psychological being. Children's ideas about the self grow more complex during the primary grade years. They realize that their minds and the minds of others are constantly active (Wellman & Hickling, 1994), regardless of whether one's thinking is obvious to an observer. Gradually, through the primary grade years and beyond, children's self-concepts include more psychological assessments (e.g., "animal lover"), characteristics uncommon to others (e.g., "the shortest kid in the class"), and descriptions of active abilities (e.g., "a really good gymnast"), as well as many of the physical characteristics cited by younger children (e.g., "curly hair"). Elementary school children also understand their own specific strengths and weaknesses, but their self-evaluations, in contrast to preschoolers' sunny reports, grow more critical. Because they can judge their often varying competencies in multiple areas (e.g., math, reading, sports, music), their self-appraisals become less sweeping and more specific (Eccles, Wigfield, Harold, & Blumenfeld, 1993).

Although primary grade children feel more like unique individuals, they also feel more closely bound to a social network (Maccoby, 1980). As a result, primary grade children are likely to include membership in a group (e.g., an ethnic group, a sports team, a scouting troop) when asked to describe themselves. Sustained experience in groups offers tremendous growth opportunities. Ethnic groups may guide children's development in many ways (e.g., expectations of how children treat their elders) and help them forge their identities. Within groups, children are also stimulated to acknowledge how their behavior appears to others (e.g., bossiness is not valued), to monitor their behavior, and gradually to make appropriate adjustments.

Children gain "extensive knowledge of gender stereotypes" and gradually become aware that "both males and females *can* have the same traits or engage in the same activities and occupations" (Serbin, Powlishta, & Gulko, 1993, p. 64, emphasis in original). Young children (and adolescents) regard "the crossing of stereotyped gender boundaries as more wrong and expressed a greater personal commitment to sex-role regularity, than do children in middle childhood" (Stoddart & Turiel, 1985, p. 1241). Primary grade children's increased freedom from rigid adherence to gender stereotypes stems partly from their secure understanding that their gender is constant and that gender roles are societal conventions rather than absolute requirements. As Western society formally and informally continues to reduce its gender-stereotyped expectations and restrictions, children may recognize and embrace their life options wholeheartedly.

Self-esteem is the evaluative component of the sense of self, and positive self-esteem is possible when children's physiological needs and needs for safety, belonging, and love have been met (Maslow, 1970). Two essential ingredients that contribute to self-esteem are the warmth, acceptance, and respectful treatment given a child, as well as the child's success as "measured against personal goals and standards" (Coopersmith, 1967, p. 242). Thus, the origins of self-esteem lie not only with how children are treated by the important people in their lives but also with how well they do in the world. Children need not excel in everything they do in order to feel good about themselves, but reasonable competence in selected arenas is important to self-esteem. In addition, children's beliefs in their own motivation and learning abilities fuel their performance accomplishments (Bandura, Barbaranelli, Caprara, & Pastorelli, 1996; Measelle, Ablow, Cowan, & Cowan, 1998).

A person's self-esteem is linked to his or her aspirations in specific fields of interest. If you try an unfamiliar activity and do not do well, you might be mildly embarrassed, but your self-esteem should not suffer. After all, you are a fish out of water. However, you care very much about your performance in areas in which you have chosen to compete—perhaps child observation. This is your pond, and your performance is connected to how you feel about yourself.

The same process is true for children. Children, however, are just beginning to find their ponds, and adults need to assist them in their searches by exposing them to a wide range of experiences. Trying out new activities includes the possibility of failure, so adults working with primary grade children can encourage this risk-taking by being low-key and minimizing pressure. Mallory, age 6, made a list of all the things she wanted to try—soccer, softball, ballet, violin, Brownies, jazz dancing, horseback riding, and gymnastics. Her parents supported her interests with the stipulation that she had to commit for a season or school year and not have too many activities going at once. At the end of first grade, she crossed off three of the four activities she had tried that year: soccer (too hot and too much running), softball (too boring), and ballet (too embarrassing), and anticipated sticking with Brownies and trying out jazz in the second grade. Through this process Mallory learned more about the kinds of activities she enjoys and can do well. Her self-esteem will be enhanced as she discovers the ponds in which she wants to swim, develops competence, and is encouraged by those who love and teach her. Box 4.10 lists indicators of the growth of self-concept and self-esteem in primary grade children.

Advances in Play

During the elementary school years, we see a decline of pretend and rough-and-tumble play. "Replacing these forms of interactions are games with or without formal rules, and activities structured by adults" (Rubin et al., 1998, p. 639). Board games are popular as primary grade children readily learn rules and understand they should apply equally to all players. Even in children's unstructured play (e.g., school, spies, house), rules command an increasingly prominent role. Cooperative play is sustained as maturation and experiences stimulate children to give and take actively in their encounters. Part of the ability to do so stems from their improved theory of mind that allows them to understand the mental states of others (Jenkins & Astington, 2000) (see Box 4.11 for growth indicators of play).

Box 4.10

Growth Indicators of Self-Concept and Self-Esteem

Growth Indicator	Example
Includes psychological assessments, uncommon characteristics, and active abilities as well as concrete characteristics in descriptions of self and others	Heidi reports to her parent after school, "I really like the new kid in my class; she's kinda shy like me, and I think she likes the monkey bars too!"
Considers group ties as part of self-definition	Stavros proudly wears a scouting uniform to school. Child shares photos of the Aroma Pueblo. "I'm this kind of Native American, just like my mom, who lived here when she was 10."
Does not rigidly adhere to all stereotyped gender roles	"I'm really good in math," Nellie proudly tells her mother after school.
Becomes aware that gender roles are societal customs	Spencer reads *Little House in the Big Woods* and compares the diversity of his sister's activities to those of Laura Ingalls.
Searches out areas of interest that contribute to self-esteem	Much to the children's delight, a second grade class plans a hobby/collection/interest day so that each child may share her or his personal "passion."
Gains more accurate understanding of strengths and weaknesses	"I bet Mr. Yonce will say something really good about me in reading on my report card," anticipates Stacey.

Moral Reasoning and Prosocial Behavior

Young preschool children tend to base moral judgments on the material outcome of an action rather than on the intent of the person involved, but by the age of 4, children evaluate some lies (e.g., an antisocial lie intending to hurt someone's feelings) as worse than others (e.g., a "white" lie that does not hurt anyone) (Bussey, 1999). Primary grade children expand their understanding that many moral questions pivot around a person's intent. Their earlier preoccupation with surface details (e.g., how much paint was spilled) is gradually abandoned for a deeper evaluation of the situation's complexities and relevant issues (e.g., Was the spill accidental? Was the person being careless? Were any rules broken? Was anyone hurt?). Developmental changes in moral reasoning generally parallel cognitive development, but children's

Box 4.11

Growth Indicators of Advances in Play

Growth Indicator	*Example*
Participates in cooperative play	"Ya wanna play fort?" Meleah calls to two friends. "I'll build the walls, and you can build the roof, and we can all decorate it. OK?"
Participates in and makes up games with rules	"You're out!" several children call to a child hit by the ball in dodge ball.
	Let's say you don't really have to go to jail when you land here," says George to Duncan while playing Monopoly®.

Cooperative play and games with rules characterize play during the primary years.

levels of sympathy and the social context are also factors (Carlo, Koller, Eisenberg, DaSilva, & Frolich, 1996). In addition, their maturing theories of mind help them become adept at understanding the perspectives of others.

Although children gain increasing maturity in judging what is the right thing to do in hypothetical situations, whether they choose the right thing in a real-life situation is another matter. Recall from Chapter 3 that prosocial behaviors (e.g., cooperating, helping, sharing, comforting, and interacting positively with others) are related to the regulation of one's own behavior (Eisenberg et al., 1999); as children gain control over their own impulses, they are more likely to engage in these other-oriented behaviors. Further, "prosocial behaviors have been linked with peer acceptance" (Stormshak et al., 1999, p. 169) and support both the establishment and maintenance of friendships. See Box 4.12 for growth indicators of moral reasoning and prosocial behavior.

What can be done to promote children's prosocial behavior, particularly in a time when "the broader culture is increasingly shaping the lives of our children" (Pipher, 1996, p. 19)? First, adults can stimulate children's growth of social competence by working within their zones of proximal development (Maccoby, 1992). Seizing opportunities to help children think about others builds and challenges their perspective-taking skills. For example, parents may talk about others' experiences or discuss inferences from stories or television programs; such

---

Box 4.12

Growth Indicators of Moral Reasoning and Prosocial Behavior

Growth Indicator	*Example*
Increasingly evaluates the intent of the actor	"We know you told us to stand still," a brave child tells the substitute teacher, "but Robby would have gotten hit by the ball if Shuichi hadn't knocked it away. He really wasn't being bad."
Increasingly takes into account the relevant issues of a moral situation	"No way!" Caleb vehemently argues. "Marcin shouldn't get any treats 'cause he didn't help."
Demonstrates perspective-taking skills in many, but not all, situations	Aware that a friend dislikes scary stories, Brock advises against reading a particular book. "Come on, just jump," Jillian impatiently urges Bonnie on the swings. "There's nothing to be scared of."
Expands prosocial behavior	"Would you like to sit with me at lunch?" Renata asks Carol on her first day at a new school.

early experiences at age 3 contribute to children's understanding of emotions at age 6 (Brown & Dunn, 1996). Furthermore, adults may "promote each child's comfortable, empathic interactions with people from diverse backgrounds" (Derman-Sparks, 1994, p. 69).

Second, a reasonable amount of control over their own lives provides children with experience in responsibility. Third, power-assertive discipline that undermines children's sense of control and responsibility is rejected because conscience development is enhanced by encouraging "internalized regulation, growing empathy, and awareness of wrongdoing" (Kochanska, Padavich, & Koenig, 1996, p. 1433). Eisenberg et al. (1999) point out that using inductions to guide children, "techniques in which an adult gives explanations or reasons for requiring the child to change his or her behavior" (p. 711), and "quality early schooling and supportive relationships between children and their teachers have been associated with the development of prosocial behavior" (p. 728). Clear connections between a child's actions and their consequences, along with a history of positive relationships with adults, will help the child consider consequences and benefits to others when faced with moral choices. What is our long-term goal for children? Consider the model posed in the classic novel from South Africa, *Cry, the Beloved Country:*

> I shall no longer ask myself if this or that is expedient, but only if it is right. I shall do this, not because I am noble or unselfish, but because life slips away, and because I need for the rest of my journey a star that will not play false to me, a compass that will not lie. (Paton, 1995, p. 208)

Relationships with Peers

Children's relationships serve as important models for their future relationships. Primary grade children, now spending approximately 30% of their social-interaction time with peers (Rubin et al., 1998), increasingly choose friends who come to their aid and stick up for them, share their secrets, and engage in leisure-time experiences together. Generally, children's preferences for playing with children of the same gender increase during the primary grade years, and each gender demonstrates distinct play styles; for example, "boys' games are more competitive than girls' games" (Maccoby, 1998, p. 39).

> At preschool age, the children were spending nearly three times as much time playing with same-sex others as with opposite-sex others, although there was also a considerable amount of play in mixed-sex groups. By age 6½, the ratio of the same- to other-sex play partners had increased to 11 to 1. (p. 22)

Children tend to like children who display classic prosocial behaviors, such as sharing, helping, and offering comfort. Even in the early weeks of kindergarten, "children who engaged in higher levels of prosocial behavior . . . tended to develop more mutual friends and higher levels of peer acceptance" (Ladd, Birch, & Buhs, 1999, p. 1394). Overall, the frequency of aggressive acts declines, but boys continue to display more aggression than girls (Coie & Dodge, 1998). Physical aggression typically declines and is gradually replaced by verbal aggression (insults, derogation, threats), but unfortunately, "bullying accounts for a substantial portion of the aggression that occurs in the peer group" (Rubin et al., 1998, p. 639). To bully other children, "boys typically use force or the threat of force; girls often mock or ridicule their victims, making fun of their clothes, behavior, or appearance or revealing their most embarrassing secrets" (Berger, 2000, p. 412).

Peer relationships provide unique benefits for children. Children with friends are better able to consider others' points of view and are more altruistic than those without them (Dunn, Brown, & Maguire, 1995). "Children who see their friendships as a source of validation or aid tend to feel happier in school, see their classmates as supportive, and develop positive school attitudes" (Ladd, Kochenderfer, & Coleman, 1996, p. 1116). In addition, children's expanding psychological understanding of themselves goes hand in hand with their increasing appreciation of their friends (Hartup, 1992).

Increasingly, throughout the school-age years, peer groups offer the individual security and a sense of belonging, but they also exert pressure to conform. Much of this conformity centers around participation in activities (e.g., playing four-square at recess), clothing (e.g., wearing the "right" brand of shoes), and allegiance to peer-group members. Some peer groups expect conformity in antisocial activities. In general, children are inclined to go along with their peer groups until they reach midadolescence (Shaffer, 1999); therefore, the types of peer groups primary children are involved in warrant scrutiny. Box 4.13 lists growth indicators of primary grade children's relationships with their peers.

Box 4.13

Growth Indicators of Relationships with Peers

Growth Indicator	Example
Increasingly focuses friendships on loyalty and intimacy as well as mutual interests	"I like Melody more now 'cause she really stuck up for me at recess," Jocelyn reports.
Usually prefers same-gender playmates	Shirley only invites girls to her birthday party, and her brother asks her to invite his best friend, Charlie.
Is aware of, and sometimes is vulnerable to, peer-group influences	"I can't wear this shirt that Grandma sent me to school, Mom," Mikio whines. "All the kids will laugh."

Managing Stress

Everyone has stress in daily life, and children are no exception. How children cope depends on two factors: their competence (social, academic, and creative) and their social support (Werner & Smith, 1982). Critical problems arise when these factors are in short supply and/or when the stresses multiply (e.g., divorce plus a move plus the mother returning to work plus lower family income).

The modern tendency to pressure children to hurry through their childhoods has resulted in unnecessary stress (Elkind, 2001). Parents hold high expectations for their children's successes, but their demands may be inappropriate to the children's developmental levels. Typically, children are enrolled in an abundance (often, an overabundance) of extracurricular activities and allowed access to information (e.g., about adult problems, violence, and sex in the media) formerly reserved for the more mature. What can adults do? Here are some of Elkind's (1994, 2001) suggestions:

1. Reinvent our adulthood. Children are not born with an internal set of rules and controls; they rely on adults to set standards. "When we try to be pals with our children . . ., we deprive them of their most important source of internal rules, limits, standards, and controls" (Elkind, 1994, p. 227).

2. Cut back on the demands placed on children and increase adult supports. Look for a reasonable balance of developmentally appropriate responsibilities and adult support and commitment. For example, a teacher encourages the parents of a 7-year-old who goes home each day to an empty house for three hours to enroll their child in an after-school program. After the child becomes noticeably happier, the parents decide to devote half of a weekend day to a leisure-time activity with their child.

3. Provide opportunities for unstructured play, such as opportunities for creative expression—a natural antidote for hurrying. Competitive and instructional activities, although they may be an important part of children's lives, do not usually reduce stress. Be sure children have physical space to call their own for their projects and relaxation.

4. Identify, appreciate, and acknowledge each child's uniqueness.

5. Model living in the present and smelling the roses in your own life. Remember that children carefully observe and imitate the important adults in their lives; through example, you can model ways to enjoy life and moderate stress.

These suggestions are further supported by research on the relationship between stress and school activities. Children in developmentally inappropriate classrooms exhibited more stress than did children in appropriate classrooms; particularly stressful times were transitions, waiting, and workbook/worksheet activities (Burts et al., 1992). Moreover, "compared to children in didactic programs, children [ages 4–6] in child-centered programs rated their abilities higher, had higher expectations for success on school-like tasks, selected a more challenging math problem to do, showed less dependency on adults for permission and approval, evidenced more pride in their accomplishments, and claimed to worry less about school" (Stipek, Feiler, Daniels, & Milburn, 1995, p. 220).

Psychosocial development does not proceed in a vacuum but is inevitably linked to the other major domains. For example, "children's classroom participation, particularly the ability to behave in a cooperative/independent manner in the kindergarten milieu, is a powerful precursor of early achievement" (Ladd, Birch, & Buhs, 1999, p. 1396). Psychosocial development is affected by children's individual natures, developmental strengths and limitations, unique social surroundings (their family, friends, school, and extended social networks), and cultures. Against the backdrop of the developmental trends discussed in this section, cherish the inevitable differences among children.

SELECTED HIGHLIGHTS OF CREATIVE DEVELOPMENT

Imagination, innovation, problem-solving, rearrangement, originality, risking, inventions—these are the elements of the creative process. Creativity, as it relates to primary grade children, can be defined as "the mechanism by which people use past knowledge and learned skills to meet the needs of a new situation or to solve a [novel] problem" (Koster, 2001, p. 87). "Even though a discovery may have already occurred, if it is new to the individual, then it is a creative act" (Russ, 1996, p. 31). Feldman (1980) suggests there are two approaches to the study of creativity—the **trait approach** and the **process approach.** Recall from Chapter 3 that the trait approach proposes that people are born with various amounts of creativity; it unfolds on its own. In the process approach favored by educators (Davis & Rimm, 1998), creativity is an interaction between the person's abilities and the opportunities to explore, practice, and perfect. This chapter section focuses on identifying the growth indicators of creativity and learning how the primary grade teacher facilitates interactions with children and their environments.

Advancing from preschool to the primary grades, children's expressions of creativity become increasingly clarified and intricate. Two examples follow. A preschooler may draw a person, a house, or an animal disproportionately in space, whereas a first grader may recall and illustrate a favorite scene from a family outing using detailed figures in an organized drawing that includes a baseline and a skyline with air in between. Preschoolers may shake musical instruments to the rhythm of a favorite song; K–3 children may construct their own music-making devices. During the early elementary years, nonverbal, verbal, and written expressions become representational and more elaborate than they were during the preceding years.

Another difference between preschool and primary grade children's creative development is the more pronounced individuality in the primary grade years. Children's creative interests and strengths begin to bud during the preschool years, but they bloom during the primary years. Comparing the dictated stories of two preschoolers, Ona and Whitney, would probably have some observable differences.

If, however, Ona continues to nurture her interest and ability in writing and Whitney finds writing less appealing than science experiments, the differences in these two girls' third grade stories will become increasingly pronounced. Ona and Whitney, along with other primary grade children, begin to recognize and develop their individual creative talents through abundant and varied opportunities.

In the primary grade classroom, common forms of creative expression are writing, thinking, creating, making music, acting, dancing, building with blocks, and storytelling (Engle, 1995; Gardner, 1980). Many children this age delight in organizing and participating in plays and neighborhood circuses, building treehouses, and inventing new games or revising old ones. In the classroom, evidence of creativity is proudly displayed at open house: artwork, science and social studies projects, and original stories.

"Creativity is different from the other areas of growth that teachers try to develop in our children. It is not something we can teach directly, but we must foster it through our attitude, behavior, and activity choices" (Koster, 2001, p. 95). During these important primary grade years, maturing individual strengths can be appreciated and supported when creative interests and abilities are identified. The growth indicators of creativity (based on the creative skills identified by Gordon & Williams-Browne, 2000) listed in Box 4.14 provide the basis for teacher observation that leads to recognition of development and curriculum planning based on individual needs.

One avenue of self-expression is drawing.

Box 4.14

Primary Growth Indicators of Creativity

Growth Indicator	Example
Expands representations, moving from a single idea to interrelated ideas	Chase's preschool drawing of his family displays each member as distinct and separate, without background. Chase's second grade drawing of his family shows each member involved in roles: Mom is at the computer, Dad's cooking dinner, and his two brothers are doing homework—all in one room!
Expresses individual strengths	The child enthusiastically volunteers for the lead in the first grade play, *Are You My Mother?*
	The boy shares a poem he wrote after his kitten was run over.
Expands flexibility and fluency	"Two five-year-olds, Missy and Eric, want to build a school, but they have no blocks or pieces of wood. They consider using shoe boxes, which are fairly durable and stackable, for a base" (Schirrmacher, 1998, p. 5).
Expands sensitivity	The child leafs through a coffee-table art book on French Impressionism, looks up, and says, "Why do they paint pictures of people without their clothes on?"
Expands imagination	Tori is whirling around and clapping her hands in patty-cake fashion. She tries frantically to keep the beat of the rock music that's playing. She flaps and flops her hands over her head. Then she opens and closes her hands quickly like little signal lights. She calls out, "I'm dancing like a peacock."
Expands risk-taking	Having a lot of practice riding her two-wheeler with training wheels, Najeeba seeks out her big brother. She says, "I want you to take off these training wheels. I'm going to teach myself how to ride without them."
Expands self resourcefulness	While four children are playing an electronic memory game, the pattern with four different colored buttons becomes too difficult to duplicate. One child suggests that each child concentrate on only one color. Therefore, as a team, the group could successfully reproduce long patterns.
Expands expressiveness and skills using creative materials	"This is the best story I've every written about dinosaurs," the child says, "I think I'll illustrate it. Let's see, should I use watercolors, tempera paints, clay, markers, or block prints?"

One specific pathway, creative art, has been singled out and spotlighted over the years. Art growth has been studied and defined through adolescence (Herberholz & Hanson, 1995; Linderman, 1997; Lowenfeld & Brittain, 1987). Development of representational drawing follows a predictable pattern as children are given bountiful opportunities for unrestricted practice and experimentation. A word of caution—art activities duplicating a model are not creative; in fact, they stifle growth. "The creation of new ideas does not come from minds trained to follow doggedly what is already known. Creation comes from tinkering and playing around, from which new forms emerge" (Wassermann, 1991, p. 135).

The growth indicators in Box 4.15 are the target for observing the characteristics of representational drawing that occur in the primary grade years. The characteristics for early primary (found in Chapter 3) are repeated, together with the characteristics of middle primary. Remember that growth is continuous and ages are only general guidelines.

"Is creative expression really important?" ask educators who are pressured to demonstrate classroom proficiency in academic areas. Absolutely! Creativity assists independent thinking, fosters self-esteem, relieves emotional tension, and helps children discover that their own uniqueness is special, valued, and important in the world (Dixon & Chalmer, 1990; Hendrick, 2001).

How can creativity be promoted in the classroom? If "a primary goal of education is to enable children to develop their minds and intellectual capabilities, using all forms of creative intelligence as means for achieving this goal" (Getty Center for Education in the Arts, 1985, p. 11), then employing a curriculum design that embodies creative development becomes a critical choice for the teacher. The integrated curriculum approach, based on thematic units, is an excellent example of such a design. "A thematic curriculum is one in which many different subject areas are integrated by relating them to a carefully selected broad-based concept" (Koster, 2001, p. 121). Developmentally appropriate themes are based on the children's interests and experiences and are relevant to their lives. The theme is then supported by language arts, math, science, social studies, art, or music activities that are related to the theme; disciplines are integrated. For example, if the theme is families, one possible way to begin would be to introduce a literature story and then plan activities that branch from there. Figure 4.2 illustrates how such an approach facilitates development of creativity in the primary grades.

In summary of this chapter section, promoting creativity is one of the teacher's main challenges. The primary grade child's maturing creative expression and emerging strengths develop best when:

- Creativity is incorporated into the curriculum.
- Indicators of creative growth are fostered.
- Children's creative interests are encouraged.
- A classroom climate of support and exploration is provided.
- Ample opportunities for children to grow at their own rate are provided.

Box 4.15

Primary Grade Growth Indicators of Drawing

Early primary (ages 4–6)
- Combines shapes that become schemas (personalized representational symbols); makes intentional image repetition of schemas; develops preferred schemas
- Begins drawing representations, often of people, animals in profile letterlike forms, basic forms represented consistently—houses, flowers, boats, people
- Portrays meaning (subject matter) in an increasingly readable manner
- Repeats repertory or symbolic forms, practices, and adds new elements
- Shows beginnings of individual style (e.g., typical way of drawing a house)
- Isolates figures, each is discrete (no overlapping of whole or of parts); shows no context or baseline, and draws size and details according to perceived importance or interest (e.g., long arms)
- Presents several figures on the page; begins representing events or narratives; places schematic figures in a larger concept; for example, knowing an elephant is a four-legged animal with a trunk, the child uses a well-established routine, or schema, for drawing animals—cats, dogs, and so forth—and adds a trunk.

Middle primary (ages 5–8)
- Draws elaborations and variations of schematic figures and experiments; shows repetition of imagery by practicing "set pictures" (always drawn the same way), such as racing cars
- Produces details traditionally or formulaic, such as windows with tie-back curtains, chimneys with smoke coming out at an angle, girls with skirts and long hair
- Draws narratively, illustratively, and inventively; often shows baselines as multiples; draws "see through" houses and most figures are in their own space, without overlapping

Note: Adapted with the permission of the National Association for the Education of Young Children. From *Considering Children's Art: Why and how to value their works* by B. S. Engle. Copyright © 1995 by National Association for the Education of Young Children.

The teacher's guide (Crosswhite, 1995) contains information for reading, vocabulary, structural analysis, and guided and independent reading. Beyond reading, the following activities are some samples of using the story across the curriculum.

Themes: **Nap time, bedtime, families**

Story: *The Napping House* **by Audrey Wood**

Sample Activities:

• Have the students select rhythm instruments to represent each of the action words in the book, such as sandpaper blocks for snoring, triangle for dreaming, and drums for bumps. Read the story a second time, adding the sound effects.

• Play charades by having individual children act out bedtime/morning activities as the other students determine the activity.

• Discuss bedtime/nap time experiences. Encourage the children to share a time when a nap was disturbed or something funny happened. Then invite the children to write a story and illustrate the event.

• Assist the children in creating their own family mobiles (including pets). Discuss several ways to make a mobile, including using straws, string, and construction paper.

Figure 4.2
Integrated curriculum example.

To avoid redundancy the expanded explanation of the approaches to creativity (trait versus process), conditions of creativity, and the teacher's role are excluded from this chapter. Review the creativity section in Chapter 3 for that information.

> QUICK REVIEW <

The primary grade child is developmentally different from yet similar in many ways to the preschool child. Children within both age groups show individual maturational rates, follow general predictable patterns, and draw on their own experiences and genetic makeup. In this chapter, however, development has been highlighted as an ongoing process, making advances physically, cognitively, psychosocially, and creatively. Identified growth indicators help the teacher zero in on developmental strides through continued observation.

TAKE A MOMENT TO REFLECT

Personal Reflection

David Elkind purported (in an interview by Scherer, 1996) that the general trend of the families of today has changed from a cohesive unit to autonomous individuals. "Today soccer practice or a business meeting takes precedence over dinner because personal needs are more important than the family" (p. 7). Reflect on the implications of that idea and answer the questions below.

1. What examples have you seen in which families have replaced togetherness with autonomy? Think about your own, relatives', and television families.
2. How might the individual focus of some of today's families strengthen or limit the developmental process of their primary grade children?

Ethical Reflection

NAEYC Ideal I-1.2 is "to base program practices upon current knowledge in the field of child development and related disciplines and upon particular knowledge of each child" (Feeney & Kipnis, 1992, p. 4). Reflect on specific examples from Chapter 4 that illustrate how teachers fulfill this ethical responsibility to children.

Observing Individual Children

Chapter 5   Observing the Development of Individual Children by Using Running Records

Chapter 6   Observing the Development of Individual Children by Using Anecdotal Records

Chapter 7   Observing the Development of Individual Children by Using Checklists

Chapter 8   Observing the Development of Individual Children by Using Rating Scales

Chapter 9   Observing the Development of Individual Children by Using ABC Narrative Event Sampling

Chapter 10   Child Portfolios and Parent Conferences

5

Observing the Development of Individual Children by Using Running Records

When Fiona thinks of one of her students, Warren, her ponderings often begin with "if only." If only Warren would wander less. If only Warren would pay more attention in class. If only Warren would complete his assignments. If only Warren found school interesting. If only. If only.

Warren does, however, wander in class, and he does not pay attention or complete assignments or find school interesting. How can Fiona begin to understand this child who frustrates her best intentions as a second grade teacher?

In the midst of meeting her many teaching responsibilities in an industrious classroom, Fiona worries that she is not meeting the needs of this challenging child. She fears she has overlooked clues that help to explain Warren's behavior; perhaps there are consistencies or patterns that she does not see. Fiona plans time to observe Warren as he goes about his usual school activities to clarify how he spends his time. She is interested to discover his activities while wandering, his work procedures, his interactions with others, his interests, and his transitions between activities. The aim of this chapter is to describe how to write running records that record children's behaviors within their natural contexts; a running record is Fiona's observational method of choice.

OVERVIEW OF OBSERVING USING RUNNING RECORDS

Description

The **running record** is a "continuous observation of a 'behavior stream' for a particular period of time" (Bergen, 1997, p. 120). In a written narrative the observer writes in the present tense what the child says and does during a specified length of time or designated activity. Detailed, factual recordings are made in sequential form while the event is happening. "The observer in making a narrative record records a wide slice of life. No attempt is made to filter what occurred in any systematic way" (Evertson & Green, 1986, p. 177). The observer does not look for or interpret any specific behavior; the goal is simply to gather as much raw data as possible. Because of the high yield of **qualitative data,** the running record is a valuable observational method for teachers of young children.

Perhaps an analogy is in order. Compare the writing of running records to observing as a human video camera. Like the camera lens, the observer's eyes are focused on the subject, and the observer records what is seen and heard. The qualification of *human* is, however, essential; although the observer would like to be able to capture absolutely everything, keeping up with an active child and being as objective as possible makes recording a challenging task.

Acknowledging that recording *everything* a child says and does is impossible, the observer makes reasonable judgments about the amount of detail to record. The best guideline is to keep the purpose and setting of the observation in mind. This focus will help determine which facts are essential to record and which may be safely omitted. In a running record in Chapter 2, for example, Cyd's language in the sand area was recorded as clear evidence of his ability to seriate three objects by size; noting his clothing, however, would not have added useful information. In contrast, if a child being observed interacts with several unfamiliar children, recording what each child is wearing could be vital in distinguishing one child from another. In Figure 5.1, the observer keeps her focus on one child and does not record other children's words or actions. The observer, always improving with experience and practice, makes on-the-spot decisions regarding the appropriate amount of detail to record.

A well-written running record is a rich account of naturally occurring behavior. The observer can return again and again to its deep well of details to refresh memories or to study a child with a new purpose or from a new perspective. To heighten the future value of a running record, a conclusion is added. Written in the past tense, the conclusion briefly summarizes the development demonstrated by the behavior or activity observed and recorded in a running record. Imagine the amount of time it would take a teacher to sift through the contents of a few running records for each child while preparing for parent conferences. Conclusions at the end of each of those running records would supply the teacher with instantly accessible information. Pay attention to this valuable service provided by the conclusions in the running records in Figures 5.1 through 5.4.

Purpose

Researchers in child development depend on running records (at times called "specimen records" or "descriptive narratives") to gain insights into behavior and development. Piaget, for example, relied on his detailed observations of children to help him conceptualize and describe cognitive growth. Think back to the Off on Your Own 1.1 exercise in which you took notes about what one child did for 10 minutes during a free choice time. What did you learn about that child? Classroom teachers may use running records of children's behavior to describe all areas of development and to guide responsive instruction. The intent of the running record is to learn more about the many aspects of a child's total development from the precise recording of this child's actions and language. Running records can be particularly helpful to teachers getting to know a new child in the classroom or trying to understand individual children's problems; see Figure 5.1 for an example. Reading a running record at the end of the observation day, a week later, or two months later provides a replay option that allows the observer to note each child's developmental strengths or limitations and draw conclusions. In addition to helping teachers learn more about individual children, running records support classroom planning. Teachers may use their observations and conclusions to plan supportive and stimulating daily activities.

Teachers may also use running records to augment information contained in other observational formats. For example, in the next chapter a running record provides the data for an anecdotal record. To complete checklists or rating scales assessing children's growth (topics of Chapters 7 and 8), a teacher may draw on running records for supportive accounts. The information gathered in running records also enriches parent conferences by supplying teachers with specific, wide-ranging accounts of children's behavior, language, interests, and interactions in the classroom.

Guidelines for Writing Running Records

Typically, running record observation times are 10 minutes or less; observers first practicing their skills might begin with spans of only 3 to 5 minutes. The raw data of a language specialist's 6-minute running record in Figure 5.2 provide information about a child's difficulties keeping up with the pace of an activity and suggest teaching adjustments.

What guidelines smooth the transition from reading about running records to actually writing them? The following suggestions have been helpful to many observers viewing children's development through the observational lens of running records.

- Use the running record observational method when the details of a child's naturally occurring behavior are desired. Because this method is time-consuming and requires the observer's complete attention, it is used selectively in the early childhood classroom; anecdotal records, introduced in the next chapter, are recorded most frequently.

Running Record of Alison During Your Choice Time

Center/Age level:	Rainbow Ridge/4-Year-Olds		
Date:	9/14	Time:	8:45–9:15 A.M.
Observer:	Mary Agnes	Child/Age:	Alison/3; 11
		Teacher:	Wilt
		Assistant:	Mary Agnes

Comments

Alison sits cross-legged on the carpet next to Wilt as he announces special   *8:45*
materials available for Your Choice Time: chalk and a variety of paper in the
art area, new wood pieces for gluing in the construction area, pencils and
notepads in the house area, and aluminum foil in the block area. Alison
looks at her clasped hands and turns her plastic flower ring around and   *Listening?*
around; she does not look at Wilt or any of the children who are talking
about their plans.

    When Wilt says, "OK, have a good Your Choice Time," Alison stands up,   *8:50*
still clasping her hands and twirling her ring. She walks to the art area,
stands about 3 feet from the table, and watches four children making chalk
drawings. She looks at the children, then down at her ring, looks at the   *All spaces taken.*
children, then down at her ring. Alison repeats this looking pattern, twirling
all the time, for nearly 3 minutes.

    Alison turns her head toward the opening door and the sound of heavy
rain. She walks in that direction and enters the empty book corner. She
bends down and arranges two pillows side by side and lays on her   *8:55*
stomach on them. She fingers the carpet, then removes her ring and tries
to catch and pull carpet strands with her ring. Her efforts produce a   *Jewelry at school?*
popping sound, but the carpet stays intact! Wilt walks into the book corner
and sits beside her, holding a container of farm animals and a container of
zoo animals from the block area. He talks softly to Alison.   *Can't hear.*
  9:05
    Alison stands up, takes the zoo animal container from Wilt, and walks
directly to the block area where Sean, Annette, and Kenny are building in
the far end. She sits cross-legged with the container in her lap, facing the
shelves so that she has 12 inches of carpet between the shelves and her
knees. She puts the container in front of her and picks out a small lion with
her right index finger and thumb and an elephant with her left fist. She   *Does she know how to*
gently knocks their heads together about 8 times, then their feet, and then   *play?*
their tails. She returns the two animals to the container and, leaving it on
the floor, walks to the music area.

Figure 5.1
Preschool running record example.

Alison puts on the headphones, chooses an Ella Jenkins tape from the basket, slips it into the player, plugs her jack into the player, and adjusts the volume. She remains standing while she listens and dances in the small space allowed by the headphones cord. She claps occasionally, sways with her upper body, and moves her hands back and forth about chest height. She continues; Wilt announces Your Choice Time is over.

9:06

Competent tape player user!

Conclusions: Alison spent most of Your Choice Time engaged in onlooker behavior and solitary play. Her level of involvement with other people and materials was low, and she did not spend longer than 7 minutes with any activity. Alison did not appear to be unhappy or bored, but she did not exhibit any enthusiasm for the activities she chose. Alison's manipulation of the tape player, headphones, animals, and ring indicated competent fine motor control.

Figure 5.1 *(Continued)*
Preschool running record example.

- Begin by reviewing the general guidelines for observation in Chapter 2.
- Prepare a heading to include the setting (center or school/age level or grade, date, and time) and people present (observer, child/age, teachers). This format will also be the standard used for checklists, rating scales, ABC narrative event sampling, tally event sampling, and time sampling.
- Record only the facts. Try to minimize subjectivity, and do not add any inferences.
- Write exactly what is happening in the present tense.
- Record behaviors in sequence as they are occurring.
- Stay focused on the child being observed. Conversations, noise, or activities going on simultaneously in the classroom may be distracting; resist!
- Provide space in the right margin for comments. Use this space to jot down notes that are not a part of your running record (e.g., additional information about an activity or impressions you may want to think more about later). Also, periodically note the time (about every 5 minutes or when the activity changes). Knowing how long a child was engaged in an activity can provide information about the child's interests and attention span.
- Use abbreviations or short phrases if helpful. The flow of activities can be so rapid that even an experienced observer can have trouble keeping pace with the action; you should, however, write complete quotes of a child's language. The exact words a child said will be difficult to remember and fill in later.
- When you have completed the observation, go back and fill in the needed details as soon as possible while they are fresh in your mind. Running records are rich with description.

Running Record of Taki During Listening Lotto

Center/Age level:	Center for Speech and Language/3- to 6-Year-Olds			
Date:	7/17	Time:	10:20–10:26 A.M.	
Observer:	Naoki	Child/Age:	Taki/5; 1	
		Teacher:	Camille	

Comments

Taki is seated on the floor with Kyle (4; 8) and Camille, the teacher, in a corner of the classroom; both children have their backs to the center of the room. Taki sits with her right leg tucked under her bottom and her left leg bent with her foot flat on the floor. The Listening Lotto card is in front of her on the floor, and she holds a bunch of red plastic markers in her right hand. Camille begins the tape.

10:20

No intro of game.

    The first sound is of a baby crying. Taki looks up at Camille, who says, "What's that?" Taki looks at Kyle, who has already placed his marker on the crying baby. Camille says, "That's a baby crying," and points to the picture on Taki's card. Taki places the marker with her left hand as the next sound, beating drums, begins.

Hearing aid working.

    Taki looks at Kyle as the drumming continues. Camille points to the picture of the drums on Taki's card, and Taki places her marker.

Understands process.

    The next sound is of a toilet flushing. Taki looks at Kyle and points to the drums. Kyle says, "Good, Taki. We heard drums banging." Taki smiles. Camille says, "Do you hear the toilet flushing?" as she points to the correct picture. Taki places her marker and repositions herself to sit cross-legged. She continues to hold the markers in her right hand and place them with her left.

10:22
Kyle supportive of Taki.

    When the tape plays the sound of glass breaking, Taki looks at Kyle, Camille points to the correct picture, and Taki places the marker.

    The sound is of a bouncing ball. Same process: Taki looks at Kyle, Camille points to the picture of the ball, and Taki places the marker.

    A lion roars on the tape. Taki looks at the markers in her right hand (3 left) and scoops up more from the floor. Camille says, "Do you hear the lion?" She points to the picture, and Taki places the marker with her left hand.

    The sound is of sizzling bacon in a frying pan. "What's that, Taki?" asks Camille. Taki looks at Kyle, Camille points to the picture, and Taki places the marker.

Figure 5.2
Language specialist's running record example.

Camille looks up at another group finishing a science activity, checks the clock, and says, "One more." The sound is of a radio and the changing of stations. "Where's the radio?" She points to the radio, and Taki places a marker.

Taki behind-stop tape?
10:24

"Time to clean up," announces Camille. Taki opens the 3-inch × 6-inch plastic bag with her left hand and slides her remaining markers in from her right hand without spilling one. She picks up the last markers on the floor with her right hand and, making a troughlike shape with her right hand, slides the markers in the bag. She zips the bag closed (holding it with her right and zipping with her left), puts the bag and her game card in the box, stands, and walks to her snack table.

Conclusions: Taki's receptive language was on display when she followed the teacher's directions in Listening Lotto (put markers on the appropriate spots), but she did not demonstrate success on her own. Her fine motor control was in evidence as she adeptly handled small markers.

Figure 5.2   *(Continued)*
Language specialist's running record example.

- At the end of the running record, write a conclusion in the past tense summarizing the development (cognitive, psychosocial, physical, or creative) demonstrated by the child.
- Keep the records confidential; do not leave them lying around the classroom.
- Organize each child's running records in his or her portfolio. (More on this in Chapter 10.)

A major temptation with using running records is to write general and vague descriptions. Capturing children's developmental moments in detail is a valuable skill to cultivate and will sharpen your observational eye; using explicit words is the key. After writing a running record, the observer checks to see if some words are general or vague and need to be replaced with specific words to thoroughly describe an event. For example, a general statement might be, "The girl plays with the blocks in the carpeted area." What specific words would explain how she might have played with blocks? Did the girl stack five cylinders or form a square enclosure with two small rectangles for each side? Descriptive words can precisely characterize the child's behavior and provide the teacher with accurate developmental information. Practice Activity 5.1 presents an opportunity for you to apply your practical understanding of word choice.

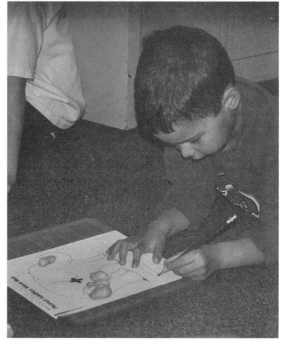

Detailed running records of these activities will provide developmental information about the children.

PRACTICE ACTIVITY 5.1

Descriptive Word Practice

Write some descriptive verbs to further specify the following activities of children. Use a thesaurus if you wish.

Example:
Looks—squints, peeks, stares, glances, scans

1. Builds

2. Colors

3. Tells – *explain, describe, narrates, informs, repeats*

4. Writes

Selecting descriptive words increases the clarity of each observation. Study the following contrasting examples, and identify the details that enable the reader to form vivid mental images of the "B" events being described.

Example 1A
Delia rolls balls down different-sized ramps made of blocks.

Example 1B
Delia (4; 2) stacks three blocks and angles a long, flat board from the top of the blocks to the ground. Then she rolls a ball down the incline, watching where it stops. Next, she adds two more blocks vertically so that the incline is even steeper and rolls another ball down the higher ramp. As the second ball races down the incline and speeds past the first ball, an ear-to-ear smile fills her face. Without hesitation, she constructs a ramp seven blocks high and again rolls a ball down the ramp.

Example 2A
Bentley likes to paint and seems to enjoy the choices we offer. He takes awhile just to arrange the containers in his easel tray.

Example 2B
Bentley (5; 3) scans the paint containers on the art table and focuses on the blue shades. He picks up two dark shades in each hand, carries them to his easel, and deposits them in the left section of the tray. He repeats the selection process with two light shades, puts them in the right section of the tray, and returns and studies the remaining options. He selects another dark shade and a medium one and returns to the easel. He holds these two containers in front of his eyes and turns slightly to his left, looking at them in stronger light. He puts the dark shade on the very left in the tray and the medium shade to the right of the other two dark shades; the blues are now seriated from dark on the left to light on the right.

Descriptive words can provide information about the child's facial expressions, movements, appearances, tones of voice, gestures, and problem-solving methods. Accurate conclusions cannot be drawn without these details.

Striving to record an accurate picture is the job of the trained observer. Avoid the pitfall of vague descriptions; and remember that details, details, details pave the way to useful observations in running records.

INTEGRATION OF DEVELOPMENTAL THEORY AND OBSERVATION

Preschool Example

A teacher committed to studying the development of her students observed a 3½-year-old boy in the dramatic play area. Jeffrey, as usual, was the first child to arrive after the child care center opened at 7:00 A.M., and his teacher, Gita, thought she would have 10 to 15 minutes to observe him working alone before she and her assistant, Dolores, would need to welcome other children and parents. After Gita hugged him good morning and he put his jacket in his cubby, he headed for the dramatic play area. This area seemed to be his favorite spot in the early morning, but Gita knew she was unaware of the fine points of his play. A running record was made to order because she was interested in observing his natural play rather than assessing a specific skill or behavior. Gita sat on a small chair next to a low shelf with her notepad and filled in her heading; she was about 12 feet away from Jeffrey where she could maintain full view of the dramatic play area and the entrance door. Read Gita's running record in Figure 5.3.

Interpreting the Data

Later in the day, when Gita reads over her running record (Figure 5.3), she is able to draw detailed conclusions about specific areas of Jeffrey's development. First, there is wonderful evidence that Jeffrey enjoys using his cognitive ability to represent. Jeffrey

Children's interest and abilities are continually on display in the classroom.

Running Record of Jeffrey in the Dramatic Play Area

Center/Age level: Peaceable Kingdom Day Care/3-Year-Old Classroom
Date: 2/8 Time: 7:10–7:20 A.M.
Observer: Gita Child/Age: Jeffrey/3; 6
 Teacher: Gita
 Assistant: Dolores

Comments

Jeffrey stands at the entrance to the dramatic play area and rubs his hair *7:10*
with both hands. Then, with his hands on his hips, he turns his head from
one end of the area to the other, looking at the materials. He stands,
without moving, looking back and forth at the area for 50 seconds. He
walks heel-to-toe to the far corner and looks down at the heap of dolls and
stuffed animals. He bends over, picks up the brown bear with his right
hand, and holds it under his left arm while he pulls out the rabbit and pink
bear. He takes this load and dumps the three animals on the round table
and walks back to the pile. This time he drops down on his knees and
rummages through the heap of mostly dolls. He extracts a dog with a torn
ear and missing eye and nose; after turning it all around, he discards it to
the side. He pulls out a stained, limp lamb and quickly puts it with the dog.
He rummages again. Lifting his head, he calls to me, "Hey teacher, we got
any more animals?"

"No," I reply, "I think you found them all." *7:13*

Standing up, Jeffrey returns to the round table. He puts the animals in
three of the four chairs around the table that are pulled out and scoots each
one in. He picks up the pile of full-sized plates from the stove with both hands
and walks to the brown bear. Holding the plates in his left hand, with fingers
gripped around the edges, he pats the brown bear on the head with his right
hand and announces, "Gregory." He puts a plate in front of Gregory. Moving
clockwise around the table, he reaches the pink bear. "Mimi," he says and
gives it a plate. He pauses with his hand on the rabbit's head for 15 seconds.
"Casey," he says with hesitation; then, "No—Wally." He gives Wally a plate.

Jeffrey walks to the cupboard and picks up the plastic fruit and a large,
long-handled spoon from the bottom shelf. Using his left hand, he places
the plastic tomato on the spoon held in his right hand and, balancing it,
side steps over to Wally.

"Here you go, Wally," Jeffrey says with a smile, enthusiasm, and a slightly
raised voice. "Your favorite, bacon an' eggs." He tips the tomato onto the plate.

(continued)

Figure 5.3
Gita's preschool running record example.

"Now for you, my little chickadee," Jeffrey sing-songs on his way back to the fruit. "What my little darlin' want to eat?" He pauses, looking through the fruit. "Oh? We got some that too." He puts the plastic apple on the spoon, carries it over to Mimi's plate, and tips it on. He briefly glances at two children who are being greeted by Dolores.

7:16

After studying the animals at the table, Jeffrey rummages through the stove, sink, and cupboard without removing anything. Wrapping his fingers around the handle, he opens the refrigerator door, smiles, and uses both hands to collect an oversized handful of real flatware from the top shelf. Walking heel-to-toe with small steps toward Gregory, he transfers the flatware to his left hand; as he tries to pull out a fork with his right hand, several pieces drop to the floor. He picks them up and tries again. Again, he loses several pieces, but this time he gives Gregory a fork before collecting the pieces. The fork he tries to pull out for Mimi gets tangled, and the whole handful tumbles to the floor. Frowning, Jeffrey scoops the flatware up with both hands and dumps the pieces in the sink.

Yipes! Clean up and sort!

7:20

Noah and Lene arrive at the entrance to the dramatic play area and are greeted by Jeffrey with a raised, eager voice, "Hi, wanna play with me? I'm feeding my babies. He got bacon an' eggs, and she got pancakes with 'nanas. I'm the dad, OK?"

Conclusions: Jeffrey's dramatic play as a dad who talked to the stuffed animals with raised intonation and prepared them pretend food demonstrated his focused representational ability. He maintained one-to-one correspondence with three animals and three plates. He displayed fine motor skills when he used his right hand to manipulate a long-handled spoon effectively, balance the plates, and open the refrigerator door. His initiation and independence allowed him to play on his own although he also welcomed other children.

Figure 5.3   *(Continued)*
Gita's preschool running record example.

allows one object to stand for another. The animals were given names and referred to as *babies.* He pretended that the tomato was bacon and eggs and the apple was pancakes with bananas. Jeffrey is able to take on a role with appropriate accompanying language. He pretended that he was the dad and talked to the animals with raised intonation. He gave each animal a plate and started to pass out forks. Perhaps he is imitating action and language he has observed. Perhaps he has heard someone use the phrase "my little chickadee" and watched the table-setting process.

Gita also finds information about Jeffrey's developing number skills. Jeffrey is able to maintain one-to-one correspondence with small numbers. He successfully passes out plates to the three animals although he took the whole stack with him to the table rather than counting out three at the stove. It appeared that he planned to give each animal a fork but abandoned the idea when the handful of flatware proved to be unwieldy.

This running record also provides information about Jeffrey's development in other areas that will not be pursued at this time. In the psychosocial realm, for example, Gita observed a child who worked beautifully by himself and yet was cordial to arriving children. Running records often provide a wealth of information in various developmental areas.

Follow-Through Plans

Practicing the observational methods presented in this book will advance your observation skills. You will learn about the potentials of the various methods and how to utilize them competently. As a teacher (future or present), however, you want to conduct observations in order to enrich the lives of the children in your classroom. You will want to press your running records and interpretations into service. Remember, "teaching is not one activity and inquiring into it another. The ultimate aim of inquiry is understanding; and understanding is the basis of action for improvement" (McKernan, 1991, p. 3).

Therefore, in anticipation of teaching responsibilities, let's examine how Gita puts her running record to practical use. She notices in the comments column how long it took (nearly 10 minutes) for Jeffrey to set up his role-play. The dolls and stuffed animals were all jumbled together. The plates, flatware, and plastic fruit seemed to be located in random places; the flatware was in the refrigerator and the plastic fruit in the cupboard. Gita wonders how much more Jeffrey's role-play might have developed if he could easily have located his props in predictable places. Consequently, Gita decides to do a general housecleaning and organization of the dramatic play area.

Gita continues to study the materials-and-equipment issue. She concludes that plastic fruit is a poor substitute for bacon and eggs or pancakes and bananas. She worries that because plastic fruit clearly represents real fruit, some children might feel constrained to use it only as fruit. Further, the plastic fruit does not allow the child to mix things together or practice fine motor skills by ladling food onto dishes. She plans to fill one canister with open-ended materials, such as various wooden shapes, to add to the ease and enjoyment of the children's pretending.

Gita ponders what else might be changed in the dramatic play area to support children's representational thought. What else could Jeffrey do as a make-believe grown-up? Are there materials to support pretending to write checks, make a shopping list, read a cookbook, take care of a baby, and chat on the telephone? If Jeffrey wants to pretend to be someone other than a family member, could the dramatic play area provide the foundation? Are props and space available to be a shopkeeper, bank teller, doctor, office worker, chef, fire fighter, and the like? Gita's running record stimulates an evaluation of the materials available and the use of space throughout the classroom.

Noticing that Jeffrey exhibits one-to-one correspondence with three animals and three plates, Gita wants to find out if this skill extends to larger numbers. She decides to ask Jeffrey to pass out napkins to the eight children at the snack table tomorrow. She plans to provide Jeffrey with opportunities to count objects so she can further evaluate and support his number development.

Gita's running record also gives her pause to appreciate Jeffrey's thoughtfulness and initiative; he did not act impulsively in the dramatic play area. He studiously surveyed the area before commencing play. He was not distracted during his cumbersome search for the stuffed animals. Jeffrey appeared to plan his role play mentally and carry it out with great deliberation. Gita recognizes the importance of being responsive to this individual characteristic by continuing to provide large blocks of time for Jeffrey to initiate and extend his complex play.

Primary Grade Example

Going one step further than being a *"human* video camera," a primary grade teacher arranged (with parental permission) for a student teacher to videotape Thienkim, a child in his kindergarten class. To minimize classroom disruption, the camera was set up near a wall, and the zoom feature was used to follow the child. Pablo, the teacher, was concerned about Thienkim's behavior in the classroom and scheduled a preliminary child-study team meeting of the principal, resource specialist, and himself to explore the necessity of special help for Thienkim. Pablo promised to supply a videotape so the team could share a common frame of reference, and he transcribed a portion of the tape in the form of a running record (Figure 5.4) to send to the team members before the meeting and for Thienkim's file.

Interpreting the Data

Supported by the running record and videotape, Pablo presents Thienkim's problems as he sees them to the child-study team. Pablo describes an insecure, timid child whose behaviors limit her potential enjoyment of friends, school, and learning. Pablo is bewildered by some of Thienkim's behaviors: Thienkim said she wanted to work with Luciano and then chose not to; further, she held up her index finger while recognizing two ducks on a Lotto card. Pablo admits feeling unsuccessful with Thienkim and begins to wonder if she should be placed in a special class where she could get more individualized attention.

Fortunately for Thienkim, the resource specialist is of Vietnamese ancestry and is able to explain some of Thienkim's behaviors to Pablo and the principal. In Thienkim's culture, shaking hands and hugging are not acceptable methods of greeting between teachers and children; a slight bow is appropriate. Indeed, "in Vietnamese culture, touching people on the head robs them of their soul" (Gonzalez-Mena, 1997, p. 23). As an indication of courtesy and comprehension, Vietnamese often answer a question with "yes" and then go on to reply to the message. Regarding Thienkim's ability to count, the resource specialist notes that Vietnamese begin counting with their thumbs—so the index finger is the usual sign for 2 (Buell, 1984).

Running Record of Thienkim During Greeting Time

School/Grade: Glade Elementary/Kindergarten
Date: 9/17   Time: 8:00–8:15 A.M.
Observer: Pablo   Child/Age: Thienkim/5; 4
                                                         Teacher: Pablo

Comments

Thienkim arrives at school, barely visible behind her mother. With a gentle   *8:00*
tug, the mother pulls Thienkim in front of her, guides her through the
doorway into the classroom and departs quietly. Thienkim stands
motionless with her eyes cast downward.

    "Good morning, Thienkim," I say cheerily and reach out to grasp her
hands, pull her close, and hug her warmly. Thienkim's body stiffens, and
she recoils from my embrace as soon as she is released.

    Thienkim goes to the cubbies via the outskirts of the classroom, without   *8:02*
making eye contact with the other arriving children. She puts her lunch
away, sits on the rug circle, and studies her hands until the class is
gathered to begin the day.

    During the calendar and counting activities, Thienkim remains
motionless and silent. I begin free choice time by asking, "Who wants to
work with blocks?" Thienkim does not volunteer nor does she express
interest in any other available activity. All other children leave to start on
self-selected activities. Only Thienkim remains on the circle.   *8:06*

    "Would you like to work with Luciano and the puzzles?" I ask.

    "Yes, I don't want to," replies Thienkim in a barely audible voice. She gets   *Works 9 minutes*
up, walks immediately to the small-toys area, chooses a Lotto game, spreads   *on this.*
the cards out on an empty table, and sits down with her back to the center of
the classroom. She studies each picture card for a second or two before
putting it in place. She completes all 12 matches on 2 cardboard sheets.

    "How many ducks are there?" I ask later, pointing to a card.   *8:15*
                                                                                    Holds up one
    "Two," answers Thienkim without hesitation, holding up her hand with   *finger—why?*
her middle, ring, and pinky fingers bent down.

Conclusions: Thienkim withdrew from friendly interactions with the teacher
and class participation and chose to work alone with a structured game,
showing her reserved relationships with adults and peers. In the
classification and number areas, she correctly matched all the Lotto cards
and enumerated two objects.

Figure 5.4
Pablo's primary grade running record example.

A running record is often the key to an expanded understanding of a child.

Follow-Through Plans

Grateful for the resource specialist's gentle and gracious cultural education, Pablo resolves to make his classroom more hospitable to Thienkim. Review Pablo's running record in Figure 5.4, and write down your suggestions in the exercise below.

PRACTICE ACTIVITY 5.2

Practical Applications of Pablo's Running Record

List ways Pablo can make use of the information from his running record of Thienkim and meeting with her child-study team.

Example:
Greet Thienkim with verbal warmth but physical restraint.

1.

2.

3.

APPLICATIONS

Strengths and Limitations

The fundamental benefit of using the running record method is the collection of detailed, narrative data, usually on one child. The data are usually gathered in short periods (5 to 10 minutes) because of the method's stringent attention demands although an experienced observer may effectively manage a longer session. Remember, however, that much can be learned from a short running record. This observational method records a child's behavior and language and allows developmental conclusions to be drawn. Running records may be saved and used throughout the year (or longer) for discovering, assessing, and marking the changes in children over time. They may also serve to stimulate plans for developmentally appropriate activities and the evaluation of the classroom.

Both experienced and inexperienced observers can easily recognize the major difficulty with the running record. The setting alone, an active early childhood environment, can be problematic. A young child may change activities frequently as the observer frantically writes or may move to a place where sight and hearing are hindered. Perhaps classroom noises or interferences distract the observer. Myriad factors might cause the observer to neglect to record some behaviors or verbalizations. Being a "human video camera" requires the constant use of imaginary blinders, a well-tuned ear, and a fast hand.

Another problem is scheduling. Even though the running record method requires only a paper and pencil, the busy classroom teacher encounters many obstacles to finding the time to observe a child. Given the daily demands on an early childhood teacher, running records are best spaced out and employed judiciously. It takes a diligent teacher who is willing to plan for (and an administration that is willing to support) the practical implementation of observation time.

Keep in mind that the payoffs of using the observational method of running records are high. A running record for Warren, the child discussed in the chapter's opening vignette, might have yielded a wealth of understanding; for example, it might have revealed his interests, his active concern with practically oriented problems, how long and under what conditions he worked on-task, and how he responded to peers. Warren's teacher, Fiona, however, probably would have required help from the principal, a specialist, or a parent to accomplish this running record. She could have asked this person to free up her time in order to give Warren her full attention for a short period, or if the person were trained in observation, Fiona might have asked him or her to use the running record method to observe Warren.

As you gain expertise in the observational methods presented throughout this book, you will become able to put the running record in perspective: one plate in a smorgasbord of observational options. You will use the running record selectively when you need raw, factual data to learn more about a child or profit from an overall picture. Then, the time investment required by the running record will pay off. Review the educational follow-through plans for Jeffrey and Thienkim if you have any doubts.

>>>

OFF ON YOUR OWN 5.1

Running Record Activity

For 3 to 5 minutes, observe a child working alone with materials or engaged in a gross motor activity outside, and record his or her actions and language in a running record. Consider using a tape recorder that you can start and stop at your convenience as you write your final copy. Remember to include the following information on your recording form.

Running Record Title

Center or School / Age level or Grade:

Date: Time:

Observer: Child / Age:

                                         Assistant:

                                         Teacher :

Running record: *Comments*

Conclusions:

>>>

> QUICK REVIEW <

1. A running record is a descriptive narrative, unhampered by premature interpretations, that reports the actions and verbalizations of a child in detail. The running record stands alone as raw, qualitative data and is available for later study—stimulating evaluation and profitable follow-through plans.

    ❑ True

    ❑ False

2. The heading of a running record includes (check all that apply):

    ❑ Center or School/Age level or Grade

    ❑ Tuition information

    ❑ Date and time of observation

    ❑ Observer

    ❑ Weather

    ❑ Child/age

    ❑ Teacher

    ❑ Assistant teacher

    ❑ Parents

    ❑ Description of child's clothes

3. The running record is written in the

    a. past tense.

    b. present tense.

    c. future tense.

4. The conclusions in a running record are written in the

    a. past tense.

    b. present tense.

    c. future tense.

5. Is the following sentence factual or subjective? "Roland (7; 3) struggles to write a short description of our trip to the nursery to buy vegetables for planting. He bothers his neighbors to detract attention from his clumsy handwriting."

    a. Factual

    b. Subjective

6. Running records provide such a wealth of information that they should be posted on the bulletin board for parents to read.

   ❑   True

   ❑   False

7. A running record of a child working in the sand area may yield conclusions about her

   a. physical development.

   b. cognitive development.

   c. psychosocial development.

   d. creative development.

   e. all of the above.

8. Write a factual sentence to describe the girl with paint in the photograph on p. 120.

9. Instead of writing that a child "says" something, an observer might use a more descriptive word, such as mumbles, exclaims, reports, describes, explains, informs, or summarizes. What are two descriptive words or phrases to use instead of "runs"?

   • runs with flat feet

   • lopes

   • _____

   • _____

10. Running records yield

    a. quantitative data.

    b. qualitative data.

TAKE A MOMENT TO REFLECT

Personal Reflection

 Frequently we have suspicions about what data our observational study will turn up, particularly if we know the children involved. Pablo, in the primary grade example, is no exception. Before he collected his running record data, he scheduled a child-study team meeting to explore the necessity of special help for Thienkim. He anticipated documenting her problems with the running record so that the other professionals in the meeting would agree with his assessment. What happened? When the resource specialist interpreted some of Thienkim's behavior within her cultural context, Pablo viewed this child in a new light. He immediately began to make plans to support Thienkim's development in his classroom and abandoned his proposal for special placement for Thienkim.

Fortunately, Pablo had an open mind and did not stubbornly stick to his preconceptions. He was able to use the new cultural information to reassess his interpretation of the data. Think about the openness of your own mind in a similar situation, and reflect on strategies to cultivate it.

1. Recall an incident in your own work life in which you were either open or closed to surprising, unanticipated information. What happened? What would you have done differently?

2. List some practical values of maintaining an open mind in the workplace and in observational settings.

Ethical Reflection

NAEYC Ideal I-4.2 is one that considers our ethical responsibilities to community and society: "To promote cooperation among agencies and professions concerned with the welfare of young children, their families, and their teachers" (Feeney & Kipnis, 1992, p. 10). Reflect on how Pablo fulfills this ethical responsibility in the primary grade example.

6

Observing the Development of Individual Children by Using Anecdotal Records

Gita, the teacher in the preschool example in Chapter 5, is sitting, notepad in hand, when Noah and Lene arrive at the entrance to the dramatic play area. Jeffrey cordially invites them to play. Gita's running record of Jeffrey's role play has progressed smoothly, and she has the time and desire to continue. She anticipates that Jeffrey's interactions with the other children will be interesting to observe. What problems do you foresee if Gita chooses to use the running record method in this situation?

While a running record is an excellent method to use when the observer wants to gather wide-ranging data on one child, can you imagine Gita's frantic attempt to write down every action, reaction, interaction, and verbalization of all three children if she chooses a running record?

Gita certainly collected an impressive display of developmental information about Jeffrey in a running record, and now she wants to extend her understanding of Jeffrey's social skills by recording the behaviors of the trio. There is, however, another observational method that can efficiently summarize incidents and is especially useful when detailed accounts are not feasible—the anecdotal record.

This chapter investigates the use of the anecdotal method as a powerful teacher's tool for building an understanding of the whole child; it is an easy way to collect and analyze significant happenings. Although this chapter features the observation of individual children, anecdotal records can also be helpful for teachers observing two or more children together (e.g., Jeffrey and friends), students observing master teachers, supervising teachers observing student teachers, or principals observing teachers. What, then, are anecdotes? Read on, and learn about one of the most popular observational methods in the early childhood classroom.

OVERVIEW OF OBSERVING USING ANECDOTAL RECORDS

After returning from a vacation or, as in this instance, a family celebration, I frequently delight in sharing memorable moments with friends. Often, the happenings are humorous or heart-warming; often, they are unusual or unfortunate. They are always anecdotal. One such anecdote is as follows:

> My nephew Ryan, who is 3 years old, goes to a church-sponsored preschool and has learned the song *Jesus Loves Me, This I Know.* When I was visiting them, I saw Ryan look up at his mom when they were snuggled on the couch, and say, "Momma I love. This I know."

Have you had similar experiences of recounting personal happenings? Most likely we all have. An anecdote, then, is not a new idea to any of us. We all seem to have a sense of what it is all about.

Description

In the early childhood classroom an **anecdote** is more than something interesting, emotive, or amusing to share. It is one directly observed incident written in a short, concise, nonjudgmental narrative. The focus of this simple recording is a specific incident or event that the teacher identifies as notable in the child's development (Diffily & Fleege, 1992). Consider the above definition while reading the following classroom anecdote:

> 10/23 Cheyanne (4; 8): While at group time discussing the season autumn, Cheyanne contributed, "It makes me feel like dancing when I watch the leaves twirling." (Creative–Imagination)

The difference, then, between a classroom anecdote and a personal anecdote is purpose; the classroom anecdote is chosen for its developmental significance, whereas the latter is usually remembered for its emotional appeal.

When writing classroom anecdotes, the teacher first observes the incident, then identifies the incident as valuable (developmentally significant), and completes the process by writing it down after it has occurred. This account, transcribed from memory, of an important classroom event preserves golden developmental moments and provides a permanent record of individual children's growth trends. Figure 6.1 shows four examples of classroom anecdotes for one child. Read through them, and appreciate the developmental significance each represents. Note that the data available for study are qualitative.

Anecdotal records are most reliable if jotted down as soon as possible after the event, thus capitalizing on a clear memory. In bustling classrooms, however, writing a detailed anecdotal entry immediately after the observed incident is not always possible. Reread the first anecdote of Kristi and the fire fighter in Figure 6.1. The teacher, in this example, having acquired the competence to spot significant behaviors, observed a noteworthy incident and had time to make only a quick memorandum using key words on a nearby scratch pad.

10/5 Kristi (3; 3): During the fire fighters' classroom visit, Kristi cried and crawled into the teacher's lap when Paul's mom (one of the fire fighters) put on her uniform. (Psychosocial—Fear)

10/7 Kristi (3; 3): While sitting on a swing outside, Kristi said to me that when she grows and her toes get bigger, she'll be able to pump herself on the swing. (Cognitive—Mental Images)

10/12 Kristi (3; 3): At the art table, Kristi chose four various-sized brushes for each hand and two different colors to paint long strokes the entire length of the paper. (Creative—Expanding Risk-Taking.)

10/15 Kristi (3; 3): Choosing the outside obstacle course, Kristi steadily walked with even paces, one foot in front of the other, on a 4-foot balance beam. (Physical—Gross Motor)

Figure 6.1
Examples of preschool anecdotes.

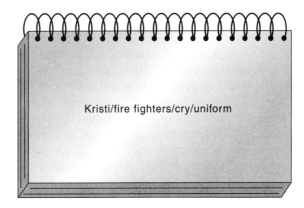

As time permitted later in the day, the teacher transcribed the key words into the few meaningful sentences shown in Figure 6.1 and placed the anecdote in the child's portfolio. This same technique, using key words, was practiced by the teacher in each of the anecdotes in Figure 6.1. What key words do you think the teacher wrote for the other anecdotes about Kristi? Many teachers find that using key words relieves the pressure of recording their anecdotal observations while they are teaching.

Anecdotes require no particular setting, no forms, and no time structures. The observer needs only to capture the essence of what occurred—the child's behaviors, actions, and reactions, during the incident (Gaustad, 1996). The observer may draw on the **journalistic approach** and record the factual accounts of the *who, what, where, when,* and *how* of a single incident. Reporting the specifics of *when* and/or *where* may not always be necessary; it is up to the observer's judgment. For example, if a

The journalistic approach assists the observer in remembering the essential components of anecdotes.

child chooses the planned art activity for the first time when it is set up outside, then stating where it transpired may be a neccessary factor and should be included.

An important component in learning to write anecdotes is what to include in the content. A well-written anecdote gives brief information to build a visual image of the setting, summarizes how the incident happened, and uses descriptive words to tell what was said and done in a factual and nonjudgmental manner. "The use of direct quotes and descriptions of the child's expressions and gestures are important to include because they provide valuable information for review" (Smith, Kuhs, & Ryan, 1993, p. 11). As additional examples, consider the language anecdotes shown in Figure 6.2 that were extracted from individual portfolios. Analyze the content. Did the observer satisfy the requirements of the journalistic approach?

Language development is one of the major growth areas in the early childhood classroom. The teacher recording the language anecdotes in Figure 6.2 considered them developmentally meaningful; in so doing, the teacher appraised the child's age, the vocabulary choice and usage, the expression of relationships, and the concise communication of a complex idea. Language anecdotes may also be collected to evaluate sentence length, articulation/clarity, word order, and conversation skills. In addition, K–3 teachers may observe and record children's use of expanded sentences, pronouns, and accurate grammar, to mention just a few examples.

Purpose

The fundamental aim of the anecdotal record is to document significant and ongoing evidence of children's development through selected observations. Teachers

---

Example 1:

10/5 Tatiana (2; 0): While sitting on the floor in the art area peeling the wrappers off crayons, she looked up as the caregiver drew near and said, "I making the crayons all naked." (Cognitive—Language)

Example 2:

1/15 Maggie (4; 8): I listened as Maggie chattered on and on while the two of us cleaned up the block area. Finally I winked and said, "It all sounds like baloney to me." Maggie quickly asked, "What's baloney?" I replied, "It's a word that means you made all that up!" She thought for a few seconds and said, "No, it's salami!" (Cognitive—Language)

Example 3:

2/24 Matthew (7; 4): While discussing *In A Dark, Dark Room and Other Scary Stories* by Alvin Schwartz, Matthew thoughtfully shared, "Do you know what kind of scary things I like best? Things that are halfway between real and imaginary." I started to ask, "I wonder what . . . " Matthew quickly replied, "Examples would be aliens, shadows, and dreams coming true." (Cognitive—Language)

Figure 6.2
Examples of language anecdotes.

observe and record behavioral patterns, changes, progress, milestones, or uncommon happenings (Kapel, Gifford, & Kapel, 1991) based on the growth indicators explained in Chapters 3 and 4. Typical topics for early childhood anecdotes are language and literacy development, social interaction patterns, problem-solving skills, fine and gross motor competencies, creative characteristics, interests, and achievements. The recordings may involve interactions with only a single child, child-child interactions, or adult-child interactions.

Portfolios (see Chapter 10) house the abundant anecdotes that chronicle a child's development and provide the basis for the teacher's planning of appropriate environmental support, activities, responses, and experiences. One or two anecdotes a week for each child gives the teacher a collection of valuable information on which to build a learning program that germinates from emerging individual needs.

"Taken regularly, anecdotal notes become not only a vehicle for planning instruction and documenting progress, but also a story about an individual" (Rhodes & Nathenson-Mejia, 1992, p. 503). Recordings gathered over time and representing all requisite domains of development (physical, cognitive, psychosocial, and creative) supply enough information to create a story and, thus, a holistic understanding of the child. In addition, parents can fully appreciate this story when well-selected anecdotes are shared at conference time.

Educators with teaching experience may believe they already know the strengths and weaknesses of the children in their classroom and conclude that they do not

Teachers observe and record anecdotes to note developmentally significant incidents.

need to write down individual observations. It is, however, impossible to remember the wonderful growth, in detail, of 8 to 15 (let alone 20 or 30) children over the course of a school year. "Memory leaves just the impression. The written word is an opportunity to check impressions and opinions against the facts" (Gordon & Williams-Brown, 2000, p. 201). Regular and systematic recording documents up-to-date information needed for individual planning and productive parent conferences.

Guidelines for Writing Anecdotes

Over the years, researchers, teachers, and observers have developed helpful hints to ensure success using each of the various observational methods. The following are suggestions to assist in writing useful anecdotal records:

- Employ the anecdotal record method when you want to document significant developmental incidents. Use the information from anecdotes to help chart developmental growth, plan curriculum (based on children's needs and interests), design environments, and write summary forms for parent conferences. Anecdotes are recorded frequently in the early childhood classroom; they are the backbone of portfolios.

- Begin with a clear understanding of the developmental characteristics of the age group being observed. (Review Chapters 3 and 4 or reread the growth indicators in Appendix A.) Be able to identify growth indicators for physical, cognitive, psychosocial, and creative development.
- Be aware of significant happenings in each child's daily activities.
- Using key words, jot down brief notes on paper or adhesive note paper or dictate into a small tape recorder as soon as possible after you directly observe an incident. Record important language passages verbatim. Tuck the notes away in a folder or in a pocket designated for anecdotal records. (Remember that all records must be kept confidential.)
- As soon as possible, transcribe the key words or cursory notes into readable sentences.
- At the beginning of each anecdote, enter the date of the observation and child's age (year; month).
- Use the journalistic approach, and write in the past tense.
- Be factual, objective as possible, and concise; summarize.
- State the developmental significance (e.g., physical, cognitive, psychosocial, or *language* creative) in the anecdote itself or in parentheses at the end. In the primary grades, cognitive development may be categorized into the relevant subject areas (e.g., language arts, math, social studies, and science).
- Guard against haphazardly tossing individual anecdotal records into a catchall file. Enter the finished anecdote in the child's portfolio of observational records.
- Commit to writing one or two anecdotes for each child on a weekly basis.
- Check portfolios periodically to verify the collection of a variety of developmental incidents for each child.

To practice using the guidelines, slowly read the anecdotal record examples listed in Practice Activity 6.1 and determine if each is a correctly or incorrectly written anecdote. For each incorrect anecdotal example, decide what changes should be made.

PRACTICE ACTIVITY 6.1

Anecdotal Examples for Analysis

If the anecdote meets the guidelines, place an X in the box marked correct. If, on the other hand, the anecdote does not meet the guidelines, place an X in the box marked incorrect. In each case, describe your reasoning in the space marked *Analysis.* While working through the following examples, ask yourself the following questions:

(continued)

PRACTICE ACTIVITY 6.1 *(Continued)*

Does this example

- use the correct form (state the date of the observation and the child's age)?
- concisely describe only one incident?
- use a journalistic summary rather than an overall appraisal?
- give too much or not enough information?
- use descriptive words to recount how the event occurred?
- provide quotations of the child's language when appropriate?
- state the developmental significance?

Example:

5/8 Willie (4; 5): Willie is cognizant and watchful while playing with others. He can communicate well. Does like to create own play with other objects but keeps his playmates in mind. (Psychosocial—Play)

☐ Correct

☒ Incorrect

Analysis:

The observer has written an overall evaluation using inferences rather than a journalistic summary of one specific incident. Recording quotes would indicate Willie's communication skills. The last sentence is subjective.

Example:

11/24 Meghan (3; 9) with Ernestina (3; 3): When Meghan saw Ernestina in the doorway crying and clinging to her mother's leg, she walked over and gently touched her cheek to Ernestina's. The girls stood quietly cheek to cheek for a few moments, and Ernestina's mom departed. (Psychosocial—Empathy)

☒ Correct

☐ Incorrect

Analysis:

The observer has identified a significant incident in the psychosocial development of Meghan and Ernestina. The narrative summary is written concisely yet contains information on the *who, what, where,* and *how* of a single incident. This anecdote could be filed in each girl's portfolio. What would the developmental significance be for Ernestina's anecdotal record?

2/15 Jeffrey (3; 6), with Noah (3; 8), and Lene (3; 3): At Jeffrey's invitation Noah and Lene joined in dramatic play. Jeffrey directed and Lene cooperated in the feeding and napping of Jeffrey's "babies." Noah dressed up in men's clothes and pretended to wash the dishes. (Psychosocial—Play)

☑ Correct

☐ Incorrect

Analysis:

how?

12/7 Hien (4; 2): Hien picks one marker out of the container with his left hand, smelling it (scrunching up his nose). "Um pink," he says. He carefully draws horizontal parallel lines with it and puts it back. He sorts through the container and picks up a thinner marker, smells it, and looks it over. Hien asks if all the markers smell as he drops the thin one back into the container. He takes out a green marker, smells it, and draws on the paper using a circular motion. He uses his right hand to steady the paper. "I'm gonna make a target for us," he says. Putting back the green marker, he takes out the red marker and bangs it on the table and then lays it down. Next, he takes out the blue marker and uses a circular motion to draw inside the green circle.

The teacher asks, "So that's a target?"

"Not yet," Hien says. He returns the blue to the container and takes out a purple marker. Quickly, he draws with purple in a circular motion inside the blue circle and says, "Now, that's a target." (Creative—Expands expressive experiences and skills using creative materials)

☐ Correct

☐ Incorrect

Analysis:

4/11 Thelma Lou (6; 4): I am quite worried about Thelma Lou's fine motor development. While working with small puzzles, she seems to have a plan to begin with but asks for help over and over.

☐ Correct

☐ Incorrect

(continued)

PRACTICE ACTIVITY 6.1 *(Continued)*

Analysis:

6/23 Cassandra (7; 11): A small, cooperative math learning group was assigned to create a new pattern using plastic links. Cassandra stood up, gathered the links that had been placed in the center of the table, unlinked each one, and announced, "We all have to have the same amount; I'm going to pass them out!" (Psychosocial—Relations with peers)

☒ Correct

☐ Incorrect

Analysis:

INTEGRATION OF DEVELOPMENTAL THEORY AND OBSERVATION

Knowledgeable teachers jot down anecdotal records that reflect all areas of development. Periodically they check each child's portfolio to see if they are collecting a variety of anecdotes in different settings. Individually or as a team, teachers read the newly added anecdotes, a sample of the old ones, and any other types of new observations in the child's portfolio to broaden their understanding of each child. They look for developmental growth patterns as they study individual recordings and plan activities based on assessed need.

Not all anecdotes necessitate follow-through plans. The following preschool and primary examples, however, beg for teacher interpretation. "Interpretations are constructed through our active mental work; they are not part of the immediately given environment. They grow out of our theories, our past experiences and our present observations" (McCutcheon, 1981, p. 5). The plans based on the preschool and primary grade examples below model the process that teachers follow when interpreting anecdotal information.

Preschool Example

> 1/3 Song (3; 3). While watching a puppet show in another classroom, Song responded with tear-filled eyes when he was mocked by the two 4-year-old boys sitting next to him. One boy poked the other and said, "Look at him; he's Chinese. He looks like this." With his hands he pulled down the corners of his eyes until they were partially closed. (Psychosocial—Self-concept)

Interpreting the Data

At the moment this incident happened, the teacher looked firmly at the two boys and only had time to say, "Song is not Chinese; he is Korean. You hurt his feelings when you make fun of his eyes. Eyes can be all different shapes." And then the teacher looked at Song and said, "It's OK to tell them that you don't like that."

After the children have gone home, the team teachers in Song's class evaluate the day. They begin by looking at the anecdotes they'd written. Song's is first. The teacher who interacted with Song and the two boys shares her feelings related to this incident. She says she is a little surprised but very pleased with her response. In the past she hadn't responded this assertively to uncomfortable situations. The other teacher readily responds that he personally has been afraid to step in when sensitive matters occurred. Both teachers spend time talking about their own discomfort. Realizing that their biggest fear is uncertainty regarding the right words to say, they review other responses teachers might make in similar situations.

> "That's very hurtful when you say _____. I can't allow you to hurt someone's feelings."

> "I'm sorry Logan and Ricardo hurt your feelings."

> "I think you're wonderful just the way you are."

The teachers agree that knowing the kind of words to say is important, but they must steer away from pat answers that become litany because those kinds of answers don't represent real feelings or responsive actions. Because each situation will be different, their responses must come from an active involvement.

The teachers then shift their attention to Song's distress and inability to stand up for himself with 4-year-olds. They discuss how they could affirm Song. In their 3-year-old classroom they continuously represent several cultures, including Korean, with dolls, pretend food, cooking tools, books, snacks, and pictures on the classroom walls. Song's mother is also a regular volunteer in their classroom and often teaches the children songs in Korean or cooks various family foods with the children. As the teachers read back through other anecdotes they have collected about Song, they see a clear picture that Song shows confidence in dealing with and communicating his feelings with children his same age in his classroom; however, he is the first child of young parents and could benefit from more exchanges with older preschoolers in their school.

Follow-Through Plans

After much discussion about Song's reticence and the other boys' insensitivity, the teachers decide to invite the same class of 4-year-olds to share a diversity aware-ness party with the help of parent volunteers. Their party will have several differ-ent activities set up throughout the room; the children will freely choose one activity to participate in, and the adults facilitating each activity will document the learning process.

Song's teachers confer with the teachers of the 4-year-old class and choose the theme, "I'm Me and I'm Special" (York, 1991, p. 73). The teachers referred to the books *Anti-Bias Curriculum* (Derman-Sparks & A.B.C. Task Force, 1989) and *Roots and Wings* (York, 1991) for some of the following ideas.

At the first table the teachers decide to have hand mirrors; skin-toned construc-tion paper; and several boxes of crayons, including assorted skin-tone crayons. The children who choose this activity will be invited to look into the mirrors and draw what they see. The teacher at this table will help the children look for and describe their unique characteristics and abundant similarities, exploring what we look like—"you and me."

At the second table there will be long pieces of butcher paper, many shades of skin-tone tempera paint, primary-color tempera paints, various sizes of paint-brushes, craft sticks for mixing paints, paint cups, crayons, pencils, scissors, and a full-length mirror. The children will be offered the big paper to trace around each others' bodies on the floor. Then, with the aid of an adult, they will mix the skin-tone paints to reflect the color of their own skin and help each other paint their por-traits on the butcher paper, adding hair, facial features, and clothes. The adults at this table will talk about our skins' many beautiful shades of color and how no two seem to be exactly alike.

At the third table will be pictures cut from magazines of eyes of various shapes and colors, along with scissors and glue for making collages. Again, mirrors will be handy to help the children identify their own eye shape and color.

At the fourth table, close to the sink, will be long strips of butcher paper, skin-tone tempera paints to be mixed to individual shades, buckets of soapy water, pa-per towels, and paintbrushes. Here, the children can take their shoes off, mix the paint the color of their feet, paint the bottoms of their feet, and make footprints on the paper. Perhaps they will also want to make hand prints. The teacher at this table can talk about the marvelous variety of sizes, colors, and shapes.

In addition, two other large tables will be available on the periphery of the room. One of these tables will be left empty for children who want to work independ-ently. The other table will be designated the resource table; it will have an array of materials that children from any table may need: yarn, crayons, markers, glue and tape, various colors of construction paper, large and small pieces of fabric, and wallpaper sample books.

The adult at each table will write a description of the process that each group ex-periences, being careful to capture some exact quotes that reflect the children's con-versations. Digital cameras will also be available to the adult to photograph the unfolding of each activity.

After all the projects are complete, the adults plan to assist the children in displaying their creations in the classroom and common spaces of the school. The mounted photographs, along with the documentation, will allow everyone to reflect on the learning process over and over again (Helm, Beneke, & Steinheimer, 1998). The teachers from both classrooms will help the children to continue to talk about and celebrate their differences and similarities.

The diversity awareness party takes place two days later and is a success for all. The teachers of the two different ages plan more times when the two ages can be mixed: a trip to the park, snack time, and a musicfest. Subsequent anecdotal records note that Song slowly and steadily gains confidence with older children. The two 4-year-old boys become more accepting of diversity, and the use of the anti-bias curriculum begins to gain momentum in the school. Daily the teachers are more aware of their own as well as the children's reactions to cultural diversity. They are watchful not to ignore subtle comments. They use opportune moments to point out differences, likenesses, options; they model acceptance of and joy in who each person is. They agree that working toward a bias-free environment is a perpetual process necessary to help children develop a positive sense of self and others.

> If teachers demonstrate that they value persons of differing characteristics and backgrounds, children will sense and emulate this attitude. Therefore, educators should model acceptance of people who look, dress, or speak differently. Educators should not tolerate children teasing others about their language or other cultural idiosyncrasies. (Boutte, 1999, p. 60)

As the year progresses the teachers in Song's school continue to explore multicultural/anti-bias education by reading new books and attending workshops. They realize they have taken only the first steps toward building a quality program that reflects diversity and equity. They want not only to respond to classroom issues as they arise but also to create a curriculum that includes encouraging children to think critically about "issues related to gender, disabilities, socioeconomic status, and the many ways of being a family, as well as issues related to ethnicity and culture" (Derman-Sparks, 1999, p. 43).

Primary Grade Example

Anecdotes are also useful in the primary grade classroom. Consider the example of Grayson during a 10-minute quiet class reading time.

> 9/12 Grayson (5; 6): During quiet reading time, Grayson aimlessly flipped through seven books and then put his head down on his desk and gazed out the window. (Cognitive—Language Arts)

Interpreting the Data

Grayson's teacher, Yana, knows the importance of children having positive experiences with books. She plans her kindergarten program to include weekly trips to the school library and stocks a library corner in her room with quality children's literature and comfortable, cozy furniture. In addition, Yana schedules 10 minutes right after lunch for everyone in the class to quietly look at books. She places big wicker baskets full of a variety of books on each table for the children to explore. During the first month of quiet reading, her goal is for the children in her class to become familiar with the basics of books: books have a beginning and an ending, a title page, an author, and an illustrator; many books are predictable by following the picture clues; and most of all, books provide both tools for learning and pleasant adventures to enjoy.

As Yana enters the above anecdote in Grayson's portfolio, she takes an extra minute to look at her checklist that records the centers children chose during the first 2 weeks. Yana sees that Grayson spent all his free choice times playing computer games. He showed no interest in the library corner or the writing center.

The next day Yana observes that Grayson's response to books during quiet reading time is the same as it was the day before. Later that day Yana finds a moment to speak privately to Grayson. She shares that he didn't seem to be interested in the books he picked during quiet reading time. He responds, "Yeah, I think books are boring." Yana continues talking with Grayson and finds that his out-of-class time interests are centered on trading and collecting cards (e.g., Pokémon cards) and playing GameBoy and that he wishes the computer programs in their classroom had more action. When Yana inquires about having books read to him at home, he tells her that they mostly watch TV at his house; in fact, he has his own TV in his bedroom.

Teachers use anecdotes to document children's appreciation of and interest in books.

Follow-Through Plans

Troubled by her conversation with Grayson, a few nights later Yana calls her mom, who is a retired early childhood teacher. They have a long conversation about children who occupy their precious, out-of-school childhood moments watching videos, playing computer games, and trading cards. Their discussion generates the following thought-provoking questions: What messages are children receiving and what values are being taught through their play? Are children's video games teaching them to associate fun, thrills, and success with violence? As parents, are we so frazzled that we don't have time to examine the messages in children's toys and are just happy our children are entertained? How often do we play with our children? Are children's imaginations, creativity, resourcefulness, and problem-solving skills being expanded in their free choice activities? Are children exploring and developing out-of-school interests that will lead to possible adult occupations? How many parents read books for pleasure and model the rich and joyful experience of reading? Are we becoming a culture preoccupied with fast action and immediate rewards? How can we incorporate the positives of technology and new fads without excluding other modes of learning that create connections with other people and reflect purposeful play? Yana and her mom discuss these questions at length and realize there are no easy answers. They finally conclude that these questions must be raised and addressed, and if educational leaders don't respond to them, who will?

Yana wrestles all week with her plan of response. How can she capture Grayson's interest and introduce him to the world of books? How can she most effectively communicate with his parents so they become partners in directing Grayson on a path of lifelong learning? On Monday the answer comes. The school principal asks Yana if she would be interested in piloting the use of a digital camera in her classroom. Yana smiles ear-to-ear as she realizes she has an opportunity to involve Grayson in writing illustrated books using the computer and the digital camera. This step could bridge the gap between his keen interest in computers and the world of reading. The camera changes hands from the principal to Yana, and Yana embraces the challenges and rewards of teaching.

As the week progresses and Grayson gets involved in the new writing project, Yana suspects there are children in her class other than Grayson who spend numerous unproductive out-of-class hours and could benefit from enriched experiences. This thought was affirmed one night when she was reading *The Irreducible Needs of Children* (Brazelton & Greenspan, 2000) and was stunned by Brazelton's study of the effect of 30 minutes of TV-watching on 3-year-olds. He states that the children came away emotionally and autonomically exhausted. He reported, "We did some heart rate and respiration tests on children and showed the effect [of TV watching] on the cortex. The child was stimulated at first, then habituated . . . Habituation is a way the brain protects the child from getting overloaded" (p. 128). Concerned and more committed than ever, Yana decides to enlist the help of the families and makes the class homework assignments for the next few months include parents and children reading books together from a carefully constructed weekly book list. The assignment will also include visiting the local library and obtaining a library card if the family does not already have one.

To raise and explore the questions that Yana and her mom discussed, Yana resolves to develop a computer chat room to engage parents in conversations. She will begin the conversation with a well-chosen quote; it is her intention to provide a neutral ground for open discussion. As she flips through one of her favorite books, *Raising Lifelong Learners,* Yana spots the perfect beginning.

> We are wise to take our children's play seriously, because how children play has everything to do with how children work. The five-year-old who often drifts around waiting for someone or something to entertain her could easily become the ten-year-old who sighs deeply as she looks at a bookshelf and says, "These books are dull." And this child could easily become the twenty-year-old who gets out of college and then drifts around waiting for the Right Job to come along. This same person could, years later, look at a spouse and think, "This marriage is dull. I need something new to be happy." It's easier to nurture qualities such as initiative, resourcefulness, tenacity, imagination, optimism, and enthusiasm in a five-year-old than it is in a twenty-year-old.
>
> The qualities that matter most in a child's education and life are nurtured first and most efficiently through play. It is important to pause and consider, "Am I doing all I can to support my child's play?" It's a rare parent indeed who questions ways in which we can support our child's play. (Calkins with Bellino, 1997, pp. 109–110)[*]

Yana's goal is that the computer forum will be a "safe" arena to bring up concerns parents have and in the long run help the school community to better understand how to support optimal development for children and how to be active participants in a changing culture. And to think that it all began with an anecdote!

ANECDOTES AND OTHER FORMS OF RECORDINGS

A cohesive portrait of each child's development is drawn through the use of many forms of classroom observation. The use of various methods allows the teacher to see through the looking glass with clarity and confidence. Some teachers find it difficult to work with the large amount of raw data collected through running records. Although many running records document abundant and varied happenings, their conclusions cannot stand alone without the running record. Running record conclusions are seeds for several anecdotes (for clarification, review the running record and conclusion in Figure 5.2). For this reason teachers pick out individual incidents in each of their running records, rewrite them as anecdotes, and file them in the child's portfolio. These shortened, one-incident recordings usually prove to be much more useful than the long descriptive passages of running records when the teacher is analyzing, planning, and conferencing.

Likewise, anecdotes are a possible source for some of the information requested by checklist or rating scale assessments discussed in the next two chapters (Bergen,

1997). For example, a child's gross motor abilities recorded in several anecdotes could be transferred to a motor development checklist or rating scale. Language anecdotes are also a likely topic. Think about other potential topics as you are introduced to checklists and rating scales in Chapters 7 and 8.

APPLICATIONS

Strengths and Limitations

In the early childhood classroom, anecdotes are one of the most widely used observational methods; their strengths are numerous. To begin with, "teachers report that they see and hear with more clarity when using anecdotal records, by focusing more intensively on how children say things and how they interact with each other" (Rhodes & Nathenson-Mejia, 1992, p. 508). Many times the teacher's attention is on whether the child is able to complete the task instead of on the process the child is using while engaged in the task. When the teacher is cognizant of growth indicators and on the lookout for significant developmental incidents, the teacher's focus is on the child's process. In these focused moments, the teacher will be able to respond appropriately to each child and can effortlessly move children ahead in their zones of proximal development (see Chapter 3). Such progress can happen when anecdotal recordings are one of the main classroom observational methods.

Developmentally appropriate programming requires that the curriculum be appropriate for the age, individual, social situation, and culture (Bredekamp & Copple, 1997). Anecdotal records are one of the vehicles teachers use to meet these criteria. Weekly anecdotal recordings supply the teacher with specific examples of each child's growth patterns and developmental characteristics; the focus is the individual rather than the group. These valuable records are then analyzed and, when suitable, used in planning to facilitate individual learning and provide a program that serves the individual needs of each member.

Many teachers maintain that an important advantage of anecdotal records is their ease of use. Writing anecdotes takes no more than paper and a pencil (or a pocket-sized tape recorder). Anecdotes are written at the teacher's convenience after the event has occurred. Because anecdotes are concise statements, little time is needed to record the major elements; they are easy to record on a daily basis (Tull, 1994). Using the key-word method to jot down significant words at the time of the observation helps teachers' memories remain accurate, especially at the end of a long day! Time can also be saved when using a computer. "This year I discovered how much easier it is to make quick notes during the day and write up the incidents later on the computer. Word processing allows anecdotal records to be created in one-quarter the time, sometimes less" (Diffily & Fleege, 1992, p. 13). Many experienced teachers also enlist the help of paid and volunteer assistants, who can be trained effectively in anecdotal record collecting; some schools provide excellent in-service training for assistants.

Trained assistant teachers are valuable cohorts in collecting anecdotal records.

Anecdotal records are a treasure chest of documented incidents that can be compared and contrasted with other recorded observations. These gems, used in conjunction with other kinds of observational records, can help the teacher form a clear understanding of each child's specific growth patterns, changes, interests, abilities, and needs. These records, when read weekly, provide the teacher with an overall, ongoing portrait of the individual developmental composition of the class. This wealth of information is the teacher's foundation for planning and conferences. Teachers report that conference preparation and participation are smooth and efficient when based on anecdotal records; parents have high regard for the teacher who offers true-to-life illustrations of their child's development.

Many would argue that teachers' biases may influence what they choose to record (Bergen, 1997; Gaustad, 1996). Teachers may fail to see an important developmental step if they have preconceived ideas (either positive or negative) about a particular child or about children in general. For example, a primary school teacher may think boys are better in math than girls. Or a preschool teacher may judge a child's behavior on the basis of a sibling's competence displayed in a previous year. Practicing anecdotal writing and receiving feedback from instructors or peers are excellent ways to uncover hidden biases and avoid this potential limitation.

On the other hand, the teacher may unknowingly miss an important milestone for one or more children because of the many demands for a teacher's attention. Teachers avoid this pitfall by using paid assistants or enlisting parent volunteers as classroom helpers, relying on well-organized systems of record keeping (more on this in Chapter 10), and offering a program that has a variety of child-directed activities. "Sand and water play, blocks, and dramatic play, for example, tend to anchor children and free teacher time for observation" (Benjamin, 1994, p. 17). In addition, devising creative classroom management techniques allows for needed "release time" to stand back, observe, and listen to individual children as they play and work.

One final note—as it is with learning any new observational method, practice, practice, practice leads to ease of use and eventually mastery of writing and recording anecdotal observations (MacDonald, 1996). Off on Your Own 6.1 will give you some of that practice.

>>

OFF ON YOUR OWN 6.1

Anecdote Exercise

You are now ready to write some anecdotes of your own. One of the best ways is to turn on a videotape of prerecorded incidents. (Beginning writers of anecdotes think that the replay button is mighty helpful!) Because we cannot play a videotape in this book, we will move to the next best option. This exercise gives you the opportunity to practice writing anecdotal records by extracting them from a running record.

Study the running record for Evan at the workbench, and then write one anecdote embedded in the scenario. Remember, an anecdote is a summary of one incident.

Write your chosen anecdotal record for Evan (5; 2) or Shaina (5; 4). Use the correct form, concisely summarize the incident, use the journalistic approach along with descriptive words, write in the past tense, and state the developmental significance.

Running Record of Evan at the Workbench

School/Grade:	Cornerstone School/Kindergarten		
Date:	9/25	Time:	10:15–10:23 A.M.
Observer:	Mariah	Child/age:	Evan/5; 2
		Teacher:	Mariah

Comments

As the door swings open to the outside yard, Evan makes a beeline to the workbench. He leans over and roots around in the large scrap-wood box, finally selecting two long (about 15 inches) rectangular pieces, one in each hand. As he grips with fingers and thumbs wrapped about the wood pieces, he places them on top of the bench and arranges one piece of

(continued)

wood perpendicular to and on top of the other, forming a T shape, both lying flat. He holds the top rectangle in place with his right hand, and his left hand retracts the hammer from its hanging position on the pegboard that is attached to the back of the workbench. He lays the hammer down on the workbench and lets go of the wood with his right hand. The two wood pieces stay in the T position without support. Evan slides open the drawer under the workbench top with both hands and picks out three nails with the index finger and thumb of his left hand and places each one on the workbench. He grasps the hammer in his left hand and a nail with his thumb and index finger of his right hand. Holding the nail at the intersection of the two wood pieces, he raises his left arm almost shoulder height and whacks the nail; he misses and instantly pulls his fingers holding the nail away. The top wooden rectangle falls off the bottom one, and Evan lets go of the nail. Still holding the hammer in his left hand, he once again repositions the wood into a T shape. He picks up another nail with his right hand using his index finger and thumb and holds it in the same place. Again, he raises the hammer shoulder height and brings it down toward the nail with great speed. Again, he misses! With the hammer in his left hand and the nail in his right, he puts both hands on his hips and sighs deeply.

Shaina (5; 4) approaches the workbench and says, "Wanna play chase?" "NO," responds Evan, "I'm making 'un airplane, but this nail's falling." Shaina walks around the workbench, looking at Evan's structure as Evan rejoins the two pieces he has been working with. "Wait, wait!" hollers Shaina as she raises her hands into the air. "You gotta use the vise." "The what?" asks Evan. "This thing," Shaina replies as she reaches up and takes the vise from its position on the pegboard. "My daddy show'd me how to use this; it works!"

Evan steps back one step with eyes glued on Shaina's actions as she clamps the two pieces of wood together and securely fastens them on the edge of the workbench with the vise. "Now it won't move. Try it and don't pound so hard," she says as a smile fills her face from ear to ear.

With his right hand he chooses another nail and moves it into position. This time, he holds the nail with his whole hand. Evan bends slightly at the knees, raises the hammer about 1 foot above the nail and, with a slower speed, taps the nail. This time he makes contact. With tongue now gripping the right side of his mouth, he lifts the hammer and strikes the nail again. He repeats his successful motion six times, each time making contact. When the nail is securely driven in, he looks up at Shaina, eyes wide, lips together, gives one nod of his head. Before Evan has time to utter one word, Shaina exclaims, "I'll bet that's a DC-10!"

Conclusion: [The conclusion has been omitted so that your selected anecdote will not be influenced]

> QUICK REVIEW<

1. An anecdotal record is an observational method used to summarize a single developmental incident after it occurs.

    ❑ True

    ❑ False

2. Observing and recording a child's developmental progress through anecdotal records requires

    a. an advanced degree.

    b. little time.

    c. an observation instrument.

    d. an abundance of details.

3. Anecdotes can easily be used to collect _____ data in all areas of growth.

4. When using the journalistic approach to writing anecdotes, the contents state what five elements of an observed behavior?

    a.

    b.

    c.

    d.

    e.

5. Using an in-the-nutshell recording format, anecdotes are written

    a. before the incident takes place.

    b. while the incident is happening.

    c. after the incident occurs.

    d. during a discussion of the incident.

6. In addition to documenting children's ongoing development, state two other purposes for using anecdotal recordings in the early childhood classroom.

    a.

    b.

7. Anecdotal record-keeping necessitates the use of minimizing _____ to the best of one's ability, a thorough _____ of child development, the _____ to proficiently write an incident in a concise form, and the _____ to regular recording for each child.

8. Read the following statements and circle the one that is considered a specific guideline for writing anecdotes.

     a. Be as inconspicuous as possible so the children don't know you're watching them.

     b. Write exactly what is happening in the present tense.

     c. Be objective, factual, and detailed.

     d. Be aware of significant happenings in each child's daily activities.

     e. All of the above.

9. Analyze the following anecdote for incorrect or correct documentation as in Practice Activity 6.1.

Nigel (6; 1) and Joelle (5; 9) were stating numbers, each topping the other's number until Nigel said, "Infinity. That's the biggest number of all!" When the teacher asked what else is infinite, Nigel replied as he gestured a tumbling motion with his hand, "Words, they just keep coming out of your mouth." (Psychosocial—Language)

Analysis:

10. Anecdotes are often considered the backbone of portfolios.
   ❑ True
   ❑ False

TAKE A MOMENT TO REFLECT

Personal Reflection

In the classroom, authentic (naturally occurring) observations take place as the child experiences the daily program; anecdotal records are authentic observations. If the teacher collects weekly anecdotes for each child in all areas of development, a comprehensive and true-to-life picture of each child's current and evolving strengths becomes apparent and is readily available. Two scenarios are given below. Read both, then reflect on one.

1. Suppose you were the only teacher at your school who was collecting anecdotes—doing authentic observations. The other teachers seem to scurry around the last week before conferences trying to get some idea where the children are developmentally. You see your colleagues pull children aside and "test" them. You feel compelled to share your knowledge about authentic assessment at the next staff meeting. You worry, however, about how to do that without offending other teachers and jeopardizing your staff relationships. You are aware that not all of the teachers have had an observation class. What approach would you take? How would you proceed to be a child advocate in this situation?

2. Search your own memories. Have you had experiences that prompted you to think everyone was out of step except you? What feelings surface as you think about a particular example or situation? If you courageously came forward and shared your thoughts or took action, what was the outcome? Explore how your past experiences may influence how you handle current and future child advocacy concerns.

Ethical Reflection

NAEYC Ideal I-2.3 is "to respect the dignity of each family and its culture, customs, and beliefs" (Feeney & Kipnis, 1992, p. 6). Think about the preschool example in this chapter and how Song's teacher fulfills this ethical responsibility.

7

Observing the Development of Individual Children by Using Checklists

Nicole feels fortunate to have three computers in her first grade classroom to augment her curriculum. Students may use a computer to type their written work, practice their math skills, or choose an educational game to play during free choice time. In October Nicole wants to be sure that all students have basic computer skills so that they can use their computer time productively. She searches for a quick and efficient observational method to provide this feedback.

Nicole surveys some observational options. She rejects the running record method because she does not need the detailed information this method yields; in addition, running records may not answer her specific questions about the children's computer skills. Anecdotal records may provide helpful information about children's individual interests and skills, but for now, she wants to find out if each child knows the basics of using the menu, mouse, and keyboard. This chapter introduces the checklist, an observational method for Nicole to consider.

Undoubtedly, checklists are familiar to you, so the study of checklists will build on what you already know. As a starter, recall how you brush your teeth at night, and check off which of the following descriptions apply to you.

The tooth-brusher

☐ uses fluoridated toothpaste.

☐ brushes for at least 1½ minutes.

☐ uses dental floss.

☐ uses a gum massager of some kind.

You have just completed a short checklist that requires no special skills other than knowledge about your tooth-brushing practices. Keep this experience in mind as this chapter progresses.

OVERVIEW OF OBSERVING USING CHECKLISTS

Description

A **checklist** is a register of behaviors, skills, or characteristics that the observer marks off if they are present; useful checklists have clear items that leave little room for personal interpretations. Checklists usually investigate easily observed behaviors or skills within their natural contexts. For example, children's motor skills or teachers' story-reading skills might be recorded on one or more occasions. In the opening vignette, Nicole wants to evaluate children's computer skills; a checklist is an appropriate observational method for her. In addition, checklists may focus on characteristics of a curriculum or an environment (e.g., do the materials and equipment reflect ethnic diversity?).

Checklists may be filled out during or after an authentic observation as children engage in their normal classroom activities. In either case, the observer brings the checklist and paper for note taking to the observational session. The quality of data recorded on checklists depends on the clarity of the items and the observer's ability to assess each item accurately. Therefore, the observer must be familiar with the content of each item and know what constitutes an earned check.

Information to complete a checklist may be gathered from a single or several observations, or the observer may want to include data from other observational records (e.g., anecdotes) on the subject. The choice depends on the purpose and type of checklist used. A one-time observation may be sufficient to assess an environment, whereas a teacher completing a checklist for a primary grade child on multiple subjects would want to draw on the widest possible information base.

This chapter examines checklist items that focus on children's development, the environment and curriculum, and explicit teaching skills. First, let's look at the first three items from a checklist Nicole put together to assess her first graders' computer skills after studying one by MacDonald (1996).

The child

- ☐ visually scans the whole screen.
- ☐ manipulates the mouse to move the arrow.
- ☐ manipulates the mouse to move the arrow to a specific place.

Nicole's items go on to assess children's abilities to use the menu, type their names, and return to the home page.

Checklists that examine environments for young children help educators evaluate the success of their curriculum. Part of the checklist developed at High/Scope Educational Research Foundation specifies details in the environment. The following item with five sub-items focuses on how materials are labeled for easy access and clean-up (Hohmann & Weikart, 1995, p. 147). (Note that lines are used instead of check boxes.)

_____ Labels make sense to children. They are made from

      _____ the materials themselves.

      _____ photographs, photocopies.

      _____ pictures.

      _____ line drawings, tracings.

      _____ written words in addition to any of the above.

These clear and straightforward items are responsive to curricular goals of accessible and well-organized materials in a print-rich environment to support children's interests, autonomy, and intentions; the observer records their presence or mentally notes their absence.

Other portions of the High/Scope checklist assess the skills of teachers in supporting the curricular goals. Building on the preschool growth indicators of seriation summarized in Chapter 3 (Box 3.8), consider these relevant items (Hohmann & Weikart, 1995, p. 472).

Comparing attributes (longer, shorter, bigger/smaller)

_____ Provide materials whose attributes children can easily compare

      _____ Sets of materials in two sizes

      _____ Materials children can shape and change

      _____ Materials with other contrasting attributes

_____ Store and label materials in a way that encourages children to compare attributes

_____ Listen for and support the comparisons children make as they play and solve problems

The High/Scope checklists focus on precise teaching skills that serve to keep teachers on track in meeting program goals.

Purpose

Checklists are primarily used to assess the current characteristics of an observational subject (child, teacher, curriculum, or environment) and to track changes in these characteristics over time. First, consider the examination of current characteristics. A child care teacher might be interested in verifying which of the children heap blocks, make stacks, or build rows, bridges, and enclosures and which are beginning to name, add details to, and pretend with block structures. Having observed children's developing building skills over the first few months of school using anecdotal records, this teacher now wants to condense these observations onto an accessible and easy-to-read form. A checklist is an appropriate observational method to meet this teacher's needs.

The following example shows the use of checklists to examine current characteristics of a different observational subject: teachers-in-training. A college professor of children's literature devises a checklist to observe students reading stories to children in the laboratory school. The initial few items on this checklist are the following.

During story time, the practicing student:

- ☐ provides a brief introduction connecting the story to the children's experiences.
- ☐ maintains eye contact with the children.
- ☐ helps children examine the illustrations to predict the plot.
- ☐ asks the children open-ended questions throughout the story.
- ☐ provides opportunities for the children to comment about the story.

After **pilot testing** the entire checklist "to test and refine procedures" (Brown, Cozby, Kee, & Worden, 1999, p. 372), the professor adds space for comments at the bottom of the form. Here, particular strengths, words of encouragement, areas of concern, examples, or suggestions may be jotted down.

Checklists are used for assessment. In this photo, a college professor consults with a student about her story-reading techniques.

The second major purpose of checklists is to track changes in characteristics over time. Nicole, from the opening vignette, will reuse the computer skills checklist every other month to monitor children's progress. The child care teacher observing block-building skills can use the same checklist periodically over the course of the year to chart children's developmental growth. Over the semester, the college professor can document the students' improvement by using the story-time checklist as a pre- and post-test.

Checklists, like all observations, can be put to work to help teachers plan supportive activities, evaluate program effectiveness, and plan appropriate curricular adjustments. Once characteristics or behaviors have been assessed and possibly tracked over time, observers have laid the foundation for enhanced program planning. For example, after an observer studies his block-building checklist results, he may conclude he needs to plan exploratory experiences for the novice builders and add more diverse building materials for the experienced builders. After Nicole reviews the computer-skills checklists, she may conclude that she needs to spend more time showing children how to use the menu to access programs. Checklists (and observations in general) are not completed just to be entered in children's portfolios or cumulative records. Rather, the information they provide about individual children and teachers, curriculums, and environments can nourish effective education.

Guidelines for Constructing a Checklist

Although many useful checklists are available to the early childhood educator, you, as a student of observation, will want to gain the ability to construct your own. Then you will gain the freedom to explore early childhood issues that are of specific interest and concern to you; see Box 7.1 for guidelines for designing a checklist.

Checklists are constructed to assess children's or teachers' skills or behaviors or the specific characteristics of programs and environments. The topic under examination is thoroughly researched, and the checklist items are carefully worded.

Box 7.1

Designing a Checklist

1. Select an appropriate topic.
2. Research the topic in libraries and classrooms.
3. Identify clear, distinct items.
4. Design a recording form with the traditional heading and check boxes.
5. Consider adding space for comments at the bottom of the form.
6. Pilot test the instrument, and revise if necessary.

"Inconsistent results will be obtained if observers interpret the categories of behavior differently; precise measurement depends on clear operational definitions" (Brown et al., 1999, p. 87). The checklist, now a form on a piece of paper, is called an **observational instrument**—"a device used to collect data, information, and evidence" (Wheeler & Haertel, 1993, p. 72). Pilot testing (trying out the observational instrument) is essential to testing and refining procedures (Brown et al., 1999) because items may not be added after data collection has begun. Chapter 13 addresses pilot testing in greater detail, but for now, participate in Practice Activity 7.1 by selecting some appropriate subjects for checklists.

PRACTICE ACTIVITY 7.1

Checklist Topics

List five topics that may be appropriately assessed by checklists. You may include topics concerning children, teachers, curricula, and/or environments.

Examples:

- Children's understanding of numbers
- Presence of culturally diverse materials

    1.

    2.

    3.

    4.

    5.

Return to the tooth-brushing checklist, which I made up after thinking about what I know about tooth-brushing. You and I have no confidence that my checklist identifies the essential components of good tooth-brushing because I failed to research my topic in the library and in the field. If I want to design a checklist that accurately assesses a person's oral hygiene, I must do some research. I might visit a school of dentistry to interview professors about proper oral hygiene and ask them to critique my checklist. I could also talk to my own dentist, observe people brushing, and then move to a literature search.

What are the possible flaws in my checklist? Perhaps to do a thorough cleaning job, the brusher needs to brush for 3 minutes rather than 1½. I simply don't know how long an effective tooth-brusher brushes, but the experts may. If not, this item should be omitted. The item "uses dental floss" lacks clarity because it does not specify if one must floss between all teeth to earn a check or just around a few troublesome teeth. Furthermore, I worry that my last two items overlap and, therefore, are not **mutually exclusive**—that is, one item might be included in another. Does flossing serve to massage the gums in addition to cleaning between the teeth? Or should a gum-massaging agent be used in addition to floss for optimal results? In addition, I do not know if the advice my dentist has given me about my own teeth is universally applicable or if mouths, like children, vary considerably.

On the surface the topic of tooth-brushing appears simple and straightforward, yet I quickly demonstrated that the construction of a checklist, regardless of the topic, requires research and care. I hope you conclude that I had no business, despite my years of brushing, constructing a checklist without researching the topic. Apply this lesson to early childhood education, and understand that all proficient researchers review the relevant literature to ensure an accurate and current list of items.

INTEGRATION OF DEVELOPMENTAL THEORY AND OBSERVATION

Preschool Example

To vicariously experience the process of constructing a checklist, we join Cecily and Dave, somewhat novice preschool teachers of 4-year-olds, who want to know what gross and fine motor abilities the children in their classroom possess. Because these teachers do not yet have a thorough understanding of the range of normal physical development, they read and take notes on several chapters about the physical abilities of preschoolers in reputable textbooks on child development. They are drawn to the convenient checklist format, which readily allows them to assess the physical skills of individual children.

Cecily and Dave read that gross and fine motor abilities show marked development over the preschool years but also that there is a great deal of normal variation among individual children. They decide to prepare a list of observable skills commonly gained by 4-year-olds and remind themselves that the items describe abilities *most* children gradually acquire during this year.

1. Rides trike smoothly
2. Climbs up and down
3. Catches a large ball with two hands and extended arms
4. Dresses self
5. Grasps and controls small objects (puzzle pieces, Legos, tape dispensers)
6. Alternates feet while walking up and down a flight of stairs
7. Fastens buttons

8. Uses pincer grip on pencil

9. Jumps up, down, and forward

10. Runs with control from start to finish and around turns

11. Gallops

12. Skips

13. Cuts with scissors with moderate precision

14. Throws small ball overhand

Although Dave and Cecily are attracted to the simplicity of this list, they decide on some changes after pilot testing and discussion. For example, they decide to re-arrange the items to clarify the distinction between gross and fine motor skills and omit the item about dressing because it is vague and would not be observed at school. Because buttons are not the only clothing closure that their children use, Cecily and Dave modify the 7th item to include fastening and unfastening a variety of items. The term *moderate* in the 13th item lacks clarity, so a rewrite is in order. More specificity is added to several items.

To monitor children's development over time, Dave and Cecily plan to use the checklist three times over the course of the year. For a week they observed the children's physical skills in their own playground and at a neighborhood park, writing related anecdotes on handy pocket notepads, and then filled out a checklist for each child. Figure 7.1 presents the checklist as completed for Gilberto. (They plan to expand their checklist in the future to include items for 3- and 5-year-olds so as to better assess 4-year-olds who are not "average." For example, they will add items about increasing kicking and ball-catching skills.) Cecily and Dave anticipate that the physical development data will not be difficult or time-consuming to collect.

Interpreting the Data

Gilberto performed every gross motor item on the checklist except alternating feet while walking up and down a flight of stairs. In contrast, he was adept at using his upper and lower body to climb ladders and jungle gyms. Because Lomas Day Care is a single-floor facility, Dave and Cecily took the children on a walk to the neighborhood park to observe #3. Very few of the children earned a check on this item. Afterward, the teachers asked them if they have stairs at home, and most, including Gilberto, reported that they do not. What a revelation!

Cecily and Dave note Gilberto's strengths in fine motor development (items 10 and 11). Because Gilberto is a young 4-year-old, his teachers are not concerned that he has trouble fastening his jean snaps and cutting precisely with scissors (items 9 and 12).

Follow-Through Plans

The checklist results stimulate Dave and Cecily to plan some walking trips to nearby places that have steps and stairs in order to provide a variety of opportunities for the children to walk up and down. Back in their play yard, the teachers

---

Physical Development of 4-Year-Olds

Center/Age Level: Lomas Day Care/4-Year-Olds

Date/Time: 10/24–10/28/various

Date/Time:

Date/Time:

Observer: Cecily   Child/Age: Gilberto/4; 3

                                          Teachers: Cecily and Dave

☑ ☐ ☐   1. Runs with balance and control; can turn, start, and stop easily
☑ ☐ ☐   2. Demonstrates a specialized gait: gallops or skips for five strides
☐ ☐ ☐   3. Alternates feet while walking up and down a flight of stairs
☑ ☐ ☐   4. Climbs up and down (e.g., ladders, jungle gyms, slides, trees)
☑ ☐ ☐   5. Jumps up, down, and forward
☑ ☐ ☐   6. Rides trike rapidly and smoothly
☑ ☐ ☐   7. Catches a large ball with two hands and extended arms
☑ ☐ ☐   8. Takes a step forward when throwing a small ball overhand
☐ ☐ ☐   9. Fastens and unfastens typical clothing closures (e.g., buttons, snaps, zippers, belts)
☑ ☐ ☐   10. Grasps and controls small objects (e.g., puzzle pieces, Legos, tape dispensers)
☑ ☐ ☐   11. Uses pincer grip on pencil
☐ ☐ ☐   12. Cuts with scissors on or close to a line

Comments:

10/24—Held railing tightly and led with his right foot when walking down a flight of six stairs. Problem with jean snap on #9.

Figure 7.1
Preschool checklist example developed by teachers.

and children build obstacle courses that include a few treads for practice. Gilberto's checklist is filed in his portfolio with a reminder tab to check his progress after several months to allow time for the effects of maturation and practice.

Other 4-year-olds in Cecily and Dave's class demonstrate motor strengths and weaknesses different from those of Gilberto. The checklist assessments heighten the teachers' awareness of individuals and stimulate them to take advantage of and plan for opportunities to practice specific skills with specific children. For example, Sarvenez (who runs with arms wide and at an uneven pace) may enjoy

The assessment of individual children's physical development leads to the planning of supportive follow-through activities.

trotting around the yard with the security of the teacher's hand to announce it is time to go inside, while Nathan, a budding athlete who needs challenges beyond the typical preschool yard, may benefit from designing an obstacle course in consultation with one of the teachers. Charlotte may be just the child to help cut out a new magazine picture of a freeway system to hang in the block area. And Hubie may be the perfect candidate to stand next to the ball bin and catch the softly tossed balls to put away at the end of outside time.

Data from checklists may thus be used to plan supportive activities for individual children; note that although specific children are targeted, others may benefit as well. The teacher trotting around the yard with Sarvenez may soon find they are accompanied by a whole herd of children becoming more proficient runners. The benefits to one often extend to many.

When teachers study the results for all of the children in the class, the checklist might also yield information about the strengths and limitations of the program and environment. Suppose almost none of the 4-year-olds can catch a ball. Dave and Cecily may scratch their heads for about a second before realizing that they hardly ever take the balls out of the storage closet! They need to correct this oversight. Or perhaps the teachers do not know if the children can manage their own fasteners because these tasks are usually done for them; after all, Cecily and Dave are so much more efficient at buttoning and snapping than the children are. This procedure, too, can change. Checklists provide valuable information about how well curriculum goals are being met.

Primary Grade Example

To facilitate the tracking of students' math progress, a kindergarten teacher, Aram, uses the detailed curriculum checklists supplied by the teacher's manual (Baratta-Lorton, 1995). He has used this curriculum for several years and attended training sessions, so Aram is thoroughly familiar with the meaning of each item, assessment procedures, and appropriate math activities to support children's growth. The checklist section on counting is presented in Figure 7.2 to begin a discussion of the usefulness of Aram's observational assessment.

Interpreting the Data

Aram assesses his students' counting skills in mid-September and determines from the checklist results that several children, including Blanca, are ready for practice in counting on.

> The skill of counting on is a useful problem-solving tool in solving addition problems. It involves the child being able to perceive the number of objects in one group and count from there to obtain the total. Children who have this skill solve addition problems more quickly. When faced with a group of four objects and a second group of three objects, for example, these children *know* there are four objects in the first group so they merely count from there: *four;* five, six, seven. Children without this skill must find the total by counting both groups: One, two, three, four, five, six, seven. A child who has this skill quickly discovers that the total can be found by counting on either group, which encourages flexibility and a concrete understanding of the associativity of addition. (Baratta-Lorton, 1995, p. 103)

Follow-Through Plans

After the September 13 assessment, Aram plans two activities from the math text (Baratta-Lorton, 1995) to give Blanca and several of her classmates the opportunity to discover and practice counting on. The first, "Bite Your Tongue," provides a gross motor experience of counting on.

> Ask the children to bend to one side two times, counting silently, then bend to the other side, counting aloud from three to six. This cycle is repeated over and over again with the children "biting their tongue" so the first two beats are silent. (p. 105)

The second activity, "Cover Up," provides practice counting on with objects after a teacher demonstration. Aram, pleased with the usefulness of the checklist, plans

Counting Checklist Items

School/Grade: Hidden Ridge Elementary/Kindergarten

Date: 9/13

Observer: Aram   Child/Age: Blanca/5; 3

                                     Teacher: Aram

1. Memorizing the sequence of number names
   - ☐ From 1–5
   - ☑ 6–10
   - ☐ 11–20
   - ☐ 20+

2. Counting objects (1:1 correspondence)
   - ☐ Groups of from 1–5
   - ☑ 6–10
   - ☐ 11–20
   - ☐ 20+

3. Invariance or conservation of number
   - ☑ With the numbers from 1–5
   - ☐ 6–10

4. Instant recognition of small groups
   - ☐ 2
   - ☐ 3
   - ☑ 4
   - ☐ 5

5. Counting on

   Verbally
   - ☐ Starting with any number between 1–10 and counting to 10
   - ☐ 11–20 and counting to 20

   To solve a problem using objects
   - ☐ Starting with any number between 1–10 and counting to 10
   - ☐ 11–20 and counting to 20

Figure 7.2
Primary grade checklist example from a teacher's math manual.

6. Counting backward (to 1)
   Verbally

   ☐ Starting at any number from 1–10

   ☐ 11–20

   To solve a problem using objects
   ☐ Starting at any number from 1–10

   ☐ 11–20

Figure 7.2 *(Continued)*
Primary grade checklist example from a teacher's math manual.
Source: From *Mathematics Their Way* by Mary Baratta-Lorton. © 1995, by Addison-Wesley. Copyright © 1995 by Addison-Wesley Publishing Company. Published by Dale Seymour Publications. Adapted with permission.

When teachers accurately assess children's current abilities, they can respond appropriately to individual needs.

to reuse it again in 2 or 3 weeks after introducing counting on and counting backward. Because he wants to keep children's math checklist results on the original paper, Aram will use a different colored marker and note the date when he assesses Blanca for the second time.

Thanks to participation in math curriculum workshops, Aram is well armed with instructional methods for using manipulative materials and activities to support children's mathematical understanding. As a result, he feels equipped to create a learning environment that encourages flexible thinking in math. He would like to share his information with parents, so he begins to plan an evening workshop in which parents can actively learn some skills. His goals are to improve the parents' understanding of his classroom math program and broaden their skills as parent tutors.

APPLICATIONS

Strengths and Limitations

A checklist is an efficient, usually convenient, observational method to assess the presence of specific behaviors, skills, or characteristics; it is valued for its simplicity and time efficiency. The observer may focus on individuals, curricula, or environments and collect useful information, which is preferably augmented by data collected by running and anecdotal records. Not only do checklists provide the observer with the opportunity to learn more about the subject through authentic observations, but the data should also help lay the foundation for responsive teaching strategies and activities as well as program fine-tuning.

When evaluating a child or a classroom, observers sometimes simply want to assess whether a skill, behavior, or program characteristic is present. Checklists provide this kind of information. Think about preparing for parent conferences: teachers may want to be able to tell parents about their children's computer skills, the progress of their gross and fine motor skills, and the details of their math development. A checklist is a useful tool for evaluation and is frequently used to record developing skills. The examination of checklist results can also promote teaching strategies and activities aimed at supporting specific areas of children's development and provide feedback about curriculum success.

Unfortunately, those who use checklists may be tempted to limit their views of the skills, behaviors, or characteristics on the checklist. The checklist only notes whether a characteristic is present; typically, it does not indicate gradations of development within an item. Think about two children who cannot gallop for five strides. An observer cannot use a checklist to document that one child has almost mastered the coordination whereas another hasn't the slightest notion of how to gallop. The checklist only marks the mastery. Consider an added complication. Suppose a child cuts jaggedly with scissors one day but then cuts on or close to a line the next day. Is one demonstration sufficient for a check? Checklists are often lax about specifying criteria for a check (e.g., "counts" versus "counts 5 objects"). This limitation can cause serious confusion among checklist users.

Observer bias may inappropriately affect the checklist user. For instance, if an observer has an overall positive impression of a child, he or she might unwittingly tend to give the child more checks than warranted by careful observation. This **halo effect** can be guarded against by checking items only if they are observed in authentic contexts.

In addition, reliance on checklists does not help educators figure out how to encourage the development of the characteristics not checked. An effective teacher will evaluate data from checklists and other observational methods to maximize understanding of individual children or programs. The well-trained and conscientious teacher will then design activities to promote the unique growth of each developing child and make adjustments to increase program effectiveness.

Each checklist is only as good as its items and cannot make accommodations for exceptional cases; an item is either present or absent. Suppose a teacher uses an age-appropriate physical development checklist to observe Sarah (5; 9), the youngest of four close-knit sisters, and discovers that Sarah does not know how to gallop. The teacher knows, however, that Sarah is a superb rope jumper and is capable of some fancy footwork. The teacher suspects that Sarah has the physical capabilities to gallop but perhaps has never been taught or bothered to learn because of a lack of interest. As an observer, the teacher may not check the galloping item but regrets that the checklist does not accurately reflect Sarah's advanced gross motor skills.

With clear objectives, planned experiences, and observation, field trips provide stimulating, educational experiences for children.

>>

OFF ON YOUR OWN 7.1

Checklist Exercise

Imagine you are a preschool or kindergarten teacher planning a field trip with clear objectives. You have parent volunteers who will accompany groups of three children, and you want to be sure that all children benefit from the varied learning experiences available. Decide on an interesting field trip, and construct a checklist that would allow the parent volunteers to assess whether the individual children in their groups experience the components of the field trip. For example, if you were planning a trip to the pumpkin patch with 3- and 4-year-olds, your checklist might include the following items.

	Child 1	Child 2	Child 3
1. Once on the bus, describes an attribute of the bus.	☐	☐	☐
2. Notices something out the window of the bus.	☐	☐	☐
3. Feels the leaves, vine, stem, and pumpkin of a plant.	☐	☐	☐
4. Compares various sizes and shapes of pumpkins before selecting.	☐	☐	☐
5. Selects, picks, and carries own pumpkin.	☐	☐	☐
6. Explores and describes own pumpkin (list vocabulary).	☐	☐	☐

In your pre–field trip meeting with the parent volunteers, you carefully discuss the objectives of the field trip and examples of each item. You clarify that although you want each child to participate as fully as possible in the field-trip activities, children's refusals (e.g., refusal to touch a rough vine) must be respected.

>>

> QUICK REVIEW <

1. Checklists produce narrative details about children's activities in the classroom.
   - ❏ True
   - ❏ False

2. A checklist is a register of items that the observer marks off if they are present.
   - ❏ True
   - ❏ False

3. Checklist users should test children individually, asking them to execute each item as it appears on the checklist.

    ❏ True

    ❏ False

4. Checklists are used primarily to assess the current characteristics of

    a. a child.

    b. a teacher.

    c. a curriculum.

    d. an environment.

    e. a child or teacher.

    f. a curriculum or environment.

    g. a child, teacher, curriculum, or environment.

5. Fill in the three missing elements of a traditional heading for a checklist on the following form.

Title

Center/Age level:

School/Grade:

_____: _____:

_____: Teacher:

---

6. Checklist designers who are familiar with their topics do not need to pilot test their instruments.

    ❏ True

    ❏ False

7. Choose the item that is most clear for a kindergarten checklist on entry knowledge about books.

    a. Child demonstrates knowledge about books.

    b. Child turns pages in a picture book from front to back.

   c. Child has been informed about the front cover, back cover, title, and author of a picture book.

   d. Child has a good understanding of the relation between illustrations and text in a picture book.

8. An observational instrument is _____

_____ .

9. Checklists are valued for

   a. producing qualitative data.

   b. being simple and time-efficient.

   c. eliminating the need to research the topic in libraries and classrooms.

10. Teachers who use checklists to assess their students' progress need not write anecdotal records.

   ❏ True

   ❏ False

TAKE A MOMENT TO REFLECT

Personal Reflection

Review the final paragraph under "Strengths and Limitations" about Sarah (5; 9), who failed the checklist item of galloping even though she is a highly skilled rope jumper. Imagine her teacher shares the checklist results at a parent conference with you, one of Sarah's parents. Like most people, you find yourself focusing on the unchecked items rather than noting Sarah's progress represented by the checked items. Reflect on the following:

1. How might you feel about the teacher's evaluation of your daughter's physical development?

2. What "red flags" do your reflections raise about writing checklist items? How can we best avoid children's and parents' feelings of unjust evaluations in early childhood education?

Ethical Reflection

NAEYC Ideal I-2.6 is "to help family members improve their understanding of their children and to enhance their skills as parents" (Feeney & Kipnis, 1992, p. 6). Think about how parenting is supported and enhanced by careful planning of a parent workshop in the primary grade example.

8

Observing the Development of Individual Children by Using Rating Scales

September is a time of rededication and fervor in America as most children and teachers return to school. The mood at South Gate School was energetic. Committed to increasing parental involvement, the staff launched an exciting new parent-involvement component. There was much enthusiasm for the development of parent partnerships. Joint projects were undertaken, parent-teacher committees were formed, and new ideas were blazed.

Now it is May, time to evaluate the parent-involvement efforts and formulate next year's goals. A new committee is organized to evaluate the home-school connection and propose changes. Members of the committee begin writing a checklist for parents' feedback but quickly become dissatisfied with the quality of the information they expect they would gather. Think about some of the committee's initial checklist items listed below.

During the current school year, did you

- ☐ receive school newsletters?

- ☐ attend parent seminars?

- ☐ volunteer at school?

- ☐ participate in the home-study program?

How would the committee's information be limited by the checklist method?

In the South Gate School vignette, the committee members soon realize they do not simply want to know if the parents received newsletters, attended parent seminars, volunteered at school, or participated in the home-study program (those would be appropriate items for a checklist). Rather, the committee wants the parents to assess the effectiveness of each of these home-school communication projects. The committee chooses to develop a rating scale, the method examined in this chapter.

Each of us has had opportunities to experience rating scales; restaurants, hotels, movies, child centers, and children's academic progress on report cards are frequently rated. Consider, even, our own casual ways of rating desserts, the neighborhoods in our communities, or the behavior of people around us.

This chapter addresses the use of rating scales in observing and recording the development of young children. First, a note of caution. Early childhood teachers are tempted to rely heavily on the itemized assessment methods of checklists or rating scales because of their familiarity and ease of use. Thus, an important lesson in this chapter is learning when the rating scale method is appropriate.

OVERVIEW OF OBSERVING USING RATING SCALES

Description

Rating scales are observational "instruments used to assess the quality of a particular trait, characteristic, or attribute with assessment usually based on pre-determined criteria (scale)" (Kapel, Gifford, & Kapel, 1991, p. 467). In the early childhood classroom, rating scales can be used to evaluate children, teachers, programs, or environments. Although this chapter concentrates on the observation of individual children, a few examples of rating teachers and programs demonstrate the versatility of this observational method.

When using a rating scale, the observer is asked to make an evaluation of the listed characteristics by assigning a value to each along a continuum; the observer estimates the frequency of occurrence or degree of intensity for each item. Judgments can be based on direct observations, on past observations (preferably documented observations, such as anecdotes or running records), or perhaps in some limited situations, on overall impressions.

Rating scales, like checklists, are assessment tools that are easy to use in the early childhood classroom (Diffily & Fleege, 1993). In addition, both tools use predesigned forms that are simple to mark, provide opportunities to observe selected characteristics, and are most reliable if based on direct observation rather than memory. They differ in one primary way—purpose. "True rating scales resemble checklists, but rather than simply indicating 'yes' or 'no,' the teacher notes the extent to which the behavior is in place or how well the task was accomplished" (Gaustad, 1996, p. 29). When the observer desires data that show progressions or gradations, rating scales are the most appropriate choice.

There are several types of rating scales, each using different organizational designs, and some using a combination of designs. Our study highlights two popularly used forms in early childhood classrooms: numerical and graphic.

The first type, the **numerical rating scale,** offers choices designated by assigned sequential number values (Brown, Cozby, Kee, & Worden, 1999). The observer simply circles the number that indicates the best choice for each item. The early childhood community is familiar with this type of rating scale because it is the observational tool used in the self-study program by teachers, directors, and parents when schools and centers are applying for accreditation through the National Academy of Early Childhood Programs. One example from the *Guide to Accreditation* (National Academy of Early Childhood Programs, 1991b) is given below. Note that this instrument uses a numerical scale from 1 to 3: marking 1 indicates not met, marking 2 indicates partially met, and marking 3 indicates fully met.

J–3 Individual descriptions of children's development and learning are written and compiled as a basis for planning appropriate activities, as a means of facilitating optimal development of each child, and as records for use in communications with parents. (p. 62)	1	2	3

Other equally familiar numerical rating scales are the series of four well-constructed and highly utilized environmental observational instruments: *Early Childhood Environment Rating Scale,* revised edition (Harms, Clifford, & Cryer, 1998); *School-Age Environment Rating Scale* (Harms, Jacobs, & White, 1996); *Infant/Toddler Environment Rating Scale* (Harms, Cryer & Clifford, 1990); and *Family Day Care Rating Scale* (Harms & Clifford, 1989). Each of these instruments uses a scale from 1 to 7, with specific characteristics assigned to every other number. As shown in the item from the *Early Childhood Environment Rating Scale,* revised edition (Figure 8.1), when rating the classroom use of TV, video, and/or computers, all observers base their judgments on the same detailed criteria for each item so that bias is minimized.

The second type of rating scale in our study is the **graphic rating scale,** "sometimes referred to as a 'visual analogue' scale" (Husén & Postlethwaite, 1994, p. 4924). The graphic rating scale "asks the survey respondent to place a check mark along a continuous line anchored by descriptive adjectives" (Brown et al., 1999). Using this graphic rating scale, the observer makes an overall assessment by marking the quality of each item using **descriptors** on the continuum. Typical sets of graphic descriptors are: never, sometimes, frequently, always—not yet, occasionally, often—never, sporadically, regularly—poor, average, excellent. Some of you may remember the descriptors on your primary grade report card (e.g., O = outstanding, exceeds grade-level expectation; S = satisfactory, meets grade level expectations; P = progressing toward grade-level; R = reinforcement needed).

Following are examples of items from a graphic rating scale that could be used to assess three areas of fine motor development based on the growth indicators from Chapter 3. Can you see that this type of rating scale got its name from the repeated visual arrangement of the descriptors?

Scoring Instruction: When scoring an item, always start reading from 1 and progress upward until the correct score is reached. A rating of 1 is the maximum score given if any part of that descriptor applies. A rating of 2 is given if no part of 1 and half or more of 3 apply. A rating of 3 or 5 is given only if all parts of the description are met. Please note that all descriptions in 3 must be met before any higher rating is given for an item. A midpoint rating of 4 or 6 is given when all of the lower and half or more of the next higher description apply. A rating of 7 is given only when all of the description in 5 plus all of the description in 7 apply.

Use of TV, video, and/or computers

Inadequate		Minimal		Good		Excellent
1	**2**	**3**	**4**	**5**	**6**	**7**
1.1 Materials used are not developmentally appropriate (Ex. violent or sexually explicit content, frightening characters or stories, computer game too difficult).		3.1 All materials used are nonviolent and culturally sensitive.		5.1 Materials used are limited to those considered "good for children" (Ex. Sesame Street, educational video and computer games, but not most cartoons).		7.1 Some of the computer software encourages creativity (Ex. creative drawing or painting program, opportunities to solve problems in computer game). *NA permitted.*
1.2 No alternative activity is allowed while TV/computer is being used (Ex. all children must watch video program at same time).		3.2 Alternative activities accessible while TV/computer is being used.		5.2 Computer used as one of many free choice activities. *NA permitted.*		7.2 Materials used to support and extend classroom themes and activities (Ex. CD ROM or video on insects adds information on nature theme; video on farms prepares children for fieldtrip).
		3.3 Time children allowed to use TV/video or computer is limited (Ex. TV/videos limited to one hour daily in full-day program; computer turns limited to 20 minutes daily).		5.3 Most of the materials encourage active involvement (Ex. children can dance, sing, or exercise to video; computer software encourages children to think and make decisions.).		
				5.4 Staff are actively involved in use of TV, video, or computer (Ex. watch and discuss video with children; do activity suggested in educational TV program; help child learn to use computer program).		

Figure 8.1
Numerical rating scale.

Source: Reprinted by permission of the publisher from Harms, T., Clifford, R., & Cryer, D. *Early Childhood Environment Rating Scale,* revised edition. (New York: Teachers College Press, © 1998 by Teachers College, Columbia University. All rights reserved.) p. 35.

	Never	Occasionally	Frequently	Always
Demonstrates the ability to use the pincer grip and/or pick up small objects with finger tips				
Demonstrates the ability to insert and remove small pieces				
Demonstrates the ability to string or lace items				

 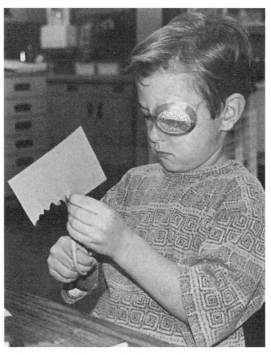

Understanding of children's growth can be bolstered by the appropriate use of rating scales.

When using the graphic rating scale design, be aware of one potential problem—personal interpretations. Imagine how different observers might translate the meaning of the descriptors used in the preceding example of fine motor development.

We have briefly introduced two rating scale designs. When constructing your own instrument or choosing an existing instrument, check that the format yields clear results. Practice Activity 8.1 provides just such practice.

PRACTICE ACTIVITY 8.1

Examination of Rating Scale Design

Select one item from the following list of creative characteristics based on the growth indicators for primary grade children in Chapter 4 and construct a numerical and graphic rating scale for that item. Write clear descriptors.

Creative characteristics:
- Exhibits mental flexibility
- Exhibits sensitivity
- Exhibits imagination
- Exhibits risk taking
- Exhibits resourcefulness
- Participates in expressive experiences
- Exhibits skills using creative materials

The following is an example of one item on a numerical and a graphic rating scale (i.e., "exhibits risk taking").

Numerical Example:

1	2	3	4
Shows no signs of risk taking	Takes risks if an adult suggests them	Takes risks when working with a group	Engages in risk taking to complete a personal project

Graphic Example:

Exhibits risk taking	Never	Sporadically	Regularly

After you have constructed the rating scales for Practice Activity 8.1, evaluate both rating scale designs for clarity, developmental results obtained, ease of use, and personal preference.

Purpose

Rating scales are used to evaluate children, teachers, environments, or programs in a specified area(s) by positioning the items to be observed on a continuum. This method can best be used for assessing individuals once or on repeated occasions throughout the year.

"Assessment provides teachers with useful information to successfully fulfill their responsibilities: to support children's learning and development, to plan for individuals and groups, and to communicate with parents" (National Association for the Education of Young Children and the National Association of Early Childhood Specialists in State Departments of Education, 1991, p. 32). Repeated use of rating scales for individual children can provide information about developmental change over time. For instance, rating scales can be used throughout the year to assess the advancement of fine and gross motor skills, a child's degree of social maturity, the growth of language, the intensity of aggressive behaviors, or a child's reading stages. The same rating scale administered more than once a year can provide pre/post-growth comparisons, often on one rating scale using different colored marks to indicate the pre and post ratings.

The most authentic results are obtained when assessments are based on several observed incidents that occur naturally within the classroom over a period of time; this process is in contrast to a testing procedure in which children are pulled aside and asked to perform. Naturally occurring incidents are best remembered when they have been preserved as running records or anecdotes.

Individual rating scales may compile large amounts of information, usually categorized by developmental areas. Discerning practitioners do not simply file those completed forms in the child's portfolio and wait for the end of the year to reassess. Instead, when evaluations are complete, they analyze each form, look for patterns, compare it with other records, and plan follow-up observations or classroom experiences as the year progresses.

Guidelines for Constructing Rating Scales

Although well-designed rating scales are available, a teacher may not be able to find an existing scale for a selected area of concern or one that the teacher can use to observe specific developmental goals to meet individual needs. Another option is illustrated in the example of the teacher-developed scale of fine motor development shown in the previous description of graphic rating scales.

Practice Activity 8.1 gave a first-hand opportunity to construct at least one item of a rating scale. Was the task deceptive? The rating scale form appears simple, but the process of writing items and choosing descriptors that are clear, comprehensive, and as free of observer bias as possible can be a tedious and often complex task, even for a seasoned researcher. Indeed, construction of a rating scale is not a task to embark upon halfheartedly. Allow plenty of time for

Rating scales may provide one method of assessing stages of creative development.

designing and pilot testing. To develop productive rating scales, follow the guidelines given in Box 8.1.

If, as a classroom teacher, you choose to use a ready-made instrument, be sure to check it against the given guidelines. Many available rating scales are poorly constructed. Using such an instrument could produce faulty judgments and conclusions.

INTEGRATION OF DEVELOPMENTAL THEORY AND OBSERVATION

Preschool Example

During the preschool years, quality programs assist children in mastering self-help skills, such as dressing, toileting, and cleaning up materials. A child's sense of autonomy is developed through the young child's acts of independence, self-assertion, and decision making (Hendrick, 2001). Let's explore how a teacher uses

---

Box 8.1

Designing a Rating Scale

1. Select an appropriate topic.
2. Research the topic in libraries and classrooms.
3. Identify clear and distinct items to be rated. Reject ambiguous terms. Select terms that can be interpreted the same way by all observers.
4. Design a recording form.
   - Choose the rating scale design that best suits your needs, preferences, and subject matter: numerical or graphic.
   - Use a heading similar to that introduced in Chapter 5.

     Center or School/Age level or Grade:

     Date:

     Observer: Child/Age:

                                            Teacher(s):

     Add instructions if needed.
   - Assign clear meanings to the scale descriptors. Be careful that the descriptors do not overlap.
   - Choose the number of descriptors that give an accurate picture of each item.
   - Be aware of the **error of central tendency.** If an odd number of descriptors is chosen, observers may tend to rate in the middle "to avoid making difficult decisions" (Borg & Gall, 1989, p. 493). Exercise caution or use an even number.
5. Pilot test the first-draft rating scale, and make any necessary corrections.

---

rating scale observations in assessment and planning to facilitate children's developing autonomy.

Treasured Times Preschool has established a policy that all parents must attend four parent education sessions per year. One session covers Erikson's stages of emotional development (Hendrick, 2001) with an emphasis on the development of autonomy in the preschool years. Another session trains the parents in anecdotal record keeping. Consequently, the parent volunteers in Billy Ray's 3-year-old classroom are well equipped to help him gather anecdotal records in the area of autonomy. He assigns different children to each of the volunteers on the days they help. Before long many anecdotes are logged for all of the children.

Organized classroom materials foster autonomy.

Billy Ray also contributes anecdotes and running records to each child's portfolio. Using this observational data bank and a few instances of perceived behavior from his memory, Billy Ray is able to fill out the autonomy graphic rating scale (developed by his center) for each of the 12 children in his class. Figure 8.2 offers the results for Rosey. How can this rating scale information help Billy Ray promote Rosey's optimal growth? What suggestions for follow-up plans are in order?

Interpreting the Data

Billy Ray begins by checking each rating scale for any possible error of central tendency. Finding none, he compares the children's rating scales, looking for threads of similarity. His group, overall, is quite capable and acts with autonomy. On occasion, boots or new jackets require assistance; that's understandable. From the rating scales Billy Ray can see that all of the children appeared to have difficulty remembering to wash their hands. He will investigate that tomorrow.

Billy Ray singles out Rosey's rating scale (see Figure 8.2) for further study. He notices that Rosey "engages in self-selected activities" but "asks for assistance in

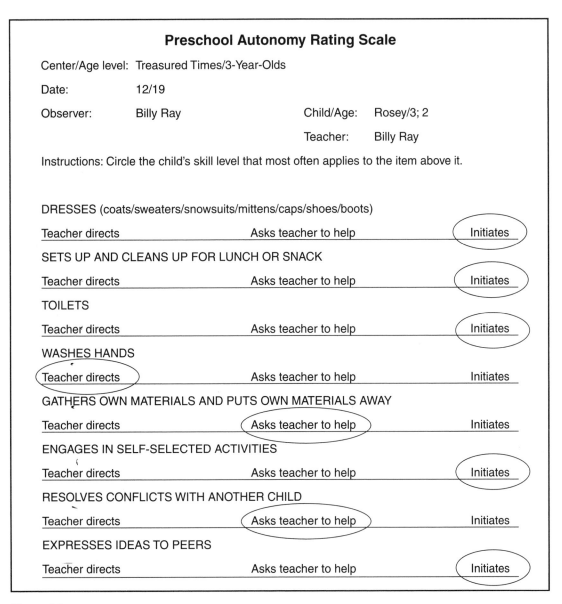

Preschool Autonomy Rating Scale

Center/Age level: Treasured Times/3-Year-Olds

Date: 12/19

Observer: Billy Ray   Child/Age: Rosey/3; 2

                                            Teacher: Billy Ray

Instructions: Circle the child's skill level that most often applies to the item above it.

DRESSES (coats/sweaters/snowsuits/mittens/caps/shoes/boots)

Teacher directs   Asks teacher to help   Initiates

SETS UP AND CLEANS UP FOR LUNCH OR SNACK

Teacher directs   Asks teacher to help   Initiates

TOILETS

Teacher directs   Asks teacher to help   Initiates

WASHES HANDS

Teacher directs   Asks teacher to help   Initiates

GATHERS OWN MATERIALS AND PUTS OWN MATERIALS AWAY

Teacher directs   Asks teacher to help   Initiates

ENGAGES IN SELF-SELECTED ACTIVITIES

Teacher directs   Asks teacher to help   Initiates

RESOLVES CONFLICTS WITH ANOTHER CHILD

Teacher directs   Asks teacher to help   Initiates

EXPRESSES IDEAS TO PEERS

Teacher directs   Asks teacher to help   Initiates

Figure 8.2
Preschool graphic rating scale for Rosey.

gathering and putting away materials." He questions, "Why the dichotomy?" Billy Ray would like to encourage Rosey's full autonomy. The next item reads "asks for assistance in conflict resolution." This behavior, suitable for a child of Rosey's age, will continue to develop. Billy Ray plans to keep ongoing anecdotes to ensure that conflict resolution remains an observational priority. In particular, he will watch for times when Rosey is successful on her own.

Follow-Through Plans

Billy Ray surveys the classroom environment and keeps Rosey in mind as he thinks about 3-year-olds' abilities. He immediately spots a possible deterrent to individual autonomy. Although Billy Ray has organized and labeled the block center and a parent helper recently arranged the housekeeping center in the same fashion, Rosey's favorite centers (the art and reading areas) are not so serviceable. Billy Ray resolves to add a labeled help-yourself art shelf so that Rosey and others can independently select and put away materials of their choice.

Billy Ray assembles a low shelf to hold materials that need minimal supervision, such as crayons, markers, paper, scissors, paste, paper punch, yarn, and magazines. He invites Rosey to help him arrange the beginnings of the newly assembled help-yourself art shelf; for better success, they start out with only a few items on the shelf. Rosey eagerly points out the best place for the markers and the paper. A few weeks later as Billy Ray expands the number of materials on the shelf, he puts each item in a marked storage container with its picture and corresponding word and invites Rosey to arrange them. He can see that she has no hesitations. As time passes, Rosey popularizes the use of the help-yourself art shelf and seems to adopt a personal interest in cleaning up this area.

In the reading corner Billy Ray's class has an extraordinary number of books; unfortunately, they are shelved in disarray. To promote autonomy in this area, Billy Ray classifies many of the books into a few popular topics. For instance, all animal books get a piece of red tape on the binding and are filed in the red-painted section of the bookshelf. Billy Ray puts an animal picture on the front of the red section and so on, until the color/picture coding is complete. Now it is much easier for everyone to find and return books. Billy Ray puts another child who also had difficulty initiating cleanup in charge of this center. Using the information drawn from a rating scale evaluation, this teacher improved the classroom environment so that several children were able to become more autonomous over the course of the year.

Primary Grade Example

Rating scales can be used at any time throughout the year. Some teachers prefer to use the same scale at several different intervals, dating each mark and/or changing marker colors. Melana first used her teacher-designed graphic rating scale during the third week of school (Figure 8.3). She wanted to assess the children's current work habits so that she could begin to form a comprehensive picture of each child, thus enabling her to plan and meet individual needs better. Figure 8.3 is a completed rating scale for a child named Andrew. As you read this observational assessment, be aware of your initial interpretations.

Primary Grade Work Habits Rating Scale

School/Grade: Meadowbrook Elementary/Third Grade
Date: 10/7
Observer: Melana   Child/Age: Andrew/8; 2
                                                               Teacher: Melana

Instruction: Put an X under the rating that applies on each line.

KEY: Rarely =   0–2 out of 10 times
        Sometimes =   At least 5 out of 10 times
        Usually =   At least 8 out of 10 times
        Always =   10 out of 10 times

	Rarely	Sometimes	Usually	Always
Listens attentively	X			
Follows oral directions		X		
Stays on task when working independently	X			
Shows self-confidence in independent work; does not need to consult others	X			
Stays on task when working in a group			X	
Does assignments legibly		X		
Completes work			X	
Works cooperatively with others				X

Figure 8.3
Primary grade rating scale for Andrew.

Interpreting the Data

> After analyzing the ratings of Andrew's work habits, what did you infer about his classroom behavior? Did you picture a child who is out of his seat often or constantly talking with other children? Or perhaps you saw him as being confused and needing to ask other classmates what to do on assigned work. Might Andrew be a typical example of a "problem kid"?
>
> Melana, Andrew's teacher, is trained in observational methods. As she sits down to interpret the ratings, she is aware of the serious danger of labeling, which is inherent in using rating scales as a final evaluation of children. Melana's

approach is to use the rating scale as a beginning point in assessing, understanding, and planning. She looks closely at the results. Andrew's inconsistent ratings raise immediate questions. How could Andrew usually complete his work yet have trouble listening to directions and working independently? Melana had based her ratings on her grade book and her collected anecdotes. She is aware of Andrew's inattention and excessive talking, but he seems to complete most of his work with satisfactory answers; legibility, however, is a problem. What is going on?

Melana checks the anecdotes in Andrew's portfolio; several record Andrew's eagerness to contribute terrific ideas to class discussions. Melana also notes that he is often a leader in group projects. He is well liked by his classmates and is frequently chosen first in team games. He shows a definite strength in social development and many characteristics of a strong leader. To gain a more accurate picture, Melana pulls together all the information she has recorded to date. She reviews her grade book once again. It documents another strength—finishes work with excellent understanding. Included in Andrew's portfolio is a recent profile (this is the first chance Melana has had to review the results) that shows Andrew's learning preference as visual/kinesthetic. That means his best channels for processing information are through his eyes and body. The profile also reveals that Andrew's ears are his weakest processing channel. No wonder he rarely appears to listen and has trouble following oral directions! The marks on the rating scale begin to make sense to Melana.

Follow-Through Plans

The teacher-constructed rating scale helps Melana gain a more precise image of Andrew's work habits, but it also leads her to explore other pertinent observations. Her classroom philosophy is evident—the program should fit the child—rather than the child should fit the program.

Keeping with her philosophy, Melana is now ready to plan teaching/learning strategies based on Andrew's individual needs. Melana makes the following immediate plans:

- *Directions:* Stand by Andrew or have eye contact when giving short oral directions for a kinesthetic connection. Capitalize on his visual mode of learning by writing lengthy directions on the board. Have a student read the written directions a second time aloud. Underline the key words in the directions.

- *Work improvement:* Label assignments in grade book OD or WD (oral or written directions). In those two columns keep a tally of times Andrew's papers were neat and not neat. See if there is a relationship between written directions and neat work. Perhaps he hurries after he has had to spend time figuring out what to do (when oral directions are given), usually by asking others.

The issue of Andrew's productivity and independent work is difficult for Melana. She does not want to squelch Andrew's gregarious personality and his natural interpersonal skills. She wants to encourage these strengths as she helps him develop the weak area—independent work. How to do that is the task at hand. After much thought, Melana comes to the conclusion that her teaching strategies seldom allow for partner learning. From her past experience she knows that interpersonally adept children are more comfortable when they are able to share new insights with other children.

Melana prides herself on having a quiet classroom despite all of the times she has to remind Andrew to quit talking. Looking back through Andrew's portfolio, she finds some anecdotes of incidents when Andrew seemed so excited from reading about science in his self-chosen books that he shared newfound information with the child next to him. Perhaps if she gave Andrew a specific time he could count on each day to have conversations, he would grow toward using independent work time appropriately. Melana develops her plans further as follows:

- *Group work:* Set up daily cooperative reading experiences. Using small groups, plan activities in which the children can read favorite stories to each other, share stories they have written, or discuss story characters they are reading about. Suggest that the shared reading groups, especially ones whose members are kinesthetic learners, develop skits or puppet shows together.

Oh yes, the whole picture is becoming very clear to her. Melana has not allowed the children enough social exchange; Andrew is trying to meet his own need. She feels fortunate that it is early in the year and that she has uncovered a necessary adjustment in her teaching strategies by observing and studying Andrew's portfolio. So, where else can she adjust?

- *Math tasks:* Andrew shows a special interest in math. Melana does not want to miss the opportunity to reinforce Andrew's critical-thinking skills. In addition to the small group instruction and independent work in math, Melana decides to add a box full of "brain teasers." At first, the activity will be part of the group math work. Eventually, the teasers will be made available for children to work on in pairs when they have finished their independent work. Melana will reserve a portion of one bulletin board wall for children to share their analytical projects.

Melana sees a definite change in Andrew's work habits almost immediately when he is given written instructions and more time to work cooperatively. Melana confers with Andrew, and they discuss the new plan before its inauguration. Andrew likes the idea of written directions and suggests that the paired reading experience follow the independent reading time. He tells Melana that occasionally he writes stories or has an idea that he just has to tell someone during independent work time.

After another 6 weeks Melana repeats the rating scale. All of Andrew's marks are in the *always* or *usually* column. Melana is satisfied with Andrew's progress and with the new learning environment. Not only are Andrew's strong social needs supported, but according to her latest class rating scales, children who were somewhat withdrawn are beginning to take a more active part in cooperative or paired work times.

What other ideas can be added to Melana's beginning plans? There is rarely just one right way. The sky is the limit as long as the plans effectively fit the child's needs and are integrated with the teacher's style.

APPLICATIONS

Strengths and Limitations

Rating scales and checklists share many strengths. Like checklists, rating scales require less time to complete than do other observational methods. With high classroom demands and hectic schedules, teachers appreciate the simplicity of these two methods. Rating scales and checklists can be based on prerecorded anecdotes and running records and can therefore be completed at the teacher's convenience. Both methods are relatively easy to mark and usually require no special training. These orderly forms may also offer a developmental summary for parent conferences.

In the early childhood classroom, rating scales are especially useful to easily assess multiple characteristics within a given area or multiple areas. Unlike the checklist, which records only the presence or absence of a characteristic, the rating scale allows the observer to measure the degree or frequency of behavioral characteristics (Diffily & Fleege, 1993). We have already looked at how an instrument assessing autonomy can quickly give a detailed picture, thus allowing the teacher to compare children within the classroom or to evaluate one child. "Convenience and efficiency are primary reasons for the widespread use of rating scales" (Witt, Heffer, & Pheiffer, 1990, p. 368).

The many advantages of rating scales, however, are often overshadowed by the disadvantages. The first limitation, error of central tendency, has already been pointed out in Box 8.1. In addition to unconsciously rating down the middle if there is an uneven number of descriptors, Husén and Postlethwaite (1994) warned: "Some raters exhibit caution and tend to make ratings in the region of the center of the score distribution, while other raters seem to make great use of the extreme categories" (p. 4928).

The second limitation is the possible subjectivity of ratings. If the descriptors are ambiguous, "a summary of the observer's opinion is produced rather than actual observed events" (Stallings & Mohlmar, 1990, p. 640). In the section on graphic rating scales, the difficulty of descriptor interpretation when assigning ratings has already been mentioned. Practice Activity 8.1 illustrated the flip side of that limitation; constructing any of the rating scale designs with clearly defined items and descriptors that represent the observer's true assessment is challenging but achievable. Once again, caution is needed.

A third limitation is present in the process of assessment because the observer, unless she or he has constructed the scale, is asked to pigeonhole the evaluation by using limited, preselected choices on the rating scale continuum, perhaps restricting a response. This forced choice limitation is a common frustration and reminds me of the discussion at my house following the "eggplant soup dinner." I love to experiment making new kinds of soup once a week. We've enjoyed my adventurous culinary practices—until I made the eggplant soup. That soup was certainly memorable! I asked my husband how he would rate it. "On a scale of what?" he asked, having been highly schooled in research. "Oh, 1 to 3," I answered, trying to decide if I'd ever make it again. "I'd prefer more choices; I'll use 1 to 6," he countered as he continued to develop his own numerical descriptors as follows:

1. Would cause sickness.
2. Wouldn't eat it unless starving.
3. Was tolerable.
4. Just average; would choose to have it occasionally.
5. Would enjoy having it a couple times a month.
6. Wow! I'd tell everyone about it. A true culinary pleasure.

I listened with delight and thought of the abbreviated numerical descriptors I use on all my recipes.

1. No clean bowls.
2. No comments.
3. Crowd pleaser.

I refer to the shortened scale to decide whether the dish is worth making again. I would find the six-point system time-consuming and cumbersome. (In case you are curious, my husband rated the eggplant soup a 4 on his scale. I gave it a 1 on my scale; I wouldn't make it again!) So you see, each rater can have a preferred scale. If you don't construct your own scale, however, you are asked to make a choice that may not be as representative of your evaluation as you would like. To counteract this restriction, many teachers use spaces between the items or, as in checklists, space at the bottom for written comments. This is particularly useful when the topic of rating scales is development.

In addition, when assigning ratings, another caution must be kept in mind.

> Since rating scales are attempts to quantify observation, the validity of such ratings depends largely on the adequacy of observations that the ratings are based on. The adequacy is determined by the amount of time spent observing the child as well as by the number of different settings and situations in which he is observed. (Medinnus, 1976, p. 25)

Thus, as in the checklist method, observers should know the child's abilities well and refrain from judgments based on only one observation.

A fourth limitation is the influence of **observer bias.** For instance, observers may rate a child who has well-developed language skills as a leader or may rate a child as uncooperative because the child's older sibling was. The ratings then are based on an impression. "If this impression is favorable, they tend to rate every item high; if it is unfavorable, to rate every item low" (Alkin with Linden, Noel, & Ray, 1992, p. 1348). This bias, known as the *halo effect,* was discussed in Chapter 6. Please note, if the characteristics being rated are unclear or too complex, the halo effect may be unavoidable, rendering the validity of the ratings questionable.

The final limitation is that rating scales, like checklists, do not tell the conditions that surround the evaluation. The skills, behaviors, or conditions being rated are lifted out of their context, thus leaving an overall evaluation of isolated items (Jablon, Dombro, & Dichtelmiller, 1999). If rating scale assessments are coordinated with running records or anecdotal records, however, they become a useful summary for planning and conferences.

OFF ON YOUR OWN 8.1

Practice in Using a Rating Scale

Design a rating scale that evaluates one of the following areas of children's development: impulse control, prosocial moral reasoning, or language.

- Review the guidelines for construction in Box 8.1.
- Refer to Chapter 3 or 4 or a child-development textbook for background information.
- Select your rating scale design and construct your instrument.
- Guard against observer bias.
- Pilot test the rating scale.

With the newly constructed rating scale in hand, locate a preschool or K–3 teacher who will work with you in trying out your observational instrument in the classroom. To ensure that all items are clearly written, ask a friend to accompany you and try out your newly constructed instrument, too. Observe the same child. After the observation, discuss your first attempt at designing an instrument. Did either of you have any problems using the rating scale? Were your results the same? If not, why not? Share your results and thoughts about revision in class.

> QUICK REVIEW <

1. Rating scales are a useful observational tool when teachers want to assess the _____ of specific traits, characteristics, or conditions using a predesigned instrument.

2. Two of the most popular rating scale designs in the early childhood classroom are graphic and numerical.

❑ True

❑ False

3. Two cautions teachers must be watchful to avoid when constructing or using rating scales are _____ and _____.

4. One of the limitations of both rating scales and checklists is that they provide narrative descriptions based on direct observation.

❑ True

❑ False

5. The adjectives used to rate the items on the continuum are referred to as

a. authentic assessors.

b. descriptors.

c. graphic organizers.

d. category values.

6. When designing a rating scale, be sure to choose clear and distinctive items, rejecting _____ terms.

7. When rating scales have an uneven number of descriptors, the tendency to rate down the middle is called _____.

8. Rating scales can be used to assess children, teachers, _____, and _____.

9. One difference between a checklist and a rating scale is

a. a checklist records the presence or absence of an item, and a rating scale records the degree to which the item is present.

b. a checklist primarily assesses individual children, and a rating scale primarily assesses environments.

c. a checklist gathers narrative data during a specific time period, and a rating scale gathers specified data on a structured form.

d. a checklist uses descriptors on a continuum, and a rating scale uses yes or no indicators.

10. A rating scale uses a similar heading as the running record or a checklist does, but a rating scale heading more frequently includes directions.

❑ True

❑ False

TAKE A MOMENT TO REFLECT

Personal Reflection

A Quick Guide to the Internet for Child Development (Milburn & Gotthoffer, 2000) is a concise introduction to Internet use and an extensive reference for websites where information pertaining to early childhood can be accessed. The following sites are examples of early childhood URLs:

> http://www.nncc.org
> http://www.clas.uiuc.edu
> http://www.naeyc.org
> http://www.piaget.org
> http://www.theideabox.com

Log on to one of the above sites, and explore the depth of that resource. Then reflect on the following questions.

1. How could the information available at this website be useful to an early childhood educator practicing observation and curriculum planning for individual children?

2. What additional information is available at a website that is linked to the one you chose?

Ethical Reflection

NAEYC Ideal I-1.4 is "to appreciate the special vulnerability of children" (Feeney & Kipnis, 1992, p. 4). Review the primary grade example in this chapter, and reflect on how Melana fulfills this ethical responsibility.

9 Observing the Development of Individual Children by Using ABC Narrative Event Sampling

When Billy Ray evaluates the rating scales on autonomy for all the children in his preschool class (see the example in Figure 8.2), he becomes interested in yet another child, Kirby. He wonders why Kirby (4; 1) usually requires a teacher's help to express ideas to others. Billy Ray wants to discover the circumstances that motivate Kirby to ask for help and those that are conducive to his autonomous communication. Billy Ray is also curious about how other children respond to Kirby's communication. Therefore, he wants to explore the causes and consequences of this particular rating scale item.

T he review of rating scales can typically leave the observer interested in the dynamics that surround particular items; Billy Ray is no exception. The observational method introduced in this chapter will allow him to learn about Kirby's communication abilities within their natural contexts.

Two forms of event sampling are studied in *Through the Looking Glass:* ABC narrative event sampling and tally event sampling. In addition, a close cousin, time sampling, is presented in Chapter 12. For now, the focus is on the **ABC narrative event sampling** method, which investigates what precedes (the antecedents) and what follows (the consequences) an event. The study of antecedents will help Billy Ray identify the situations that prompt Kirby to request the teacher's help when expressing his ideas to others. The study of consequences focuses on how others respond to Kirby and what kinds of feedback his communications evoke from his peers. In other observational investigations, observers may wish to uncover the frequencies of events; in such cases, the tally event sampling format discussed in Chapter 11 can be used.

OVERVIEW OF OBSERVING USING ABC NARRATIVE EVENT SAMPLING

Sampling

In order to record every instance of Kirby's peer communications, Billy Ray would have to be his shadow. In most classrooms, however, teachers do not have the luxury of observing one child exclusively for an indefinite period of time. To compromise, a **sample,** or subset, of Kirby's communications is collected and allowed to represent his peer communications in general. Let's think about an analogy to explore the meanings of sampling and samples because "the strategy for selecting your sample influences the quality of your data and the inferences that you can make from it" (Mertens, 1998, p. 253).

Imagine that the quality control manager of a cereal company wants to know what proportions of cereal, pretzels, and peanuts are in a snack it sells and therefore requests your careful assistance. Of course, you cannot count every piece in the thousands of bags that are filled in the factory even in a single day. As an alternative, you place one empty snack bag identical to the ones that will be filled under the filling chute on the packaging line and count all these pieces to calculate the percentages of cereal, pretzels, and peanuts. You allow the ingredients in the bag (the sample) to represent the ingredients in all bags of this product (the population).

Consider a few potential problems. First, you think about the size of the sample, in this case the bag. You want to collect enough of the mixture to feel confident that your sample is representative of the bin, but you don't want to count hundreds of items unnecessarily. You know the bag is exactly the size of the bags sold in stores; a smaller sample, say a handful or even a cupful, might be unrepresentative just by chance, and a very large sample, say a trash can full, would not use your time efficiently. The bag is large enough that chance (random) conglomerates of ingredients (e.g., a bunch of peanuts) even out but not so large that your counting is excessive.

Because the bag was filled from the same packaging line as the product bags, you are confident that the ingredients in your sample have been as well mixed as those in the bags. Suppose, instead, you had drawn your sample from the top of a large bin feeding into the filling chute. If the peanuts were poured into this bin first, the pretzels second, and the cereal last and the ingredients were not mixed at the top, your scoop would contain only cereal and would therefore be unrepresentative. You are reassured by knowing your sample comes straight from the filling chute.

You also evaluate possible subjectivity in your work for the cereal company. If you had allowed yourself to scoop out the sample yourself, your selection might have revealed your personal biases. Imagine these scenarios. You want the cereal company to put in more of your favorite ingredient, so you purposely look for a no-peanut place to scoop. This unrepresentative sample will help make your case for adding more peanuts. Or suppose you are a loyal employee of the company and are tired of hearing complaints that there aren't enough pretzels in the mixture—so you just happen to aim your scoop toward the bunch of pretzels in view. Your data will show them! Therefore, in the interest of accuracy and objectivity, you place your bag under the filling chute and let the machine pour in a random sample of ingredients.

Now reflect on observational projects in the early childhood classroom; the same problems apply. You must be careful to observe enough examples of the behavior(s) under study to ensure that your sample is representative. You have to collect data from a well-stirred pot—consider time of day, activities, and the people in the classroom. Moreover, you must be careful that your own views, predictions, and wishes don't get in the way of collecting a truly **representative sample.** With this knowledge you can follow Kerlinger & Lee's (2000) definition: "a *representative sample* means that the sample has approximately the characteristics of the population relevant to the research in question" (pp. 165–166).

If you fail to collect a representative sample, the results may lead you to an incorrect conclusion. For example, concerns about Kirby's expressions of ideas to others pertain to the entire school day. If you observed Kirby only during outside time when he sticks close to his best friend, you might conclude he is usually competent in his communications. Just as Kirby may be more comfortable talking with some people than with others, he may also have more difficulty in large groups than in small groups or vice versa. The data will tell. To draw a representative sample of Kirby's communications to others, you observe him during each time block over several days to ensure an accurate portrait.

Description

In event sampling, the "observer records behavior only when particular events or behaviors occur" (Brown et al., 1999, p. 369). In Kirby's case, "expressing ideas to others" is the event of interest to his teacher. Through event sampling, the observer studies events in their everyday contexts and collects enough of them to draw conclusions.

Event sampling permits the observer to collect data about the targeted behavior in an efficient manner because it concentrates his or her attention on only that behavior. Although an observer is not able to see every targeted event of interest over an indefinite period of time, a sample of observations over a limited period should serve to represent the behavior. Thus, the collection of observed communications is a sample of all of Kirby's communications.

Observers using event sampling try to record an event whenever it naturally occurs during a specified limited period. Think about the logistics of exploring children's participation during cleanup time. The observer must be ready to record when cleanup times naturally occur. In this case the observational period might be limited to 10 minutes during the day, and the teacher may choose to collect a sample of observations over a week or two. In contrast, to study the effectiveness of a teacher's classroom-management methods, the observer must be watchful at various times throughout the day to attend to management events as they arise. If the events occur fairly frequently, an adequate sample might be accumulated in 4 or 5 days.

The preceding description is applicable to event sampling methods in general. Chapter 11 will introduce a tally event sampling method to study children and teachers and their interactions, but for now we turn to the individual (child or teacher) as the focus of study. Bell and Low (1977) introduced a straightforward method of observing naturally occurring events: the ABC narrative method. Although their method is not the only means of collecting narrative qualitative data for event sampling, its clear organization and ease of use (see, for example, Figure 9.2) make it worthy of special attention. The ABC method concentrates the observer's attention on the antecedent event (*A*), the behavior or event itself (*B*), and the consequence of the event (*C*) (see Figure 9.1 for the format). Therefore, the event is seen in the context of what came before and what followed. Appreciate how well this observational method will meet Billy Ray's needs in his exploration of Kirby's dependent communications.

Now consider a few more examples. A preschool teacher concerned about a child who grabs toys organizes an ABC event sampling recording form around what preceded the grabbing (*A*), the event itself (*B*), and what immediately followed (*C*). A primary grade teacher who is concerned about a child's seemingly random cruel remarks (e.g., "I knew you'd get that one wrong!") plans to do an ABC narrative event sampling to investigate what prompts the remarks (*A*), each remark itself (*B*), and how the victim of the remark and others respond (*C*). ABC narrative event sampling can be used to examine a wide range of problems.

Practice Activity 9.1 gives you a chance to suggest appropriate events to study through the ABC narrative event sampling approach. Choose behaviors or events within their naturally occurring contexts—items that you could follow from their roots to fruition.

PRACTICE ACTIVITY 9.1

Topics for ABC Narrative Event Sampling

List three topics that may be appropriately studied by ABC narrative event sampling in the early childhood classroom. Remember that this method is useful when you want to observe an event carefully in context. You will be searching for what prompts the event and what follows.

Examples:
- Wandering and unoccupied behavior
- Fearful behavior

1.

2.

3.

Purpose

When the goal of observation is to uncover the contextual causes and effects of an individual's behavior, the ABC narrative approach to event sampling is an excellent method. Suppose a child consistently throws several temper tantrums over the course of the day, and the perplexed teacher wants to explore these events in search of a possible pattern or explanation. At this point, the teacher does not write an anecdotal record about one tantrum because the goal is to evaluate the processes of many tantrums. Nor does the teacher prepare items to observe (as in checklists and rating scales) because of uncertainty about the key elements in this child's process of temper tantrums. The narrative approach to event sampling is the observational method of choice because it allows the teacher to remain unrestricted by a prepared form with predetermined categories, and free to observe the natural unfolding of the temper-tantrum events.

Let's step back for a moment and take a look at the forest rather than the trees. Why do we care about understanding the cause of an event? Many child guidance books offer creative and practical solutions to common behavior problems and are not concerned with their causes. If, however, teachers assume in this example that there is one best way to respond to a temper tantrum, they close the door on the opportunity to respond to children as individuals at their own developmental levels with their own strengths, interests, family and cultural histories, limitations, and personalities.

There are many possible causes of temper tantrums, and some will be easier to pinpoint than others. Temper tantrums might result from children's fatigue from long hours in child care or might serve as vents of frustration for young children whose language development does not yet adequately serve their needs to communicate. An observer might consistently see tantrums toward the end of the day or in response to communication difficulties. However, the observer may not be able to identify clear patterns, thus prompting inquiry beyond the classroom. Perhaps a child feels insecure on the arrival of a new baby in the family or is anxious over the recent separation of his or her parents. There are probably other situations that prompt young children to release their emotional tension—usually at the most inopportune times. Knowing what is behind individual children's temper tantrums allows teachers to reevaluate the 5:00 P.M. activities at a child care center, help verbalize the feelings of the 2½-year-old with little language, promote sociodramatic play with a child who has a new baby at home, or increase the emotional support of a child under stress. The point is that teachers explore causes of events within their natural contexts in order to devise appropriate and helpful responses for particular children.

Guidelines for ABC Narrative Event Sampling

After deciding on an appropriate event to study, the observer prepares a sheet of paper with the typical heading of information at the top and four columns below labeled *Time, Antecedent Event, Behavior,* and *Consequence.* This format is presented in Figure 9.1.

ABC Narrative Event Sampling Title

Center or School/Age level or Grade:

Date: Time:

Observer: Child/Age:

Behavior/Event: Teacher(s):

Time	Antecedent Event	Behavior	Consequence

Figure 9.1
ABC narrative event sampling recording form.

The ABC narrative event sampling method is an effective means of understanding behaviors within their natural contexts.

The observer keeps the recording sheet on a clipboard close at hand to record the event under scrutiny whenever it is observed during a specified time period or periods. Occasionally, an observer might miss seeing the antecedent event; if so, he or she continues to record the time, behavior, and consequences. This happened to Gabrielle, the observer in Figure 9.3; she used an ellipsis (. . .) to indicate the gap of information. She hopes that the remaining information, in conjunction with the observations of many complete events, will still add up to the "big picture."

INTEGRATION OF DEVELOPMENTAL THEORY AND OBSERVATION

Preschool Example

Rachel is a quiet and shy 4-year-old girl who has posed no problems for her teachers, Sal and Pam. Several anecdotal observations focusing on Rachel during large- and small-group activities and directed outside games describe a cooperative group member. In November, when the classroom of 22 children is running smoothly, however, the teachers begin to pay more attention to Rachel's behavior during free choice times. She typically stays with an activity for no more than 10 minutes and wanders the room until a new activity is suggested. Rachel rarely makes anything to take home; when she does, her artwork appears rather simple, like something a younger child could have accomplished. Sal, who is most familiar with Rachel, takes responsibility for observing Rachel's wandering behavior. The ABC form in Figure 9.2 is kept on a clipboard in the classroom for a 2-day sampling period; included in the figure is a *portion* of the data collected.

Interpreting the Data

At the end of the second day of observation, Sal and Pam read over the event descriptions on their ABC event sampling form. They are disheartened to see that in Rachel's first hour of school on 11/8, she did virtually nothing. She was not intently involved with materials or people, and she did not initiate activities or interactions. She responded agreeably to suggestions from Pam, Alex, and Betsy as if she had no plans or ideas of her own. The events recorded on 11/9 again show Rachel's willingness to go along with others' proposals. Pam and Sal worry that Peach Hill Nursery School is not optimizing this 4-year-old's development.

The 2-day sample of observations documents Rachel's wandering and unoccupied behavior during free choice times both inside and outside the classroom. Sal and Pam reread the anecdotal records that describe Rachel's interest and willing participation in structured times, such as circle and story. They suspect that they did not notice her behavior during free choice time during the first 2 months of school because she is such a cooperative group member.

ABC Analysis of Rachel's Unoccupied Behavior

Center/Age level: Peach Hill Nursery School/3- and 4-Year-Olds

Dates:	11/8	Time:	8:15-9:15 A.M.
	11/9		8:15–9:15, 10:05–10:30 A.M.
Observer:	Sal	Child/Age:	Rachel (4; 3)
		Teachers:	Sal and Pam

Behavior/Event: Wandering around the room, unoccupied

Date: 11/8

Time	Antecedent Event	Behavior	Consequence
8:15	Rachel arrives with Mom. Mom kisses her good-bye.	Wanders around room for 15 minutes, watching children.	Alex says, "Want to play cars with me?" Pushes cars on block area carpet for 6 minutes.
8:40	Watches the noisy arrival of the bus kids. Pam (teacher) says, "OK, free choice time. Find something to do."	Watches Daisy and Chloe hang up jackets and rush off to house area.	Turns attention back to kids entering room.
8:46	Sal (teacher) says to Rachel, "You need to get started now."	Walks around room with no expression on her face, looking in each area.	Goes to art area and rolls play dough with rolling pin for 4 minutes. Looks around classroom more than at her play dough.
8:54	Puts play dough away.	Walks to edge of manipulative area and watches Pam and 3 kids.	Pam says, "Would you like to join us? Here are some Bristle Blocks." Rachel silently stacks blocks for 5 minutes.
9:13	Pam leaves area.	Stops building and watches other kids. Smiles at Betsy.	Betsy smiles back and asks, "Want to play play dough?" Rachel nods. They leave the blocks on the floor and head toward the art area.

Date: 11/9

Time	Antecedent Event	Behavior	Consequence
8:15	Rachel arrives with Mom and hugs her good-bye.	Scans the room and walks toward art area where Betsy and Yiota are mixing paint. Watches from the edge of the area.	Betsy and Yiota don't appear to notice her.

Figure 9.2
ABC narrative event sampling form: Preschool example.

8:24	Remains 3 steps from the art area.	Looks through the color-labeled crayon containers on the shelf and re-sorts four crayons that are out of place.	Sal checks on the paint consistency, looks at Rachel, and says, "The paints are ready. Would you like to use them?" Rachel nods and goes to the easel next to Betsy.
8:51	Hangs painting of red and yellow lines up to dry.	Wanders around room until cleanup time.	Sal asks her to help him clean up in the manipulative area. She does not reply but gets right to work with the tinkertoys.
10:10	Outside time begins.	Circles perimeter of yard twice in 10 minutes.	On second round Pam calls out, "Rachel, do you want to push on the swing?" Rachel shakes head no and continues circling.
10:25	Children in sand box bring over two pails of water.	Stops partially behind tree and observes.	Children do not notice her.

Figure 9.2   *(Continued)*
ABC narrative event sampling form: Preschool example.

Follow-Through Plans

Sal and Pam feel bad for having overlooked Rachel's consistent wandering and unoccupied behavior during free choice times, but they concentrate their energies on the future. They put the data to use and develop several strategies for helping Rachel focus her attention and learn more from her encounters with materials and other people. The following summaries are drawn from the ABC event sampling form along with the teaching strategies they prompted in Sal and Pam.

Summary of Observation   Sal and Pam realize that neither of them personally greeted Rachel and that she responded positively to friendly overtures from Alex and Betsy.

- *Strategy:* Sal will come over to greet Rachel when she arrives and tell her about special materials out in the various areas.

Summary of Observation   Pam announced when it was free choice time and said, "Find something to do." Sal told Rachel that it was time to play and to get started. Perhaps Rachel has no clear understanding of her options or what is expected of her during free choice time. Or perhaps she is overwhelmed by her options.

- *Strategy:* When Sal greets Rachel, he will remind her that during free choice time, she can choose her own materials and friends to play with. He will also stay with her until she gets started. He might walk around the classroom with her to help her make her choice.

Summary of Observation   The data show Rachel worked superficially with materials (e.g., pushing cars, rolling play dough, painting only lines). Perhaps she is not comfortable enough with other children to concentrate on her activity, or perhaps she has not had much experience in working with many of the materials available at Peach Hill Nursery School. She did, however, respond positively to Betsy's initiative and observed Betsy mixing paint.

- *Strategy:* Betsy will join Sal's small-group time so that a friendship between Rachel and Betsy can be fostered.
- *Strategy:* Once during each free choice time, Sal will work next to Rachel with the same materials to model new ideas. He will be careful to build from her initial activity. For example, when she chooses play dough, he might roll out lots of snakes and see if Rachel is interested in shaping them into objects like bowls, log houses, or other ideas she might have.
- *Strategy:* Sal will use small-group times to explore many uses of familiar materials to widen Rachel's experience with objects. He suspects that he has overlooked the importance of exploration for other children as well. For example, he might plan an activity to explore print-making with Bristle Blocks and other small manipulatives. Dipping the objects in paint to make prints on paper, pressing them into clay to form imprints, or making rubbings with crayons and paper are all options. Another day, the children might use Bristle Blocks for building. They might first stick them together flat on the table, then form a high tower, and next build enclosures. These activities might be done individually and then in a group so that one huge flat surface, tower, and enclosure are put together. Sal would offer the children a variety of small animals to go inside their building. He will plan many small-group times that encourage the children to explore materials, make things with them, and then pretend with them.

Summary of Observation   Rachel's wandering and unoccupied behavior continued during outside time as she circled the yard and watched others.

- *Strategy:* Outside, the teachers will plan optional group games to provide some enticing structure for Rachel and encourage her to play with other children.
- *Strategy:* Sal and Pam will reuse their ABC event sampling form on Rachel in a few weeks to observe her progress. They expect to see more focused behavior during free choice and outside times.

The ABC event sampling method proved to be productive for Sal and Pam. It allowed them to observe in detail a problem of which they had only vaguely been aware. Sal's recordings of the event in context evidenced noteworthy consistencies in the child's behavior. Instead of limiting the observer's attention to the wandering and unoccupied behavior, the ABC method provided a means of observing which classroom situations prompted Rachel's wandering and what followed. The teachers took advantage of the data collected to plan strategies to enhance Rachel's development. Data collected on a different child's unfocused behavior during free choice time might well have shown different patterns, thereby suggesting the trial of different teaching strategies.

Primary Grade Example

Gabrielle teaches first grade and is nearly fed up with Adam's off-task behavior that consistently disturbs other children's work and activities. Although she knows that she has an ample reserve of surface patience, she is wearing thin inside. Some mornings, she notices herself dreading to face Adam again.

At the end of a dismal week, Gabrielle promises herself to keep an ABC narrative event sampling form close at hand beginning on Monday. She worries she will neglect the observation once she is involved in teaching, but she is motivated to try. Her reprimands, pleas, and light punishments have been to no avail. Figure 9.3 contains a *portion* of the data Gabrielle collected over the next week. (Recall that Gabrielle uses an ellipsis [. . .] to indicate a gap in the information collected.)

Interpreting the Data

By Friday lunchtime, Gabrielle can stand the suspense no longer. Anxious to confirm her growing suspicions nourished by her data collection, she eats at her desk and rereads the seven pages of event descriptions (remember, Figure 9.3 reproduces only a portion of the data). The data are voluminous, and she tries to think of some ways to make them manageable.

Gabrielle experiments with sorting Adam's off-task behaviors into categories to look for possible patterns. She finds four times during the school day that account for the bulk of the problems: math time, transitions like the end of story time, sustained silent reading time, and group math games. Then she begins to do some figuring. First she counts up all of Adam's observed off-task behaviors over the course of the 4½ days of observation and finds the sum to be 38. She tallies his off-task behaviors in each category and lumps the remaining six into an *other* category. Finally, she divides each category sum by the total number of off-task behaviors (38) to find its percentage of total off-task behaviors. For example, she divides the 17 math-time incidents by the total 38 to get .45 or 45% of the total off-task behaviors. (Notice that Gabrielle is doing some quantitative analysis with the qualitative narrative data, an option possible with lengthy samplings.) The results, displayed in Figure 9.4, would have surprised Gabrielle on Monday before she began her data collection.

Before Gabrielle systematically began to gather data on Adam's off-task behaviors, she would have predicted that they occurred at an even pace throughout the

ABC Analysis of Adam's Off-Task Behaviors

School/Grade: Jefferson Elementary/First Grade

Dates: 10/16 to 10/20   Time: Various

Observer: Gabrielle   Child/Age: Adam/6; 7

     Teacher: Gabrielle

Behavior/Event: Off-task behavior

Date 10/17

Time	Antecedent Event	Behavior	Consequence
8:20	. . . I had just started a math activity with six children.	Pokes neighbor (Marcus) with pencil.	Marcus squirms, then laughs aloud. I say, "Excuse me, Adam."
8:22	. . . Math activity.	Pretends to draw on back of Marcus' shirt (uses eraser).	Marcus yells, "Hey!" I say, "Please, Adam, pay attention."
8:25	. . . Math activity.	Grabs Marcus' eraser.	Marcus wrestles his eraser back. I ignore.
8:27	I demonstrate a subtraction problem on the board.	Is under his desk when I turn around.	I send Adam to the time-out desk isolated at the side of the classroom.
11:45	I regretfully close *Matilda* by R. Dahl and say it is time to line up for lunch.	Stays in seat and argues, "Oh come on, come on Mrs. Ambleson. Just a little more, please. We can be late for lunch; come on please. The lines are too long anyway."	I say, "I'm sorry; we'll read more tomorrow." I have to ask him two more times to line up before he follows directions.
12:40	. . . Sustained silent reading time; OK for 5 minutes. Reads *Frog and Toad* for umpteenth time.	Puts head and arms down on desk and rolls into Marcus.	Marcus rolls back. I say, "Sit up please, boys."

Figure 9.3
ABC Narrative event sampling form: Primary grade example.

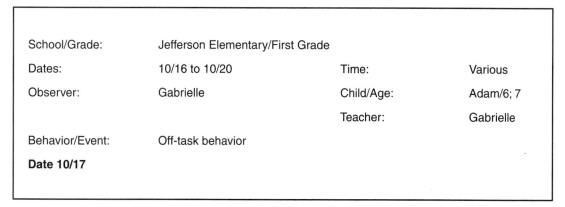

School/Grade:	Jefferson Elementary/First Grade

Dates:	10/16 to 10/20	Time:	Various
Observer:	Gabrielle	Child/Age:	Adam/6; 7
		Teacher:	Gabrielle

Behavior/Event: Off-task behavior

Date 10/17

Figure 9.3   *(Continued)*
ABC Narrative event sampling form: Primary grade example.

Adam's Off-Task Behaviors
(10/16 to 10/20)

Time	Number	Percent of Total Off-Task Behaviors
Math activity	17	45
Transitions	5	13
Sustained silent reading	6	16
Group math games	4	10
Other	<u>6</u>	<u>16</u>
	38	100

Figure 9.4
Understanding ABC event sampling data.

day. She is excited because this is not the case and feels rewarded for her week-long observation efforts that yielded objective data. Now it is time to study the contexts of Adam's off-task behaviors and search for the meaning behind the data.

Follow-Through Plans

Gabrielle's observations cluster around three major areas: math activities, sustained silent reading, and transitions. In the privacy of her classroom, this thoughtful, reflective teacher lays aside her pride and wrestles with the data staring her in the face.

Careful study of the data leads to appropriate follow-through plans.

Summary of Observation   Gabrielle considers the high proportion of off-task behaviors during math activities and realizes that problems during math time or group math games account for 55% of the total; she wonders if this is an important clue. Had Adam's off-task behaviors commenced and accelerated as math became more difficult? The grade book documents his initial average and then declining grades, and two anecdotal records describe behavioral disruptions during math time. She forms a hypothesis that Adam's disruptions during math are connected to his tentative (at best) understanding of the subject matter; disturbances are Adam's ticket out of math.

- *Strategy:* Gabrielle plans to do more spot-checking of daily math assignments to be sure the children are on the right track and to clear up confusion before frustration and failure set in. She concludes she got behind in this responsibility because she relied too heavily on parental help in correcting math assignments and tests. She rededicates herself to becoming familiar with her students' specific strengths and weaknesses.

- *Strategy:* Suspecting that Adam's problems center around subtraction, Gabrielle begins to plan next week's math using manipulatives to allow the children to experience subtraction concretely. Gabrielle, confident in her ability to teach math, is certain she can effectively reduce Adam's errors.

Summary of Observation   The disturbances during sustained silent reading time and during some transitions at the end of story time encourage Gabrielle to turn her attention to Adam's reading interests and abilities. Judging from his pleas for story time to continue, Adam relishes a compelling story. Unfortunately, this appreciation is not being satisfied by his choice to read the same book (however good) over and over. A check of her grade book reminds her that Adam's reading skills are above average for a first grader.

- *Strategy:* Gabrielle plans to build on Adam's interests and reading ability and decrease his disruptive behavior in the process. Knowing his love of Arnold Lobel's endearing characters Frog and Toad, she is convinced there are other literary characters who can also win Adam's heart. Edward Marshall's George and Martha are two who might fit the bill, as well as Elsie Fay from *Troll Country* a bit later. She will also browse through some Steven Kellogg books to check the reading difficulty and keep *The Beast in Ms. Rooney's Room* series by Patricia Reilly Giff in mind for later in the year. She is excited by the superb store of authors just waiting for Adam's discovery.

Summary of Observation   Gabrielle admits that her reprimands of Adam's off-task behaviors are neither meant nor taken seriously; she has not acted like a teacher who expects her directions to be followed. She resolves to reevaluate her classroom control and to begin this process with Adam (hopefully a manageable task).

- *Strategy:* Gabrielle will avoid the half-hearted reprimands that have been ineffective with Adam.
- *Strategy:* On Monday's plan Gabrielle schedules time for a class discussion about classroom rules; it is obviously time to revisit this issue. Her goal is for the children to brainstorm suggestions for classroom rules. When they talk about why rules are important, Gabrielle will enlist their explanations of how the welfare of the classroom depends on the actions of the individuals. The children can imagine the resulting chaos if everyone talks at once or throws erasers in the air. The rules will be evaluated and a reasonable list posted in the classroom. Gabrielle anticipates that this group experience will help the children perceive the rules as less arbitrary and more compelling.
- *Strategy:* Gabrielle also examines Adam's long complaint when story time had to end at 11:45 A.M. Whether or not she or Adam likes it, Jefferson Elementary School runs on a schedule. She realizes, however, that her typically abrupt dismissal did not acknowledge Adam's feelings of regret. She might have said that she understood his wishes to continue but that lunchtime was not something they could choose to skip or delay. On Monday she will ask Adam to keep an eye on the clock and let her know when she has to stop reading for lunch; sharing in the responsibility for keeping the class on schedule might ease his transition to the next activity. Gabrielle will continue to look for these types of opportunities to help children build self-control rather than relying on a time-out desk.

As Gabrielle relaxes during the last few moments of her lunch break and savors her feelings of accomplishment, she warmly remembers her college class on observation: time and study well spent.

APPLICATIONS

Now let's move on to an activity that asks you to solve the puzzle of an event. In Practice Activity 9.2, you will be identifying the clues of a child's behavior in order to zero in on observations that generate responsive and appropriate teaching strategies.

PRACTICE ACTIVITY 9.2

Narrative Event Sampling: Acquisition of a Second Language

You are the teacher of a preschool child who has recently arrived in the United States with her family from Taiwan. During the first week, the child said nothing; thereafter, she began to speak occasionally in Chinese. Toward the end of her third week, you notice Lin speaking a word or two in English. You are very excited and resolve to keep an ABC narrative event sampling form to observe the situations that seem to promote Lin's attempts to speak English.

Examine the following brief ABC data to identify events or situations that seem conducive to Lin's learning and speaking English. Then write down specific summaries of observations that lead to specific strategies. For example, after observing that Lin smiled and quietly said "hi" to Marion, you plan to encourage that friendship by putting their snack placemats next to one another.

ABC Analysis of Lin's Attempts to Speak English

Center/Age level:	Where the Kids Are/3-Year-Olds		
Date:	4/26	Time: 8:30–9:00 A.M. (free choice time)	
Observer:	Robbie	Child/Age:	Lin/3; 10
		Teacher:	Max
Behavior/Event:	Lin attempts to speak English		
Date:	4/26		

Time	Antecedent Event	Behavior	Consequence
8:30	Marion arrives with her mother and is holding a stuffed bear. Lin stares at the bear.	Smiles and says "hi" softly and without eye contact.	Marion smiles back and goes to the house area.

Time	Antecedent Event	Behavior	Consequence
8:40	Stands next to the house area, watching Marion and Carlota feed their bears at the table.	When noticed by the girls, raises her arms and asks a question (it sounds like "Bear?").	Carlota says, "Lin, what?" Lin does not answer. All look confused, and Lin moves away.
8:55	Max is mixing sand and water with children in the sand area to make molds. Lin wanders to the outskirts.	Max says, "Lin, would you like to play with us?" Smiles from ear to ear and says, "yes" in a loud, clear voice.	Side steps to a vacant space next to Damon, a 3-year-old. Works with the sand molds with a smile and concentration.

Summary of Observation

- *Strategy:*

Summary of Observation

- *Strategy:*

Summary of Observation

- *Strategy:*

Strengths and Limitations

The primary value of the ABC narrative event sampling method is to study a behavior in the context of its antecedents and consequences. Observers use this method to explore an event as it naturally unfolds from its causes through its outcomes. The ABC method promotes the exploration and understanding of the relevant features surrounding an event.

The ABC method also heightens awareness of children as individuals. It focuses attention on a unique person in the midst of often complex circumstances. The ABC method looks at events with a video- rather than with a still-camera lens; there is no stop-action photography here. A problem is viewed as a process with prompting conditions and results. Such scrutiny allows observers to respond with individualized strategies.

The care with which an event is analyzed can also be a drawback because the ABC method requires time and commitment. It can be a burden for overextended teachers or for those who lack support in the classroom. The observer requires time to observe the event in progress, record data, and then analyze the data. This requirement is true of all observational methods and is not so much a limitation as an admonition to teachers to work observational time into their daily schedules.

The ABC method is best used by observers with keen eyes and who strive toward objectivity. Observers with predrawn conclusions will easily shade their observations from the truth. The ABC method will illuminate an event for those who have the skills and vigilance to look.

>>>

OFF ON YOUR OWN 9.1

ABC Narrative Event Sampling

Return to the list of appropriate ABC narrative event sampling topics in Practice Activity 9.1. If you teach, try one of the examples in your classroom. If you do not teach, arrange a visit to a preschool or elementary school to practice the ABC method. Briefly explain the method to the teacher and ask for a suggestion; often a child who has difficulty with transitions will be an edifying subject. After collecting a reasonable sample of narrative data, analyze them and write down appropriate follow-through plans. Remember, to gain more than a superficial understanding of the method, you must try it out.

>>>

> QUICK REVIEW <

1. A sample should have slightly more favorable characteristics than the population it represents.

   ❑   True

   ❑   False

2. The purpose of the ABC narrative event sampling method is to

   a. describe a developmental milestone.

   b. rate the changes children make in their on-task behaviors.

   c. understand events and behaviors within the contexts of their antecedents and consequences.

   d. prepare qualitative data for a child's Individualized Education Plan (IEP).

3. The goal of ABC narrative event sampling is to uncover teaching strategies that work effectively with all children.

   ❑   True

   ❑   False

4. The four column headings on an ABC narrative event sampling form are
    _____, _____, _____, and _____.

5. Gabrielle's study of the _____ of Adam's off-task behaviors during math
    activities helped her recognize his current difficulties with subtraction, and
    her evaluation of the _____ of her half-hearted reprimands helped her plan
    more effective classroom control strategies.

    a. antecedents/consequences

    b. severity/events

    c. narration/sampling

6. Quantitative analysis should not be done with ABC narrative event
    sampling data.

    ❑   True

    ❑   False

7. Practice Activity 9.2 that focuses on the acquisition of a second language
    demonstrates that the ABC narrative event sampling method is not
    restricted to the study of problem behaviors.

    ❑   True

    ❑   False

8. The goal of the observer using the ABC format is to

    a. document individual children's development.

    b. assess individual children's development.

    c. understand patterns of behavior.

9. The ABC narrative event sampling method is a good example of authentic
    observation as introduced in Chapter 1.

    ❑   True

    ❑   False

10. An appropriate topic to study with the ABC narrative event sampling
    method is

    a. the frequency of off-task behaviors of three first-graders.

    b. all child–parent separations in a child care center on Mondays.

    c. preschool teachers' strategies during transitions.

    d. the aggressive acts of Nathan during outside time.

TAKE A MOMENT TO REFLECT

Personal Reflection

 Observation projects are due in a child development practicum class, and two graduating seniors compare experiences. Pat volunteered in an ethnically diverse elementary school and was asked by a teacher to observe a third grader, Danny. Usually cooperative and competent in all subjects, Danny recently began to display an overall lack of attention. An entire school day served as the sample; Pat employed the ABC narrative event sampling method and then examined the data for patterns. She found Danny was inattentive when the attention of the class was on the front of the room (e.g., on the chalk board or a book), but when he was moved from his rear seat to the front, he worked productively. Discussion with the teacher provided the information that a recently broken copy machine had necessitated math problems being written on the board and that Danny had complained of headaches. You guessed it: Danny needs glasses. The teacher responded to Pat's report with guilt that was fortunately overshadowed by a sense of relief, gratitude to Pat, and plans for a vision check.

Shannon chose to do her internship in the child life specialist department of a children's hospital. One of her responsibilities involved working in the children's playroom that should serve as a safe haven from medical procedures (e.g., checks of vital signs and delivery of medications). Shannon was frustrated, however, by the frequent interruptions of medical staff that intruded on the children's play. She created a tally event sampling instrument (see Chapter 11) to study the agents of the interruptions. Shannon found that 17% of the interruptions were committed by registered nurses, 24% by licensed vocational nurses, and 57% by clinical assistants; the more highly trained nursing staff better protected the sanctuary of the playroom. Shannon's final meeting with her Child Life Specialist supervisor is tomorrow, and she has begun to plan how she will present her findings.

Reflect on strategies to present information effectively to one's supervisors.

1. Pat was fortunate because Danny's teacher requested the observation and was receptive to the results. How might she have handled the situation if the teacher had been defensive about or resistant to the information about Danny?
2. Assuming that Shannon's supervisor agrees with the conclusion that the playroom should be off limits to medical procedures, how might they convince their nursing co-workers that supportive changes should be made?
3. Sometimes you might have to give negative feedback to your supervisor. Recall a few supervisors you have had. How might they have responded to unfavorable information? Did you ever have to give your supervisor negative information? What are some productive communication strategies?

Ethical Reflection

NAEYC Ideal I-13 is "to recognize and respect the uniqueness and the potential of each child" (Feeney & Kipnis, 1992, p. 4). Reflect on how Gabrielle fulfilled this ethical responsibility.

10 Child Portfolios and Parent Conferences

As we end Part II of *Through the Looking Glass,* recall with affection some of the children you've met so far in this book:

- Annie, who seized the red tractor for reasons unknown, in Chapter 1
- Taki, who played listening lotto, in Chapter 5
- Song, whose teacher confronted the insensitivity of a few classmates, in Chapter 6
- Gilberto, as yet unable to alternate feet when walking up and down stairs, in Chapter 7
- Andrew, whose work habits were unproductive, in Chapter 8
- Rachel, who spent most of free choice time wandering, in Chapter 9

Each of these children resonates with individuality; each is unique and multifaceted in development. They will blossom in supportive early childhood classrooms, and most have at least one parent or guardian who wants and needs to know how they are progressing in school. How can their teachers organize their observations and retrieve necessary information for planning and effectively communicating the results to these children's parents?

U sing a variety of observational methods, the trained early childhood professional keeps comprehensive observational records for all children. These observational treasures will have limited value unless the records can be accessed easily for classroom and conference use. There is, however, another aspect of observation to explore.

The goal of this chapter is to answer the question posed at the end of the opening vignette: how can teachers organize observations and retrieve information for classroom planning and parent conferences? You will become acquainted with options in organizing bountiful classroom observational records and sow the seeds for successful family–teacher partnerships. The first part of this chapter discusses designing and personalizing child portfolios and record-keeping procedures for ease in usability. The second part of the chapter presents the topic of family–teacher conferences—preparation, content, and leadership. Although the teacher-in-training cannot apply this information immediately and comprehensively, this chapter develops tools that help guide professional growth.

OVERVIEW OF CHILD PORTFOLIOS

The word *portfolio* is not new to you. You were first introduced to portfolios in Chapter 2, and they have been referred to in several other chapters throughout the book. Recall that the definition for a **portfolio** is a collection of observational records and work samples for one child that reflect developmental growth, usually kept for 1 year. The contents of specific portfolios vary from one child to another as the teacher chooses from several observational methods to best document children's growth and the ways children exhibit a variety of interests and participate in an array of activities.

Throughout the year early childhood teachers may complete running records, anecdotal records, checklists, rating scales, and ABC narrative event samplings for individual children in their classrooms. Occasionally, a tally event sampling or time sampling (Chapters 11 and 12), usually recorded for groups, is kept for a single child. As a result, early childhood educators gather a great deal of observational documentation over the course of a year. Some of these records note specific developmental milestones. Some records are used immediately to plan activities and teaching strategies. Other records are saved to illustrate points during parent conferences or to develop an **Individualized Education Plan** (IEP) and an **Individual Family Service Plan** (IFSP). All records are used to understand the overall developmental progress of each child.

> In developmentally appropriate early childhood programs, curriculum, assessment, and teaching cannot be separated; they are integrally connected. Teachers continually engage in observational assessment and documentation of children's learning for the primary purpose of improving teaching and learning. (Bredekamp & Shepard, 1998, p. 93)

In addition to an abundance of teacher observations, selected samples of children's work are kept throughout the year to illustrate developmental growth over time. "At the preschool level, as at later age levels, *portfolios* of the child's work—drawings, writings, constructions—allow children to demonstrate their abilities and knowledge in unique ways, which can reveal strengths that formal tests would not have shown" (Elkind, 1998, p. 120). Work samples for the preschool child may include artwork; dictated stories; writing samples; photographs of block structures, science activities, and dramatic play episodes; and any other examples that show the child's most outstanding strengths, unique capabilities, and continuous development (Benjamin, 1994; Shores & Grace, 1998). The teacher may want to help the primary grade child select pieces of work that represent progress and accomplishment in all areas of study. Samples may include selected classroom assignments/projects that are of special interest or show skill mastery (health, social studies, science, math), an assignment that was revised, a favorite piece of creative writing and/or artwork, printouts of activities completed using the computer, a register of books read, language audiotapes, and child-written journals that are written reflections of growth assessments in art, math, science, and language arts (McAfee & Leong, 1997; Mindes, Ireton, & Mardell-Czudnowski, 1996). These multidimensional concrete learning examples augment teacher observations and provide for the child's involvement in the record-keeping process.

It is easy to visualize the organizational challenge presented by these mounds of observational records and work samples (the contents of portfolios) that require storage. This challenge can be as overwhelming as filing income taxes is to some people. Organizing, however, does not have to produce anxiety if the teacher chooses a workable record-keeping system for the portfolio. Remember, the point is to organize early childhood records for simple access, not to store the records away as we do with our tax records for once-a-year retrieval.

To understand the paramount importance of organization, let's examine the advantages of using a record-keeping system. First, an efficient system retains and orders documents in the child's portfolio illustrating his/her developmental growth; it is a priceless memory bank, easily accessed by the teacher. In contrast, unorganized observations become an explosion of papers piled high or tossed into a file folder or desk drawer. Consequently, shuffling through these records to understand individual development becomes time-consuming, difficult, and often frustrating. Second, an organized storehouse of observations allows for smooth, consistent planning of classroom activities that respond to individual needs. Masses of unorganized observations often result in abandonment of planning to meet individual needs; curricula become haphazard or uniformly prescribed for all children. Third, using portfolios that have systematic record keeping, teachers have abundant information at their fingertips and can prepare for conferences expediently and confidently. In summary, organizing observations is essential for first-rate teaching!

Portfolio System Description

A **record-keeping system** for portfolios is a specific procedure used to organize the selected samples of children's work and the many observations and documentations of learning activities written by the teacher throughout the year. An organized system acts as a frame within which to assemble the developmental puzzle pieces for each child. Once the teacher has chosen or created an arrangement for keeping observational records, all of the children's records are stored in like fashion. The system allows the teacher to collect as much individual observational/documentational information as is wanted; the system also allows the teacher to arrange this information in logical order and to protect the child's privacy.

We begin the process for creating a personally workable and efficient portfolio system by exploring three possible storage methods (card file box, file folder case, or notebook) for keeping teachers' observational records. We then discuss how children's work samples can be included or kept separately. The storage container and the procedure for storing the teachers' observational records plus the children's work samples become the portfolio record-keeping system.

The farsighted teacher-in-training will explore and compare the systems, noting the strengths and limitations of each. Time spent in examining workable systems provides the foundation for determining a preference and, eventually, a confident choice once the teacher is inside the classroom. On the other hand, experienced teachers may have other ideas that have worked for them. There is much room for additions, improvements, and diversity.

Storage Choices for Teachers' Observations

The teachers' observational records for 12 or 15 children can be housed in three large file boxes for 3-by-5-inch cards, a file folder carrying case, or a 3-inch three-ring binder. Throughout the year, the teacher will store a variety of observational records, anecdotes being the most numerous. Because of their abundance and the key role they play in facilitating weekly planning, the first consideration in choosing a storage system is the ease with which anecdotes are accommodated.

To conserve space, instead of using a blank page or index card for each section, put an index tab on the first observation page or card you put in each section. This advice will help when managing 60 or more index tabs! In addition, color coding the index tabs proves to be time-efficient.

First index tab: Child's Name and Birth Date

                                                      Physical

Second index tab, indented:

                                                      Cognitive

Third index tab, indented:

                                                      Psychosocial

Fourth index tab, indented:

                                                      Creative

If the card file box is the container of choice, the teacher begins by recording anecdotal records for each child on 3-by-5-inch index cards. These individual anecdotal records are then stored in the card file box behind the index divider for the appropriate child (see sketch). The box is further sectioned off behind each child's name, using tabs on dividers labeling the major developmental areas discussed in Chapters 3 and 4: *physical, cognitive, psychosocial,* and *creative.* (The order of the areas makes no difference as long as they are consistent for each child.) Valuable space is saved if the child's name and birth date are placed on the first tab with the title of the first developmental area. This advice will be helpful when managing 48 or more index tabs.

Not all teachers choose to use the traditional developmental areas listed above. Because of the monumental importance of language during the preschool years, many preschool teachers prefer to have a separate index for it. Other teachers choose to include language development under the cognitive index. Some teachers prefer to have a separate index for perceptual development; others cover this aspect of development under *cognitive* and *physical.* The primary grade teacher may want to subcategorize cognitive development by using color-coded cards for reading, writing, math, and other subjects.

Regardless of how the categories are organized, all anecdotes can be filed behind the corresponding developmental index tab when using the card file box system. In fact some observations may be duplicated and filed behind more than one section (e.g., an anecdote about a child's easel painting that shows creative, cognitive, and/or fine motor advances). Each separately filed anecdote is dated and filed in chronological order. This method of organization simplifies filing and retrieval.

Some teachers think the card file box system is the most convenient of the three options because file boxes kept on a book shelf are always within the teacher's reach. One teacher, a proponent of the card file box system, sought to facilitate collecting and filing of observations. She purchased a three-quarter-length apron with two big pockets able to hold the observational tools she was using; that way, she could keep a pen and several empty file cards handy for writing her daily observations. Using the handy pockets, she could quickly slip the completed cards away and file them when she had a few extra moments.

Large pockets in aprons act as temporary housing for observations during a teacher's busy day.

In primary grades, teachers may also use apron pockets to keep handy cards with checklists of skills in math and literacy. If all observational records are kept on or transferred to index cards, the card file box system is simple to use because all of the cards are the same size and fit behind the index dividers.

The second storage option is the file folder case system. The teacher chooses the appropriately sized file case (plastic or metal) that will accommodate the classroom observational records. One manila file folder is labeled with each child's name and birth date. (Alphabetizing the file folders permits quick reference.) Inside each file folder are four anecdotal recording sheets (Figures 10.1 or 10.2) that contain the following headings: *Cognitive Development, Psychosocial Development, Physical Development,* and *Creative Development.* Take a minute to familiarize yourself with these samples of preschool and primary grade recording sheets. Each of the four boxes represents one entire page in each child's file folder. Color-coding the recording sheets is an effective organizational strategy.

Within each child's file folder, anecdotes are written on these sheets (or stuck on, if the teacher uses peel-off labels). Other observational records and relevant information available to the teacher (e.g., running records, checklists, rating scales, ABC narrative event samplings, documentations of activities, primary grade reading and writing inventories, and cross-references for photographs and videotapes— more on this later in the chapter) are filed behind the appropriate developmental sheets. If the observational record contains running records or possibly a checklist

Page 1

Cognitive Development

Representational Abilities

Language   Seriation

Reasoning   Number
                        Development

Social Cognition   Memory

Classification   Other
_____

Entry 1—Date. Anecdote

Entry 2—Date. Anecdote

. . . and so forth with each entry

on the 8½-by-11 inch pages

Page 2

Psychosocial Development

Relationships with adults and peers

Self-concept

Play

Fears   Impulse control

Aggression   Other
_____

Entry 1—Date. Anecdote

Entry 2—Date. Anecdote

. . . and so forth with each entry

on the 8½-by-11 inch pages

Page 3

Physical Development

FINE MOTOR: GROSS MOTOR:

Grasp/control   Run
Fasten/unfasten   Jump
Insert/remove   Hop
String/lace   Gallop
Use scissors   Skip
Other   Climb
                        Balance
                        Catch
                        Throw
                        Kick
_____

Entry 1—Date. Anecdote

Entry 2—Date. Anecdote

. . . and so forth with each entry

on the 8½-by-11 inch pages

Page 4

Creative Development

Flexibility   Risk-taking

Sensitivity   Imagination

Resourcefulness

Expressive experiences and skills in
using creative materials (two-
dimensional and three-dimensional art,
music, dramatic play, blocks)
_____

Entry 1—Date. Anecdote
Entry 2—Date. Anecdote
. . . and so forth with each entry on the
8½-by-11 inch pages

Figure 10.1
Preschool anecdotal recording sheets using subcategories (condensed in size).

Page 1	Page 2
Cognitive Development	**Psychosocial Development**
Representational abilities	Self-concept and self esteem
Language Classification	Advances in play
Logical thought Number development	Moral Reasoning and Prosocial behavior
Metacognition Memory	Relationships with peers
Subject areas Other	Other
Entry 1—Date. Anecdote	Entry 1—Date. Anecdote
Entry 2—Date. Anecdote	Entry 2—Date. Anecdote
. . . and so forth with each entry on the 8½-by-11 inch pages	. . . and so forth with each entry on the 8½-by-11 inch pages

Reading order of the four boxes:

Page 1

Cognitive Development

Representational abilities

Language   Classification

Logical thought   Number development

Metacognition   Memory

Subject areas   Other

Entry 1—Date. Anecdote

Entry 2—Date. Anecdote

. . . and so forth with each entry on the 8½-by-11 inch pages

Page 2

Psychosocial Development

Self-concept and self esteem

Advances in play

Moral Reasoning and Prosocial behavior

Relationships with peers

Other

Entry 1—Date. Anecdote

Entry 2—Date. Anecdote

. . . and so forth with each entry on the 8½-by-11 inch pages

Page 3

Physical Development

FINE MOTOR: GROSS MOTOR:

Use of tools   Arm/leg strength

Uniformity of letters   Speed

and numbers   Coordination

Eye–hand   Agility

coordination   Endurance

                Specialized

                Skills in sports

                Other

Entry 1—Date. Anecdote

Entry 2—Date. Anecdote

. . . and so forth with each entry on the 8½-by-11 inch pages

Page 4

Creative Development

Flexibility   Risk-taking

Sensitivity   Imagination

Resourcefulness

Expressive experiences and skills in using creative materials (two-dimensional and three-dimensional art, music, creative dramatics, writing, block play)

Other

Entry 1—Date. Anecdote

Entry 2—Date. Anecdote

. . . and so forth with each entry on the 8½ -by-11 inch pages

Figure 10.2

Primary grade anecdotal recording sheets using subcategories (condensed in size).

or a rating scale, those records are placed at the back of the child's individual file folder behind the anecdotal sheets.

The recording sheets in Figures 10.1 and 10.2 provide a flexible, expandable organizational framework. For teachers who prefer a more detailed and thorough system, the subcategories listed under each of the four developmental areas can be used. (Many of the subcategories are the growth indicators described in Chapters 3 and 4.) The system may be personalized by adding or deleting categories based on the classroom goals.

The purpose of the subcategories is to present the teacher with a quick check-off system to ensure that records have been gathered in all domains of development, thus giving an expansive picture of the child's developmental progress. As the teacher records an entry for one of the major developmental areas, a check is made next to the appropriate subcategory on the top of the sheet. For example, if the teacher observed a child who was fearful when the fire fighter visited the class, the anecdote would be recorded on the sheet headed *Psychosocial Development* and one check made before the subcategory of fears. Because of their own interests and strengths, teachers may find themselves collecting observations that concentrate on certain areas and subcategories of a child's development and neglect others.

> Do you have a tendency to be drawn to the most verbal children in your group, the children who help others solve problems, or the children who never break program rules? Observational assessment will point out to you on a day-by-day basis how much or how little you know about all the children in your program. (High/Scope Educational Research Foundation, 1992b, p. 4)

By adopting a detailed system that provides check-offs for observational entries, a teacher can merely glance at the sheets to see if the total picture for each child has been captured.

Practicing teachers report that using the anecdotal recording sheets with subcategories is a major support to the teaching process. The built-in organization of recording sheets (with other observations appropriately filed behind one of the four developmental headings) saves precious hours when studying growth patterns, planning activities, and preparing for conferences.

When using the file folder system, choose the appropriate size file folder to ease the potential storage problem. Large file folders are recommended if children's work samples, such as unwieldy representations like easel paintings, are to be included in the teacher storage container. The file folders, regardless of size, can be conveniently stored and transported, if necessary, in a sturdy carrying case obtained from an office supply store.

The third storage option for teachers' observations is the notebook. This system closely resembles the file folder organization, but the contents are housed in a different type of container. Instead of using file folders for each child's developmental records, the notebook is divided by section pages that have individual index tabs with each child's name. The same four anecdotal recording pages as used in the file folder system (see Figures 10.1 and 10.2) are placed behind each child's name tab. Recording anecdotes and other observations are done in the same fashion as for the file folders. The notebook, like the file folder case, is often the choice for teachers who prefer to write anecdotes on a clipboard, a pad of paper, or large peel-off labels. Moreover, developmental checklists or rating scales, assessments, or inventories fit nicely in a notebook or a file folder but are too bulky for a card file box. Those who choose the notebook system instead of the file folder case system state that they are simply more comfortable with the notebook—maybe it's all those college classes!

No matter what storage container is chosen, a summary of the child's entrance information can be helpful when included in the portfolio along with the observational records. Note that licensing regulations and educational standards in many states require each child's medical forms and personal information to be filed separately in a central office. If permitted, however, the competent teacher takes time to review these files, summarizing pertinent and appropriate information for classroom records, and stores this information on a recording sheet or index card labeled *General Data*. This sheet can be added as a first item in any of the storage containers.

Three different record-keeping systems for organizing and storing teachers' observational records have been surveyed: card file box, file folder case, and notebook. A system tailored to meet personal teaching needs will be concise, orderly, and workable. Study the advantages and disadvantages of the three systems compared in Figure 10.3. As you read through this figure, you may also want to keep a mental tally of the strengths and limitations of keeping children's work samples separate.

Storage Choices for Children's Work

The last portfolio design decision is to determine if the children's work samples will be included in the teacher-kept storage container or if the children will keep their work separately. If the teacher chooses the expandable file folder case system and uses legal size folders, then the children's work samples could be kept together with the teacher's observational records within the same folder. This feature is unique to the file folder case system. Oversized work samples (e.g., easel paintings) and access for the children, however, are two reasons that many teachers prefer to keep the children's work samples separately from the teachers' observational records, no matter what system is used.

Children's work samples, if housed separately, may be stored in large (18 by 24 inches) construction paper or newspaper envelopes (usually put together by the teacher and decorated by the child), legal-sized file folders, metal file bins, roll-away racks for hanging files, tote trays, or scrap books (McAfee & Leong, 1997; Mindes et al., 1996). These expandable files can hold all subject matter examples, including math. "Children as early as preschool can help prepare their own portfolios by choosing which materials they want to present to their parents" (Billman & Sherman, 1996, p. 37). In choosing a separate work sample container, explore the following questions:

Advantages

Card File Box	File Folder Case	Notebook
Expandable	Expandable	Expandable
Closed cover keeps observations confidential	File keeps observations confidential	Closed cover keeps observations confidential
Durable	Easy to transport in carry case	Easy to transport
Quick filing using index tabs	Planning at a glance using recording sheets	Planning at a glance using recording sheets
Cards fit in pockets for classroom mobility	Compact and comprehensive recording sheets	Compact and comprehensive recording sheets
	Least amount of storage space	Held in place with rings
	Large files hold oversized work samples	

Disadvantages

Card File Box	File Folder Case	Notebook
One box per four to six children	Papers are loose in each file	Takes time to file using rings
Cannot store work samples in box	Less durable than other two	Cannot store oversized work samples
Cannot fit other observational records in file box		
Cumbersome to transport		

Figure 10.3
Advantages/disadvantages of teacher record-keeping storage systems.

- Is access easy for the children? Consider the storage location within the room and the procedure children will use to independently file samples.
- How will various-sized work samples be accommodated? Are group projects to be included?
- Can each child personalize the cover?
- How will photographs of the children's work samples be protected if they are included in this container rather than housed with the teacher's observations?

Again, there is no one right procedure for systematizing portfolios. Whether the teacher uses a system separate from the children's or keeps all the observations and work samples in one folder is a personal choice. Proponents of the separate systems,

There are many ways to systematize records; here a teacher organizes her observations in a notebook.

however, profess that when children are given the opportunity to choose and contribute to the record-keeping process, ownership in the learning process is strengthened and self-esteem is enhanced (Freeman & Freeman, 1991).

What system initially strikes your fancy? You may want to do further research. Ask experienced teachers what type of portfolio system works best for them and why. Perhaps the school you choose to work in already has a system in place; if so, you may need only to experiment with modifications to suit your individual preferences. If you are selecting the system, however, you may want to try out several types and then base your decision on your own needs. Don't be in a hurry. Use the first 6 months to create a serviceable system; it must work for you or you won't use it. Remember, "portfolios are a means of collecting, organizing and reviewing authentic-assessment evidence gathered over time" (Gaustad, 1996, p. 32). A functional portfolio system is one of the early childhood educator's most prized possessions!

Guidelines for Designing a Portfolio System

At this point you may have some ideas of your own for keeping your records organized. Some helpful hints follow.

- Choose a portfolio format that accommodates all methods of observation used in the classroom (e.g., running records, anecdotes, checklists, rating scales, ABC narrative event sampling).
- Check the format for ease in filing and planning.
- Label one index tab for each child. Arrange sections behind each name using major developmental areas. To save tabs, write the first area label on the same tab as the child's name.
- Use color-coding whenever advantageous. Color-coding the recording sheets saves time when filing (e.g., all physical recording sheets are printed on red paper, all cognitive recording sheets are printed on green paper, etc.).
- If the storage container for the teachers' observation records does not include space for samples of children's work, determine how those will be filed and stored.
- Ensure that your system protects confidentiality.
- Understand that parents have legal access to all school records on their children. This law promotes an open-door policy and facilitates parental involvement in informed decision making.

There are many ways to organize and store observations rather than haphazardly collecting them in one big file folder for the entire class. Without a filing system, those valuable observations will serve little use in planning and conducting conferences.

OVERVIEW OF PARENT CONFERENCES

Parent conferences are scheduled appointments for teachers and family members to share their support of and concerns about the growth of these families' children. Whether the conference is the traditional fall/spring event or if it has been specially called to discuss a child's specific problem, the attitude of partnership prevails (Nilsen, 1997). "Schools must recognize and applaud the home as the foundation of the child's learning. Teachers must make every effort to bridge the gap between home and school. Effective communication between teachers and parents can and will bridge the gap" (Lawler, 1991, p. 89).

The teacher plays a key role in the development of the partnership. A positive tone is maintained, and leadership is provided by a teacher who is prepared and trained. Read on to see how the teacher who has made comprehensive observations, filed them in an efficient manner, and used them to support children's learning prepares for a conference confidently and proficiently.

Conference Preparation and Content

The child's developmental level and the goals of the educational program guide the conference content. For example, the content of a conference with a family whose toddler is in child care is very different from that of a conference with the family whose child is in a primary grade. Likewise, the conference content for various programs within the same age range may emphasize different aspects of the overall goals, thus influencing the content (e.g., the emphasis of the conference content for a child in a Montessori program may differ from that for a child in a Head Start program).

Regardless of the program type, the teacher begins to prepare for the conference by filling out a **conference form** for each child (see examples in Figures 10.4 and 10.5). The teacher summarizes the child's development in all four areas (physical, cognitive, psychosocial, and creative), drawing on the teacher's records and the child's work samples that have been systematically stored in the child's portfolio. The completed form establishes a focus for the conference.

Figure 10.4 is an example of a fall half-day preschool developmental conference form (a spring conference form does not include goals). Most families of children in half-day programs are familiar with the typical day. Many parents stay and observe on various occasions. Several have the luxury of helping out in their children's classroom. However, all-day child development programs for children 2½ to 5 years of age will want to include a description of the typical day in their conference reports because most all-day children have full-time working parents.

Primary grade conferences traditionally have centered around a report card concentrating on the child's proficiency in the subject matter and behavior in school. Developmentally appropriate curricula have become, however, increasingly implemented in K–3 classrooms. In these classrooms teachers and family members are concerned with the child's comprehensive growth and development. At conferences the graded report card is replaced or augmented with a more expansive reporting form (Figure 10.5). The National Association for the Education of Young Children guidelines for developmentally appropriate practices for 6- through 8-year-olds (Bredekamp & Copple, 1997) make the following suggestions for evaluations:

> Teachers and parents share useful, specific feedback about individual children's learning and developmental strengths and needs. Children's progress is shared with parents in the form of narrative comments following an outline of topics and in language that parents understand. A child's progress is reported in comparison to his or her own previous performance, and parents are given general information about how the child compares to age-related expectations. Letter or numerical grades are considered inadequate reflections of children's ongoing learning. (p. 176)

Figure 10.5 suggests a developmentally appropriate conference form for the primary grade years. As in Figure 10.4, the teacher uses the form to write comprehensive summaries. Keeping a well-designed portfolio system pays high dividends when you are preparing conference forms!

In addition to preparing a conference summary form for either preschool or primary grades, some teachers send home a short questionnaire (four or five open-ended questions) to help the families begin to think about their children's school experiences, topics to discuss, and goals to formulate. Two sample questions are offered by Mindes et al. (1996): "When you think about it, what excited Willard most about second grade? Were there assignments or activities that he seemed excited to do and couldn't wait to go to school that day?" (p. 153).

Preschool's Name

Fall Conference

Child: Age:

Teacher: Date:

The child's noteworthy developmental strength:

The child's current interest at preschool:

Developmental Overview

- Physical Development—This domain includes gross and fine motor development.

Family/Teacher Goals:

- Psychosocial Development—This domain includes social and emotional development.

Family/Teacher Goals:

- Cognitive—This domain includes language; problem-solving skills; readiness skills; memory; representation, number, classification, and seriation abilities.

Family/Teacher Goals:

- Creative—This domain includes indicators of creativity as well as evidence of creative abilities in art, music, drama, block-building, or dictated stories.

Family/Teacher Goals:

Figure 10.4
Sample preschool conference form.

Primary School's Name

Fall Conference

Child: Age/Grade:

Teacher: Date:

Cognitive: Covers the academic areas of reading, writing, math, science, social studies, health, language, and listening/speaking. Also includes problem-solving abilities, logical thought, classification, seriation, memory, and perspective-taking.

Psychosocial: Includes personal and social development, such as peer and adult relationships, impulse control, motivation, self-concept, self-esteem, and moral reasoning.

Physical: Discusses both gross and fine motor development. Includes child's abilities in physical skill development.

Creative: Includes music, art, writing, block play, and dramatics.

Goals:

Figure 10.5
Sample primary grade conference form.

Recognizing that most families have terrifically busy lives, some speak English as a second language, some are single parents, and others may have negative school memories, short preconference questionnaires can encourage focused thinking and help parents to participate confidently in a productive discussion.

Getting Started

Even though "a conference with family members is the most prevalent way of sharing information and planning how to mutually support the child's development" (Feeney, Christensen, & Moravcik, 2001, p. 165), it is the teacher's responsibility to facilitate productive communications from start to finish. How is that done? It's accomplished by understanding the main purposes of a conference: listening, sharing, and strengthening the family–teacher partnership as it relates to the children's growth and development.

Now let's look at how a conference is generally carried out. First, the teacher welcomes the family members and sees that everyone is comfortably seated. (Be sure there are enough adult chairs!) Hendrick (2001) suggests that the time limit be mentioned early on, in a conversational manner. An example would be, "Time to talk together never seems long enough; I'm so pleased we were able to arrange this 30-minute meeting." Then the teacher begins the discussion by setting a positive tone—sharing about an outstanding strength the child possesses or a recent accomplishment. Here are two examples:

- It's a real joy to see how Keara has grown in her ability to use words to solve problems independently. We've worked very hard on this. She seems so much more confident in this area at school. What do you see at home?
- Omar has such well-developed motor skills. I often observe his agility and coordination when he runs, hops, and skips. He's a great skipper. I've noticed recently that he doesn't seem to have the interest in the trikes that he used to. I think he's ready to try a two-wheeler. What do you think?

The opening positive statement does not have to detail a monumental achievement. For the child who seems "lacking in strengths," the teacher looks for the small positives, such as an expanding friendship, a special interest, a hobby, or a family trip or excursion that the child talked about. The discussion of the child's overall development can begin in any area as long as it is positive.

After the teacher breaks the ice by setting a positive tone and inviting interaction with the family member(s), the discussion continues via the content of the conference form (see Figures 10.4 and 10.5). The teacher, well prepared with examples of pertinent anecdotes and samples of the child's work, leads the family members through an informal conversation on all the areas of the child's development summarized on the form. This process is enhanced when both the teacher and the family members have a copy of the written conference summary form in front of them.

Throughout the conference the teacher asks the family members if they've noticed similar or the same developmental strengths or weaknesses that may need to be addressed. Usually family members relate stories that correlate with what the teacher has seen at school. On occasion, family members are surprised and report that their child is different at home. The teacher listens attentively and jots down this important input. The teacher can then summarize joint concerns. During the fall conference, the teacher and family members can then establish specific goals for the child.

> Parents' observations, made at home or at school, are invaluable. Parents know their child better than anyone else. They see their child under every imaginable circumstance. They are aware of the child's likes and dislikes, joys and anxieties. Most importantly, they know what they want for their child. (Allen & Marotz, 1999, between pp. 132 and 133)

The teacher and the family bring their own perspectives to the conference table, interpreting the child's growth through their own observational prisms. Together they peer through the looking glass, often doubling the visibility. The conference is a collaboration; it sets in place the desired family–school partnership.

Supporting Documentation

Effective conferences require sharing of selected observations (often anecdotes) to augment the summaries. The trained teacher also selects samples of the child's work (e.g., drawings, stories, primary grade math, or writing papers) to illustrate various topics on the conference form. For example, the teacher may present a painting or a collage that shows the child's ability to represent or a child's unfinished math assignments as evidence of weak work habits. Families appreciate documentation in the form of children's work samples and can more clearly understand their children's developmental advances or impediments when samples accompany the written summaries.

Another way to widen the perspective and document written comments is to present an audiotape, a videotape, and photographs (Helm, Beneke, & Steinheimer, 1998). Digital cameras now afford teachers the opportunity to embed classroom photos within the summary form itself! More common is the use of instant photographs. One teacher shares her experience by telling about Juanita, a child who always responded with, "I don't know," when her parents asked her what she did at preschool:

> During the parent conference I brought out some photos of Juanita's science discoveries using magnets and balances along with photos of her block-building feats, and her favorite dramatic play scenario—the office. Her parents were delighted to see her emerging science interest and her active classroom participation. Those pictures were worth a thousand words!

Not to be overlooked as an effective tool during the conference is the appropriate use of videotapes. When teachers, who have the equipment, take the time to film children at work in the classroom and choose selected vignettes to share at the conference, parents are offered an enlightening and rewarding view of their child. A videotape can be useful in clarifying a child's strengths and weaknesses or portraying developmental progress. For example, video clips can be chosen to show a young preschooler's growing ability to interact with other children. As the children progress in years, video clips can highlight leadership skills. Let's look at how one teacher integrated videotapes into a conference.

> I once taught a 4-year-old, Bethany, who was precocious in her artwork. By the second or third month, Bethany ventured out into the block area, where she became as interested in pursuing social contacts as in building. Her time in the art area declined, and she took less time and care with her projects. Unfortunately (from my perspective), her parents grew increasingly dissatisfied with the "quality" of work Bethany brought home from preschool!
>
> My verbal explanations of Bethany's change in pursuits were not as effective as a videotape of Bethany during free choice time in persuading her parents that her time was being well spent. Once they recovered from their initial surprise and disappointment (remember, their expectations were not being met), they began to appreciate how hard Bethany was working to expand her social networks. In the short term the videotape lessened the parents' anxieties about

unproductive time in preschool and, in the long run, helped to allow Bethany the time needed to achieve a balanced life at school.

"Photographs and audio or video recording provide concrete evidence of young children's performance in the classroom . . . [They] document performances with an accuracy and competence not possible with written records" (Smith, Kuhs, & Ryan, 1993, p. 12). These selected pieces of media can provide value insights during the family–teacher conference. Family members value the opportunity to see their children on their own and leave the conference with a broadened understanding of the educational program.

Guidelines for Parent Conferences

Frequency

Preschools, child care programs, and primary grades typically offer two yearly conferences for each child. To strengthen the family partnership and develop joint goals for the child, a fall conference is offered about a month after school has begun. To discuss the child's growth, goal realizations, and next year's educational plans, another conference is offered near the end of the school year. Conferences offered only on a volunteer basis that are left up to the parents' request place total responsibility on the parents and miss the intended goal of partnership, thus robbing the child of an optimal developmental environment.

Preparation

Treat each child individually. Carefully review portfolios of observational records and children's work samples. Write each child's developmental summary on a conference form. Write with your mind and your heart. Remember to be tactful and gentle, gentle, gentle with your words. Choose items to discuss, such as children's work, photos, and anecdotes. Organize.

Planning

Set a time that is convenient for the teacher and the family. Aim for a 30-minute session. Invite the parent(s) or guardian.

Setup

Arrange a comfortable place for the parent(s) or guardian to wait. Provide adult-sized chairs and a table with reading materials. Early childhood magazines, class photo albums, or stories children have dictated or written help early arrivals pass the time. A pitcher of ice water or a pot of coffee with disposable cups is always appreciated. In addition, give attention to the physical setting you have chosen for the conference.

The environment must help parents feel more relaxed and less intimidated. Having adult-sized furniture and seating arranged so that parents and the teacher can sit side by side will help parents feel welcome. Provide paper and pencils for note taking. (Rockwell, Andre, & Hawley, 1996, p. 213)

Appointment

Start the conference on time! Keep track of the time so that others are not inconvenienced. During the conference be friendly, positive, and open. Listen and exchange views. Keep your purpose in mind. Develop fall goals with the parent(s) on the basis of shared information. Send home a copy of the conference form with the family.

Follow-up

Make a phone call, send a note home with the child, or informally chat at departure time to keep the lines of communication open. Schedule another conference or make a home visit if a concern requires additional attention. Let your sincere interest be known; continue to build partnerships.

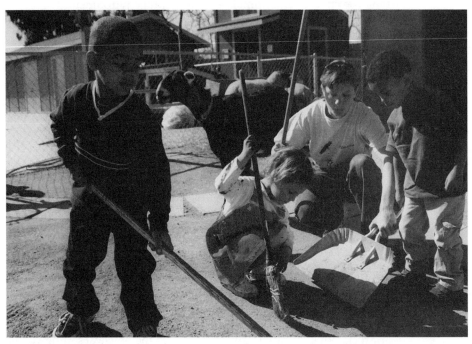

Photographs of children's activities in the early childhood classroom strengthen parent conferences.

Guidelines for Using Videotapes During Parent Conferences

Know the equipment

> Valuable conference time will be wasted if the you cannot work the equipment efficiently.

Plan the program

> Select which tape clips of each child to show and know where to find them. Carefully preview each tape and record the counter numbers of each clip.

Utilize videotapes to make substantive points to the families

> Videotapes can illustrate how children work in groups, their interests, their strengths, and so forth. Think about each selection and how you want to use it during the conference. Planning time will be shortened if the video clips depicting more than one child are cross-referenced in each child's portfolio.

Present a balanced view of each child

> Try to show families at least two clips of their child to document the variety of activities and experiences that are part of early childhood education. Remember that the clip may be short yet effective.

> In summary, it is the process illustrated in the cycle of observing, recording, planning, evaluating, and communicating (see Chapter 2) that surrounds conferences. The child is the focus, and the intention is to build a partnership with the family to support the child's development and learning.

> During a responsive and supportive conference, family members readily furnish additional information, offer new insights, ask questions, and make suggestions. Their family perspectives help give the teacher the broadest possible view of the child. As family members and the teacher share their own perspectives of the child's current and developing abilities, a valuable partnership is created. Throughout the year this partnership is developed by keeping the lines of communication open and staying in touch.

APPLICATIONS

To exemplify the conference process, let's get acquainted with Sierra (4; 4). Before the conference day, Sierra's teacher compiled the conference form summaries using the observations from Sierra's portfolio; the documents in Sierra's portfolio are displayed in Figure 10.6.

With the purpose of the conference in mind (to enhance the family–teacher team approach by listening, discussing, and sharing joys and concerns regarding Sierra's developmental progress), read through the summary (Figure 10.7) and begin to answer the following questions. What topics would you, as a teacher, be sure to discuss with her parents? What would be your tentative plans and goals for Sierra? Conference dialogue will ultimately determine joint goals; however, effective teachers come prepared with some possible goal suggestions. Practice Activity 10.1 will give you an opportunity to make some preconference goal suggestions based on the information in Figure 10.7.

---

12 *anecdotes* representing physical, cognitive, psychosocial, and creative development dated as follows: 9/9, 9/14, 9/15, 9/17, 9/18, 9/25, 9/28, 10/1, 10/5, 10/8, 10/12, 10/13
2 *running records* (one inside and one outside) dated 9/11 and 9/16, each 5 minutes
COR (Child Observation Record) *rating scale* completed 10/14 based on above records
1 *video clip* of dramatic play
work samples of her writing and drawing

Figure 10.6
Portfolio documents.

To optimally communicate children's learning during parent–teacher conferences, teachers videotape classroom experiences when they are best displayed in action rather than words.

Seaside Preschool
Fall Conference

Child: Sierra   Age: 4; 4
Teacher: Mrs. Morrow   Date: 10/16

Child's noteworthy developmental strengths: Sierra's most precious quality is her ability to be a wonderful, caring friend; she is liked by all and can easily be considered a "people person." Her refined leadership skills, vivid imagination, sensitivity to others, and confident language ability support this strength.
Child's current interest at preschool: Sierra most frequently chooses the dramatic play area where she is surrounded by others who also enjoy role play.

Developmental Overview

Physical Development

Gross Motor: Sierra thoroughly enjoys the time we spend outdoors. She runs, hops, and gallops with ease and control. Sierra takes pride in her ability to hop on one foot. She often hops on our walks from one place to another and, with her exuberant confidence, announces, "Hey look at me! I can hop on one foot!" She is exploring a new skill: skipping. With practice she will master it in no time. Sierra likes riding the tricycle and smoothly maneuvers the curves on the track. Sierra is able to catch a large red ball that is bounced to her. Sierra displays rhythm with her body during music time. She heartily enjoys doing the hand and body movements that go with the songs and has a feel for the beat of the music.

Sierra uses caution in walking down stairs, holding onto the handrail and stepping with one foot and then the other on each step. We walk down 10 steps on the way back from the playground and down 3 steps on the way back from the bathroom. She is cautious on both sets of steps.

Fine Motor: Sierra shows a lot of interest in writing, drawing, and painting. She is very adept at using tools such as pencils, markers, crayons, and paint brushes. She holds writing utensils correctly between the thumb and index finger, resting against the middle finger; she is right-handed. She writes her own name, the names of her family members, and those of some of her friends.

Sierra's hand-eye coordination is evidenced in her ability to string small items (Cheerios or pony beads) with the use of a plastic needle. She holds and uses scissors properly but gets a bit frustrated if the item to be cut (i.e., a large oval) is too big.

Figure 10.7
Completed preschool conference form.

(continued)

Family/Teacher Goals:

Cognitive

Sierra has a positive attitude toward learning and confidently shares the knowledge she has about the world around her. Her perceptiveness of language never ceases to amuse and delight me. One of my favorites was something she said in the bathroom while washing her hands: "Yikes! This water is cold. It feels like wintertime on my hands!" She has a wide-ranging imagination and shares this through her charming vocabulary. She engages in conversation with her friends and contributes new ideas during circle time. Last week while we were reading a book about bugs, she stated, "I know about termites. They eat wood."

Sierra can identify and name numbers, letters, colors, and shapes. She can count with one-to-one correspondence up to 12. She makes comparisons regarding larger and smaller and sorts things by color.

Sierra exhibits recall abilities daily as she remembers to follow our classroom rules, often reminding her classmates to do the same. Her use of language is a great asset to her.

Family/Teacher Goals:

Psychosocial Development

As I wrote, her most noteworthy strength is her ability to be a friend. She is sensitive and caring and always considerate of others' feelings. When asked one day by a child if she would sit with her at lunch, Sierra replied, "Yes, I'll sit by you, but I already promised to sit by Jessica, so I'll sit in the middle—I have two sides!" She is very well liked by the other children and seems to enjoy the friendships she has made. She tends to play primarily with girls but is not opposed to sitting next to a boy.

Sierra is confident in herself. She has announced that when she grows up she wants to be "a singer and a dancer and a doctor who takes care of animals and a detective." Wow! Sierra speaks often (with sparkly eyes) of her family; she obviously has a great love for them. She is, however, quite comfortable at preschool for her 4 hours away from them and doesn't experience any anxiety when they leave in the morning.

Sierra's use of language is also helpful in her social skills. She is able to resolve conflicts through verbal communication; she's never shown hostile or physical

Figure 10.7 *(Continued)*
Completed preschool conference form.

aggression. She rarely needs to seek teacher intervention, but if there is an injustice she can't solve, she feels comfortable in approaching us for help.

Family/Teacher Goals:

Creative Development

Sierra uses creativity in many aspects of her play. She spends much of her free choice time in the housekeeping area, using her imagination and taking on various roles (she usually plays the mom). Sierra draws pictures of her family, complete with smiling suns. I have attached some samples of her drawings. She also enjoys art activities and has no fear of getting her hands right into the paint.

She has not yet shown much interest in block-building. During free choice time, Sierra enjoys the housekeeping, art, or writing centers.

Sierra extends her creativity to our outdoor playtime. She creates a variety of cakes, soups, and pies in the sandbox.

Family/Teacher Goals:

Figure 10.7   *(Continued)*
Completed preschool conference form.

Source: Courtesy of Susan Morrow, Mission Viejo, California. Copyright © 2000 by Susan Morrow. Adapted with permission.

As you finished reading the conference summary in Figure 10.7, you might have wondered how long it took the teacher to write a comprehensive summary. Or you might have asked: "How does a teacher have time to complete summaries for 12 to 15 children?" There's no doubt that summary writing does take time. The good news is that it gets easier and goes more quickly with practice. It is, however, time well spent; the rewards come at conference time when the partnership is affirmed. Recently I overheard a dad speaking to a teacher after reading the conference summary. He said, "You certainly know my son. I couldn't have written the summary better if I'd done it myself!" The teacher, a bit embarrassed, answered, "Well, communicating to parents is my job." To which the dad replied, "I hope I do my job as well as you do yours." The dad is a doctor.

PRACTICE ACTIVITY 10.1

Suggestions for Teacher Goals

The goals recorded on each child's conference form are jointly set by the teacher and the parent(s) during the conference. The teacher, however, prepares for the conference by writing (on a separate piece of paper) some ideas for possible goals that address strengths and weaknesses. Depending on the child, most teachers like to prepare two to four preconference goals in each developmental area.

After reviewing Figure 10.7, try your hand at writing preconference goals as if you were Sierra's teacher. Write one for each developmental area.

Physical goals:

Example: To provide experiences to further her gross motor skills by introducing jump roping accompanied by new jump rope jingles. Her interest in others and her strong language skills may act as invitations to this activity.

Cognitive goals:

Psychosocial goals:

Creative goals:

To implement successful conferences, the teacher must be skilled in writing goals and summaries. Practice Activity 10.2 offers practice in writing summaries.

PRACTICE ACTIVITY 10.2

Practice in Writing Summaries

It is time to prepare for fall conferences at Eighth Street Elementary. The teacher thoughtfully fills in the conference form (modeled in Figure 10.7) to discuss Sawyer's (5; 3) development. The teacher praises Sawyer's advanced gross motor skill abilities, all executed with coordination, speed, and agility. The teacher also applauds Sawyer's extensive vocabulary, which he effectively uses to explore ideas, ask questions, and relate experiences during group time. In all areas, Sawyer is inquisitive, curious, and adventurous. The teacher is concerned, however, about Sawyer's frequent outbursts of anger, his rough play, and his inability to enter groups without using force (e.g., knocking over someone's block structure, taking the ball away). Children have already begun to avoid and reject him in their play.

Using the form modeled in Figure 10.7, imagine that you are Sawyer's teacher preparing for a fall conference. Write the psychosocial paragraph addressing Sawyer's exuberance when he is playing with other children. Be positive, clear, and concise when conveying this information. Include the strategies the teacher uses to support his growth.

Eighth Street Elementary
Fall Conference

Child: Sawyer   Age: 5; 3
Teacher: Date:

Psychosocial:

>>>

OFF ON YOUR OWN 10.1

Evaluation of Portfolio Systems

Option 1

Choose two schools that serve the age group you are interested in (2½- to 8-year-olds). Call ahead and request *blank* copies of their observation sheets, record-keeping sheets, and conference forms. If each school can meet your need, stop by and pick up the forms. (If a school cannot meet your request, choose another that can.) On examination of your collections from the schools, answer the following questions by writing down your findings.

- What information about each child do the various forms collect, and what information do they omit? How are they similar and different?
- Do the forms meet the guidelines given in this chapter for designing your own system? If not, what modifications would you suggest?

Option 2

Visit one school that serves children of the age you are interested in (2½- to 8-year-olds) and uses written observations. Obtain *blank* copies of the observation sheets, record-keeping sheets, and conference forms. Make an appointment and discuss them with a teacher or teachers at the school. Learn how the sheets and forms are used at that school. Find out what the teacher(s) considers the benefits and drawbacks of the samples you've collected. Write down your findings.

> QUICK REVIEW <

1. The contents of a portfolio are
   a. a combination of letter grades and teacher comments.
   b. a month's worth of work samples created by the child.
   c. an organized collection of classroom observations.
   d. a combination of the child's work samples and the teachers' observations over a year's time.

2. Teachers may create their own record-keeping systems, modify others' systems or use one of the three presented in this chapter. The three organizational systems discussed were,

a.

b.

c.

3. One of the features of an effective record-keeping system is that it expedites classroom planning and parent conferences.

❑   True

❑   False

4. _____ records are the most abundant observations kept by a teacher and are often referred to as the backbone of portfolios.

5. Name three samples of children's work that could be included in the portfolio to represent more than one area of development.

a.

b.

c.

6. Which one of the following guidelines for designing a portfolio system is NOT accurate?

a. Choose a system that accommodates all methods of observation used in the classroom.

b. Be sure to keep portfolios in a locked cabinet to ensure confidentiality, allowing for teacher access only.

c. Check the format for ease in filing and planning.

d. If the storage container selected for the teachers' observational records does not include space for samples of children's work, determine how those will be filed and stored.

7. One of the goals of a family-teacher conference is to build a _____ that ensures optimal progress for the child.

8. During a family-teacher conference the teacher should open with a _____ statement about the child.

9. Tools to effectively enhance the written comments in a family-teacher conference are audiotapes, videotapes, and photographs.

❑   True

❑   False

10. Conference forms should be written from the head and the _____ .

TAKE A MOMENT TO REFLECT

Personal Reflection

As adults, we have the opportunity to collect and store documentation for a variety of activities: checking and savings accounts, recipes, photographs, mileage, grades, car repairs, monthly bills, doctor and dentist visits, insurance claims—the list goes on and on. Reflect on how you systematize your personal records and answer the following questions.

1. What type(s) of record-keeping system(s) has been most successful in your personal life experiences?
2. Would that type be a usable form for classroom observations?
3. In what areas of your life is record keeping difficult? Can you identify any negative habits that could possibly creep into your classroom record-keeping process?

Ethical Reflection

NAEYC Ideal I-2.5 is "to interpret each child's progress to parents within the framework of a developmental perspective and to help families understand and appreciate the value of developmentally appropriate early childhood programs" (Feeney & Kipnis, 1992, p. 6). Reflect on how Sierra's teacher fulfills this ethical responsibility in the conference summary.

Observing Children, Teachers, Interactions, and Environments

Chapter 11   Observing Children and Teachers at Work by Using Tally Event Sampling

Chapter 12   Observing Children and Teachers at Work by Using Time Sampling

Chapter 13   Designing Observational Instruments to Use in the Early Childhood Classroom

Chapter 14   Selecting Methods to Observe, Plan, and Enrich the Physical Environment

11

Observing Children and Teachers at Work by Using Tally Event Sampling

At the end of each week, the teachers at Canyon Primary School set aside time for individual class evaluations and general planning for the next week. They record and file observations in well-used portfolios. On these Friday afternoons, they spend the bulk of their planning time rereading observations, identifying emerging patterns, setting curriculum goals, and planning appropriate activities and teaching strategies.

Today in Room 3, one team of teachers is pondering how to stimulate more divergent thinking during class discussions. The two teachers are disturbed because observational records in many of the children's portfolios describe quick, short answers during discussions of potentially interesting and complex topics. As the teachers brainstorm further, attention turns to their own teaching techniques. Could they be setting up the same kind of patterns that Calkins (1997) warned about?

> Teachers ask an average of 1 question every 11 seconds. It's not unusual for a teacher to speak like this: "Today, in class, we're going to study what, class?" The class chimes in the correct answer, "Haikus." "Good; haikus" (The teacher begins to write on the board.) "How do you spell haikus, class? And what country originated the haiku? Japan, good. How do you spell Japan? That's right. And what book did we recently read on Japan?" (p. 27)

The teachers begin to suspect that the way they lead discussions, specifically the types of questions they ask, could contribute to the children's short recorded responses. The teachers decide to observe how often they ask questions that promote divergent thinking and extend language as opposed to questions that elicit one-word responses. What observational method could these teachers use to explore their own question-asking patterns over a 2-week period?

Observations in the early childhood classroom usually focus on behaviors of *individual children*. In the preceding vignette, however, you are asked to elect a method to observe how *teachers* could explore their question-asking patterns. The time has come to broaden our observational scope by expanding the subject of our observations to include more than one person; the looking glass widens.

As you puzzle over the question posed in the opening vignette and search your current knowledge for an appropriate method, you may think about using a checklist to observe and examine the frequency of teachers' questions that promote divergent thinking and those questions that elicit a one-word response. A checklist only documents the presence or absence of the two types of questions for one teacher at a time. The Canyon Primary teachers, however, wish to investigate, analyze, and compare two or more teachers' questioning patterns on several occasions. These teachers want to evaluate one aspect of their teaching methodology—question-asking. In order to obtain the information requested in the vignette, we will explore a new method—**tally event sampling.**

OVERVIEW OF OBSERVING USING TALLY EVENT SAMPLING

Description

Event sampling—does it sound familiar? It certainly does. Chapter 9 introduced *ABC narrative event sampling*. This chapter presents another event sampling method: *tally event sampling*. These two methods are similar in two ways. First, they both observe specified **events** (identified behaviors or situations). Second, they both use an observational period known as a *sampling*, "the method used to select a given number of people (or things) from a population" (Mertens, 1998, p. 253). As stated in Chapter 9, the data gleaned from a sampling is generalized to represent the whole; thus the results are drawn from this representative sample.

ABC narrative event sampling and tally event sampling differ in purpose, form, and data. The ABC approach is used to study the causes and effects of individual children's behaviors. The tally approach (sometimes called frequency counts or frequency event sampling) is used to determine how often a specified event occurs. "With a tally system, an observer puts down a tally or tick *every time* a particular event occurs, e.g. every time the teacher asks a question or gives praise" (Hopkins, 1993, p. 100; emphasis in original). The subjects of an ABC narrative event sampling are always individuals and the subject(s) of tally event sampling can be individuals but are generally groups. The ABC method uses an A–B–C form that records written episodes; the tally approach uses a form called a grid to collect the tally marks (see Figure 11.1). The ABC approach yields qualitative data, whereas the tally approach provides quantitative data. "Quantitative analysis involves converting information to numbers—the number of times a person spoke in a group, the number of correct responses to specific questions, or the number of words in a composition" (Brause & Mayher, 1991, p. 136).

Let's return to the opening vignette of this chapter. The two Canyon Primary teachers ultimately chose tally event sampling because they wanted to find out the number of times during group discussions each of them asked an **open question** (a question that has many possible answers) or a **closed question** (a question that elicits a single correct answer, usually a one-word response). Using this method, the observer at Canyon Primary inscribed one tally mark each time one of the two types of questions was asked by a teacher during a group discussion—the focus of this observation. The tally marks were recorded on a grid that organized and simplified the potentially cumbersome task of observing several subjects (teachers) and recording abundant data (questions asked). Figure 11.1 exhibits the tally event sampling instrument developed by the two Canyon Primary teachers.

This form may be expanded vertically to include additional teachers and horizontally to include other subjects. When observing preschools, room areas or

---

Tally Event Sampling of Teachers' Open/Closed Questions

School/Grade:

Date: Time:

Observer: Teachers:

                                                 Children:

Event: Open questions (O)—have many possible answers that allow the child an opportunity to expand and explain.

              Closed questions (C)—have one correct answer.

Instructions: Make one tally mark in the appropriate column each time a teacher asks a question during specific discussion times.

Discussion Time	Science		Social Studies		Math		Shared Reading		Small Group	
Question / Teacher	O	C	O	C	O	C	O	C	O	C
Xavier										
Nadia										

Figure 11.1

Tally event sampling: Teachers' questions.

activities can be substituted for the subject categories. This tally form enables the teachers to summarize and compare their overall patterns of open or closed questioning throughout the day. The results will undoubtedly promote conversation among these teachers about the value and implications of open and closed questions during class discussions.

The tally approach can be used to examine a wide range of topics and is versatile because of its flexibility in choice of subject. The observer can measure the frequency of events involving *one person* (e.g., a teacher's repeated use of classroom-management techniques or the number of times a child is out of her or his seat during work periods), events involving *groups* (e.g., teachers' questioning patterns or children's use of **power words**—profanity or other offensive words such as "shut up"), or events involving *interactions* (e.g., children's language exchanges).

Keep in mind that tally event sampling can be used to record various **overt** (observable and apparent) behaviors that occur infrequently or with moderate frequency. What about events that occur rapidly, incessantly, or with very high frequency? Those require yet another method—time sampling—which is explained in Chapter 12.

What events or behaviors that recur moderately often would teachers want to examine? Think about appropriate topics that can be observed using the tally event sampling method (Practice Activity 11.1).

PRACTICE ACTIVITY 11.1

Tally Event Sampling Topics

Identify four topics that could be studied using tally event sampling.

Examples:

- Frequency of children's use of selected classroom centers
- Frequency of teachers' use of direct method instruction
- Frequency of staff members sharing resources and information with co-workers during weekly staff meetings

1.

2.

3.

4.

As discussed in previous chapters, no matter what topic (or method) is selected, the confidentiality of observational records and portfolios must be respected. The format and the size of observational instruments, such as tally event sampling or time sampling (studied in Chapter 12), can pose more of a problem. If using a clipboard, take special care to keep a cover sheet over the instrument; on the other hand, if using a notebook, keep it closed when not in use. Attention to confidentiality is a significant component of professionalism.

Purpose

Tally event sampling is most useful for teachers when they want to know how frequently a specific event occurs. Employing this approach, teachers can quickly and easily obtain quantitative information to be used in analyzing classroom problems and then in planning or revising teaching strategies, activities, and materials (Hintze & Shapiro, 1995). For example, one teacher concerned with meeting individual needs was interested in exploring how often each child used various methods to gain teachers' attention. With tally event sampling data the teacher could analyze possible age and cultural preferences and apply the findings to better meet individual needs.

Teachers can use tally sampled data to monitor developmental changes and the effectiveness of teaching strategies. Suppose a preschool teacher, Noi, who is exasperated with a child's use of power words, uses tally event sampling to check the child's frequency of power words use before and after intervention strategies. (Note: The subject of this tally event sampling is one child as opposed to a group.) In the first tally sampling period of 1 week, this child used power words an average of nine times a day. (Noi expected 50!) As Noi sets into practice a plan to help the child control this behavior, she knows that the process of behavior change may be long and difficult . And because the use of power words particularly irritates Noi, it seems as if no progress is being made. Nevertheless, after 2 weeks of concerted effort, Noi uses a second sampling period of 1 week to record the child's use of power words and finds that it has diminished to an average of twice a day! Encouraged by the positive results, she continues the corrective practices and looks forward to additional progress. Another power words sampling is planned for 3 weeks later.

Teachers are often shocked at the findings of tally event sampling, especially in the area of teacher and child behaviors. Teachers' perceptions of classroom behaviors, particularly in large classrooms, are easily distorted. With quantitative information procured from the samplings, however, teachers can analyze patterns and plan for adjustments. Responding to the recorded data can facilitate, enrich, and promote an exceptional early childhood program.

Recording Time

Two common concerns for observers using the tally approach are how to determine the sampling period and how to gather information throughout an extended span of time. After all, the early childhood classroom is bursting with activity. How can the teacher predetermine the length of time it will take to gather sufficient data? How can a teacher manage the collection of data on one topic over several days?

The length of the sampling period is determined by the event studied, specifically how long the teacher thinks it will take to gather sufficient data for a representative sample. For instance, the teacher may need to record tallies daily for a week when sampling aggression in the classroom but only a few days when sampling direct teaching methods. Remember, tally marks are made on the recording form only when the event occurs.

Kerlinger & Lee (2000) offered this advice about managing the collection of data: "The investigator who is pursuing events must either know when the events are going to occur and be present when they occur, as with classroom events, or wait until they occur, as with quarrels" (p. 734). The teacher keeps the form close at hand (a clipboard is a popular prop) for the duration of the sampling period and records marks whenever the event occurs. Classrooms equipped with video cameras allow the teacher another option. By leaving the camera on continuously or selecting specific periods during which to record and using the replay button, the teacher can mark the tallies on the instrument at his or her leisure.

Guidelines for Constructing Tally Event Sampling Instruments

Users may design tally event sampling instruments to suit their observational needs. To ensure that the resulting grids can be used as objectively as possible to collect the necessary quantitative data and produce sound information, certain steps must be taken. Box 11.1 presents an overview to assist in the process of devising a tally event sampling instrument.

To illustrate this process, two examples follow. The preschool example demonstrates how to design an instrument to record the frequency of children's participation in circle time. The primary grade example asks you to participate in constructing an instrument to research the question "Do teachers call on boys more than on girls?"

INTEGRATION OF CLASSROOM SITUATIONS AND OBSERVATION

Preschool Example

The scene for the six-step process of designing a tally event sampling instrument unfolds as follows. Molly, a new preschool teacher, is about 10 minutes into her 3-month evaluation with her director, Camisha. Up to this point, Camisha has praised Molly for her eager participation in staff meetings; she certainly is a good team member! Camisha has also commented about Molly's effective room arrangement, supportive relationships with families, and well-planned daily activities. Camisha now shifts the focus of the discussion and asks for Molly's assessment of her first 3 months on the job.

Box 11.1

Designing and Using a Tally Event Sampling Instrument

1. Select an appropriate topic, formulate an observational question, and define the event.
2. Research the topic in libraries and classrooms. Review what others have already done in the selected area.
3. Identify clear, distinct categories.
   - Generate sets of categories, vertical and horizontal.
   - Define each set of categories when necessary.
   - Select a **sign** or a **category system**.
   - Decide if category codes are needed.
4. Design a recording form.
   - Use the heading modeled in Figure 11.1.
   - Use the categories to construct the **grid**.
   - Label a space for comments at the bottom of the form.
5. Pilot test the instrument. Revise, if necessary, and pilot test again.
6. Establish **inter-rater reliability.**

Molly takes a few minutes and shares the positive happenings within her classroom. She mentions the trust and relationship she is building with the children, her feeling of acceptance with other staff members, and the joy and professional pride she experiences in working at an accredited school. Then she takes a deep breath and says that she is pleased to have an invitation to discuss a "troublesome area" that she has been thinking about for several weeks. As Molly tells Camisha about her concern for the acting-out behaviors at circle time, Camisha nods her head and concurs that this is an area Molly could work on. Camisha says, "I think you will better understand the dynamics of your circle times if you zero in on when children participate and when they don't." After discussion, Camisha and Molly agree on the following plan of action. Molly will design an instrument to record circle participation and ask a classmate from an early childhood curriculum class to observe her circle times for a week. Following the observation period, Molly and Camisha will meet to discuss the results.

Molly returns to her classroom and confidently begins work on her instrument. Having taken a college class in observation, she is armed with the appropriate know-how and soon realizes that she needs to collect data not only on who participates productively, but also on the frequency of the misbehaviors. Therefore, she identifies her question as, "How often do the children in this classroom participate productively

Circle time can be enhanced by observation.

and counterproductively during specific circle activities?" Molly reviews the possible observational methods, and because she wants to count frequencies, she chooses the most appropriate one—tally event sampling. The process of designing a tally event sampling instrument (based on the steps in Box 11.1) is set in motion.

Step 1   With her observational topic selected and her question clearly stated, Molly completes Step 1 by defining the event so that it is open to only one interpretation.

> *Circle time participation*—the child joins in teacher-planned group activities in a productive or counterproductive manner.

Step 2   Choosing the horizontal and vertical categories (components of the chosen event) is the next step and requires Molly to research the topic of circle time. Letting her question guide her, she checks her curriculum books and current journal articles on the topic in the library. She also reflects on her own experiences in this area. This important step determines what data will actually be collected.

Step 3   Molly determines that one set of categories is the children's names and the other set (given below) is the types of activities during circle time. Based on her research, she carefully selects categories that do not overlap.

- Calendar activities
- Topical discussions
- Fingerplays or action activities that are not sung
- Games (e.g., teacher-planned cognitive, movement, auditory discrimination activities)
- Sharing (e.g., item from home, information, an experience)
- Songs sung with or without actions
- Stories or poetry read from books, presented on flannel boards, or told by an adult

Molly chooses subcategories to indicate whether each child's participation is productive or counterproductive by dividing each of the above categories into two parts (see Figure 11.2).

Molly considers the use of a category or sign system while choosing categories.

Category System	**Sign System**
Categories must be mutually exclusive; each category is distinct and separate from the others.	Categories must be mutually exclusive; each category is distinct and separate from the others.
AND	BUT
Categories must be exhaustive; a category is listed for every possible observed behavior. Nothing is left out.	Categories do not have to be exhaustive. Allows the observer to select only pertinent categories.

For the first set of categories, Molly has selected specific circle activities typical of her classroom. This set is not exhaustive, so she uses a sign system. For the other set, Molly plans to list every child in her classroom; she uses a category system for this set.

Molly quickly sketches out the grid and notes that codes are in order. Some of the category descriptors contain many letters and will be difficult to fit in the small spaces on the grid. She could use abbreviations, letters, numbers, or symbols. She settles for the efficiency of letters; they will serve to jog her memory if necessary:

C   = calendar activities

TD   = topical discussions

F   = fingerplays or action activities that are not sung

G   = games (e.g., teacher-planned cognitive, movement, auditory-discrimination activities)

Sh   = sharing (e.g., item from home, information, an experience)

So   = songs sung with or without actions

St/P = stories or poetry read from books, presented on flannel boards, or told by an adult

p   = productive participation (e.g., comments or asks questions related to topic, takes part in movement or song activity)

cp   = counterproductive participation (e.g., impulsively jumps up, blurts out comments or questions off the subject, distracts another)

When codes are used, the observer tries to memorize them before going into the classroom to observe. In the construction of Molly's form, she has room to include the code meanings in her heading for quick reference. Code definitions ensure that others can use and understand the form; they may be printed in the heading or, if lengthy, on a separate sheet or on the back.

Step 4   Molly begins the construction of the tally event sampling form by filling in the heading. She then uses some scratch paper to try out a grid-arrangement pattern. Taking the size of the paper into account, she places the longest set of categories (children's names) down the left side of the recording sheet and the shortest set (circle activities) along the top; she positions the subcategories (p and cp) below each circle activity. With this arrangement, all the categories can fit on one sheet.

The tally event sampling grid is complete, with the matrix that displays the intersection of the two sets of categories. The grid is placed below the heading and definitions (shown in Figure 11.2 without data).

Step 5   To check that the form is efficient, is easy to use, and collects the desired information, Molly pilot tests her instrument while visiting an afternoon classroom.

Tally Event Sampling
of Preschoolers' Participation in
Selected Circle Time Activities

Center/Age level:

Date: Time:

Observer: Teacher:

                                 Children:

Event: Circle time participation—the child joins in teacher-planned group activities in a productive or counterproductive manner.

Codes: C = calendar activities, TD = topical discussion, F = fingerplays or action activities not sung, G = games, Sh = sharing, So = songs with or without actions, St/P = stories or poetry read from books, presented on flannel boards, or told by an adult.

              p = productive participation, cp = counterproductive participation.

Instructions: Mark one tally mark in the appropriate box each time a child joins in during one of the specified circle activities. Record the tally within each category under productive (p) or counterproductive (cp) participation.

Circle Activity / Child	C		TD		F		G		Sh		So		St/P	
	p	cp	p	cp	p	cp	p	cp	p	cp	p	cp	p	cp
Child 1														
Child 2														
Child 3														
and so forth														

Figure 11.2
Tally event sampling preschool example: Circle participation.

Conc.
Follow up-

Molly has no difficulty using her instrument. She is pleased with the organization of the instrument but adds the comment row she had forgotten (see Figure 11.3 for revision).

Step 6   The final step in instrument construction, the inter-rater reliability check (this process is explained in Chapter 13), is executed using paired observers. Molly enlists the help of Al, a fellow student from her evening class in early childhood education. They look over the instrument together. Molly foresees a possible problem and takes the time to train her inter-rater partner. Molly points out the difference between a movement game and a song sung with action. For example, a record with movement instructions and music in the background would be recorded under the G category as a teacher-planned movement activity. In contrast, the Hokie Pokie is a song sung with actions; it would be recorded under the So category.

With confidence in the category definitions, Molly and Al proceed to obtain inter-rater reliability by observing the same classroom during circle time, each using the tally instrument (as in Figure 11.3). When the observation time is complete, they check for consistency in what they recorded.

Inter-rater reliability is a measure between two or more observers resulting in a percentage that indicates the amount of agreement; exact agreement is 100 percent (Boehm, 1992). Molly and her partner compute 94% agreement. The high percentage (above 80%) indicates that these two observers are likely to produce similar results in different situations while using this instrument. If inter-rater reliability were low (below 80%), Molly would reevaluate the instrument to clarify categories or definitions or provide Al, her partner, with additional training.

Interpreting the Data

Al agrees to observe and collect participation tallies in Molly's preschool classroom for 5 days, recording each day during circle time (10:00 to 10:20 A.M.). The results have been compiled onto one form (Figure 11.3) for manageable analysis.

As Molly studies the results that Al gives her on Friday (Figure 11.3), she quickly sees some concerns. Molly, however, has studied observation and knows the importance of computing the results so that detailed conclusions can be drawn from the quantitative data.

Adding down the column tallies shows the amount of productive and counterproductive participation in each circle activity for the week of observation. For example, there were 5 productive participations and 11 counterproductive participations during calendar activities. Adding across the rows shows the number of times each child participates in circle activities. For example, Roman had 11 tallies; 9 were productive and 2 counterproductive.

When Molly adds all the counterproductive columns, the data reveal that 40% (55 of the total 139) of the participation was counterproductive. Molly knows that

Tally Event Sampling
of Preschoolers' Participation
in Selected Circle Time Activities

Center/Age level: University Heights Children's Center/4-year-olds
Date: 1/10 to 1/15   Time: About 10:00–10:20 A.M.
Observer: Al   Teacher: Molly
    Children: Twelve—7 boys and 5 girls

Event: Circle time participation—the child joins in teacher-planned group activities in a productive or counterproductive manner.

Codes: C = calendar activities, TD = topical discussions, F = fingerplays or action activities not sung, G = games, Sh = sharing, So = songs with or without actions, St/P = stories or poetry read from books, presented on flannel boards, or told by an adult.

p = productive participation, cp = counterproductive participation.

Instructions: Mark one tally mark in the appropriate box each time a child joins in during one of the specified circle activities. Record the tally within each category under productive (p) or counterproductive (cp) participation.

Circle Activity / Child	C p	C cp	TD p	TD cp	F p	F cp	G p	G cp	Sh p	Sh cp	So p	So cp	St/P p	St/P cp
Roman		/	/		///		/		/	/	///			
Hasana	/		/		///		//			/	///		///	/
Bailey		///		//			/	/		///		//		///
Mora		/			//		//	/			///	/		/
Davey	/	///		//			/	/		/	///	/		/
Vito		/			///	/	/		/		/	/		/
Dusty	/				///	/	/				///			///

Figure 11.3   (continued)
Tally event sampling preschool example: Circle participation (data).

Circle Activity / Child	C		TD		F		G		Sh		So		St/P	
	p	cp	p	cp	p	cp	p	cp	p	cp	p	cp	p	cp
Luella		//	/	///	/	/					/	/		///
Yong	/				///	/	/				///			//
Zane	/		/		///	/					///		/	/
Caren			/	/	//		/		/		///		/	/
Martha Sue					//		/				/		/	
	5	11	3	7	27	5	13	3	3	6	27	6	6	17

Comments:

Bailey and Davey never get to circle time until after the opening fingerplay because they slowly pick up and, in the process, play with the blocks.

One child shares per day on M/W/F.

One designated helper does calendar each day.

Songs are sung on M/W/F, fingerplays on T/Th.

Stories are read on T/W/Th/F, flannel board on M.

One auditory discrimination game is played on Tuesday; one movement game is played on Thursday.

One play yard problem is discussed on Tuesday.

On four of five days, circle time lasts for 25–30 minutes.

Figure 11.3 *(Continued)*
Tally event sampling preschool example: Circle participation (data).

is high! She studies totals of each row and column, computing each child's balance of productive and counterproductive participation in circle time, as well as productive and counterproductive participation during each specific activity. Then she surveys the results and forms the following initial conclusions:

1. There is more counterproductive than productive participation during calendar activities, topical discussion, sharing, and stories. Stories that take place at the end of the circle time had the most counterproductive participation. There are two activities out of the seven that only one child per day can participate in—calendar and sharing.

2. There is more productive than counterproductive participation during fingerplays, games, and songs—the activities that involve all the children.

3. The average number of times a child participated (either productively or counterproductively) over the week is 11 times. All children except one participated counterproductively at least once. The most counterproductive participation by one child is 14; the average is 4.

As planned, Molly takes her tallied instrument and initial conclusions to Camisha's office to discuss the results. Camisha greets her in the doorway and apologizes, saying that she is unavailable for about 3 days because of state reports but suggests that in the meantime Molly visit the college's lab school to observe a model circle time. Camisha adds that she would be able to provide a substitute for 1 day. Molly is delighted in the opportunity to use her instrument to gather further information for possible follow-through plans.

Follow-Through Plans

When Molly meets with Camisha, she enthusiastically shares her tallied data (Figure 11.3), initial conclusions, and the following insights from her observational visit to the lab school.

- Buck, the teacher of the 4-year-old group at the lab school, had two 10-minute circle times: one just before and one after outdoor time. Each began with action songs. Molly observed only 2% counterproductive participation.

- With the children shoulder-to-shoulder as they sat on the floor in a circle, the first circle time began with a lively song then engaged all children in a unique sharing experience. The child whose name had been drawn the day before had taken home the instant camera to snap a picture of an activity shared with someone else. As the child explained the scenario, the children seemed interested to hear every word about the adventure as they passed the photo around; they asked questions and made comments. With Buck's help the children then wrote the adventure in a group dictated story. Buck wrote the story on a large tablet and clipped the photo to the story so that children could "reread" the story all day. The next day, Buck typed the story, photocopied the picture, and entered it into the class book that could be reread throughout the year in the language center.

- The second circle time was arranged to help the children transition from outdoors to indoors, as well as to develop language and social skills. Buck divided this circle time into two smaller groups using the teacher assistant to lead one of the groups; the children participated in various combinations of singing songs or participating in fingerplays, games, story time, or discussions.

- Buck told Molly that shortening the duration; preparing ahead of time and having all the needed materials gathered; varying the activities; personalizing and modifying the songs, games, and activities; giving the children props to use whenever possible; choosing activities based on the children's interests and need for active involvement; and asking the child(ren) who had counterproductive behaviors to assist in planning circle time helped him have productive circle times.

- Molly also noticed that Buck's wall calendar had the name of the helper-of-the-day printed on each square. Buck told Molly that he eliminated the traditional calendar activity during circle time because he had observed too many counterproductive behaviors while children were asked to sit and wait for this abstract experience.

Camisha smiles as she listens to Molly's insights and acknowledges that Molly has paired two important steps. First, she found out what the participation looked like in her room and analyzed what was and wasn't working. Then she took the opportunity to learn new ideas. Molly thanks Camisha for sending her to see Buck's successful circle time. She says that she has gotten many worthwhile suggestions and that she would like to try out some of them. The children in Buck's class were developing the sense of togetherness that Molly hopes her group will develop from productive circle participation.

Molly and Camisha both agree that small changes are most effective for the children and the teacher. Camisha proposes that Molly begin her circle changes by decreasing the time to 10 minutes and planning activities that involve the children in movement. Molly agrees and adds that she thought she would enlist the help of Bailey, the child with the most counterproductive participation, to choose the games and/or book. Molly decides to have the circle time when the children come in from outside—offering a movement activity followed by a short story, flannelboard, or game. Camisha and Molly agree to meet again in 2 weeks to review the circle participation. Molly plans to eventually have two circles times as Buck modeled. Her 4-year-olds could benefit from more group activities.

As Molly walks back to her classroom, she feels empowered by Camisha. From the start, Camisha let her disclose her area of concern and suggested she gather the data and visit another school for modeling. Camisha put Molly in charge of her own learning, and now Molly is on her way to facilitating productive and successful circle times.

Primary Grade Example

Lee, the principal of Fitzgerald School (grades K–3), provides dynamic leadership through effective use of staff meetings. In today's meeting, Lee reports the highlights from last week's regional workshop for preschool directors and primary school principals in which the discussion topic was based on the article from *Young Children* entitled, "Gender Equity in Early Childhood Education" (Marshall, Robeson, & Keefe, 1999). Lee extends the conversation with his staff, and many opinions regarding how teachers foster gender equity are shared. The principal then shows some videotape clips of teachers leading small group discussions in another school. Lee directs his teachers to look at whom the video teachers call on when questions are asked. He points out that even though teachers intend to be unbiased and perceive themselves to be unbiased when choosing either a girl or a boy to call on, gender fairness is an area that needs constant review. The teachers begin to wonder if unintended preferences can creep into their goal to choose children equitably.

Much discussion is generated by the teachers about their own personal experiences with gender fairness in their classrooms. One teacher, Dakota, suspects that the subject being taught may produce unconscious biases (e.g., subscribing to stereotypes of boys being better and more interested in math than girls). She suggests that a classroom study could help raise consciousness. Another teacher, Giancarlo, thinks that teachers may call on boys more often than girls as a way to manage the class; in his experiences, boys have often been the eager hand-wavers. He is interested in

Do teachers call on boys more than on girls?

finding out whether girls raise their hands as often as boys and if teachers call on children of one gender more often than those of the other. Practice Activity 11.2 will help you to construct an instrument to collect these data.

PRACTICE ACTIVITY 11.2

Construction of a Tally Event Sampling Instrument

In this activity you will have the opportunity to apply your understanding of tally event sampling. Your task will be to design an effective grid to collect the requested information for the Fitzgerald School teachers.

Let's return to the teachers' meeting for more details. The team of teachers decides to gather data to analyze the gender distribution of student responses to teachers' questions in their school. (The principal is enlisted to collect the data on the instrument designed by the teachers. He will use the observation windows so that the teachers will not be aware of when they are being observed.) The teachers choose tally event sampling to determine how many times girls and boys raise their hands in response to teachers' questions and the relative frequency with which each teacher calls on boys or girls. In order to compare the results, the data

(continued)

will be collected during math time in each classroom over a period of a month, and each teacher will be observed four times.

Having agreed on the event and determining that no event terms need to be defined, the next step is to develop the categories. The following categories are chosen:

HAND-RAISERS:　　　　　girls/boys
TEACHER CALLS ON:　　　girls/boys

Using the categories defined above, construct a grid and fill in the following skeleton form. Give thought to using two levels of horizontal or vertical categories (see Figure 11.2 for use of subcategories creating a second horizontal level).

Tally Event Sampling of Boy/Girl Hand-Raising and Teachers' Responses

School/Grade:

Date: Time:

Observer: Teachers:

                                             Children:

Event: (Define the event.)

Codes: (Fill in codes and meanings, if any are used.)

Instructions:

_____

(Fill in horizontal categories, then add vertical lines between categories.)

_____

Teacher 1

_____

Teacher 2

_____

Teacher 3

_____

Teacher 4 and so on listing the primary grade teachers

_____

Comments:

Interpreting the Data

After the pilot test of the grid and measurement of inter-rater reliability, the data can be collected and examined to further the teachers' understanding of gender fairness in one subject area (math) at their school. The staff will have a precise picture of the gender-related question-and-answer patterns by asking the following types of questions.

- Given the boy:girl ratios, does one gender in an individual classroom account for a disproportionate share of hand-raisers?
- What is the relationship between the gender of hand-raisers and the gender of those who are chosen?
- Do individual teachers have gender-preference patterns?
- Are there changes that the entire staff wants to work on?
- Are there teachers who seem to be gender equitable and could act as role models for teachers who may want to improve in this area?

Suppose the data from a classroom with an even number of boys and girls show that the teachers called on girls 28 times during math but called on boys 46 times; thus, the girls answered questions 38% of the time and the boys answered questions 62% of the time. The hypothetical data also show that the girls raised their hands 10% less often than the boys did. The staff for this classroom are astounded and disturbed by these typical results. As a group, they examine individual teacher data and find that the boy-choice trend is fairly equally distributed throughout all the classrooms. The principal continues his investigation by sampling during other times of the day, using both small and total class groups. Comparing the responses during different curriculum times will provide information about consistency in gender response choices during the entire day. Additional data will help the teachers draw sound conclusions. With a broad understanding the teachers can then develop strategies to foster gender equity throughout the curriculum areas.

The results of this gender inquiry may also lead to additional teaching strategies beyond calling on boys and girls equally; the teachers may consider checking gender access to computers, providing girl and boy models of achievement in every area, balancing female–male language usage, and monitoring children's reactions to others' mistakes. Striving to reduce biases and audit gender equity adds another dimension, or perhaps for some a renewed awareness, to the teacher's role. In this instance the consciousness raising was generated from observations using tally event sampling.

APPLICATIONS

Strengths and Limitations

The greatest strengths of tally event sampling are efficiency and simplicity, whether the observer is the teacher or someone else. Once the instrument has been constructed, making tally marks takes little time. If the observation does not include the teacher's behaviors, then the teacher can keep the form nearby on a clipboard or condense the form to fit on a large index card and keep it in a pocket until complete. Event sampling is time-saving because it allows the teacher to continue classroom activities while waiting for the selected event to happen. Tally marks can be collected easily, even in the busiest of classrooms.

The quantitative data collected through tally event sampling can be compared and analyzed quickly and impartially. The preschool circle participation example afforded a beginning experience. Chapters 12 and particularly 13 discuss quantitative analysis further.

Quantitative data allow the observer to compare changes over time when the systematic observation follows the process of initial observation, then intervention strategies, then follow-up observation. In the preschool example, if Molly had Al come back and observe her circle time after she'd implemented her planned changes for a fair amount of time (perhaps 3 months later), her quantitative analysis of the observational data would be different, showing improved productive circle time participation. When this process is used, another advantage emerges—confirmation of effective teaching strategies (Hintze & Shapiro, 1995).

The versatility of this approach provides for observations of one teacher or child, but more often for groups of teachers, children, or their interactions. Tally event sampling can be used with a wide variety of moderate or infrequently occurring topics. Think back through this chapter's examples; this method can be used by teachers for individual classrooms or by entire staffs for identified events schoolwide. Using event sampling to improve teacher effectiveness or the school environment is a potent way to build teamwork.

The major limitation of tally event sampling is that recording frequencies generally takes the behavior out of context. The tally approach method does not record what takes place before or after the event. Tally event sampling does not identify the cause of the event; it is limited to recording how often an identified event occurs.

>>

OFF ON YOUR OWN 11.1

Preschool/Kindergarten Tally Event Sampling: Motor Development

Many educators believe that children will develop gross motor skills on their own if the equipment is available (although it is usually available only outdoors). According to Miller's study of preschool children's motor development (as cited in Poest, Williams, Witt, & Atwood, 1990), however, "children allowed to play in well-equipped motor play areas scored significantly below normal in motor development compared to those provided with planned motor activity centers and guided movement experiences" (p. 4).

Suppose the teachers at Center X observe that children often use the equipment for specified purposes, such as the climbing structures for dramatic play and the tire swing (with little motion) for socializing. As a preliminary step before designing a planned motor development program, the teachers need a detailed understanding of how the children are using the outside equipment so that the motor development program can be planned according to the children's needs. The teachers' task, then, is to determine how often the children in the center use the outside equipment for motor development and how often it is used for other specified purposes unrelated to motor skills. The data collection will require specific information regarding what other uses the children have for the equipment. For this action project you are invited to construct a tally event sampling grid on which these teachers may record the requested information.

>>>

> QUICK REVIEW <

1. Explain how the purposes for using tally event sampling and ABC narrative event sampling differ.

2. Observers appropriately select the tally event sampling method when they want to determine how _____ an identified event occurs.

3. The tally event sampling method is used primarily to observe individuals.
    ❑ True

    ❑ False

4. What kind of data is collected with tally event sampling?
    ❑ Qualitative

    ❑ Quantitative

5. Which one of the following is *not* a possible topic for tally event sampling?
    a. Teacher's use of conflict resolution
    b. Children's requests for help from adults in classroom
    c. Types of questions teachers ask during and after reading stories
    d. Children's language interactions (who speaks to whom in what language)

6. When observers choose to design their own tally event sampling instrument, they choose two sets of categories (horizontal and vertical) that intersect to form a _____ in which the tallies are collected.

7. Inter-rater reliability is
   a. the degree of agreement between observers when they observe the same setting at the same time using the same instrument.
   b. the frequency with which observers engage in observation using a stop watch.
   c. the process of trying out an observational instrument to assess its workability.
   d. an educational concern that is to be studied and is stated as an interrogatory.

8. A major strength of the tally event sampling method is efficiency and simplicity in recording.
   ❏ True
   ❏ False

9. The principal limitation of the tally event sampling method is that it generally takes the behavior under study out of _____.

10. The tally event sampling instrument collects data using a predetermined sampling period.
    ❏ True
    ❏ False

TAKE A MOMENT TO REFLECT

Personal Reflection

Do you remember in the preschool example, Camisha (the director) empowered Molly by asking Molly to identify her own teaching problem, giving her tools to solve the problem, and offering support that facilitated the process? Empowerment is further exemplified in this reflection.

After Sophie's (5; 2) first few days in kindergarten, she was unhappy to go to school because she was teased by two boys that her father called "bullies." When Sophie's mother picked her up from school on the fourth day and Sophie was in tears, her mom knew Sophie needed help in learning how to handle this difficult situation. After arriving home, her mom said, "Sophie when those boys bother you again you just walk up to them and yell NO right in their faces!" Then Sophie's mom role-played with her until Sophie felt confident in her new skill. When Sophie's mom picked her up from school the next day, Sophie beamed from ear to ear and reported, "Mom, it really worked. When I yelled NO, the boys took off running."

Sophie is fortunate to have a mom who understands how to support and empower children. This parenting scenario may be an extraordinary case, but it is not an isolated one. Children often experience empowerment in school; teachers are alert to such opportunities moment by moment. Think about empowerment in your life and reflect on the following questions.

1. Recall a childhood incident in which you felt empowered or wished you had felt empowered to stand up for yourself. What was the situation, the empowerment, and the skill learned in the situation you recalled?

2. Is this situation an example of a topic that could be used for a tally event sampling in an early childhood classroom? If so, sketch the grid.

Ethical Reflection

NAEYC Ideal I-3A.1 is "to establish and maintain relationships of trust and cooperation with co-workers" (Feeney & Kipnis, 1992, p. 6). Reflect on the primary grade example in this chapter and think about how the teachers at Fitzgerald School fulfill this ethical responsibility.

12 Observing Children and Teachers at Work by Using Time Sampling

Aimee, a student teacher in early childhood education, would like to observe what teachers say in the classroom. Her initial items include:

- Provides new information
- Gives directions
- Restates what child said
- Asks questions
- Answers questions
- Praises
- Encourages
- Greets
- Criticizes
- Talks with other adults

What problems might be encountered if Aimee uses tally event sampling to observe teacher verbalizations in a dynamic classroom? Imagine if there were more than one teacher in the classroom.

N o doubt you can imagine Aimee's weary hand and frazzled mind as she tries to observe and tally everything the teacher says; tally event sampling is not a practical means of studying events that occur rapidly. Fortunately, there is a more feasible observational method to apply in such cases—**time sampling**—which is the focus of this chapter.

OVERVIEW OF OBSERVING USING TIME SAMPLING

Description

Tally event sampling and time sampling are close cousins. Both methods are appropriate for studying one or more than one child's or teacher's behaviors and interactions. The distinction to bear in mind is that time sampling is used when observing behaviors or interactions that occur too frequently for efficient tally event sampling. In the vignette example, you realized that an observer using the tally event sampling method could not keep up with the continuous flow of data generated by teachers' verbalizations. Therefore, if data would be missed by using tally event sampling because the behaviors or events under study occur in rapid succession, time sampling is the observational method of choice.

The unique component of time sampling is the use of time samples (predetermined units of time) to guide the observer's attention throughout the observational period. These time samples may be specified in two ways. In the first, which we shall call the **concurrent time-sampling technique,** a single time unit stipulates how long the observer observes and records before moving on to the next subject. In other words, observation and coding are done concurrently within the same time unit. For example, an observer might observe and code a child's social play for 30 seconds before moving on to the next child on the list. Figure 12.1, drawing on Parten's (1932) classic study, illustrates the concurrent technique of time sampling.

The second technique of specifying time sampling units, which we'll call the **delayed time-sampling technique,** identifies two separate time units: the first specifies how long the observer observes and the second how long the observer codes. The observer watches intently through the first time unit and then turns his or her attention to coding; thus the coding is delayed until after the behavior has been observed. Using this format, an observer might listen to one teacher for 20 seconds and then use 10 seconds to code the verbalization(s); following this system for all teachers in the classroom, the observer rotates observations in a prearranged order. This technique is preferred when the observer might have difficulty observing and coding simultaneously; an example is presented in Figure 12.2.

Once the time sampling units have been specified, the time sampling method is much like tally event sampling. Figures 12.1 and 12.2 illustrate easy-to-use recording grids (introduced in Chapter 11) to collect information in clear sets of defined categories. These sets of categories are arranged horizontally or vertically to produce the best fit. In Figure 12.1, the categories of social play were listed horizontally and the list of children vertically, whereas in Figure 12.2, the teachers were listed horizontally and the types of verbalizations vertically.

Time sampling yields quantitative data about the group as a whole and about individuals. Thus, while observers may compile information about a group of children in general (e.g., the incidence of types of social play in a preschool classroom), they may also learn specific information about individuals (e.g., the predominance of individuals' social play types).

Time Sampling of Children's Social Play

Center or School/Age level or Grade:
Date: Time:
Observer: Teacher:
                                         Children:

Event: Children's social play using Parten's (1932) categories (see reverse side for
                definitions)

Instructions: Observe each child for 30 seconds, and mark a tally for type of social play
                demonstrated. Rotate 30-second observational and coding time units from child-to-
                child throughout observational period.

Type of social play / Child	Onlooker Play	Parallel Play	Associative Play	Cooperative Play
Child 1				
Child 2				
Child 3				
And so on				

Figure 12.1
Concurrent technique of time sampling example.

Purpose

Time sampling observations are used for the methodical investigation of behaviors that occur in rapid succession. The procedures of time sampling help observers efficiently collect representative data that may be used to learn more about children and to refine teaching strategies, the curriculum, or the environment. Time sampling can be a systematic and efficient observational method that produces quantitative data.

Guidelines for Constructing Time Sampling Instruments

The thoughtful construction of time sampling instruments can produce the means to study rapidly occurring behaviors. The steps discussed in this section are summarized in Box 12.1.

Time Sampling of Teachers' Verbalizations

Center or School/Age level or Grade:

Date: Time:

Observer: Teacher:

                                                            Children:

Event: Teacher verbalizations

Instructions: Observe each teacher for 20 seconds, and then take 10 seconds to mark a tally for
                      each verbalization demonstrated. Rotate 30-second focus from teacher-to-teacher
                      throughout observational period.

Teacher / Verbalization	Teacher	Teacher Assistant	Student Teacher
Provides new information			
Gives directions			
Restates what child said			
Asks questions			
Answers questions			
Praises			
Encourages			
Criticizes			
Greets			
Talks with other adults			
Other			

Figure 12.2
Delayed technique of time sampling example.

Box 12.1

Designing a Time Sampling Instrument

1. Select an appropriate topic, formulate an observational question, and define the event.
2. Research the topic in libraries and classrooms.
3. Identify clear, distinct categories.
   - Generate sets of categories, vertical and horizontal.
   - Define the categories when necessary.
   - Select a sign or category system.
   - Decide if category codes are needed.
4. Design a recording form.
   - Use the heading modeled in Figures 12.1 and 12.2.
   - Use the categories to construct a grid.
   - Specify the time sampling units.
   - Plan to collect the data in the form of tallies or durations.
   - Label a space for comments at the bottom of the form.
5. Pilot test the instrument. Revise, if necessary, and pilot test again.
6. Establish inter-rater reliability.

The selection of an appropriate topic to study is the first step in using time sampling. The topic should focus on overt behaviors that occur rapidly. For example, the types of children's play are overt behaviors because the observer can easily see if children are playing alone or with others and, with a bit more attention, if they are merely playing next to one another or are truly engaging in cooperative play. The causes of children's derogatory comments about other children on the playground are usually not apparent to an observer and are therefore inappropriate for time sampling (and other observational methods). Utilizing the time sampling method, observers may study such diverse topics as gross motor activity during recess, child–child interactions, and teacher responses to children.

In Practice Activity 12.1 you will generate a short list of topics appropriate for the time sampling observational method.

PRACTICE ACTIVITY 12.1

Appropriate Topics for the Time Sampling Observational Method

List three topics that can best be studied through the time sampling observational method. Remember that the behaviors to be observed must be overt and must occur rapidly. You may include topics focusing on children and/or teachers.

(continued)

Examples:

• Child–child verbalizations

• Types of interactions among children in an inclusive classroom

• Primary grade teachers' verbalizations during math time

1.

2.

3.

After choosing time sampling for the topic at hand, the observer formulates an observational question. A clear question specifies a manageable portion of the topic to observe. For example, a teacher who is committed to an anti-bias curriculum may ask, "What types of play do children engage in with culturally diverse materials during free choice time?"

Library research time, classroom observation, and the application of previous experience help the constructor of a time sampling instrument to investigate the topic and identify the precise categories to be observed. The categories should be mutually exclusive, but they may represent either a sign or category system (see Chapter 11), whichever provides the most appropriate information. Once selected, the behavioral categories should be clearly defined so that all users of the instrument interpret them in the same way. If category definitions are lengthy, they are usually printed on a separate sheet or on the back of the recording form so as not to take up valuable space. Definitions are reviewed before the observation so that once in the classroom the observer will need to refer to them only for occasional reminders or clarifications. If the labels are long or cumbersome and would take up needed space on the recording form, the observer may use codes or abbreviations for the categories to be observed.

Working with well-defined categories, the observer is ready to design a recording form (e.g., Figures 12.1 and 12.2). Space is provided at the top for the heading. Then one set of categories is listed horizontally near the top of the grid (e.g., types of social play), and the other set of categories is listed vertically down the left side of the page where there is more room (e.g., names of children). Lines are drawn horizontally and vertically to mark off the two sets of categories, and a grid is completed as in Chapter 11. In many studies observers employ more than two sets of categories, so additional organization and detailing may be necessary.

The most difficult tasks in constructing a time sampling instrument are choosing either the concurrent or delayed technique and specifying the length of the time sampling units. To create a feasible observational schedule that produces the requisite information, the observer must do some pilot testing. Previous experience and best guesses may help, but the greatest aid will be trying out the

Time sampling is an appropriate observational method to use when the behaviors or events under study occur in rapid succession.

time sampling schedule under real conditions. There is no substitute for hands-on experience.

The observer considers the type of time sampling data that will best answer the observational question. If the observer is interested in the frequency of behaviors, recording tallies is appropriate. For example, an observer using the instrument in Figure 12.2 is interested in how often teachers exhibit various verbalizations to children; tallies would specify the frequencies for easy comparisons among types of verbalizations and among teachers. As an alternative, the observer may choose to monitor observed behaviors with a stopwatch to answer questions about the pro-portionate duration of each (e.g., time of teacher talk versus student talk in a third grade classroom). Instructions may also be given to combine tally- and duration-recording as in Figure 12.3.

Once the time sampling units are in place, a judgment needs to be made about how long to observe and during which parts of the day. If a study focuses on teach-ers' behaviors, the observer will sample their behaviors during all parts of the day and an abundance of data may be collected within a week. Note, however, that the high mental concentration necessary for observation may prompt the observer to visit the classroom at various times over the course of several weeks rather than a whole day per visit; the goal may be to observe each time period (free play, snack, outside time, etc.) three times. If, on the other hand, a primary grade teacher's math instruction skills are examined, the observer would collect data only during math time but on several different occasions.

The instrument is now ready for pilot testing so that any weaknesses may be identified. After adjustments are complete and the pilot test is successful, the observer establishes inter-rater reliability (detailed in Chapter 13) in preparation for data collection in a real classroom.

INTEGRATION OF CLASSROOM SITUATIONS AND OBSERVATION

Preschool Example

Blocks and preschool go together like apple blossoms and spring, and of course, there are good reasons why blocks are a staple of early childhood centers (Hirsch, 1996). The mere presence of blocks in a classroom, however, does not guarantee that children use them and learn from them. Teachers are responsible for organizing blocks and making them accessible to children, providing additional interesting materials to use with blocks, and extending children's work with blocks. Blocks offer endless learning potentials, but skilled teachers are required to fulfill them.

A child care director attended a directors' workshop on designing observational instruments and worked with a small group on an instrument to observe specific ways classroom teams of teachers interact with children in the block area. The directors sketched out a time sampling instrument, using the delayed technique (see Figure 12.3), to systematically observe staffs' teaching strategies in the block area, pilot tested the instrument in one of the host's classrooms, and then established inter-rater reliability. Why did the directors select time sampling as an observational method when focusing on a teacher and assistants? You now know the answer—think about the frequency and types of behaviors to observe, and you will be on your way.

The directors decided to use a sign rather than category system when selecting teacher behaviors to observe in the block area because they were not interested in tallying every possible behavior they might see. Rather, the directors were motivated to record behaviors that support and extend children's block activities. Utilizing the delayed technique, they planned to systematically rotate their focus from one teacher to the next, observing each for 30 seconds and then coding for 30 seconds. A stopwatch was a critical piece of equipment; each observer started her or his stopwatch when beginning to observe, noted when the 30-second observational period was over, and then used the next 30 seconds to code (and write comments if desired). After the observer moved to the next teacher, the stopwatch was restarted and the observation/coding process was repeated. Pilot testing and the inter-rater reliability check proved this system to be productive.

To collect information about the duration of time teachers spend in and out of the block area, the directors elected to circle the tally marks in the "not present in the block area" category when the teacher was not in the block area for all of the

*Blocks offer children a wealth of learning
experiences in the early childhood classroom.*

observational time unit. Thus, a circled tally mark would indicate that the teacher was not present in the block area for all 30 seconds of a time unit. A simple tally would indicate that the teacher was not present in the block area for part of a 30-second observational time unit.

A few days after her return, the director tells her child care teachers and assistants that she wants to observe during free choice time to collect information for future staff discussions. She uses the same instrument to collect data during free choice periods in each classroom on three different days; Figure 12.3 presents the results from the 4-year-olds' room, staffed by a head teacher and two assistants.

Interpreting the Data

In the 4-year-old classroom taught by Evelyn and her two assistants, Dante and Mari, the director, Kemlyn, observes 1 hour of free choice time for 3 days using the observational form shown in Figure 12.3. During each day, she rotates her focus from teacher to teacher, observing for 30 seconds and then coding for 30 seconds. Thus, in 60 total minutes of daily observation in this classroom, she concentrates her attention on each of the three teachers for 20 minutes; of those 20 minutes, she observes for 10 minutes and codes for 10 minutes. Consequently, over the course of 3 days, she collects 30 minutes of data on each teacher and assistant.

While studying the data, Kemlyn is stunned to discover how infrequently children had the pleasure of an adult's company in the well-used block area. During her 90 minutes of observation (30 minutes per teacher and assistant), she made circled tallies (indicating not present in the block area for the entire 30-second observational time unit) for 61 minutes. She is particularly dissatisfied with her observations of Evelyn, the head teacher who was not present in the block area for 26 minutes. Perhaps her teaching skills in the block area are severely limited so she tends to avoid this area. It is also possible that as a head teacher she focuses on the children as a class rather than as individuals with unique strengths and interests. Whatever the reasons, Kemlyn realizes that the head teacher in the 4-year-olds' classroom is not modeling effective teaching strategies in the block area.

On the other hand, Kemlyn was delighted to see Dante frequently down on the carpet building with the children. For example, on one day he was involved in planning and constructing an elaborate cityscape with two boys. He was generous with his encouragement and asked two open questions ("What are you going to build next?" and "Where should I build my trade center?"). Dante wrapped a block in aluminum foil to simulate reflective building materials, thus modeling a new idea, and offered the roll of foil to the boys with the restriction that they could use it for only one building. The time sampling observations lead Kemlyn to conclude that Dante enjoys playing with the children but that his methods of extending children's activities in the block area are minimal (he extended his own very well). Kemlyn wants Dante to be able to step back from his involvement, observe the building in progress, and think about how he can best support the *children's* ideas rather than his own. At present, the children are only following his lead.

Time Sampling of Teaching Strategies in the Block Area

Center/Age Level: Mesa Office Park Child Care/4-year-olds

Dates: 11/18 to 11/20   Time: 9:30–10:30 A.M.

Observer: Kemlyn   Free choice (7 centers available)

                                                    Teacher: Evelyn

                                                    Assistants: Dante, Mari

                                                    Children: Twenty 4-year-olds

Event: Teaching strategies in the block area—teacher behaviors that support and extend children's block activities.

Instructions: Use the delayed technique with a stopwatch to observe one teacher for 30 seconds and then code for 30 seconds; rotate observations of teachers, and repeat throughout free choice time. Mark a tally for each behavior observed in the block area. Circle tally mark when teacher is "not present in block area" for an entire 30-second observational period.

Teacher / Behavior	Evelyn	Dante	Mari
Builds with child		⁄⁄⁄⁄ ⁄⁄⁄⁄ ⁄⁄⁄⁄ ⁄⁄⁄⁄ ⁄⁄⁄⁄ 29	
Offers materials		⁄⁄ 2	⁄⁄⁄⁄ ⁄ 6
Encourages	⁄⁄ 2	⁄⁄⁄⁄ ⁄⁄⁄⁄ ⁄⁄⁄⁄ ⁄ 16	⁄⁄⁄⁄ ⁄⁄⁄⁄ ⁄⁄⁄⁄ ⁄⁄⁄⁄ ⁄⁄ 22
Asks open questions	⁄ 1	⁄⁄⁄⁄ ⁄⁄⁄ 8	⁄⁄⁄⁄ ⁄⁄⁄⁄ ⁄⁄⁄⁄ ⁄⁄ 17
Models new ideas		⁄ 1	
Observes	⁄⁄ 2		
Not present in block area	⁄⁄		⁄⁄⁄⁄ ⁄⁄⁄⁄ ⁄⁄⁄
	Ⓘ = 26 min. + 2 partial time units	Ⓘ = 15 min.	Ⓘ = 20 min. + 13 partial time units

Figure 12.3
Time sampling: Block area teaching strategies.

(continued)

Comments:

Evelyn: *"How pretty!" "Good job!" "Remember, only waist high." (Lots of reminders about building rules, mediations of minor quarrels, some empty praise)*

Dante: *"What are you going to build next?" "Where should I build my trade center?"*

Mari: *"I wonder if the little counting bears in the manipulative area would fit inside your 'teensy' houses."*

Figure 12.3 *(Continued)*
Time sampling: Block area teaching strategies.

Mari floated in and out of the block area during all three of Kemlyn's visits. Although she never stopped to build with a child or take a few moments for observation, she did ask open questions to inquire about what the children were doing, encourage their constructions, and offer additional materials (e.g., "I wonder if the little counting teddy bears in the manipulative area would fit inside your 'teensy' houses"). Mari seems to support children in their activities, and Kemlyn hopes that her teaching skills will blossom with information and guidance.

Kemlyn is glad she included the "not present in block area" category; her idea of circling tally marks to specify 30-second periods not in the block area allows her to document the durations of teachers' absences from the area. In the "comments" section, she recorded verbatim quotes and other specifics she wanted to recall. For example, she noted that most of Evelyn's attention was on reminding children of the rules (e.g., height limits on building), mediating minor disputes about materials, and giving evaluative praise.

Follow-Through Plans

The data from the 4-year-olds' classroom are fairly typical of the data Kemlyn collected in the other classrooms. Kemlyn speculates that there are two major factors behind teachers' inability to work effectively in the block areas at Mesa Children's Center:

- *Teachers may not have the requisite knowledge to identify children's growth in the block area.* They may not know how building skills progress and what children might learn in the block area. Further, the teachers may not know how to interact with children in order to promote this growth.

- *Teachers lack observational skills.* Sound observational skills should enable teachers to assess individual children's building skills and interests and then aid in the formation of supportive strategies. In her center, however, Kemlyn concludes that there are no consistent efforts to collect information about children's growth in the block area.

Kemlyn decides to tackle the two parts of the block area problem through her bi-weekly staff meetings and continued education. She calls a friend on the board of the county chapter of the National Association for the Education of Young Children to ask for a speaker recommendation. She requests a person who is knowledgeable about stages of block building and learning opportunities in the block area and who will be able to guide teachers in planning supportive teaching strategies. This meeting will provide much needed information for the teachers. Two weeks later, Kemlyn will follow up with a workshop on anecdotal record keeping to begin the observational process. She makes plans to videotape children working in the block area in each classroom; clips will provide the basis for integrating the speaker's information about block building into the classrooms and for practicing anecdotal records. Finally, Kemlyn contacts the early childhood education department at the local college for course information and begins to consider how best to encourage her staff to continue professional training. Kemlyn enthusiastically anticipates collecting "new and improved" data on her time sampling instrument in 2 or 3 months.

Practice Activity 12.2 gives you a chance to try out a time sampling instrument for block area teaching strategies.

PRACTICE ACTIVITY 12.2

Block Area Teaching Strategies in a Kindergarten, First Grade, or Second Grade Classroom

Pilot test a copy of the time sampling instrument on block area teaching strategies in a kindergarten, first grade, or second grade classroom. Write down any modifications you would make. Remember that blocks are not the exclusive domain of children under age 5; their qualities extend far beyond.

Time Sampling of Teaching Strategies in the Block Area

Center/Age Level:
Dates: Time:
Observer: Teacher:
                                                   Assistants:
                                                   Children:

Event: Teaching strategies in the block area—teacher behaviors that
                  support and extend children's block activities.

Instructions: Use the delayed technique with a stopwatch to observe one
                  teacher for 30 seconds and then code for 30 seconds; rotate
                  observations of teachers, and repeat throughout free choice time.
                  Mark a tally for each behavior observed in the block area. Circle
                  tally mark when teacher is "not present in block area" for an entire
                  30-second observational period.

                                                              (continued)

Behavior \ Teacher			
Builds with child			
Offers materials			
Encourages			
Asks open questions			
Models new ideas			
Observes			
Not present in block area			
Comments:			

Primary Grade Example

A second grade teacher, Jorge, was intrigued by his summer reading, *The Art of Teaching Writing* (Calkins, 1994) and *How's It Going?* (Anderson, 2000), which sent his mind spinning with questions and ideas. He found Calkins' book well-stocked with thought-provoking commentary on the nourishment of children's writing, research and experience to back up the author's conclusions, and marvelous anecdotes selected from a wide diversity of children. Jorge found validation in his zeal to read to his students on a daily basis, for Calkins, too, believes that touching children with fabulous literature is a critical key to their own writing futures. He also gained encouragement to set aside predictable and generous time for his class to write three afternoons a week: Tuesdays, Wednesdays, and Fridays. Finally, Jorge welcomed Calkins' understanding of the mix of writing levels within his single classroom; she is familiar with the real world.

> Many second graders can just barely read their names; others are devouring the entire works of Roald Dahl and Patricia MacLachlan. Some write only captions underneath drawings; others write long chapter books and research reports. Some children

write with big, wobbly letters; others write with tiny, neat rows of cursive. (Calkins, 1994, p. 109)

In Anderson's book, Jorge found specific guidance for structuring effective writing conferences in which the teacher and student first converse "about the work the child is doing as a writer" and then "about how the child can become a better writer" (Anderson, 2000, p. 17). Jorge's goals were clarified after reading how Anderson taught his students to actively participate in writing conferences, how the students learned and used the vocabulary of writing, and how specific and useful his instruction was. Jorge's professional goal for the school year is to improve his own writing conferencing skills.

Once school is underway in the fall, Jorge wants to assess the types of feedback and guidance he currently gives to his second graders as the first step to expanding his skills as a writing teacher. He cares very much about the processes of teaching and learning in his classroom because he believes that both *what* and *how* he teaches is part of the same whole and that "the processes through which ideas are grasped and understood, which themselves are influenced by the conditions of teaching, give meaning to the content learned" (Eisner, 1998, p. 178). Jorge formulates the observational question, "What types of input do I give to children during the writing process?" and begins to work on an observational instrument to evaluate his responses to students' writing.

First Jorge considers possible behaviors to observe during writing periods. Drawing both on his reading and experience, he categorizes the "teacher's verbalizations" as follows:

Teacher's Verbalizations

- *Listens*—Teacher listens attentively to a child to help the child become a more critical reader of her or his own writing. *Example:* "Mr. Mendoza, listen to the end of my story: 'Aren't you glad an ankylosaurus won't bother your plants?' "

- *Praises descriptively*—Teacher is descriptive in his or her praise to pinpoint the writing skill the child demonstrated. *Example:* "Your question at the end of your story gives the reader a connection to you. As your reader, I felt as if you were talking just to me."

- *Gives information*—Teacher builds on a child's piece to help the child learn more about the craft of writing. *Example:* "Question-asking gives the reader something to think about. Writers use questions like this one at the end of their story to grab the readers' attention."

- *Refers to a published author*—Teacher points out how the writing skill under discussion has been effectively used by an author the child is familiar with. *Example:* "Roald Dahl used a technique similar to your question in *The BFG* when he spoke directly to his reader. Listen to this: 'If you can think of anything more terrifying than that happening to you in the middle of the night, then let's hear about it' (1988, p. 17). He really makes his readers pause and think."

- *Asks questions*—Teacher asks a child a question. *Example:* "I see you have written four different endings for your piece. Why don't you tell me how you plan to choose the best one for your report about the ankylosaurus?"
- *Answers question*—Teacher answers a child's question. *Example:* "Yes, I do think your question is an interesting way to end your report because it relates something that lived long ago to our present lives. Your question gives your reader a bit of a surprise."
- *Suggests an option*—Teacher suggests a change or addition to the child's writing. *Example:* "Sometimes authors end their piece with a question to give the reader something to think about. Why don't you try it?"
- *Gives opinionated approval without substance*—Teacher praises a child's writing while focusing on its subjective worth, not its substance. *Example:* "What a neat idea!"
- *Directs*—Teacher directs a change or addition to the child's writing. *Example:* "This question at the end doesn't have much to do with your report. Either take it out or show more of a connection."
- *Corrects*—Teacher corrects a child's writing. *Example:* This question at the end of your story needs a question mark."
- *Criticizes*—Teacher criticizes a child's writing. *Example:* "Oh my, you forgot an important punctuation point at the very end of your story."

Jorge's reading also encourages him to specify the object of a teacher's focus in writing conferences. His second set of categories includes the content of the writing, the design of the piece, the writing process, and editing; Jorge defines them as follows:

Focuses of Teacher's Attention

- *Content*—Teacher focuses on the subject matter of the child's writing. *Example:* "Your description of the frog on the ferris wheel makes me laugh!"
- *Design*—Teacher focuses on how the child has organized and shaped the piece (e.g., chronologically, thematically, snapshots), what the child emphasizes, and the pace of the piece. *Example:* "You have written three stories about your dog to tell about her personality and special abilities. Do you remember how Bernard Waber wrote several stories about Arthur? I'd like you to look at how his beginning and ending framed his stories, how the beginning and ending are linked. You might like to use this same technique from *An Anteater Named Arthur* (1999) to frame your stories about your dog."
- *Writing process*—Teacher focuses on the child's writing strategies through the drafting and revision processes. *Example:* "You planned to work on some different leads for your newspaper article. Tell me how that work is going."

- *Editing*—Teacher focuses on the child's use of paragraphs, sentence structure, word choice, grammar, punctuation, or spelling. *Example:* "Listen to the suspenseful first sentence of your story: 'My most vived memore of my childhood was when I saw the misterys Zorf here is where my story begins.' I needed to pause and take a breath after 'Zorf.' A period there will tell your reader to pause and get ready for the next sentence."

Next, Jorge begins to think about how to put his observational instrument together. Knowing that teachers may speak continuously for short periods and realizing that an observer cannot record or remember every statement, Jorge decides to construct a time sampling instrument with the delayed technique to deal with these rapidly occurring behaviors. He specifies the time sampling units as 20 seconds for observation and 30 seconds for coding. The 20 seconds for observation will provide time to observe the content of the teacher's comments, and the 30 seconds for coding will allow time for accurate coding of potentially complex verbalizations.

To obtain a comprehensive view of the writing instruction methods in place within his classroom, Jorge plans to collect data during three writing periods on different days. He designates the use of tallies on the recording sheet to document the frequency of each targeted teacher behavior. He rejects duration recording because of the impracticality of trying to record the duration of each statement; further, he is confident that the content of his messages to children, not their length, will be the key to his skills.

Jorge constructs the grid shown in Figure 12.4. He puts the smaller set of categories (focuses of teacher's attention) along the top and the more numerous set (teacher's verbalizations) down the side. Because there are many targeted behaviors, Jorge prints their definitions with examples on an attached sheet for reference. He pilot tests the instrument in a colleague's class when his students are with the music teacher and finds it to be satisfactory.

An immediate problem for Jorge is that he will not be able to observe himself. He decides not to use a tape recorder because he feels self-conscious about being on tape. Fortunately, Jorge is resourceful. He contacts the teacher-credentialing program at the area college and enlists the help of a student, Faranak. During a primary recess, they observe a fourth grade writing lesson and easily establish inter-rater reliability. Faranak visits Jorge during three writing lessons and collects the data in Figure 12.4. He obviously knows what Faranak is observing since he constructed the instrument and undoubtedly tries to demonstrate his best teaching strategies; this inherent limitation of self-evaluation, however, should not dissuade teachers from the process. Jorge still gains valuable information from the experience.

Interpreting the Data

Together, Jorge and Faranak compile the data from the three observations and total the rows and columns. Jorge is immediately critical of his emphasis on children's editing (42 inputs) and the content of their writing (41) rather than on the

Time Sampling of a Teacher's Input During Writing Time

School/Grade: Longfellow Elementary/Second Grade
Dates: 10/17, 10/18, 10/20
Observer: Faranak

Time: 1:00–1:40 P.M.
Teacher: Jorge
Children: 19

Event: Teacher's input during writing time—behaviors demonstrating type of teacher verbalization and focus of attention.

Instructions: Observe teacher for 20 seconds and code for 30 seconds; repeat throughout writing period. Mark each teacher input with a tally in the appropriate box.

Teacher's Verbalization \ Focus of Teacher's Attention	Content	Design	Writing Process	Editing	
Listens	///				3
Praises descriptively	‖‖ ///	//	‖‖ //	‖‖ ////	26
Gives information	‖‖ ‖‖ ///			‖‖ ‖‖ ‖‖ /	29
Refers to a published author		/			1
Asks question	////		‖‖ ///	‖‖	17
Answers question	‖‖ //				7
Suggests an option			////		4

Figure 12.4
Time sampling primary grade example: Teaching writing.

Gives opinionated approval w/o substance	✗✗/ /		✗✗/ ✗✗/	////	20
Directs			//	✗✗/ ///	10
Corrects					0
Criticizes					0
	41	3	31	42	
Comments:					

Figure 12.4 *(Continued)*
Time sampling primary grade example: Teaching writing.

design of their pieces (3) or their writing processes (31). He knows from reading Anderson's (2000) book that talking about the content of a piece does not usually help a child become a better writer. Jorge acknowledges how little information and concrete suggestions he gave to children about their designs and writing skills. Surely he has resources to share and can scaffold children's learning about writing. Although he is pleased to see that his descriptive praise outweighed his approval without substance, he plans to reduce the latter even further. He can just hear himself murmuring, "Oh, good; that's very nice." Such empty praise gives children nothing to hold on to, nothing to help them appreciate the substantive qualities of their writing.

Follow-Through Plans

Jorge's first plan is to collect 10 or 12 familiar books that have clear demonstrations of writing skills to have on hand for writing conferences. Jorge will review them in advance so that he can efficiently suggest concrete options to children. For example, he will include *When I Was Young in the Mountains* by Cynthia Rylant (1992) as a model for writing in the first person.

Frankly, Jorge needs to learn more about design issues. His students rarely vary from the pattern of writing their stories chronologically. At least Jorge wants to open their eyes to other possibilities: poems, letters, memoirs, and journalistic

The observational method of time sampling can collect data on rapidly occurring behaviors—for example, a teacher's inputs during writing conferences with children.

articles. A child can write about an idea in many different formats; being aware of one's choices is the first step.

Jorge plans to use note cards to collect explicit questions to ask and points to make. Jorge looks forward to inviting Faranak to check his progress in several months.

Your turn! In Practice Activity 12.3, you will study the data in Figure 12.4 and plan some specifics in Jorge's quest to improve his teaching of writing. Remember that observational instruments are only good if they increase knowledge about teachers and children and lead the way toward developmental practices.

PRACTICE ACTIVITY 12.3

Follow-Through Plans Based on a Time Sampling Instrument

Using the data in Figure 12.4, think about precise ways in which Jorge can improve his teaching of writing, and record three follow-through plans in the space that follows. You may wish to study box, row, or column totals.

Example: Since Jorge's writing conferences often featured discussions about content, explain to the entire class that the focus of writing conferences is on the student's work as a writer not on the content of a piece.

1.

2.

3.

APPLICATIONS

Strengths and Limitations

The time sampling observational method is adaptable to various subjects (e.g., one or more teachers or children) and can be an efficient and systematic means of observing rapidly occurring behaviors. A large number of observations can be collected in a short time with reasonable confidence that the samples are representative. The data collected are quantitative and are therefore useful for computing, studying, and comparing frequencies and percentages (more information in Chapter 13). The observer can remain unobtrusive and limit interference with the natural flow of events.

The limitations of time sampling revolve around the collection of quantitative data within predetermined units of time. The observer records frequencies but not qualities of events; therefore, the behaviors are not observed in context. Researchers further caution that time sampling may overestimate frequencies of behaviors and inaccurately record durations (Mann, Ten Have, Plunkett, & Meisels, 1991). The observer, as always, needs to match the information required with the most appropriate observational method.

>>

OFF ON YOUR OWN 12.1

Constructing a Time Sampling Form to Observe Stages of Children's Block Play

Study the following summary of stages of block building (Hirsch, 1996):

Stage 1:   Blocks are carried around, not used for construction. This stage applies to the very young child.

Stage 2:   Building begins. Children make mostly rows, either horizontal (on the floor) or vertical (stacking). There is much repetition in this early block building.

Stage 3: Bridging—two blocks with a space between them, connected by a third block—is used.

Stage 4: Enclosures—blocks placed in such a way that they enclose a space—are made. Bridging and enclosures are among the earliest technical building problems that children have to solve. They occur soon after a child begins to use blocks regularly.

Stage 5: With age, children become steadily more facile and imaginative in their block building. They use more blocks and create more elaborate designs, using pattern and balance.

Stage 6: Naming of structures for dramatic play begins. Before this stage, children also may have named their structures, but the names were not necessarily related to the function of the building.

Stage 7: Block buildings often reproduce or symbolize actual structures the children know, and there is a strong impulse toward dramatic play around the block structures. (pp. 142–148)*

Construct a time sampling instrument to systematically observe many children's stages of block building within a classroom. The tasks are as follows:

- State your specific observational question, and define the event.
- Decide on labels or codes for each stage.
- Specify the use of the concurrent or delayed technique and the length of the time units.
- Elect to use tallies or observe the durations of the behaviors. Consider the advantages and disadvantages of each.
- Determine how long you will observe during which portions of the day and over what period of time.
- Construct a recording instrument; the following will get you started.

Stages of Block Building

Center/Age level:

Date: Time:

Observer: Teacher:

                                               Children:

Definitions and Codes:

Event:

Instructions:

Stage Child	Stage 1	Stage 2	Stage 3	Stage 4	Stage 5	Stage 6	Stage 7
Child 1							
Child 2							
Child 3							
And so on							

Comments:

Arrange to observe a preschool when children have access to the block area. Pilot test your instrument, and then answer the following questions:

- Were your definitions and codes clear, or were you unsure of how to code some behaviors?
- How did your specification of observational and coding time units work out?
- Do you need to make some adjustments? If so, describe.

Next, choose the data from two children to discuss. Begin by responding to the following questions:

- What stages of block building did each child demonstrate? Was one stage most descriptive of her or his play?
- If you were each child's teacher, how could you best support his or her block play?

> QUICK REVIEW <

1. In this chapter the observational method of time sampling was introduced as a means of collecting representative samples of data on

   a. antecedents, behaviors, and consequences.

   b. rapidly occurring behaviors.

   c. developmental milestones.

   d. materials and environments.

2. An appropriate behavior to observe with a time sampling instrument is the autonomous behavior of one preschool child during free choice time.

   ❑ True

   ❑ False

3. An appropriate behavior to observe with a time sampling instrument is the choice of recess activities for all first grade children.

   ❑ True

   ❑ False

4. A time sampling instrument specifies that the observer observe for 20 seconds and then code for 10 seconds. This format is an example of the

   a. concurrent technique.

   b. delayed technique.

5. A time sampling instrument specifies that the observer observe and code for 20 seconds. This format is an example of the

   a. concurrent technique.

   b. delayed technique.

6. Data collected on a time sampling instrument in the form of tallies is quantitative.

   ❑ True

   ❑ False

7. In the preschool example, Kemlyn wanted to focus on teaching strategies that support and extend children's block area activities rather than on all possible behaviors. Her teacher behavior categories were thus an example of

   a. a sign system.

   b. a category system.

8. When using the time sampling method, observers focus on naturally occurring behaviors.

   ❑ True

   ❑ False

9. The time sampling method is an appropriate choice for observing the block activities of a single child.

   ❑ True

   ❑ False

10. Time sampling lends itself to a quantitative analysis of data and is therefore best suited to topics in which the observer wants to compare frequencies.

   ❑ True

   ❑ False

TAKE A MOMENT TO REFLECT

Personal Reflection

Evelyn, Dante, and Mari are fortunate to have a director who will plan for and support their professional development. Kemlyn's organization of workshops to present information about developmental growth in the block area and anecdotal record keeping promotes learning on the job. Reflect on your own similar experiences.

1. Recall colleagues or supervisors who have stimulated your professional development. Specifically, what did you learn from them? If you have not had practical work experience, describe one or two teachers who have tangibly contributed to your knowledge bank and personal growth.

2. What relationship do you see between professional development and job burnout?

Ethical Reflection

NAEYC Ideal I-3A.3 is "to support co-workers in meeting their professional needs and in their professional development" (Feeney & Kipnis, 1992, p. 8). Think about two or three efforts Kemlyn made in the preschool example to fulfill this ethical responsibility.

13

Designing Observational Instruments to Use in the Early Childhood Classroom

Students in an observation class are asked to think of a variety of classroom topics that hold personal interest. Recall in Chapter 12, for example, that a child care director was concerned about teachers' interactions with children in the block area and that a second grade teacher wanted to evaluate his strategies for teaching writing.

Some students consider topics regarding children's physical, cognitive, psychosocial, and creative development in the classroom. Other students consider topics regarding teachers' strategies, roles, and management approaches. Still other students have questions about the effectiveness of a curriculum or environment. What one topic holds substantial interest for you?

A s an active reader of the previous chapters, you have probably raised some of your own questions about children and classroom processes—even without the prompt in the above vignette. Because appropriate previously-constructed instruments will not always be available, you will need the observational tools and skills to respond to questions and problems that arise for you. This chapter is devoted to the process of designing and using an observational instrument to find answers to specific questions. Box 13.1 lists the critical steps in designing and using observational instruments.

Box 13.1

Steps in Designing and Using Observational Instruments

1. Select an appropriate topic, and formulate an observational question.
2. Select an appropriate method of observation. If using the tally event sampling or time sampling method, define the event.
3. Research the topic in libraries and classrooms.
4. Identify clear, distinct categories.
5. Design a recording form.
6. Pilot test the instrument. Revise, if necessary, and pilot test again.
7. Establish inter-rater reliability.
8. Collect data.
9. Analyze and present the data.
10. Interpret the data.
11. Formulate follow-through plans.

Although the steps in Box 13.1 are presented in a sequential order, observers may need to backtrack several times during the design process. For example, after doing some pilot testing (Step 6), an observer may discover that the original observational question (Step 1) is unclear and requires refinement or that some confusing definitions need to be reworked (Step 4). Such backtracking is a valuable component of the design process; thoughtful observers frequently reevaluate previous work and remain open to productive adjustments.

The steps of designing an observational instrument are described in this chapter, and an instrument to study parent and child separations at child care centers will be constructed as the classroom example to illustrate each step. Most terms are not defined because very little of the information is new. This chapter, rather, serves to synthesize the information presented in previous chapters. The steps may be applied to the design of a checklist, rating scale, tally event sampling instrument, or time sampling instrument, but of course, an observer beginning with an observational question considers the workability of a greater variety of methods (i.e., running records, anecdotal records, and ABC narrative event sampling).

SELECT AN APPROPRIATE TOPIC, AND FORMULATE AN OBSERVATIONAL QUESTION

A useful observational topic is explicit and manageable rather than general and vague; as a result, the topic suggests specific categories to observe. For example, studying how

Observational questions may focus on children, teachers, programs, and environments. Each observer has unique questions and concerns.

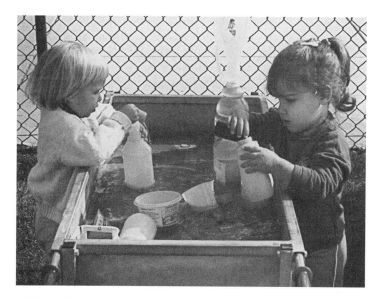

parents and children separate at a child care center adequately suggests observable categories, whereas studying *imagination* does not. A productive technique of further narrowing the topic is to form a question to study. One question represents a workable initial focus and leads to a precise delineation of the specifics to be observed.

Classroom Example

At the conclusion of the staff meeting at High Street Child Care Center, Winona, a first year teacher quietly asks her mentor, Bessie, if she can spare a few minutes. In the privacy of Bessie's room, Winona's lower lip trembles as she explains how the children in her class don't seem to like her. Her evidence is that most of the children don't want to stay at school, cling to their parents in the morning, and cry when their parents leave. She pleadingly asks Bessie if she will observe her to see what she is doing wrong.

Bessie puts an arm around Winona's shoulders and reminds her that it is only the third week of school and that many young children find separating from their parents difficult, particularly if it is a relatively new experience. Bessie, however, also acknowledges Winona's assessment that most of the children are having separation problems and suspects there are teacher and parent strategies to help children feel comfortable and welcome when they first arrive at school. Bessie tells Winona she needs a few days to work on an observation instrument but that she will be ready next week.

Bessie sets to work, eager to help the new teacher placed under her mentoring wing. She devises the following observational question: How frequently do Winona and the parents demonstrate strategies to help children successfully separate from their parents and transition to school?

SELECT AN APPROPRIATE METHOD OF OBSERVATION

After formulating an observational question, the appropriate method of observation may be quickly apparent to observers or the potential effectiveness of each method may need to be evaluated. This book presents the following methods:

- Running records
- Anecdotal records
- Checklists
- Rating scales
- ABC narrative event sampling
- Tally event sampling
- Time sampling

After a review of each method's strengths and limitations, the choice is made on the basis of which method will best answer the observational question.

Classroom Example

As Bessie reviews the observational methods familiar to her, she quickly rules out the methods of running records, anecdotal records, and ABC narrative event sampling because these will not accommodate group data or yield the quantitative data needed to answer the observational question. She also rejects checklists and rating scales; these methods will not produce the frequency data Bessie wants for a fair evaluation of Winona over several days. The list of methods is narrowed to tally event sampling and time sampling. A reassessment of her question helps Bessie make the final choice (How frequently do Winona and the parents demonstrate strategies to help children successfully separate from their parents and transition to school?). She knows parents bring their children to school individually over a 15-minute period, so she anticipates she can record data for each arrival; tally event sampling is the observational method of choice.

Bessie specifies child–parent separation as the event to observe and defines it as the process of children separating from their parents upon arrival at school.

RESEARCH THE TOPIC IN LIBRARIES AND CLASSROOMS

Library research, classroom observation, and previous experience help identify the behaviors and characteristics that effectively answer an observational question.

Classroom Example

Over the next two days, Bessie consciously studies the separation processes in her own classroom and reflects on her past experiences with children reluctant to have their parents leave them. She jots down ideas of behaviors to observe. While searching the literature, Bessie is reminded of how important successful separations are to communicate confidence in children's abilities to handle their school experiences (Kettman, 1994). She finds Brazelton's advice (1992) particularly helpful in identifying effective parent strategies.

IDENTIFY CLEAR, DISTINCT CATEGORIES

Categories are clear and unambiguous but still might need to be defined. Depending on the scope of the focus, observers may choose a sign or category system (see Chapter 11 for definitions), but in either case the categories must not overlap. Codes for categories may be specified to save space on the recording form.

Classroom Example

After reading and thinking about her topic, Bessie decides to focus on teacher and parent strategies to help children separate from their parents and transition to school and children's successful and unsuccessful separations. As a result, she identifies and defines two sets of categories to observe: children (the set of children includes the names of all children in the class) and strategies/separations. Bessie lists the following categories (with codes and definitions) under the strategies/separations set. She uses category codes to save space on the recording form and prints their definitions on the reverse side.

Teacher Strategies

- *T-G*—Teacher greets child verbally and/or physically.
- *T-CEH*—Teacher comments about the room, activities, or other children; encourages the child to begin an activity; or helps the child to do so.
- *T-P*—Teacher establishes physical proximity to the child.
- *T-D*—Teacher acknowledges parent's departure (says good-bye and/or encourages child to do so), reminds child of parents' return, expresses confidence in child, or suggests the child look at concrete keepsake of parents (e.g., photo).

Although Bessie hopes her list is comprehensive, she adds an "other" category to provide the means to record additional unanticipated strategies. She therefore uses a category system for the set of teacher categories.

- *T-O*—Teacher uses a different strategy. (Since Bessie already has a T-D label, she uses T-O for "other.")

Parent Strategies

- *P-W*—Parent expresses warmth toward child verbally and/or by physical contact (e.g., holding a hand).
- *P-CEH*—Parent comments about the room, activities, or other children; encourages the child to put belongings in cubby and begin an activity; or helps the child to do so.
- *P-D*—Parent acknowledges own departure verbally (e.g., saying good-bye) or physically (e.g., gives a farewell hug and kiss).
- *P-O*—Parent uses a different strategy.

Children's Successful/Unsuccessful Separations

- *C-SS*—Child successfully separates from parent.
- *C-US*—Child does not successfully separate from parent within 10 minutes.

Note: Bessie uses category systems for the sets of parent strategies and children's separations.

DESIGN A RECORDING FORM

Instrument recording forms begin with the heading used throughout this book, which includes the name of the center or school, the age level or grade, the dates and times of observation, the observer, and the person(s) being observed. Some forms require the definitions of the event observed, definitions of the categories and/or codes, and clear instructions to the observer; in addition, observers appreciate space at the bottom for relevant comments. The specific format of the remainder of the form must be compatible with the method used. A checklist, for example, would contain items preceded by check boxes, whereas a time sampling instrument would be based on a grid recording sheet.

Classroom Example

Bessie designs the recording form presented in Figure 13.1 and defines the codes on p. 310 on the reverse side.

PILOT TEST THE INSTRUMENT

Although an observational instrument may appear adequate on paper, the process of trying it out in a classroom is essential to assessing its workability. Taking time to make adjustments in and additions to an instrument streamlines the future collection of useful information.

Classroom Example

Because High Street Child Care Center provides both preschool and full-day child care services, Bessie is able to leave her napping full-day children with her assistant teacher and observe a class of 4-year-olds who arrive at 1:00 P.M. Her pilot testing raises two problems with her instrument. First she discovers that her category of unsuccessful separation within 10 minutes is too limited. She observed one child–mother pair who spent 15 leisurely minutes together putting away belongings, walking around the classroom, and chatting with children and parents. The child's transition to school was happy, but Bessie's first draft of her instrument requires that the transition be tallied "unsuccessful." She removes the time restriction from the category description and rewrites the category definition as follows:

- *C-US*—Child does not successfully separate from parent.

The second problem is simply visual. Bessie found all the small grid boxes visually uncomfortable, so she enlarges them. She pilot tests the revised instrument the next morning and is satisfied. A completed version of revised form (with data) may be seen in Figure 13.3.

ESTABLISH INTER-RATER RELIABILITY

Observers and designers of instruments want to have confidence that observers agree about how to use the instrument; all observers collecting data with an instrument should produce consistent, accurate, dependable—in short, reliable—data (Kerlinger & Lee, 2000). To explore the agreement between observers when they observe the same setting at the same time, the percentage of agreement may be calculated to represent the level of **inter-rater reliability.** "This is an index of

Child–Parent Separations

Center/Age Level:

Dates: Time:

Observer: Teacher:

                                                         Children:

Event: Child–parent separation—the process of children separating from their parents
                    upon arrival at school.

Codes: See reverse side.

Instructions: Mark one tally in the appropriate box for each teacher strategy, parent strategy,
                    and child separation observed.

Strategy and Separation / Child	Teacher Strategies					Parent Strategies				Child Separations	
	T-G	T-CEH	T-P	T-D	T-O	P-W	P-CEH	P-D	P-O	C-SS	C-US
Child 1											
Child 2											
Child 3											
Child 4											
Child 5											
Child 6											
Child 7											
Child 8											
Child 9											
Child 10											
Child 11											
Child 12											

Comments:

Figure 13.1
Sample recording form design: Child–parent separations.

how closely two observers agree when coding the same observations" (Cozby, 1997, p. 84). If the observers can demonstrate that their collected data are very similar, then they are ready to go out into various classrooms to observe on their own.

Agreement of 80% or higher (Cozby, 1997) provides confidence in the data collected. If the instrument is not reliable between raters, the instrument itself may need adjustments or the observers may need further training. Typical causes of low inter-rater reliability are unclear categories or instructions and insufficient training of observers. Although there are a few cautions about using percent agreement among observers as a measure of inter-rater reliability (see Dooley, 1990), this calculation is sufficient for an initial evaluation of the clarity and effectiveness of observational instruments.

A straightforward formula to compute the rate of agreement between two observers ascertains their reliability (Boehm & Weinberg, 1997). The computational procedure is given in Figure 13.2 (always rounding numbers off to the nearest hundredth) along with an analysis of Bessie's and her partner's data. Columns for additional observers may be added on the right-hand side in order to compute the agreement among more than two observers, and periodically rechecking inter-rater reliability reevaluates the observers' consistency over time.

Classroom Example

To establish inter-rater reliability, Bessie asks her director to read the instrument and category code definitions and then, using the instrument, observe with her the arrival of the children in an afternoon preschool class. The data collected by Bessie and the director are used to compute their rate of agreement; Figure 13.2 shows their step-by-step computational process of inter-rater reliability. If desired, the rate (.76) may be multiplied by 100 to yield a percent agreement between observers (76%).

The observers' .76 rate of agreement is unsatisfactory, and Bessie and the director discuss their use of the observation instrument to identify possible problems. Two are immediately obvious. First, there are glaring discrepancies between their observations in the T-CEH and P-CEH categories; the director observed many more demonstrations of commenting, encouraging, and helping behaviors than Bessie. For each teacher–child and parent–child pair, Bessie put one tally in the appropriate box regardless of the number of such behaviors while the director tallied every one she saw.

Bessie realizes her directions are unclear, and she and the director review these categories in detail. If a mother said to her child, "Oh look, honey, there's Randy already busy with the trucks in the block area. Would you like to play with him?" and then walked with the child toward the blocks, how many tallies should be marked? Bessie would have marked one. The director, on the other hand, would have marked one or two tallies for the comments about Randy and the blocks, another for the encouraging question, and another for walking to the block area with the child. Upon reflection, the director concludes that trying to mark every comment, encouragement, or help within 10 child–parent separations would render the

Step	Category	Observer A (Bessie)		Observer B (Director)
1. Count the number of instances in each category for observers A and B.	T-G	12		10
	T-CEH	7		22
	T-P	9		10
	T-D	5		4
	T-O	0		5
	P-W	9		9
	P-CEH	6		17
	P-D	10		10
	P-O	0		6
	C-SS	10		10
	C-US	2		2
2. Total the number of observations for A and B	Total	70	+	105 = 175
3. Count the number of agreements in each category and over categories for both observers.	T-G	10		
	T-CEH	7		
	T-P	9		
	T-D	4		
	T-O	0		
	P-W	9		
	P-CEH	6		
	P-D	10		
	P-O	0		
	C-SS	10		
	C-US	2		
	Total	67		
4. Divide the number of agreements by the total number of observations.		67	÷	175 = .38
5. Multiply the quotient by the number of observers; in this example there are two.		.38	×	2 = .76
Rate of agreement = .76				

Figure 13.2
Inter-rater reliability formula and computation.

Source: Adapted by permission of the publisher from Boehm, A. E., and Weinberg, R. A., *The Classroom Observer: A Guide for Developing Observation Skills.* (3rd ed.) (New York: Teachers College Press, © 1997 by Teachers College, Columbia University. All rights reserved.), p. 80 (Figure 7.2).

instrument unworkable. Given overlapping arrivals, the observer cannot observe each child's experience in such detail. A time sampling instrument would address this event frequency issue, but Bessie does not want the restrictions imposed by the time sampling units. She prefers the tally event sampling method that allows her to consistently gather data on which teacher and parent strategies are used. Bessie changes the instructions to eliminate the confusion (see Figure 13.3).

The second problem revolves around the *other* categories that specify different strategies used, T-O and P-O, with Bessie recording 0 in each category and the director observing 4 and 6, respectively. Most frequently, the director marked a tally when she overheard teacher and parent comments about the child, such as "Alyssa, I put your drawing on my refrigerator, and my husband said your sky-scrapers reminded him of growing up in Chicago." That comment pleased Alyssa and added to her happy transition to school, and Bessie appreciates the value of recording such comments in some way. She suggests the T-CEH and P-CEH category descriptions be amended to include comments about the child. The two observers also decide to eliminate the *other* categories (thus they now use sign systems for the teacher and parent sets of categories); observers can note helpful strategies under the comments section. Their revised category descriptions for T-CEH and P-CEH are as follows:

- *T-CEH*—Teacher comments about the child, room, activities, or other children; encourages the child to begin an activity; or helps the child to do so.

- *P-CEH*—Parent comments about the child, room, activities, or other children; encourages the child to put belongings in cubby and begin an activity; or helps the child to do so.

Using the revised instrument, Bessie and the director observe together the next morning and accomplish a 96% agreement. Bessie is ready to observe Winona's classroom.

COLLECT DATA

A reasonable amount of data is collected to provide a fair sample of the behaviors being studied. Observers plan when during the classroom schedule to observe and how much data to collect. A clear observational question and a concise recording form facilitate data collection.

Classroom Example

Bessie arranges for the director to cover her class for 15 minutes for the next five mornings so that she can observe the arrival of Winona's children. She wants to paint a thorough and well-balanced picture of the separation and transition processes. The data for the 5 days are compiled in Figure 13.3.

Child–Parent Separations

Center/Age level: High Street Child Care/3-Year-Old Preschool Room

Dates:	9/28–30, 10/1–2	Time: 8:45–9:00 A.M.
Observer:	Bessie	Teacher: Winona
		Children: 10 children

Event: Child–parent separations—the process of children separating from their parents upon arrival at school.

Codes: See reverse side.

Instructions: Mark one tally in the appropriate box for each teacher strategy, parent strategy, and child separation observed. Mark only one tally per box for each session.

Strategy & Separation / Child	Teacher Strategies				Parent Strategies			Child Separations	
	T-G	T-CEH	T-P	T-D	P-W	P-CEH	P-D	C-SS	C-US
Alyssa	/	//	//		卌		卌	/	////
Connor	//	/	/	/	///	//	////	//	///
Kailey	///			卌	////		卌	/	////
Kayl	//	/			/			///	//
Parker	/	///	///	//	////	//	卌	卌	
Elaine	卌	///	卌	///	卌	卌	卌	卌	
Rosemary	////		///	/	///	//	////	////	/
George	//	//			//	///	///		卌
Noel	///		/		/			///	//
Tak	卌	///	///		卌	//		//	///

Comments: 28

Figure 13.3
Data: Child–parent separations

ANALYZE AND PRESENT THE DATA

The collected data may be analyzed through various procedures, and computer programs offer a multitude of shortcuts for this process. Observers select data analysis procedures that will provide information relevant to the observational question and present the data in clear formats. Then the observers will be able to interpret what the data mean for real children and teachers in real classrooms. An assortment of data analysis and presentation procedures is given below; not all of these procedures need to be used in any one observational study.

Frequencies

Frequencies allow observers to answer questions about how often behaviors, events, or strategies occur (e.g., How often do children quarrel during outside time? How often do children use materials for classification during free play time? How often do children participate in circle time?). To compute frequencies on a grid, (horizontal) row tallies or (vertical) column tallies are simply added. Computing frequencies is a productive way to begin studying the data.

Classroom Example

By computing the column totals, Bessie can easily determine how frequently each teacher and parent strategy was used per session and how frequently children successfully and unsuccessfully transitioned to school. Remember that each box may be tallied only once per day, so each column total can have a maximum of 50 tallies; for example, if Winona greeted each child every day for 5 days (10 children × 5 days), Bessie would have marked 50 tallies in the T-G column. Practice Activity 13.1 gives you practice counting the frequencies of observations.

PRACTICE ACTIVITY 13.1

Counting Frequencies of Observations

Working with the data presented in Figure 13.3, count the column frequencies. You may write the totals directly on the recording form.

Example: T-G total: 1 + 2 + 3 + 2 + 1 + 5 + 4 + 2 + 3 + 5 = 28

Percentages

Frequencies show the sheer magnitude of observed behaviors, but they do not lend themselves to easy comparisons. Observing that primary grade children make 53 visits to the science center over the course of a week, for example, does not produce useful information in isolation. Computing the percentages of children's visits to all of the classroom areas, however, begins to describe how the science center is used in the context of children's available choices. Percentages help put the data in perspective.

Classroom Example

Bessie can easily compute the percentages of teacher and parent strategies used as well as the proportions of successful and unsuccessful separations as you will see in Practice Activities 13.2 and 13.3. Percentages will quickly convey the overall picture.

PRACTICE ACTIVITY 13.2

Computing Percentages

Using the column totals, compute the percentages of Winona's use of each strategy. For example, to compute the percentage of times Winona greeted the children, divide the column total (28) by the possible greetings (50) and multiply by 100. Now you see that over the course of 5 days with 10 children, Winona greeted them 56% of the time and, conversely, did not greet them 44% of the time. Record your calculations in the following chart.

Percentages of Teacher's Separation Strategy Use

Strategy	Frequency	Percentage
T-G	28	56 (28 ÷ 50 × 100)
T-CEH		
T-P		
T-D		

Next, again using the column totals, compute the percentages of the parents' uses of strategies to help their children successfully separate and transition to school. In the example given, you see that over the week, parents demonstrated warmth to their children 66% of the time.

Percentages of Parents' Separation Strategy Use

Strategy	Frequency	Percentage
P-W	33	66 (33 ÷ 50 × 100)
P-CEH		
P-D		

Finally, using the last two column totals, compute the percentages of children's successful and unsuccessful separations from their parents.

Percentages of Children's Successful and Unsuccessful Separations

Transition	Frequency	Percentage
C-SS	26	
C-US		

PRACTICE ACTIVITY 13.3

Computing More Percentages

Bessie also wants a clear picture of Winona's *relative* use of the teacher separation strategies to guide helpful follow-through plans. She adds up all of Winona's strategies using the column totals (28 + 15 + 18 + 12 = 73) and then computes the percentage of each strategy used. Complete the following computations in the following chart, and then do the same for parents' strategies. Note that your percentages will add up to 100% with these calculations.

Percentages of Teacher Strategies

Strategy	Frequency	Percentage
T-G	28	38 (28 ÷ 73 × 100)
T-CEH		
T-P		
T-D		

Percentages of Parent Strategies

Strategy	Frequency	Percentage
P-W	33	41 (33 ÷ 80 × 100)
P-CEH		
P-D		

Visual Presentations

Data presented visually are often clear and memorable; tables and graphs are frequently used to display data. "Perhaps the most common way to present data to show relations is in tables" (Kerlinger Lee, 2000, p. 88). Tables promote the clear presentation of information most often as frequencies, percentages, and means (averages), and typically the variables are presented horizontally along the top and vertically down the side of the table with the data in the table itself. "A *graph* is a two-dimensional representation of a relation or relations" (Kerlinger Lee, 2000, p. 200) and also serves to highlight important results often embedded in the data on recording sheets. A few options are reviewed below.

Classroom Example

Bessie wants Winona to understand how infrequently teachers and parents used strategies to help children separate from their parents (the percentages you computed in Practice Activity 13.2). Bessie wants to present both sets of data together (she could have prepared two separate tables) so Winona will readily see both she and the parents have room for improvement. She prepares the table shown in Figure 13.4. (Other tables throughout the method chapters present clear contrasts between teachers or children when the categories are the same for all. See, for example, Figure 12.3: Time Sampling of Teaching Strategies in the Block Area.)

Percentages of Teacher and Parent Use of Separation Strategies		
Teacher/Parents Strategy	Teacher	Parents
T-Greets	56	
T-Comments, encourages, helps	33	
T-Establishes physical proximity	36	
T-Acknowledges parents' departure	24	
P-Expresses warmth		60
P-Comments, encourages, helps		32
P-Acknowledges own departure		62

Figure 13.4
Percentages presented in a table.

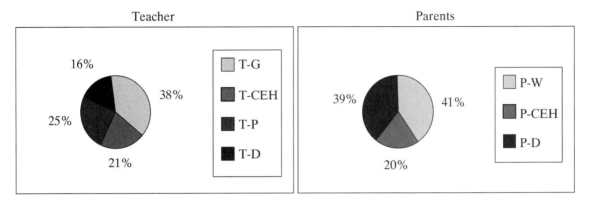

Figure 13.5
Percentages of teacher's and parents' relative use of separation strategies. Data presentation in pie charts.

Given the observed data, Bessie wants to illustrate the relative proportion of strategies on which Winona and the parents relied. Pie charts display percentages of data in sections of a circle. In Figure 13.5, Bessie presents Winona's and the parents' relative use of the strategies observed (you computed these percentages in Practice Activity 13.3).

Conclusion

The preceding methods of data analysis and presentation represent options for the observer. All need not be used, and additional methods might be helpful to some observers. For example, the analysis of some data may be enhanced by computing means or plotting changes in behaviors over time on a graph. Remember that the primary goals of data analysis and presentation are to use the data to answer the observational question and to present the information in clear, visual formats.

INTERPRET THE DATA

Uninterpreted data are of no use. After the data are collected, data interpretation is the next step in the process of designing and using an observational instrument.

Classroom Example

Bessie and Winona sit down together with a block of time and Figures 13.3, 13.4, and 13.5 in front of them. Bessie carefully describes the categories on the instrument and reviews their definitions on the reverse side. She explains that each box could receive only one tally per day and uses Alyssa as an example of the data collected:

- "Let's look at Alyssa's boxes one by one. First, one tally in the T-G box means you greeted her one day out of five."
- "You commented about Alyssa, the room, the activities, or the other children; encouraged Alyssa to begin an activity; or helped her to do so on two days."
- "You established physical proximity after Alyssa's arrival on two days as well."
- "You never, however, acknowledged Alyssa's mom's departure."
- "Alyssa's mom expressed warmth and said good-bye to Alyssa all five days."
- "The mom, however, never used a P-CEH strategy."
- "Each day the mom acknowledged her own departure to Alyssa either verbally or physically."
- "Alyssa made only one successful transition to school during the week I observed."

Already Winona begins to make notes of strategies she and the mom can try to ease Alyssa's transition to school. Using Figures 13.3, 13.4, and 13.5, Bessie and Winona draw additional specific conclusions. Do the same in Practice Activity 13.4.

PRACTICE ACTIVITY 13.4

Interpreting the Data

- Study the raw data in Figure 13.3, and state two conclusions about the separation processes of individual children.

Example: Elaine received the most teacher and parent helpful strategies and successfully transitioned to school each day.

1.

2.

- Study the percentages in Figure 13.4, and state two conclusions about Winona's and the parents' uses of separation strategies.

Example: Winona greeted children 56% of the time.

Example: Parents acknowledged their own departures to their children 62% of the time.

1.

2.

- Study the percentages in Figure 13.5, and state two conclusions about Winona's and the parents' relative uses of helpful strategies.

Example: Winona's uses of helpful strategies were fairly even (38%, 21%, 25%, and 16%).

1.

2.

FORMULATE FOLLOW-THROUGH PLANS

Observation in the early childhood classroom provides information about children, teachers, the environment, and sometimes parents to evaluate current development and practices and to plan appropriate activities and adjustments. The detailing of follow-through plans is the culmination of the observational process.

Observations of child–parent separations in the early childhood classroom can lead to supportive follow-through plans.

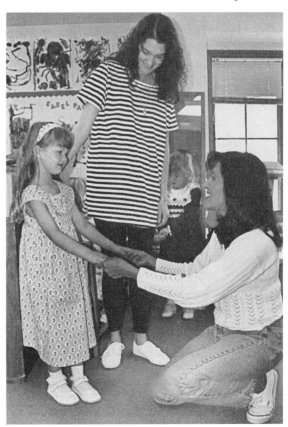

Classroom Example

Bessie's warm and supportive discussion of her observation ends with attention to the "What next?" question. Knowing that observation is often the best teacher, Bessie arranges to have Winona observe a morning class with her, using the same observational instrument. She selects a class known for its smooth separations; Winona will witness clear demonstrations of the teacher's and parents' helpful strategies in action. This is the first follow-through plan implemented. Read additional examples below, and add your own in Practice Activity 13.5.

PRACTICE ACTIVITY 13.5

Detailing Follow-Through Plans

Use the interpretations from Practice Activity 13.4 to stimulate ideas for effective follow-through plans for Winona.

Example: Winona will put a notecard of the teacher strategies in her pocket for quick reminders and easy access.

Example: Bessie and Winona will jointly write a brief article for the parent newsletter about child–parent separations at school. They will encourage parents to view separation as a transition, not an event, and to consciously try the following strategies from Bessie's observational instrument.

- Express warmth to the child verbally and/or by physical contact (e.g., hold a hand).
- Comment about the child, room, activities, or other children; encourage the child to begin an activity; or help the child to do so.
- Acknowledge own departure verbally (e.g., say good-bye) or physically (e.g., give a farewell hug and kiss).

1.

2.

OFF ON YOUR OWN 13.1

Designing and Using an Observational Instrument

Replicate the steps of designing an observational instrument as discussed in this chapter and as exemplified by Bessie and Winona. Design a checklist, rating scale, tally event sampling instrument, or time sampling instrument to answer a specific question about children or classroom processes. Pilot test the completed instrument, and establish inter-rater reliability. Collect data in a classroom or classrooms (whichever is appropriate) to gain the experience of analyzing and interpreting real data. Finally, put the data to practical use and formulate follow-through plans. Be sure to refer to and follow all 11 steps presented in this chapter.

>>

> QUICK REVIEW <

1. The value of learning how to design an observational instrument is to
   a. avoid using other educators' instruments.
   b. pursue an observational question of personal interest and possible importance in one's own classroom.
   c. find a favorite observational method.
   d. practice one's observational skills.

2. The first step in designing an observational instrument is to select a method.
   ❏ True
   ❏ False

3. The steps of designing observational instruments presented in this chapter are applicable to the design of
   a. checklists and rating scales.
   b. tally event sampling and time sampling.
   c. ABC narrative event sampling.
   d. a and b.
   e. a, b, and c.

4. Which of the following is a clearly written observational question?
   a. Do the third graders in Room 11 have good attention spans?
   b. Do the third graders in Room 11 have good work habits?
   c. How frequently do the third graders in Room 11 work on individual writing projects?
      • 5 minutes or less
      • more than 5 minutes but 10 minutes or less
      • more than 10 minutes
   d. How frequently do the third graders in Room 11 demonstrate sustained focus on individual writing projects?

- 5 minutes or less
- more than 5 minutes but 10 minutes or less
- more than 10 minutes

5. Research in _____ and _____ as well as previous experience help identify the behaviors and characteristics that effectively answer an observational question.

6. The process of trying an observational instrument out in a classroom to assess its workability is called _____.

7. Because the designer of an observational instrument is very familiar with the categories, establishing inter-rater reliability ensures that the categories are clear and distinct to other observers.

   ❑ True

   ❑ False

8. A check of inter-rater reliability never needs to be done more than once.

   ❑ True

   ❑ False

9. Data collected from an observational instrument are commonly presented as frequencies and percentages.

   ❑ True

   ❑ False

10. The culmination of the observational process is

    a. the formulation of follow-through plans.

    b. publishing a new observational instrument.

    c. determining the best teacher in a school.

    d. utilizing data analysis skills.

TAKE A MOMENT TO REFLECT

Personal Reflection

The 3-year-olds in Winona's classroom are new to school. They are leaving the familiarity of their home environments for the unknown experiences of school. Hopefully these experiences will be interesting, fun, challenging, supportive, and rewarding on many levels. For the first few weeks, however, the processes of separating from parents may dominate many children's feelings about school. Try to empathize with their experiences by reflecting on the following:

1. Recall a first experience in your own life. Perhaps you may not remember your first day of school, but you probably remember your introduction to a group experience during childhood (swimming lessons, scouts, religious instruction, camp, team sports). Articulate your initial feelings, and note if you felt any discomfort or wariness.

2. Describe your eventual adjustment to the preceding group experience. Was it generally positive or negative? What factors were critical to your successful or unsuccessful adjustment? What suggestions would you now give to the adults responsible for children beginning new experiences?

Ethical Reflection

NAEYC Ideal I-2.2 is "to acknowledge and build upon strengths and competencies as we support families in their task of nurturing children" (Feeney & Kipnis, 1992, p. 6). Think about how Winona and Bessie's newsletter article about child–parent separations might benefit and support families.

14

Selecting Methods to Observe, Plan, and Enrich the Physical Environment

Kirin, a college student who is enrolled in an observation class, designs an observational instrument around a topic near and dear to her heart. As an aide in a preschool classroom, she encounters relentless problems in trying to get children's attention at the end of free choice time. She wonders if the children don't respect her because she is an aide or if she works with an exceptionally difficult group. In any case, they seem oblivious to her attempts to get their attention. Before Kirin gets much of a start on her project, the head teacher rearranges the classroom and the transition problems disappear! Is this coincidence, or might some classroom problems be solved by observing, evaluating, and changing the physical environment rather than by studying children's and teachers' behaviors in isolation?

Do teachers gain children's attention more easily in some room arrangements than in others? What are the potential attention-getting problems in a classroom with a 5-foot-tall room divider in the writing area and the book nook behind the piano? How could the placement of children's interest centers help or hinder the process? What impact does the physical environment actually have on teachers' ability to get the children's attention in a modern complex classroom? Some teachers endure unnecessary problems because they overlook the effect the physical environment has on teaching and learning. Once again we gaze through the looking glass, but this time the focus is on the setting itself.

The goal of this chapter is to supply a knowledge base for environmental observation, an often overlooked but important observational subject. The first half of the chapter explores the major elements that produce an effective learning environment, both indoors and outdoors. The latter part of the chapter examines observational strategies used to assess the functional design of the physical setting. Using observational data, the teacher can assess how well the environmental elements support the educational process. If changes are warranted, the teacher can use the results of the observational data to make instructional decisions.

INDOOR ENVIRONMENTS

Recall an indoor place in which you felt right at home the minute you set foot inside. Perhaps it was a cafe or restaurant, a friend's family room, your grandma's porch, a library corner, or a ski lodge. What did it look like? What made you feel so welcome?

Now think for a moment of indoor places in which you did not feel comfortable—places that were cold, alienating, or unwelcoming. What did the uncomfortable rooms look like? What did those places have in common? Pause and identify specific factors that contributed to a sense of disfavor or uneasiness.

Our first reaction to a physical environment is emotional. Although the initial impression may be influenced by the purpose of the visit, the function of the facility, or the people within the space, the welcome feeling is fundamentally associated with the physical setting itself. All environments have the potential to enhance and support comfort levels.

Let's move the investigation into the early childhood classroom. Figure 14.1 illustrates portions of two different room arrangements for a specific preschool classroom. Take a moment to examine them. What observations can you make about these learning environments? What are your first impressions?

Now look more closely. Do the rooms welcome children's play? What can be said about the choice and location of interest centers, boundaries, traffic flow, visual stimulation, accessibility of materials, equipment choice, and storage? Imagine a young child and then a teacher working and communicating in these two different arrangements.

The room arrangement in the top photograph in Figure 14.1 appears confusing and lacks an overall organizational plan utilizing area boundaries. Visualize this room with energetic children actively engaged in free play. Could a child move easily from one area to another? Suppose two children were role-playing, dressed up in high heels and swishy dresses, cuddling their baby dolls wrapped in blankets. Imagine them clomping off to the grocery store. Using this scenario, these children might be wondering where the market could be. If the children could find an unoccupied area, could they get there without interfering with block builders, puzzle assemblers, or book readers?

Take a look at the visual stimuli in the top photograph in Figure 14.1. Young children working in this setting may be overstimulated by the wall clutter. If the

Limited room arrangement

Effective room arrangement

Figure 14.1
Two photographs of the same preschool classroom.

photograph had been reproduced in color, you would see that the color scheme contributes to overstimulation by using bright and vibrant reds, blues, and yellows. Examine the textures and surfaces. Where is the softness?

On the other hand, the bottom photograph in Figure 14.1 represents the same room rearranged to create a physical environment supported by research findings—designed to enhance learning, provide comfort, and increase the usability of space. Study the clear flow of the traffic pattern, the distinct separation of quiet and noisy areas, and the strategic placement of dividers. Take another glance. What can be said about the display of children's work, accessibility of materials, and additional touches of texture? If the teachers in this classroom were able to repaint, they would have chosen a light shade of peach. Room accents would have been in a delicate pastel green, thus giving a balance of warm and cool colors.

Compare the rooms presented in Figure 14.1. Is there a difference in coziness and emotional warmth? What growth opportunities for children are promoted by these two room arrangements? What evidence is there that the room at the bottom of Figure 14.1 was planned according to developmental goals—to encourage children's autonomy, initiative, competence, exploration, discovery, cooperation, and interactions with others?

A well-planned environment is an effective teaching strategy. Many potential problems can be eliminated by room design. Consider possible arrangements that reflect the following management concerns: capturing children's attention, providing smooth transitions, increasing the possibility of cooperative play, creating a sense of community, decreasing opportunities for potential quarrels, and minimizing wandering.

Poysner (1983) advised us, "The physical environment of the classroom is a web of micro-variables, which are highly interrelated and in many instances interdependent. Each factor of the classroom environment can and should be examined independently" (p. 36). This chapter discusses three key indoor factors in detail: room arrangement, lighting, and visual appeal.

Room Arrangement

Classrooms come in an assortment of sizes and shapes, and seldom are two arranged exactly alike; classroom organization has no prescribed formula. Unless teachers are fortunate enough to build their own schools, options in room arrangements are restricted by the fixed space—the direction the room faces, configuration of the room and the placement of the electrical outlets, plumbing, floor coverings, windows, doors, and built-in shelves and closets. Certain elements, however, necessitate special consideration. This section of the chapter emphasizes room arrangement: relationship to program goals, layout, traffic patterns, and material selection and equipment location.

Relation to Program Goals

As we explore the implications of program goals on room arrangement, recall the top photograph in Figure 14.1. Do you think the teacher in this classroom coordinated the design of the room arrangement with developmental principles and program goals? An incongruity occurs when the program plan and the classroom environment are in conflict. In contrast, room arrangements backed by developmental principles and congruent with school goals result in conducive and supportive learning conditions. Figure 14.2 gives an extensive list of program goals and their implications for preschool classroom planning. While reading through

Preschool Program Goals	Implications for Classroom Arrangements
To support children's active learning through exploration and interaction with other children, adults, and concrete materials, thus strengthening children's construction of knowledge	Diverse materials are available, organized, labeled, and accessible to children. There are places and spaces to work alone or with others. Dramatic play centers are present. Varied and abundant props are changed on the basis of the children's interests. The arrangement allows for overflow and opportunities for conversations. Every interest center provides materials to stimulate cognitive development.
To create a sense of security and promote trust	The door to the classroom opens into a cozy welcoming area that reflects children's interests. Materials for children's use are arranged on low, open shelves. Interest center boundaries are well defined. The paths leading to the centers are easy to view and unobstructed. Safe plants and fabrics with soft textures are present. Wall colors are a balance of warm and cool colors. Room decorations reflect the children's work and are carefully selected to avoid an environment that is overstimulating.
To enhance children's autonomy	Furniture is child sized. Drinking fountains, sinks, and toilets are child height. Cubbies are labeled with names and pictures. Classroom areas are well defined and labeled with words and pictures. Materials are accessible for the children's choice. Empty tables or work spaces are available for child-planned activities using self-chosen materials.
To foster children's natural curiosity	Traffic flow takes children past centers of possible interest. Center content changes to reflect the children's emerging interests.

(continued)

Figure 14.2
Foundations of preschool room arrangements.

To encourage initiative-taking (children explore and act on their own ideas)	Materials can be manipulated and reformed. Materials and props are open-ended, varied, abundant, organized, and accessible to the children. There is space to safely arrange and rearrange materials.
To recognize each child's importance and uniqueness	Bulletin boards and room decorations are at the children's eye level. Wall decorations involve the children and display their work.
To allow children to develop at their own individual rates	Various materials and centers based on the children's developmental needs, cultural heritages, interests, and town/city/rural orientation are available.
To allow children to be physically active	Adequate space is supplied in all areas and traffic paths; attention is given to the needs of children who have limited physical abilities.
To support literacy development through the child's own experiences	Literacy-rich environment is supplied. Listening, writing, and reading centers; experience stories; dictated stories; poetry charts; typewriters; and computers are visible. Housekeeping area includes cookbooks, note pads and pencils, telephone books, etc. Centers have enough space for children to converse easily with each other.
To enhance children's creativity and appreciation of fine art	Art, music, writing, and dramatic play materials are readily available and accessible. Pictures of artists, musicians, authors, and actors/actresses are displayed at child's eye level and frequently changed.

Figure 14.2   *(Continued)*
Foundations of preschool room arrangements.

the list, think about what additions, deletions, expansions, or revisions would be necessary for primary grade classrooms (e.g., *Program goal*—To assist children in understanding the meaning, as well as the mechanics, of math. *Implication for classroom arrangements*—Variety of math manipulatives available at math center and on the children's resource shelf).

Within the field of early childhood, there are many variations in programs. Not all have the same developmental goals. All programs, however, are enhanced when the underlying principles and stated goals work together with the room arrangement in mutual support. In Off on Your Own 14.1, try your hand at identifying program goals and the corresponding implications for classroom arrangements.

>>>

OFF ON YOUR OWN 14.1

Program Goals and Classroom Implications

Choose two different schools from the list below:

Private half-day preschool	Campus laboratory school
Parent cooperative preschool	Employer-related preschool
Head Start	All-day child care
Family child care	Montessori
Private primary (K–3)	Public primary (K–3)

A school with a High/Scope curriculum

A school with a Waldorf curriculum

A school with a Reggio Emilio approach

A school with a curriculum based on Gardner's Intelligences

Arrange visits to your two selections. Obtain a copy of each school's goals; perhaps an introductory brochure provides this information. Observe one class at each site for approximately 30 minutes to 1 hour, and watch for environmental implications of the stated goals. Using the information from your observation, fill in the form below by stating two goals for each school and the corresponding implications.

Example:

School: Growing and Learning: Center for Early Childhood Development

Program type: Parent cooperative preschool

Goal	Implications for Classroom Arrangements
1. To provide an anti-bias curriculum	Pictures, books, and materials on walls or shelves reflect diversity, are free of stereotypes, and are authentic representations of the cultures they depict. Dramatic play areas reflect a variety of gender-role options.

School:

Program type:

(continued)

Goals   **Implications for Classroom Arrangements**

1.

2.

School:

Program type:

Goals   **Implications for Classroom Arrangements**

1.

2.

>>

Layout

"Establishing well-defined interest areas is one concrete way to foster children's capacities for initiative, autonomy, and social relationships" (Hohmann & Weikart, 1995, p. 115). Using the interest center approach, Greenman (1988) identified three plans for room layouts: the *maze* (defined areas are separate and placed throughout the room—sides, corners, and middle area), the *perimeter strategy* (areas are placed around the outside with the central space left open for traffic access and overflow from centers), and the *central activity area strategy* (areas are grouped together in the center of the room with open space on the outer edges). One layout is not superior to another, and indeed many teachers design their own classroom layouts using modifications of these plans. However, a well-designed layout will reflect the program goals and maximize the use of classroom space.

After the general layout has been chosen, the designation of specific centers within the classroom should follow "some guiding principle or principles, such as importance, frequency of use, functional relationships, or sequence of use" (McCormick & Ilgen, 1980, p. 355). Examples associated with the principle of functional relationships are shown below.

- Noisy areas are adjacent (e.g., blocks and housekeeping).
- Quiet areas are adjacent (e.g., independent reading and computers or manipulatives).

- Areas that flow into one another are adjacent (e.g., reading and science or writing and independent reading).
- Areas that need access to the sink or electrical outlets are adjacent (e.g., art and science or music and science).

Traffic Patterns

Traffic patterns, which are planned concurrently with the location of areas, also affect the room arrangement. "Traffic should flow smoothly between learning centers so that classroom noise and the potential for accidents are reduced" (White & Coleman, 2000, p. 308). While looking at the top photograph in Figure 14.1, you thought about potential mobility problems. The skilled teacher plans traffic patterns that minimize interference in interest centers and leave pathways and doorways unobstructed. Special attention is given to the width of pathways when children with wheelchairs or physical challenges are included in the program.

> Children need to know where they are going, how to get through a space, and the quickest way to an activity area. Hard-to-reach areas receive less use; paths that cut through an area interfere with "work in progress" and create distractions; and narrow pathways cause congestion. Therefore, create a network of pathways that connect activity areas. This network should also limit the access to areas; for instance, one entrance to an area. There should be no dead ends . . . Define the edges of pathways with furniture and changes in floor covering. (Vergeront, 1987, p. 5)

Kudos go to teachers who map out the traffic flow between centers or desk areas and during cleanup and transitions. The final test, however, comes when the teacher bends down to see whether the planned traffic routes and spatial organization are visible from the child's eye.

As with any other component of the room arrangement, traffic paths need to be observed periodically and then analyzed for workability. Children's and teachers' comments may give clues about the need to adjust traffic patterns.

> When caregivers hear comments such as "She knocked over my building," or "Tell those feet to walk," or "Where is . . . ?" or when all the children are in only one part of the room, it is time to reevaluate the environment. If those feet need to be told to walk, there is too much open space and the children are running. New traffic patterns need to be established by repositioning storage cabinets. (Fisher, 1995, p. 37)

Material Selection and Equipment Location

Also adding to the room-arrangement design are the selection and placement of materials within an area. The knowledgeable practitioner selects classroom materials that reflect the program goals, developmental appropriateness, and the assessed needs and interests of individuals. For example, one study (Petrakos & Howe, 1996) found that materials and equipment choice in the dramatic play area affected children's opportunities to enter into solitary or interactive play.

In addition teachers carefully select equitable representations of gender, culture, ethnic backgrounds, and abilities. "What isn't seen can be as powerful a contributor to attitudes as what is seen" (Derman-Sparks & the A.B.C. Task Force, 1989). In order to build positive identity and self-esteem, special emphasis is given to classroom materials and equipment that represent the specific classroom populations.

> It [the environment] also contributes to the feeling of homeyness and comfort when the ethnic and cultural backgrounds of children are matter-of-factly represented in the physical environment of the school. The inclusion of multiethnic pictures, books, and artifacts will contribute to the children's overall feelings of being valued for their own cultural richness, but the inclusion of such things should constitute just the bare beginnings of multicultural experiences. (Hendrick, 1998, p. 90)

Effective room arrangements take into consideration shelving and storage for materials. Children can exercise initiative, responsibility, and creativity when materials are labeled clearly, organized systematically, and accessed easily. Greenman (1998) summarized the following characteristics for maximizing effective storage:

- Good storage is located close to the point of use.
- Good storage comfortably holds and distinctly displays the contents when open.
- Good storage is the right size and shape for the space.
- Good storage is aesthetically pleasing.
- Good storage has a visible order, clear and understandable to its user.
- Good storage is safe. (p. 78)

Researchers (DeLong, Tegano, Moran, Brickey, Morrow, & Houser, 1991) offered another dimension to consider for placing materials as they compared children's attention spans and levels of play in relation to small and large spaces. The data indicated that in smaller places preschool children "enter complex forms of play more quickly, engage in complex play segments of longer duration and tend to spend a slightly greater percentage of their overall play time in complex play" (p. 8). For classrooms that are large and open, this study has clear suggestions. Dividers and different colored floor areas create smaller spaces within an often overwhelming large setting. Some pieces of equipment and furniture can double as natural dividers or boundaries when thoughtfully placed (see Figure 14.1). Smaller defined spaces can also be created by the use of small rugs within an area; many Montessori schools effectively use this principle

In addition to providing small places within larger spaces, room arrangements offer **private spaces** for children to be alone during emotional regrouping or to take a break from groups and the stimulation of active rooms. Some children arrive at school not quite awake and need a private place to wake up. Other children benefit from a few chosen moments away from groups, just as adults do. Private spaces include areas just for one; a cardboard barrel with a cutaway door and a decorated interior just big enough for a single child is a welcomed addition to all-day child care settings. Niches under a desk or up in a small loft can serve the same purpose.

A special designated private space can be a child's retreat where no one else can enter, not even the teacher.

Effective room arrangement reflects numerous components. It requires the teacher to articulate sound program goals and philosophy. Then the following elements can be thoughtfully woven into the classroom design: layout, traffic patterns, and material selection and equipment location.

Lighting

"Lighting? That's not a matter for teachers," early childhood educators may say. "Lighting is an architect's job; it's determined before teachers first walk into the classroom." This may be the case, but what if research revealed that lighting affects the learning process? Would it then become an educator's issue? Let's investigate how the amount and types of lighting influence the early childhood classroom.

"Few of us choose to live in windowless basements or light our homes uniformly with banks of **fluorescent lighting.** Uniform fluorescent lighting washes out colors and flattens perceptions; there is no focus and all subtlety is lost" (Greenman, 1998, pp. 110–111). In our homes, visual comfort is met by sunlight streaming through windows and bright lights focused on desks and night stands for doing paperwork and reading, whereas a more diffused light is placed on ceilings. How effectively is lighting used as a tool in the early childhood classroom? Are there sufficient windows, and are lights bright in the areas requiring close-up work, such as in the art, manipulative, and language areas? Or is the amount of lighting the same throughout—even in areas where less intensity is required (e.g., cubby, coat storage, or lunch area)?

In the past the artificial lighting systems in schools supplied invariably bright light—the lighting was basically the same throughout the entire school. As lighting becomes appreciated as a teaching tool, educators are looking to challenge this approach; two important facts have been disclosed through research. First, the amount of lighting needed for children's and teachers' comfortable vision depends on the number of windows, the size of the room, and the color of and reflection from the walls, tops of tables, floor, ceiling, and mirrors (Greenman, 1988; Walter, 1996). Second, eye fatigue is reduced when light levels are responsive to the activities within the room and the action required by the activities (Rudd, 1978).

The National Task Force on Day Care Interior Design (1992) noted several environmental recommendations; two apply to lighting. "Storytelling in a lower lighting level can settle children down. It also signals to them a new activity is about to occur and renews their attention" (p. 52). The Task Force also recommended varying the lights—for example, adding soft spotlights to specific areas.

Lighting choice can also contribute to a feeling of homeyness. Try adding a lamp in the check-in area, entrance hall, or director/principal's office to embrace a sense of warmth. Use "wall-mounted sconces or indirect cove lighting" (Walter, 1996, p. 44) to meet varied classroom lighting needs, such as in the reading corner. What about installing a skylight in rooms with limited windows or adding dimmer switches to vary the intensity of overhead lighting?

Now let's turn our attention to some practical information on types of classroom lighting. Three kinds of lighting are traditionally used in classrooms: natural, **incandescent,** and fluorescent. Beginning with natural light, we can observe that most preschool and primary grade classrooms are designed with at least a few windows to let in sunlight. The amount of natural light prescribed by design engineers, however, has fluctuated over the years. In a recent study conducted for California's Energy Efficiency Board and Pacific Gas & Electric (Folmer, 2000), researchers measured the amount of sunlight in classrooms in San Juan Capistrano, California; Seattle, Washington; and Ft. Collins, Colorado and compared the children's scores in reading and math with various levels of sunlight in the classrooms. "Elementary students in classrooms with more natural illuminations scored up to 26% higher on standardized tests in reading and up to 20% higher in math" (pp. B1, B4). Research such as this may have an impact on future schools. Perhaps the decisions for lighting will be made based on pedagogy rather than on past practices, such as those of economics—saving on air-conditioning or heating bills.

Some classrooms, however, cannot be redesigned or renovated to expand the window space. And consider the many schools in Alaska, northern Canada, and Scotland, where the winter sunlight hours are minimal. An alternative source of artificial light has been developed and is now available for home, school, and work use. It's called **full-spectrum lighting,** "yielding the closest solar match in commercially available light, [and] is perhaps the 'state of the art' in present-day lighting technology" (Liberman, 1991, p. 55). Full-spectrum lighting can best be understood by comparing lighting sources using the *color rendering index* (**CRI**). This evaluative measure "was developed to describe how well colors are rendered by artificial light sources compared with natural light" (Mahnke, 1996, p. 122). According to the specifications of the International Commission on Illumination, outdoor sunlight has a perfect CRI of 100, fluorescent full-spectrum 90 and above, fluorescent cool white 62, fluorescent warm white 56, and incandescent light about 40.

Experiments comparing the effects of the various light sources conclude that lighting with high CRI and trace amounts of ultraviolet (UV) provides increased visual acuity, less fatigue, improved academic performance, increased attendance, and decreased hyperactivity (Grangaard, 1993; Hathaway, 1995; Hathaway, Hargreaves, Thompson, & Novitsky, 1992; Küller & Lindsten, 1992; Papa-Lewis & Cornell, 1987; Yizhong, 1984). Imagine assisting the learning process by simply changing the light bulb! One teacher at Banks Street College Family Center reported that she "often left the center with headaches and feelings of fatigue" (Schreiber, 1996, p. 11). When she installed full-spectrum lighting in her classroom, the headaches and fatigue disappeared.

Ultraviolet light (which is present in full-spectrum lighting and sunlight) plays a key role in visual acuity, but because ordinary window glass filters out ultraviolet light (Mahnke, 1996), all classrooms, even ones with large windows, could benefit from full-spectrum lighting. The increased sharpness of black-and-white images in natural and full-spectrum lighting (Duro-test, 1988) has important implications. Print, after all, is black and white. Perhaps full-spectrum light may assist in the development of literacy. Educators can begin by adding full-spectrum lighting to specific rooms or changing the already existing fluorescents to full-spectrum lights.

The early childhood educator can help facilitate positive learning conditions by observing children's vision needs, providing sufficient but not excessive lighting, planning lighting systems with variation, and using full-spectrum lighting.

Visual Appeal

> A school's values are made explicit in the visual "face" that is put forward for the public view. When you enter a school the first sensory impact you may receive is the smell of the disinfectant used to cleanse the halls, but the one that remains longer in memory is the visual information you receive (Fredette, 1994, p. 236).

When children and teachers enter a classroom and spend a great deal of time in it, the visual face of the environment should provide a feeling of balance and comfort so that children can grow in all areas of development. Venolia (1988) suggested that individuals should be "both relaxed and stimulated, reassured and invited to expand" (p. 7). In order to satisfy that request, the indoor environment must have an organized and wisely planned room arrangement, sufficient and appropriate lighting, and pleasing visual appeal. This section has already discussed the first two aspects—room arrangement and lighting. We now turn our attention to the concept of visual appeal.

Certainly, every classroom is different and deserves to be examined on an individual basis. This section is meant to serve as an information base from which the reader can apply general knowledge to specific situations. It is broken down into four parts: color, visual clutter, unity and complexity, and emotional warmth and texture.

Color

"Man responds to form with his intellect and to color with his emotions; he can be said to survive by form and to live by color" (Sharpe, 1974, p. 123). Many have studied the psychological effects of color on people and their behavior (Birren, 1978; Grangaard, 1993; Hamid & Newport, 1989; Torrice & Logrippo, 1989; Wohlfarth, 1981). Architects, educators, hospital administrators, surgeons, optometrists, beauticians, industrialists, and military personnel have applied these findings about color effects to their respective occupations. Scores of fascinating studies have been done on this topic; Hathaway (1982) reviewed several and summarized their results as follows:

- Color can alter perception of temperature, room size, weight, and the passage of time.
- Color can influence work speed, moods, pulse rate, blood pressure, muscle reactions, and psychomotor performance.
- Colors affect our emotions; cool colors (blues and greens) initially relax whereas warm colors (reds and oranges) initially stimulate.

Wohlfarth (1981) found that by changing the standard color and lighting in a classroom of severely handicapped children to a psychodynamically prescribed environment (using a coordinated color scheme and full-spectrum lighting), the children exhibited fewer aggressive behaviors, a significant drop in blood pressure, and a decrease in nonattentive behaviors—indicating that children were more on task in the planned environment.

Based on applied color psychology (Mahnke, 1996), Figure 14.3 enables teachers to begin to apply color associations to early childhood classroom environments.

Color	Effect	Implications for Classroom
Red	Draws attention, can alarm	Large, red butcher paper on table under new materials or new activity
	Suggests strength/importance	Background or letter color on a parent board or notice when a communicable disease or other information needs highlighting
		Background for emergency rules
	Stimulates activity	Motor development equipment, bean bags, and balls
Orange	Stimulates activity	Motor development equipment
	Cheers	Light tints on interior walls
Yellow	Emits light, luminous	The bathroom door or frame around it, yellow line on floor leading to bathroom in young preschoolers' classrooms
		Baskets for completed work in grades K–3
	Cheers	Warm soft tints on interior walls
Green	Reduces muscle tension, reflects nature/growth, refreshes, calms	Water table, play dough Science area accents Room accent color Inside color of a "private space"
Blue	Reduces weight perception (if pale in color)	Baskets for picking up blocks, bean bags
	Reduces time perception	Napping cots
	Calms/comforts	Water table, play dough Rug or cushions in reading corner Inside color of a "private space" Room accent color
Brown	Suggests stability	Natural wood used in high climbing equipment or lofts

Figure 14.3
Color effects and their classroom implications.

Color adds dimensionality to young children's space. It gives them a point of spatial reference, as does shape. Mahnke (1996) reported that "color is the major factor in establishing a desired room experience. It contributes heavily to the 'emotional loading' a space exhibits" (p. 130). The main classroom color choice is the interior color scheme. Many classrooms boast primary colors, assuming that these vivid colors are pleasing to spirited young children. Birren (1972) warns, "When the colors chosen are too bright, the combinations too dramatic, the effect may be wholly out of place, and the observer may actually be distracted from his tasks or made uncomfortable in his environment" (p. 256). Instead, designers and color consultants for young children's classrooms prefer to complement youngster's extroverted nature by using "light salmon, soft, warm yellow, pale yellow-orange, coral, and peach" for walls (Mahnke, 1996, p. 183); accents are in either green or blue shades (calming colors). There are many possible color combinations when balancing both warm and cool colors to equalize the emotional climate and avoid a specific mood. Ideally, the classroom colors blend well together and with the room rather than stand out on their own, grabbing the child's attention when first entering the room. Birren (1972) also warns about neutral white shades for walls.

> Despite the fact that some lighting engineers may freely recommend white and off-white colors for working environments (to gain as much light as possible per watt consumed) the bright environment is quite objectionable. White walls may close the pupil opening, making seeing difficult, and set up annoying distractions. For the sake of 5 or 10 percent increase in lighting efficiency, there may be a drop of 25 percent or more in human efficiency. (pp. 246–247)

Choosing the exact color scheme for the classroom is not a task to be entered into lightly. Aside from consideration for balance of warm and cool colors, several other factors help determine the intensity of color choices. Some of the influences in color selection listed by Walter (1996) are existing equipment colors and architectural features, lighting (including variation in sunlight throughout the day), backdrop colors outside the windows, color reflectance, and room size.

The influence of color in children's environments is just beginning to receive research attention. Watch for new information in this area. When reading on the subject of the psychological effects of color, however, be sure to check the author's sources. Some books and articles are not based on research and cannot support their claims with regard to color.

Visual Clutter

Think about visits to early childhood classrooms. Many have several different colors throughout each room as well as numerous items decorating the walls or hanging from the ceiling, sometimes in disarray.

> Some programs seem kaleidoscopic: one is assaulted by colors and shapes—brightly clad children moving around bright primary colored plastic furniture and toys, encircled by bright graphics, murals, and children's art. Pictures, bright colors, and contrasting shapes are targets for attention. Too many targets create a sensory overload

and exact their toll in fatigue or dulled senses, no matter how acclimated everyone becomes. (Greenman, 1998, p. 111)

When some parents or administrators first walk into a classroom that is overly decorated and filled with bright colors, they often remark, "Isn't this a happy room." This may be the initial reaction, but teachers and children must live in these high-visual-impact environments for many hours each day.

Together, disharmonious colors and numerous, unorganized wall displays can overstimulate and give a circus appearance. Moreover, if teachers laminate materials displayed on the walls, glare results, irritating vision clarity. Thus a case of visual clutter is created.

One study (Tegano, Moran, DeLong, Brickey, & Ramassini, 1996) compared the length of time children spent in play when two walls were covered with either a large geometric pattern or a small geometric pattern. The study concluded that when children felt smaller within their environment (sensation created by a large geometric wall pattern as opposed to a small pattern), they spent less time in play. The question raised by the study is this: Could excessive wall displays not only overstimulate children but also decrease their play duration?

Choosing what to display and where to place selected items is an important consideration when the intent is to avoid visual clutter. As with the pictures in our homes, school wall decorations are best when treated as accessories that help give the message of ownership to the children. Most classrooms, particularly preschool centers, choose children's artwork for wall displays. The sections about creative development in Chapters 3 and 4 made the point that ownership is felt when a child's art is original to the child and not a reproduction of the teacher's model. The realization of this point is reflected in the following example. After cutting out look-alike art patterns for hours on end, one teacher-in-training came to the conclusion, "When I become a teacher, I now know that if I want penguins that look alike for a bulletin board I will buy wallpaper!"

Having chosen wall items appropriately, framing children's work in colors that coordinate with the room scheme helps to unify the overall design and give a calming effect. The wise teacher also places wall displays of children's work or important learning concepts (e.g., alphabet letters or numbers) at the child's eye level. Visual appeal is enhanced when the arrangement of the wall items is ordered in a specific pattern.

Unity and Complexity

"Unity involves various components and parts fitting together into a coherent unit. Complexity involves more variation. Extreme unity (monotony or sensory deprivation) can lead to understimulation, and extreme complexity to overstimulation" (Mahnke, 1996, p. 23). For example, in an early childhood classroom, choosing only blue for carpets, tile, wood trim, and valences would be unifying but boring. Using too many colors throughout would be distracting and fatiguing. Healthy environments strive for harmony through balance.

Unity with variety can be achieved through the use of an appropriate color scheme. For example, walls may be painted different shades of the same color (Colby, 1990). On a lesser scale, mounting pictures in the same size and shape of frames, but using different colors coordinating with the overall color scheme, can also add to the desired effect. Another example is the use of labeling for classroom materials. By using the same size and color of cards for labels in the various centers, unity is accomplished. Changing the way the item is pictured on the label beside the word (e.g., cut out catalog picture, sketch, outline of the item, the item itself) creates variety. Some teachers have augmented harmony as well as autonomy by using colored plastic trays to store materials, color-coding each area (e.g., all art materials classified by item and kept in green trays). The trick here is to keep the color choices within the classroom color scheme; otherwise, the variety of colored trays can contribute to visual clutter.

There is no exact formula for the amount of environmental stimulation children need (Walter, 1996). Each classroom must be continually examined to monitor the need for changes. The goal for interior spaces for children is to reflect safety and comfort and foster development. This goal becomes increasingly important when planning for children who have been exposed to drugs or have attention deficit disorder.

Texture and Warmth

Recall the discussion early on in this chapter about comfortable and uncomfortable places. Did you identify two of the essential comfort qualities as softness and variation in textures? In early childhood classrooms, a simple look around the room can check for applications of softness and variations in texture.

Children applaud softness; it seems to go hand-in-hand with security. Visualize children plopping down on a lap, petting the classroom bunny, or taking their blankets to nap.

> A soft, responsive, physical environment reaches out to children. It helps children feel more secure, enabling them to venture out and explore the world, much like homes provide adults the haven from which they can face an often difficult and heartless world. (Greenman, 1988, p. 74)

In classrooms equipped with colorful, easy-care, durable plastic furniture, softness and texture may be added by introducing a few small rugs, bean bag chairs, oversized floor pillows, cushions for the seats or fabric slipcovers on the backs of the plastic chairs paired with tables, and fire-retardant valances to windows. (Of course, selections are compatible with the classroom color scheme.)

Plants of various sizes can add softness and texture within the early childhood classroom; "the presence of plants can also modulate our indoor atmosphere, influencing temperatures, humidity, and air quality" (Venolia, 1988, p. 130). Many teachers not only integrate plants in the science area but also place them around the room, as we would do in our homes. The use of plants brings living things indoors, enhances the feeling of coziness and homeyness, and adds an opportunity to experience responsibility. Extreme caution must be exercised when selecting plants for the classroom; some have poisonous leaves, bulbs, or other parts.

In discussions of classroom warmth, an important consideration is children's height in relationship to the ceiling. One effective way to visually lower the ceiling to the children's level is to use dados (a decorative wallpaper or paint border) that coordinates with the classroom color scheme. "The best way to determine placement of a dado is to estimate the average height of the children occupying the room. The dado should then be placed one adult-hand's measure above that height" (Center Management Staff, 1990, p. 14).

Another idea in providing psychological warmth and security in the classroom setting is offered by Janina, a primary teacher. While doing home visits, she observes and listens attentively. She watches to identify what the child favors in her or his home that can be added to the classroom. This is a golden opportunity to say to the child, "You are special"; simple ideas help create a magnetic ambience.

"Where noise is a problem, minimize hard, nonporous surfaces such as plaster, glass, concrete, and sheet plastics that reflect sound" (Venolia, 1988, p. 94). Choosing soft, dense materials (e.g., carpet, large area rugs, fabrics on the walls, upholstery, quilts used as wall hangings) can add to comfort levels by helping to reduce the noise level. This is significant in many classrooms that have an institutional design.

Ceilings appear lower and rooms become cozier when dado borders are applied.

OUTDOOR ENVIRONMENTS

More than ever before, the early childhood outdoor play yard of today is of major significance for the healthy development of children (Senda, 1992). At home, parents are often concerned about their children's safety if they are allowed to play outdoors unsupervised. Many children living in cities have small yards or no yards and unsafe parks. In addition, many children are lured into spending their free time inside by an endless supply of computer games, videos, and television programs. With this in mind, Greenman (1993) warned that we are becoming an "indoor culture" (p. 36). Children's time on school playgrounds is therefore highly prized.

This section of the chapter emphasizes the value of outdoor school environments by examining the developmental benefits, the design factors, the teacher's role, and the material and equipment selection. As you read on, keep in mind these wise words: "the best playgrounds are never finished. Rather, they are constantly changing as new challenges replace old ones and as play equipment and materials are used in fresh combinations" (Frost, 1992, p. 102).

Developmental Benefits

"Children demonstrate different abilities in the outdoor setting than they do inside. They may show themselves, for example, to be skilled climbers and balancers, or imaginative large-scale builders" (Hohmann & Weikart, 1995, p. 144). The big difference between indoor and outdoor environments is the amount of opportunities, equipment, and planned experiences for children's gross motor development. Motor activities are emphasized in the outdoor environment because of the greater area per child. "For playgrounds to incorporate active motor play, 100 square feet per child is a reasonable playground minimum" (Greenman, 1988, p. 187). In contrast, recommended minimum space indoors is "35 square feet of usable playroom floor space per child" (National Academy of Early Childhood Programs, 1991a, p. 43).

Outdoor play yards are usually furnished with permanent structures and pieces of movable equipment that promote large motor development. Preschools and kindergartens generally offer swings, climbers, a sandbox, a hard surface for tricycle riding, an empty table or two, and perhaps a slide. Grades 1 through 3 often have climbers, bars, slides, swings, and open spaces for group games in place of riding toys.

Play spaces outside can also be designed to provide opportunities for sensory experiences and emotional, social, and cognitive development (Theemes, 1999). Picture what a play yard looks like as a group of youngsters moves from the indoors to the outdoors. See them gleefully spread out, choosing a variety of activities; some choose to play on permanent equipment or ride those ever-popular tricycles, whereas others choose open-ended materials or activities that have been thoughtfully set up by the teacher. In these activities, children are learning to problem-solve, communicate ideas to one another and adults, improve small motor skills and eye–hand coordination, trust their own ideas, play cooperatively, use their imaginations, expand their vocabularies, recognize similarities and differences, form friendships, overcome fears; and the list goes on and on.

Outdoor play spaces can offer developmental benefits that are difficult to facilitate in the indoor environment. In grades 1 through 3, " it is difficult, for example, in most classrooms to evaluate how a child spontaneously interacts with other children. On the playground, with its natural and free environment, the child as explorer and social being becomes more visible" (Brett, Moore, & Provenzo, 1993, p. 164). On the majority of the playground exuberant play abounds. If, however, nature is incorporated into the setting, a relaxing ambience invites children to slow down the tempo every now and then and take time to wonder, make discoveries about insects and other living things, and have lazy daydreams. Activities that relieve stress, such as fingerpainting, water play, and woodworking can be given larger work spaces and are easy to clean up outside.

The key to maximizing the full range of developmental benefits is providing a variety of equipment, materials, activities, and experiences within a natural setting that are age and individually appropriate.

Outdoor Design Factors

Whether the teacher is embarking on the adventure of designing a new outdoor environment, expanding or renovating an existing yard, or simply observing to evaluate the present condition of the outdoor setting, there are several factors to consider. The basic list that follows is built on this framework: All play yard designs are developed within the shape and size of a given plot of land. Each space has its own unique features, and generally all yard designs have monetary limitations.

- Outdoor arrangements welcome children. Landscaping, such as hills for rolling or climbing and dirt or sand for digging, enhances the developmental processes. Surfaces are varied in texture, shape, and height. Some choices are wood, concrete, sand, grass, dirt, rubber, fabric, brick, or stones.

- Micro-climates are created using vegetation and man-made structures. Children can play in "sunny and shady spots, breezy spaces, still spaces" (Greenman, 1993, p. 40).

- Nature is woven throughout the play space. Incorporating trees, plants, and flowers on playgrounds extends the scope of play; provides shade or winter sunlight (deciduous trees); illustrates the cycle of seasons; assists in surface runoff and erosion control; furnishes a variety of shape and form for the area or entire playground enclosures; contributes sensory variety through plants that differ in texture, color, size, and smell; and supplies gentle indoor–outdoor transitions, gradually exposing the child to a change in light levels (Moore, Goltsman, & Iacofano, 1992). A Swedish study (Lindholm, 1995) found that children between the ages of 6 and 12 participated in more activities in playgrounds that had natural areas than in playgrounds that lacked natural areas.

- The entire outside area is fenced for safety (with secure gates) but allows children to see out.
- Boundaries (e.g., change in ground covering, landscape elevation, use of plants or shrubs) within the designated plot of land define specific areas or play zones.
- Traffic patterns are clear, safe, and direct. Bike paths do not cross pedestrian paths.
- All play zones are easily supervised; no blind spots exist.
- Play zones provide for a variety of physical activity—open spaces for mastering gross motor skills or child-initiated activities and protected quiet spaces for resting, dreaming, or watching. Play zones also provide for a variety of interactions. Spaces are designed for playing in small groups, in pairs, or alone.
- A small "parking lot" near the bike path is designated for returning large wheeled toys (e.g., tricycles, wagons, scooters) when the rider is finished so that vehicles are not left on the path, creating an unsafe condition.
- A variety of sturdy, size-appropriate equipment is provided to accommodate gross motor play activities (e.g., variety of climbing structures, swings), constructive play activities (e.g., woodworking tools, sand), dramatic play activities (e.g., playhouse and props), and group games (e.g., balls, jump rope, follow-the-leader, ring toss) (Frost, 1992).
- Impermanent activities are selected based on children's developmental needs and interests, space, staff, and weather conditions. They are teacher-planned and set up on a daily basis (e.g., small plastic buckets of water and large paintbrushes for wall or sidewalk painting, a blanket under a shade tree and a basket of manipulatives or books brought from the inside, an obstacle course).
- An abundance and variety of equipment and materials are available for different developmental levels, interests, and abilities. Examples are sandbox and water table tools for emptying, filling, and pouring as well as tools that can be used for representing. "Raised sandboxes and garden boxes of different heights can be used by children who have difficulty bending or standing" (White & Coleman, 2000, p. 318). On the primary grade playground, climbing bars, ladders, and structures of varying heights can be available. Consideration should be given to accommodating wheelchairs by offering "wide door and gate openings, ramps, and oversized paths" (White & Coleman, 2000, p. 318).
- Materials, equipment, and experiences in the various play zones offer the children gradual and continuous challenges (Henniger, 1994b).
- All equipment is kept in safe condition; cushioned materials are provided under swings and climbing structures. Sand is kept clean. All plants, flowers, and shrubs are nontoxic. A locked storage facility secures movable equipment when school is not in session.

Teacher's Role

"Teachers, administrators and others generally consider playgrounds and the activities that occur there less important than indoor spaces in the lives of young children" (Henniger, 1994a, p. 87). Moreover, some teachers perceive their roles indoors very differently from their roles outdoors. These teachers spend their planning time focused on indoor activities. When they are outside, they act only as safety supervisors. To support a child's developmental growth both indoors and outdoors, informed teachers base environmental plans on program goals, view the outdoor physical setting as an extension of the indoor setting, and act accordingly. Theemes (1999) suggested the following teaching strategies to enhance outdoor learning opportunities within the framework of safety:

- Encourage children to think about their activities. Adults can assist children in planning their outdoor activities simply by asking them, before or during outdoor time, what they would like to do.
- Observe and note children's interests and activities.
- Provide a variety of toys and materials . . . By offering these materials [loose manipulatives] in addition to the permanent structures on the playground, children have a rich variety of props and objects to inspire and support their play.
- Participate actively in children's play and conversations when appropriate.
- Assist children in resolving conflicts.
- Watch for dangerous situations. Setting limits and having simple, clear rules for children to follow when playing outside will help prevent many hazardous situations; however, adults always need to be alert for unsafe situations as children play.
- Provide sufficient time for play and cleanup" (excerpted from pp. 68–74).

Special emphasis needs to be made regarding the teacher's role in providing a framework of safety—it must be the teacher's number one responsibility. Many schools report that most playground accidents are caused by inappropriate supervision. When play yards are designed so that children are challenged and can take healthy risks, teachers must give the children space to explore yet anticipate possible mishaps, always seeing the big picture.

Outdoor Materials and Equipment Selection

When choosing outdoor equipment and materials, Kritchevsky and Prescott, with Walling (1977) suggested considering both the variety and the complexity of the play units. They defined variety as "the number of different kinds of units" (p. 12) and complexity as "the extent to which they [play units] contain potential for active manipulation and alteration by children" (p. 11). Think about these two points and inspect the two playgrounds pictured in Figure 14.4.

Figure 14.4
Playgrounds. *Top*, preschool;
bottom, primary grade.

Figure 14.4 presents photographs of outdoor play areas not yet set up for a particular day. Before bringing out additional activities or equipment, teachers informally assess the play space by considering the following:

- Equipment or space provisions for children to develop and practice the motor skills of running, hopping, jumping, climbing, balancing, throwing, and catching.

- A variety of climbing equipment (e.g., ropes, ladders, platforms, poles, or nets) and variations of specific kinds of equipment (e.g., tire swings, rope swings, or swings with seats).

- Different levels of difficulty offered through materials and equipment that can be used in simple and complex ways.
- Enough equipment so children won't have long waits for turns. (Long waits rob children of the very purpose of outdoor time.)

When evaluating a play yard, also appraise the open-endedness of the materials. Outdoor yards that supply only simple equipment often entice children to seek out the prized equipment (e.g., tricycles) on a preschool play yard. Several children will race to see who gets them first, and unless the teacher intervenes, a few children may spend the entire outside time cruising bike paths on shiny, pedaled vehicles. In this case, the environment limits the child's chance at well-rounded motor development and sets the stage for much quarreling.

In contrast, if the materials are open-ended and always accessible for children's use, the children will design their own complex units. Materials that can be moved, manipulated, and changed feed developmental needs. Material flexibility and availability, however, make some teachers very nervous. They worry about safety as the children enthusiastically drag materials and build creations. Certainly, watchful supervision and occasional advisement are necessary as children solve problems and create. Greenman (1988), however, cautioned that on playgrounds that have only simple play units, "children will add risk and daring in order to cope with boredom. They will jump off inappropriate equipment like slide ladders, play chicken, and test the limits of people and things" (p. 188).

PRACTICE ACTIVITY 14.1

Outdoor Developmental Opportunities

List additional equipment (fixed or portable) that could be added to the outdoor yards shown in Figure 14.4, and state a brief justification. Think about furthering children's development of gross motor, imagination, creativity, communication, and investigative skills.

Example:

In the preschool yard:

Tire swing—provides variety and promotes the development of coordination, strength and communication.

Garden—promotes the understanding of the growth cycle, provides "an excellent setting for integrating children with and without disabilities" (Moore et al., 1992, p. 142).

1.

2.

3.

4.

This section would not be complete without a discussion of the drinking fountain. Some states have licensing regulations requiring child care centers to have drinking water readily available to young children. Permitting each child to get drinks as needed is preferred to asking the child to wait and then making one long line to get a drink before going inside (recall information on impulse control in Chapter 3). Allowing children free access encourages autonomy and independence as well as good health practices.

OBSERVING THE PHYSICAL ENVIRONMENT

Up to this point, the details of the major elements of the physical environment (indoors and outdoors) have been examined. The importance of various factors in promoting positive learning conditions has been discussed. Now the focus of the chapter shifts to the use of observational strategies in the physical environment.

"From observation, teachers can learn whether more time, space, or play materials are needed, whether certain materials are beyond a child's ability, or if the play situation is not sufficiently stimulating" (Brett et al., 1993, p. 163). Checklists, rating scales, tally event sampling, and time samplings are the observational methods most commonly used for environmental assessments. In previous chapters you have read about these methods and have already had some practice assessing environments (e.g., autonomy in Chapter 8). Using your experiences and the information in this chapter, think for a moment about possible topics for observation of the physical environment and appropriate methods to use in assessment; then proceed to Practice Activity 14.2.

PRACTICE ACTIVITY 14.2

Environmental Observation Topics

This activity has three parts. First, list four possible topics that early childhood teachers could observe either outside or inside. Second, after each topic form a specific observational question. Third, suggest an observational method that could be used to collect information systematically to answer the question.

1) Topic	2) Question	3) Method
Examples:		
Traffic paths	Which traffic paths are used most often, and are they congested or free flowing?	Tally event or time sampling
Safety	Are the outdoor equipment, materials, and environment in safe condition?	Checklist
1.		
2.		
3.		
4.		

Classroom Example

An early childhood art professor enlisted her college students in a variety of class projects. One project, in conjunction with a local school, was to construct a checklist of art materials and make recommendations to the school staff for yearly art supply orders and requests for donations.

Five students eagerly chose this project option. The college students responsibly constructed an art checklist utilizing the guidelines in Chapter 7 and the knowledge gained in their college creative art class. As they selected items to put on the list, they were mindful to choose items that were not so small that the youngest children in the school could swallow them or put them in their ears or noses. Realizing that material choice is often restricted by limited budgets, they included items that can be obtained free-of-charge. Figure 14.5 is the students' form and the results of their art inventory.

Art Materials Inventory

School/Grade: Cypress School/Preschool–Third Grade
Date: 5/15   Time: 4:00 P.M.
Observers: Star, Lalaynia, Clark,   Child/Age: N/A
                       Mihoko, Buffy

Instructions: Check the box in front of the items that the school has in sufficient supply.

Background Materials:
- ☑ Construction paper
- ☑ Poster board/cardboard
- ☐ Butcher paper
- ☑ Fingerpaint paper
- ☑ Watercolor paper
- ☑ Newsprint paper
- ☑ Fabric
- ☐ Aluminum foil
- ☐ Paper plates
- ☑ Clear ConTact
- ☑ Tissue paper
- ☑ Tagboard
- ☐ Computer paper*
- ☐ Lined paper
- ☐ Magazines*

Drawing and Writing Materials:
- ☑ Crayons
- ☑ Pencils/colored pencils
- ☑ Tempera paints
- ☑ Watercolors

- ☑ Fat chalks
- ☑ Markers
- ☑ Shaving cream
- ☑ Fingerpaints
- ☑ Biocolor® paints

Tools for Detaching:
- ☐ Scissors (left- and (right-handed)) *only*

Collage Box Items:
- ☑ Fabric pieces*
- ☑ Paper scraps*
- ☑ Wallpaper samples*
- ☑ Corrugated cardboard scraps*
- ☐ Lace and leather scraps
- ☑ (Ribbons,) yarn, and used gift wrappings* *only*
- ☐ Dried flowers*
- ☐ Carpet/padding scraps*
- ☑ Assorted donations*

(continued)

Figure 14.5
Inventory checklist.

Items for Fastening:
- ☑ Glue and paste
- ☑ Hole punch and yarn
- ☑ Tape/scotch or masking
- ☐ Gummed labels or stickers
- ☐ Pipe cleaners
- ☑ Large plastic needles/thin yarn
- ☑ Clean ConTact

Just for teacher's use

Tools for Painting:
- ☑ 3/4- and 1-inch paintbrushes
- ☑ Watercolor brushes
- ☐ Toothbrushes
- ☑ Dabbers (Cotton wrapped in fabric and attached to tongue depressor with rubber bands)
- ☑ Cotton swabs
- ☑ Feather dusters/feathers
- ☑ Small cars
- ☑ Roll-on deodorant bottles with pop-off lids*
- ☑ Golf balls*

Three-Dimensional Items:
- ☐ Craft sticks
- ☐ Gummed paper strips
- ☐ Clay and plasticine
- ☐ Wood scraps*

- ☑ Styrofoam pieces (all sizes)*
- ☐ Nature items (branches, pine cones, etc.)*
- ☑ Play dough
- ☐ Cardboard cylinder tubes (all sizes)*
- ☐ Small cardboard boxes*
- ☐ Cotton balls
- ☐ Braid and fabric trims*
- ☐ Wooden or plastic spools (all sizes)*
- ☐ Broom straws/drinking straws*
- ☐ Bottle caps*
- ☐ Wood shavings*
- ☐ Rocks*
- ☐ Empty yogurt containers, berry baskets*
- ☐ Feathers

Tools for Printing:
- ☑ Gadgets*
- ☑ Sponges*
- ☑ Items of different shapes*

Other:
- ☑ Easels
- ☑ Smocks
- ☑ Drying area or rack

*Donated or free materials

Comments: *Organizing the supply cupboard by the categories presented above would expedite restocking. Check the usability of markers. No skin-tone crayons, markers, or paints are available.*

Figure 14.5 *(Continued)*
Inventory checklist.

Observational data assist teachers in selecting materials and planning activities.

The Cypress School staff felt fortunate to have the input from the college students. The teachers, however, were surprised to see that they had not considered **three-dimensional materials** prior to the inventory check using a designed list. Coincidentally, the school had only a few items on the three-dimensional shelf; the teachers were acutely embarrassed to admit they had overlooked the importance of obtaining and offering three-dimensional materials for the development of spatial relations and increased opportunities for creative expression. The teachers had never had an organized inventory appraisal form. In fact, they had never used systematic observation to look at the physical environment. Instead, they had used the "Mother Hubbard" approach: look in and see what is or isn't left. The teachers were grateful to have a checklist that would ensure a well-rounded collection of art materials that contribute to a comprehensive developmental program.

>>>

OFF ON YOUR OWN 14.2

Outdoor Environment Assessment

Assess the outside yard of a preschool or kindergarten using Section I of the "Playground Rating System" (Frost, 1992, pp. 107–108) that follows. Utilizing your observation and the information in this chapter on outdoor environments, make suggestions for improvement. State your rationale for suggestions. (*Note:* In Chapter 8, two types of rating scale designs were discussed. This rating scale provides another possible configuration.)

Outdoor Rating Scale

Center/Age level or School/Grade:
Date: Time:
Observer: Teachers:
                                                         Number of Children:

Instructions: Rate each item on a scale from 0–5. High score possible on Section I is 100 points.

Playground Rating System (Ages 3–8)

Section I. What does the playground contain?

Rate each item for degree of existence and function on a scale of 0–5 (0 = not existent; 1 = some elements exist but not functional; 2 = poor; 3 = average; 4 = good; 5 = all elements exist, excellent (function).

_____ 1. A hard-surfaced area with space for games and a network of paths for wheeled toys.

_____ 2. Sand and sand equipment.

_____ 3. Dramatic play structures (play house, car or boat with complementary equipment, such as adjacent sand and water and housekeeping equipment).

_____ 4. A superstructure with room for many children at a time and with a variety of challenges and exercise options (entries, exits, and levels).

_____ 5. Mound(s) of earth for climbing and digging.

_____ 6. Trees and natural areas for shade, nature study, and play.

_____ 7. Zoning to provide continuous challenge; linkage of areas, functional physical boundaries, vertical and horizontal treatment (hills and valleys).

_____ 8. Water play areas, with fountains, pools and sprinklers.

_____ 9. Construction area with junk materials such as tires, crates, planks, boards, bricks, and nails; tools should be provided and demolition and construction allowed.

_____ 10. An old (or built) vehicle, airplane, boat, car that has been made safe, but not stripped of its play value (should be changed or relocated after a period of time to renew interest).

_____ 11. Equipment for active play: a slide with a large platform at the top (slide may be built into a side of a hill); swings that can be used safely in a variety of ways (soft material for seats); climbing trees (mature dead trees that are horizontally positioned); climbing nets.

_____ 12. A large soft area (grass, bark mulch, etc.) for organized games.

_____ 13. Small semi-private spaces at the child's own scale: tunnels, niches, playhouses, hiding places.

_____ 14. Fences, gates, walls, and windows that provide security for young children and are adaptable for learning/play.

_____ 15. A garden and flowers located so that they are protected from play, but with easy access for the child to tend them. Gardening tools are available.

_____ 16. Provisions for the housing of pets. Pets and supplies are available.

_____ 17. A transitional space from outdoors to indoors. This could be a covered play area immediately adjoining the playroom which will protect the children from the sun and rain and extend indoor activities to the outside.

_____ 18. Adequate protected storage for outdoor play equipment, tools for construction and garden areas, and maintenance tools. Storage can be separate: wheel toys stored near the wheeled vehicle track; sand equipment near the sand enclosure; tools near the construction area. Storage can be in separate structures next to the building or fence. Storage should aid in children's picking-up and putting equipment away at the end of each play period.

_____ 19. Easy access from outdoor play areas to coats, toilets, and drinking fountains. Shaded areas and benches for adults and children to sit within the outdoor play area.

_____ 20. Tables and support materials for group activities (art, reading, etc.).

Source: From Complete Playground Rating System in _Play and Playscapes,_ by Joe L. Frost, 1992, Albany, NY: Delmar. Reprinted by permission of Joe L. Frost.

Suggestions: **Rationale:**

1.

2.

3.

4.

> QUICK REVIEW <

1. Significant factors to consider, observe, and assess in the indoor classroom setting are:

   a.

   b.

   c.

2. Important outdoor elements to consider, observe, and assess are:

   a.

   b.

   c.

   d.

3. Room arrangements are best when based on the program _____.

4. Effective room arrangements take into consideration traffic patterns, classroom layout, and material selection and equipment location.

   ❑   True

   ❑   False

5. An artificial light source that has a range of colors similar to sunlight is

   a. halogen.

   b. full-spectrum.

   c. incandescent.

   d. flash light.

6. Three ways to add softness to an indoor environment are:

   a.

   b.

   c.

7. The key to using color in a classroom is to use a balance of _____ and _____ colors.

8. In the outdoor play environment, _____ can be moved, manipulated, and changed, thus feeding developmental needs.

   a. open-ended materials

   b. swings

   c. natural areas

   d. lighting

9. Teachers tend to consider outdoor playground experiences more important than indoor experiences.

   ❑   True

   ❑   False

10. Circle the observational methods most commonly used to assess environments.

   a. running records

   b. anecdotes

   c. checklists

   d. rating scales

   e. ABC narrative event sampling

   f. tally event sampling

   g. time sampling

TAKE A MOMENT TO REFLECT

Personal Reflection

Picture in your mind a real place you go or would like to go when you want to study or do paperwork that requires concentration. Visualize the conditions that surround your choice. Try to be as specific as possible. In addition to the location, analyze the climate. Give attention to colors, lighting and windows, floor coverings, room arrangement, wall decorations, furniture, temperature, and sounds. After you have a clear image of your favorite learning environment ask two or three other people to visualize and describe their preferred place. Compare your findings. Then reflect on the following questions.

1. How are these learning environments alike and different?

2. Reflect on an ideal, imaginary place you would create for studying or doing paperwork that requires concentration. Based on that picture, what additions, deletions, or changes would you recommend for your real place?

Ethical Reflection

NAEYC Ideal I-3A.2 is "to share resources and information with co-workers" (Feeney & Kipnis, 1992, p. 8). Reflect on how the college students and the Cypress School teachers in the classroom example fulfill this ethical responsibility.

Observing Clearly

Chapter 15   Through the Looking Glass

15

Through the
Looking Glass

T.G.I.F.—Friday already, and three good friends and fellow recent graduates with degrees in early childhood education share a monthly dinner. Maliha is teaching young 5-year-olds in a classroom on an elementary school campus. Clay has remained with his beloved parent participation program and is now a teacher, rather than an aide, in the 3- and 4-year-old classroom. Heather is reeling from the exhaustion and exhilaration of adjusting to teaching first grade after doing her student teaching in a university laboratory school.

The three friends catch up, and inevitably the conversation turns to their classrooms and the people who bring them to life. Maliha describes a child who is angry and resentful that she is not in kindergarten with her next-door neighbor and the ABC narrative event sampling results that helped Maliha identify which activities and interactions with other children support the child's self-esteem. Clay relates the uncomfortable entry of a new child with limited English and the exciting plans that resulted from a timely parent conference. Heather shares her feelings of jubilation that her aide now engages in activities with children ever since they agreed to videotape him in the classroom and then view the results together. Think about these remarkable teachers and the role observation plays in their success.

Marian Wright Edelman (1992), a tireless advocate for children, seemed to know Maliha, Clay, and Heather as she wrote: "Focus on what you have, not what you don't have; on what you can do rather than what you cannot do" (p. 102). These teachers bring their knowledge of child development, appropriate curriculum, and observation to a full embrace of their teaching responsibilities. They know in their hearts and minds that their teaching matters to each child in their classrooms. Edelman urges us all to have confidence that we can make a difference. Let this message ring true for the educators of young children who practice observation in their classroom. Let each teacher strive to be remarkable for all the Annies and Songs and Blancas of the world.

So we come to the end of this book and rely on the final chapter to complete and summarize the journey begun in Chapter 1. Our passage followed the introduction of highlights of development during the preschool and primary grade years, methods for observing the development of individual children, and guidelines for organizing portfolios and planning effective parent conferences. The route then turned to methods for observing children and teachers at work in early childhood classrooms and included the processes of selecting and designing observational instruments and enriching environments through observation. As you now stand before the observational looking glass, appreciate your sharp and developed vision.

- Your study of developmental growth indicators and observational methods has strengthened your knowledge of *what* to observe in the early childhood classroom and *how* to observe.

- You understand that observational methods are varied and require specific procedures; choice is driven by the purpose of your inquiry. All methods are equally applicable for preschool and primary grade use.

- Your observations of children, teachers, interactions, programs, and environments are recorded as objectively as possible.

- You are prepared to select a portfolio system and plan parent conferences that enrich home/school partnerships.

- Your proficient applications of the various methods introduced in this book have resulted in satisfying results.

- You understand the processes of designing instruments and analyzing and presenting data that allow teachers to find the answers to specific observational questions.

- Above all, your practice in applications has prepared you to plan for each child's unique growth based on sound observations.

Your well-earned observational skills offer a broad perspective, not readily available to the untrained eye, of children, teachers, and the early childhood classroom. You now enter preschools or primary grade classrooms armed with the ability to recognize and meet each child's individual developmental needs by applying observational methods and planning appropriately. You are able to examine specific classroom questions and concerns using instruments that you designed. Experience will offer additional practice and further refine and mature your observational skills. Here is an account of one teacher's transition:

> In thinking about what my own experience can contribute to ideas about deepening a teacher's understanding about children and teaching, I would probably point to the gradual shift of emphasis from What and how do I teach? to What can I learn about teaching from children? Watching children learn, studying them, documenting what we see and hear, and becoming researchers in our own classrooms gives us the raw materials from which to evolve our own ways of teaching. (Martin, 1994, p. 195)

The greater part of the journey in this book provided an in-depth study of seven different observational methods within the framework of child development (Chapters 5 through 9, 11, and 12). Now is the time to cement together an overall view of observation in the early childhood classroom by clearly comparing the distinctive features of each method. Figure 15.1 provides the mortar, and Practice Activity 15.1 offers some practice.

Method	Subjects	Purpose	Date Produced	Frequency of Use
Running records	Individual children	Observe and document developmental growth; gain overall picture	Qualitative	As necessary
Anecdotes	Individual children	Document developmental growth and significant incidents	Qualitative	Daily
Checklists	Individual children or teachers, programs, and environments	Assess presence or absence of specific characteristics; assess changes over time	Qualitative*	Periodically
Rating Scales	Individual children or teachers, programs, and environments	Assess strengths of specific characteristics; assess changes over time	Qualitative*	Periodically
ABC narrative event sampling	Individual children	Observe specific concerns and developmental growth in context	Qualitative	As necessary
Tally event sampling	Individual children or teachers and groups; programs and environments indirectly	Study frequencies of predetermined events	Qualitative	As necessary
Time sampling	Individual children or teachers and groups; programs and environments indirectly	Study frequencies of events within predetermined time sampling units	Qualitative	As necessary

*This book discussed only the qualitative analysis of checklist and rating scale data. Occasionally you might see quantitative data produced and analyzed when using checklists and rating scales.

Figure 15.1
Comparison of observational methods for early childhood classrooms.

PRACTICE ACTIVITY 15.1

Selecting Observational Methods

Read the following scenarios from early childhood classrooms. Write down an appropriate observational method for responding to each.

Scenario: A preschool teacher, Beverly, realizes she thinks about some children in her classroom more than others and worries that she does not support their growth equally. She asks the director to plan an observation to answer the question, "How frequently does Beverly interact with each child during a preschool session?"

Method:

Scenario: A child has just arrived in Costa's child care program in the middle of the year and is having difficulty adjusting. Costa wants to begin observing his adjustment.

Method:

Scenario: An early childhood education student, Lida, would like to begin to learn about classroom management techniques. She plans to observe several different classrooms in order to answer the question, "How do teachers deal with children's conflicts?"

Method:

THE TEACHER'S COMMITMENT TO OBSERVATION

The ability to understand children through observation might be compared to the ability to judge fine art. We all respond to art—positively, negatively, indifferently—but the person with experience and training can better assess the aesthetic value of a

The benefits of observation return to individual children.

> work of art. Similarly, we all form impressions of children, but for the inexperienced observer, the impression may be inaccurate, biased, or limited in scope. (Phinney, 1982, pp. 23–24)

To best serve the education of all children in a classroom, the teacher demonstrates an active commitment to observation. The wheels of observation do not turn alone. They require the leadership of a teacher willing to plan observations of each child, the program, and the environment. Observation is a continuous process; to successfully integrate observation into the classroom, the teacher builds time into the daily schedule.

Although based on the teacher's commitment and leadership, observation need not be a solitary activity. Teachers will find support by sharing efforts with directors, principals, colleagues, aides, parents, child study teams, and college students. Burdens of scheduling and time allocations are eased by involving the energies of others. The rewards of observation justify the commitment and follow-through of remarkable teachers.

THE BENEFITS OF OBSERVATION IN THE EARLY CHILDHOOD CLASSROOM

The benefits of observation in preschool and primary grade classrooms are plentiful and have been noted throughout this book. Observation serves individual children by providing their teachers with information to chart their developmental growth, plan appropriate activities to support continued growth, uncover the roots of problems, and prepare useful feedback to their parents. Multiple observational methods offer the teacher a realistic view of the whole child. Observation renews the energies of teachers, who can monitor their own effectiveness and make productive adjustments. Observation helps teachers evaluate programs and environments to improve the quality of education offered to children.

In closing, the benefits of observation return to children. All children have individual strengths and emerging interests and aspirations. The headwaters that nourish a vital commitment to a life's work might hardly be noticed during early childhood but, nonetheless, may contribute to later choices. Corey, a young graduate student in Spanish literature, traces his interest in the subject to his experience in a bilingual kindergarten program. Early childhood is a time for initial exploring and experimenting with possible areas of enjoyment and interest. Look beyond the young child for a moment. A complex society such as ours requires the diverse talents of its citizens to function and progress; fostering and supporting individual abilities thus serves society as well as the individual.

How can early childhood educators advance the development of each child? You know:

- By understanding each child as an individual within the context of a family and culture.

And how can these educators learn about each child? You know so well:

- By watching, listening to, and recording what each child does and says.
- By using the information gathered to plan developmentally appropriate experiences and to adjust the program and environment.
- By using a record-keeping system and designing portfolios that bear witness to individuality and then by sharing treasures and concerns with parents.
- By observing through the looking glass with affection, competence, and commitment.

May your vision always be clear as you observe through the looking glass in an early childhood classroom.

TAKE A MOMENT TO REFLECT

Personal Reflection

Over the past 15 years, new advances in microcomputer technology have made assessment and data collection less time-consuming, simpler, more sensitive, and more useful in classroom environments. These microcomputer systems, traditionally geared for researchers, are becoming more "user-friendly" and have important applications for assisting educators in assessment and data summation (Johnson, Brady, & Larson, 1996, p. 254).

As you look toward the future, reflect on the following:

1. Data may be collected using a small hand-held remote control that transmits information to a nearby computer. Speculate on the differences between being an observer in an early childhood classroom with a clipboard and pencil and being an observer with a hand-held remote control easily carried in a pocket.

2. Observers can currently rely on computer programs to collect data using the ABC narrative event sampling, tally event sampling, and time sampling methods. Reflect on your own initial reactions to technology. Think about your own responses to change in general. While studying this book, for example, what were some of your responses to suggested changes in your observation practices? What positive results did you experience when you tried an unfamiliar teaching strategy or observational method? Change is not always easy and comfortable. Reflect on processes that ease transitions toward professional growth and expertise.

Ethical Reflection

The last ideal from NAEYC's Code of Ethical Conduct to consider in this book is I-4.5: "to promote knowledge and understanding of young children and their needs. To work toward greater social acknowledgment of children's rights and greater social acceptance of responsibility for their well-being" (Feeney & Kipnis, 1992, p. 10). Reflect on the critical role of observation in meeting this ideal.

Appendix A
Growth Indicators

PRESCHOOL PHYSICAL DEVELOPMENT

**Growth Indicators of
Gross Motor Development**

Increases competency in running
Increases competency in jumping
Increases competency in hopping
Increases competency in galloping
Increases competency in skipping
Increases competency in climbing
Increases competency in balancing
Increases competency in catching
Increases competency in one-hand throwing
Increases competency in kicking

**Growth Indicators of
Fine Motor Development**

Increases ability to grasp and control small
objects
Increases ability to fasten and unfasten
Increases ability to insert and remove small
pieces
Increases ability to string or lace
Increases ability to cut with scissors

PRIMARY GRADE PHYSICAL DEVELOPMENT

**Growth Indicators of
Gross Motor Development**

Increases strength of legs and arms
Increases speed
Increases coordination
Increases agility
Increases endurance
Increases specialized movement skills in
activities, such as sports, dance, and
recreational games

**Growth Indicators of
Fine Motor Development**

Increases ability to use writing tools, scissors,
and small objects skillfully

Increases ability to arrange numbers and letters
uniformly
Increases eye–hand coordination

PRESCHOOL COGNITIVE DEVELOPMENT

**Growth Indicators of
Representational Abilities**

Forms mental images
Imitates
Uses language
Pretends
Role plays
Represents in two dimensions
Represents in three dimensions
Decodes others' representations

**Growth Indicators of
Language Development**

Advances, but does not complete,
understanding of grammar
Progresses in articulation, but limitations
remain
Expands vocabulary
Constructs increasingly complex sentences
(structure and length)
Converses with increasing competence with
adults and peers

Growth Indicators of Reasoning

Often reasons and problem-solves thoughtfully
Often reasons on the basis of perceptions (not
logic)
Thinks in concrete or tangible terms

**Growth Indicators of
Social Cognition**

Understands that thinking is an internal,
mental process
Understands that others have their own
emotional, social, and cognitive points of
view
Demonstrates limited interpretations of others'
emotional, social, and cognitive points of view

**Growth Indicators of
Classification**

Explores diverse attributes of objects
Recognizes similarities and differences
Sorts objects with increasing sophistication

Growth Indicators of Seriation

Makes comparisons
Seriates a limited number of objects

**Growth Indicators of
Number Development**

Compares quantities of small sets
Learns number names
Understands numbers as representations of
quantities
Counts limited number of objects with one-to-
one correspondence

Growth Indicators of Memory

Remembers by recognizing
Remembers by recalling
Demonstrates individual knowledge

PRIMARY GRADE COGNITIVE DEVELOPMENT

**Growth Indicators of
Representational Abilities**

Expands complexity of preschool growth
indicators
- Forms mental images
- Imitates
- Uses language
- Pretends
- Role plays
- Represents in two dimensions
- Represents in three dimensions
- Decodes others' representations

Decodes and uses abstract symbols (letters and
numbers)

Growth Indicators of Language

Expands vocabulary
Understands there can be literal and figurative
meanings of words
Discerns subtle differences among words
Uses and understands many grammatical rules
and exceptions
Becomes a proficient communicator with
adults and peers
Constructs increasingly complex sentences
(structure and length)
Learns to decode words and comprehend their
meanings

Writes with increasing proficiency

**Growth Indicators of
Logical Thought**

Often reasons flexibly and logically about
tangible problems
Continues to demonstrate concrete thinking

**Growth Indicators of
Metacognition**

Demonstrates increasing knowledge about
people as cognitive processors
Demonstrates increasing knowledge about
cognitive requirements of tasks
Demonstrates increasing knowledge about
cognitive strategies

**Growth Indicators of
Classification**

Sorts and re-sorts objects flexibly and usually
by concrete attributes
Compares whole class with its parts with
increasing accuracy

**Growth Indicators of
Number Development**

Counts increasingly large sets of objects
Understands cardinality
Develops measurement strategies
Adds and subtracts objects and numbers;
begins to multiply and divide

**Growth Indicators of
Memory**

Increasingly uses memory strategies
spontaneously and deliberately
Exhibits early development of metamemory,
including knowledge about people as
rememberers, varying task difficulty, and
appropriate memory strategies
Benefits from increased knowledge base

PRESCHOOL PSYCHOSOCIAL DEVELOPMENT

**Growth Indicators of Expanding
Relationships with Adults and
Peers**

Demonstrates strong attachment to parents and
family

Establishes emotional bonds to nonfamilial
people
Forms friendships
Exhibits concern and empathy

Growth Indicators of Self-Concept

Understands the self has physical and
psychological attributes
Aware of private, thinking self
Overestimates own abilities
Correctly identifies own gender
Often rigidly applies gender roles

Growth Indicators of Play

Explores materials on own
Engages in physical play
Expands social interactions
Engages in dramatic play with increasing
attention to roles, rules, and themes

Growth Indicators of Fears

Fears of real objects, people, and experiences
Fears of the unknown or the imagined

Growth Indicators of Aggression

Instrumental aggression
Hostile aggression
Increasing reliance on communication to settle
disputes

Growth Indicators of Impulse Control

Usually acts before considering consequences
Has difficulty waiting
Makes choices at own developmental level
Benefits from joint activities with adults

PRIMARY GRADE PSYCHOSOCIAL DEVELOPMENT

Growth Indicators of Self-Concept and Self-Esteem

Includes psychological assessment, uncommon
characteristics, and active abilities as well as
concrete characteristics in descriptions of
self and others
Considers group ties as part of self-definition
Does not rigidly adhere to all stereotyped
gender roles

Becomes aware that gender roles are societal
customs
Searches out areas of interest that contribute to
self-esteem
Gains more accurate understanding of
strengths and weaknesses

Growth Indicators of Play

Participates in cooperative play
Participates in and makes up games with rules

Growth Indicators of Moral Reasoning and Prosocial Behavior

Increasingly evaluates the intent of the actor
Increasingly takes into account the relevant
issues of a moral situation
Demonstrates perspective-taking skills in
many, but not all, situations
Expands prosocial behavior

Growth Indicators of Relationships with Peers

Increasingly focuses friendships on loyalty and
intimacy as well as mutual interests
Usually prefers same-gender playmates
Is aware of and sometimes vulnerable to peer-
group influences

PRESCHOOL CREATIVE DEVELOPMENT

Growth Indicators of Creativity

Expands mental flexibility
Expands sensitivity
Expands imagination
Expands risk-taking
Expands resourcefulness
Expands expressiveness and skills using
creative materials

Growth Indicators of Drawing

Preschool stages
Early primary stages

Growth Indicators of Block Play

Stage 1	Child carries blocks around
Stage 2	Child repetitiously makes horizontal (on floor) and vertical stacking rows
Stage 3	Child makes bridges
Stage 4	Child makes enclosures

Stage 5   Child makes elaborate designs using pattern and balance

Stage 6   Child names structures related to their functions

Stage 7   Child reproduces or symbolizes familiar structures with buildings

PRIMARY GRADE CREATIVE DEVELOPMENT

Growth Indicators of Creativity

Expands representations, moving from single idea to interrelated ideas

Expresses individual strengths

Expands flexibility and fluency

Expands sensitivity

Expands imagination

Expands risk-taking

Expands self-resourcefulness

Expands expressiveness and skills using creative materials

Growth Indicators of Drawing

Early primary stage

Middle primary stage

Appendix B

Quick Review Answers

CHAPTER 1

1. vignette
2. True
3. True
4. National Association for the Education of Young Children
5. Association for Childhood Education International
6. Core values in NAEYC's Code of Ethical Conduct

    Appreciating childhood as a unique and valuable stage of the human life-cycle

    Basing our work with children on knowledge of child development

    Appreciating and supporting the close ties between the child and family

    Recognizing that children are best understood and supported in the context of family, culture, community, and society

    Respecting the dignity, worth, and uniqueness of each individual (child, family member, and colleague)

    Helping children and adults achieve their full potential in the context of relationships that are based on trust, respect, and positive regard (Feeney & Kipnis, 1992, p. 2)

7. False
8. differentiated instruction
9. Reasons for observing in the early childhood classroom
    - Chart developmental growth (physical, cognitive, psychosocial, and creative) for each child.
    - Evaluate each child's strengths and limitations from a realistic perspective.
    - Analyze specific problems.
    - Plan appropriate curriculum, materials, responses, strategies, and interactions based on individual needs.
    - Plan responsive environments indoors and outdoors.
    - Maintain records for study teams, conferences, and ongoing feedback to parents.
    - Arrive at a comprehensive understanding of each child or a teacher through the application of several observational methods.
    - Appraise teacher practices, and design staff development.
10. d

CHAPTER 2

1. True
2. observing, recording, planning, communicating
3. flexibility, commitment
4. portfolio
5. b
6. Any two of the following:

    Clarify the purpose of your observation.

    Schedule the visit.

    Come equipped with the necessary materials.

    Select a position from which to observe.

    Note the "lay of the land."

    Check your bias and emotional responses.

    Respond in a natural way to children's inquiries.

7. True
8. a

9. subjective
10. d, seldom

CHAPTER 5

1. True
2. Center or School/Age level or Grade
   Date and time of observation
   Observer
   Child/age
   Teacher
   Assistant teacher
3. b
4. a
5. b
6. False
7. e
8. With her left arm bent at the elbow and fingers spread, the girl spreads paint over her left hand and lower arm with her right hand.
9. runs with short strides
   runs with extended strides
   gallops
   runs with arms held stiffly at sides
   runs with arms pumping
10. b

CHAPTER 6

1. True
2. b
3. qualitative
4. who, what, how, where, and when
5. c
6. planning and parent conferences
7. subjectivity, understanding, ability, commitment
8. d
9. correct. Uses quotes for a language anecdote and records who, what, and how. Recording where and when are not essential.
10. True

CHAPTER 7

1. False
2. True
3. False
4. g

5. Date: Child/Age:
   Observer:
6. False
7. b
8. a device used to collect data, information, and evidence
9. b
10. False

CHAPTER 8

1. quality
2. True
3. observer bias, error of central tendency, ambiguous terms (any two of the three)
4. False
5. b
6. ambiguous
7. error of central tendency
8. programs, environments
9. a
10. True

CHAPTER 9

1. False
2. c
3. False
4. Time, Antecedent Event, Behavior, Consequence
5. a
6. False (See primary grade example)
7. True
8. c
9. True
10. d

CHAPTER 10

1. d
2. card file box, file folder case, notebook
3. True
4. Anecdotal
5. Any three of the following:
   dictated stories
   written stories
   art work
   photographs of block building, science experiences, field trips, dramatic play, and other classroom activities

samples of subject matter assignments (e.g., math)

6. b
7. partnership
8. positive
9. True
10. heart

CHAPTER 11

1. The purpose of tally event sampling is to record how often a behavior or event happens, and the purpose of ABC narrative event sampling is to study the antecedents and the consequences of a behavior or event to unlock the causes.
2. frequently
3. False
4. Quantitative
5. d
6. grid
7. a
8. True
9. context
10. True

CHAPTER 12

1. b
2. False
3. True
4. b
5. a
6. True
7. a
8. True
9. False
10. True

CHAPTER 13

1. b
2. False
3. d
4. d
5. libraries, classrooms
6. pilot testing
7. True
8. False
9. True
10. a

CHAPTER 14

1. room arrangement, lighting, visual appeal
2. developmental benefit, design factors, teacher's role, materials and selection
3. goals
4. True
5. b
6. Any of the following three:
   valances, plants, rugs, bean bag chairs, pillows, cushions, slipcovers over plastic chair backs, pets, blankets
7. warm, cool
8. a
9. False
10. c, d, f, g

Glossary

ABC narrative event sampling
An observational method used to explore the antecedents and consequences of individual children's behaviors within their naturally occurring contexts. Four columns on the recording sheet are labeled *Time, Antecedent Event, Behavior,* and *Consequence.*

Anecdotal record
An observational method used to summarize a single developmental incident after it occurs. The summary recounts *who, what, how,* and sometimes *when* and/or *where.* This method documents incidents involving individual children and groups of children.

Anti-bias curriculum
A proactive approach including materials, experiences, teacher attitudes, and interventions that works toward freeing children of prejudice and stereotypes regarding gender roles, race, culture, handicaps, and social class. It empowers children to like themselves and to respect and appreciate diversity.

Assessment
An appraisal based on observations or other measurements.

Autonomy
An ability to act independently.

Axiom
Principle recognized as truth.

Cardinality
The understanding that the last number counted in a set represents its total number of objects.

Category system
An approach used when selecting the types of items to be observed (e.g., in tally event or time sampling). In this approach all categories must be mutually exclusive, each category must be distinct and separate from the others, and the categories must be exhaustive.

Cephalocaudal
The physical growth pattern characterized by development from head to tail.

Checklist
An observational method containing a register of items that, if present, the observer marks off on a predesigned instrument. This method is used to assess the current characteristics of a child, teacher, curriculum, or environment; to track changes in these characteristics over time; and to support program planning.

Classification
The sorting of objects into classes and subclasses according to similarities and differences.

Closed question
An interrogative that has a single correct answer.

Cognitive development
The changing and expanding intellectual processes of human beings.

Collaborative apprenticeship
The process of peer teaching.

Concurrent time sampling technique
A single time unit stipulates how long the observer observes and records before moving on to the next subject. In other words, observation and coding are done concurrently within the same time unit.

Conference form
The written framework for reporting a child's development and arriving at joint parent/teacher goals.

Conservation
The concept that something remains the same if nothing is added or taken away (includes conservation of number, length, mass, volume, area, and volume displacement).

Cooperative learning group
An assigned number of children given a task to complete together.

Creativity
The process of self-expression as it relates to unique ideas in art, music, movement, drama, and thinking. According to theorists, expressing is creative if it is new to the individual; others may have expressed the same or similar ideas independently.

CRI

The color rendering index is a measure used to compare artificial light sources with natural light; the higher the number, the closer the artificial light shows colors as they would look under natural light. CRI is reported as a percentage.

Cultural diversity

A variety of ethnic and social groups.

Delayed time sampling technique

Identifies two separate time units: the first specifies how long the observer observes and the second how long the observer codes. The observer watches intently through the first time unit and then turns his or her attention to coding; thus, the coding is delayed until after the behavior has been observed.

Descriptors

The adjectives used to rate the items on a rating scale continuum.

Developmentally appropriate

Results from knowledge about "human development and learning, individual characteristics and experiences, and social and cultural contexts" (Bredekamp & Copple, 1997, p. 9).

Differentiated instruction

Instruction that responds to individual children by considering their readiness levels, learning preferences, and interests.

Divergent thinking

Cognitively being open to new alternatives, exploring possibilities, and evaluating information from many perspectives.

Educational practitioner

A trained adult who teaches in a setting for learning.

Environment (physical, indoors)

Refers in general to the room arrangement (layout, traffic patterns, material selection, and equipment location); lighting; and visual appeal (color, visual clutter, unity and complexity, texture and warmth).

Error of central tendency

The inclination for an observer to rate in the middle when using an odd number of descriptors in a rating scale.

Event

An identified behavior or incident.

Fast mapping

A vocabulary-building process through which children add new words to their mental maps of interconnected categories. Initially, children frequently construct limited or erroneous understandings of new words.

Fine motor development

The maturing of small muscles (e.g., fingers).

Fluorescent lighting

An artificial light source in a glass tube that gives off light through the interaction of mercury vapor and electrons.

Full-spectrum lighting

A fluorescent lighting source that has a range of colors similar to that of sunlight.

Gender identity

Knowing one's own gender.

Graphic rating scale

A specific type of rating scale design used to appraise selected characteristics; the observer assigns each item a value on a given horizontal or vertical continuum.

Grid

The graphed box that is formed by the intersection of horizontal rows of categories with vertical columns of categories. A grid is used in tally event sampling and time sampling.

Gross motor development

The maturing of large muscles (e.g., upper arms).

Growth indicators

The markers of development that denote and describe advancement. They are generally the focus for observations.

Halo effect

The susceptibility of an observer to be influenced by preconceived ideas or impressions.

Hand dominance

A preference for the use of the left or the right hand for single-handed tasks.

Help-yourself art shelf

An organized, categorized, and designated low cabinet filled with materials for creating. Children may independently use these materials at their own discretion during free choice times.

Hostile aggression
Aggression in which the intent is to hurt or dominate another.

Impulse control
Self-control of actions and emotions.

Incandescent lighting
An artificial light source in a vacuum bulb.

Inclusive education
An approach embracing children's special needs within the classroom and demonstrating commitment to the values of acceptance, belonging, and community.

Individual Family Services Plan (IFSP)
A multidisciplinary team-written program for the optimal development of a specific handicapped infant, toddler, or preschool child. The program includes support, instruction, and counseling for the family and a comprehensive program for the child.

Individualized Education Plan (IEP)
A team-written instructional program designed for a specific special needs child, based on the child's unique needs, interests, impairment, and abilities. The team usually includes a diagnostic specialist, the teacher, the parent(s), other specified professionals, and the child (if appropriate).

Instrument
(See *Observational instrument*.)

Instrumental aggression
Aggression in which the intent is not to hurt but to gain possession of an object, territory, or privilege.

Integrated curriculum approach
A program design that incorporates all subjects or disciplines around a central topic or theme.

Interest centers
Areas of the room set up around an organizational feature (e.g., housekeeping, manipulatives, blocks).

Inter-rater reliability
The degree of agreement (expressed in a percentage or decimal) between observers when they observe the same setting at the same time using the same instrument.

Journalistic approach
A technique used to select the contents of anecdotes; the observer records the *who, what, how,* and sometimes *when,* and/or *where* of an incident.

Maturation
The process of physical development involving the central nervous system.

Metacognition
Knowledge about thinking, including knowledge about cognitive tasks, cognitive strategies, and people as thinkers.

Metamemory
Knowledge about memory, including knowledge about people as rememberers, varying difficulty of memory tasks, and appropriate memory strategies.

Motor development
The maturing of small and large muscles (fine and gross motor development, respectively); this maturing is characterized by fluid movements.

Mutually exclusive
Items or categories that do not overlap.

Numerical rating scale
A specific type of rating scale design used to appraise selected characteristics; the observer assesses each characteristic by choosing one of the given number values for each item.

Observation
Watching and recording significant behaviors, characteristics, situations, events, or surroundings.

Observational instrument
The predesigned form on which an observer records the data for checklists, rating scales, and tally event and time sampling. The instrument includes a heading, space for data, and other pertinent information (e.g., instructions, definitions, codes, comments).

Observational question
An educational problem or concern to be studied that is stated as an interrogatory.

Observational records
Entries of accounts that have been witnessed and noted.

Observer bias

A prejudice or judgment based on the feelings or impressions of the one who is assessing or recording.

One-to-one correspondence

The ability to count objects in sequence, labeling each object with the correct number.

Open question

An interrogative that has many possible answers and allows the respondent an opportunity to expand and explain.

Operationally defined

A description based on the function of the item.

Overt

Observable and apparent.

Parent conference

An arranged meeting between a teacher and family member(s) for the purpose of establishing a partnership in the child's education to discuss progress and support the child's development.

Pilot testing

The process of trying out an observational instrument to assess its workability.

Portfolio

A collection of observational records and work samples for one child, usually kept for a period of 1 year.

Power words

Child-spoken profanity or words that stretch the acceptable limits within a school environment.

Preschool

Planned learning experiences in a developmental environment for children ages 2 to 5 years old. Usually scheduled for 2½ hours in the morning or afternoon.

Primary grade

Kindergarten through third grade.

Private spaces

Areas in a classroom designed to be big enough for a single child and used as a child-chosen retreat.

Process approach to creativity

A belief that creativity is the result of possessing abilities and having conditions that allow for practice and improvement.

Prosocial behavior

Behavior that reflects a concern for others (e.g., cooperating, helping, sharing, comforting, and interacting positively with others).

Proximodistal

Physical growth pattern characterized by development from the center of the body to the outside.

Psychosocial development

The changes in human beings involving self-understanding, emotions, personality, and social relationships.

Qualitative data

Information that yields narrative results.

Quantitative data

Information that yields numerical results.

Rating scale

An observational method in which the observer, using a predesigned instrument, selects a value for each of the listed characteristics. This method is used to evaluate specific characteristics of a child, teacher, curriculum, or environment and monitor changes over time.

Recall memory

Remembering without a cue being present.

Recognition memory

Remembering by recognizing something familiar.

Recording form

A document used to collect observational data (e.g., running records or ABC narrative event sampling).

Record-keeping system

An organizational method used for systematically storing observations.

Representational thought

The cognitive ability to allow a mental symbol, word, or object to stand for something else (e.g., a child's drawing may represent a house).

Representative sample

A sample is representative when it has "approximately the characteristics of the population relevant to the research in question" (Kerlinger & Lee, 2000, pp. 165–166).

Running record

An observational method used to explore the development of individual children; the observer writes a detailed, factual, sequential narrative of events in progress and adds a brief (summary of development) conclusion.

Sample
A subset of data to represent the behaviors or events under investigation.

Sampling behaviors or events
The process of collecting a subset of data to represent the behaviors or events under investigation.

Scaffolding
A metaphor to describe the necessary assistance for children's learning within the zone of proximal development that is responsive to their individual developmental levels.

Self-concept
The psychological construct of the self, nourished by expanding cognitive and social maturity.

Self-esteem
The evaluative component of the sense of self, deriving from the warmth, acceptance, and respectful treatment given a child and from the child's success in selected areas of interest.

Seriation
Arranging objects in order along one characteristic (e.g., arranging four pieces of sandpaper from smooth to rough).

Sign system
An approach used when selecting the types of items to be observed (e.g., in tally event or time sampling). In this approach all categories must be mutually exclusive, but they do not need to be exhaustive.

Social cognition
Thinking and knowledge about humans and human affairs, such as their desires, emotions, intentions, visual perspectives, and thoughts.

Systematized
Organized in an orderly fashion.

Tally event sampling
An observational method used to systematically record the frequency of occurrence for an identified behavior or situation within a designated period. This method collects quantitative data about children, teachers, or interactions on a predesigned instrument.

Technological records
Media for maintaining data other than paper and pencil (e.g., videotape, computer diskette).

Thematic units
A curriculum approach that integrates all content areas by organizing instructional objectives, materials, and activities around a specific topic or theme.

Theory of mind
An expanding understanding of human mental processes, one's own and others' mental states, mental activities, perceptions, and emotions.

Three-dimensional materials
Items that have depth (e.g., cylinders, wood blocks).

Time sampling
An observational method used to methodically investigate behaviors that occur in rapid succession. Predetermined units of time and a recording grid guide the observer's collection of quantitative data on a predesigned instrument dealing with children, teachers, or groups. Time sampling units may be specified by the concurrent or delayed time sampling techniques.

Trait approach to creativity
A belief that creativity is innate and unfolds in a natural fashion.

Vignette
A short story or scenario.

Visual acuity
Clarity of sight.

Visual appeal (classroom)
Pleasing and comfortable to the eyes.

Zone of proximal development
The hypothetical, dynamic distance between the level of children's independent functioning and the level of their functioning with the help of adults or more competent peers.

References

ACEI. (2000). *Association for Childhood Education International.* Retrieved November 15, 2000, from http://www.acei.org.

Adams, M. J., Treiman, R., & Pressley, M. (1998). Reading, writing, and literacy. In W. Damon (Ed.), *Handbook of child psychology* (5th ed.) (Vol. 4, pp. 275–355). New York: Wiley.

Alkin, M. C., with Linden, M., Noel, J., & Ray, K. (Eds.). (1992). *Encyclopedia of educational research* (6th ed.). New York: Macmillan.

Allen, K. L., & Marotz, L. R. (1999). *Developmental profiles: Pre-birth through eight* (3rd ed.). Albany, NY: Delmar.

Amabile, T. M. (1989). *Growing up creative: Nurturing a lifetime of creativity.* New York: Crown.

Anderson, C. (2000). *How's it going? A practical guide to conferring with student writers.* Portsmouth, NH: Heinemann.

Bandura, A., Barbaranelli, C., Caprara, G. V., & Pastorelli, C. (1996). Multifaceted impact of self-efficacy beliefs on academic functioning. *Child Development, 67,* 1206–1222.

Baratta-Lorton, M. (1995). *Mathematics their way.* Menlo Park, CA: Addison-Wesley.

Bell, D., & Low, R. M. (1977). *Observing and recording children's behavior.* Richland, WA: Performance Associates.

Bem, S. (1989). Genital knowledge and gender constancy in preschool children. *Child Development, 60,* 649–662.

Benelli, C., & Yongue, B. (1995). Supporting young children's motor skill development. *Childhood Education, 71,* 217–220.

Benjamin, A. C. (1994). Observations in early childhood classrooms: Advice from the field. *Young Children, 49,* 14–19.

Bergen, D. (1997). Using observational techniques for evaluating young children's learning. In B. Spodek & O. Saracho (Eds.), *Issues in early childhood assessment and evaluation.* (Vol. 7, pp. 108–128). New York: Teachers College Press.

Berger, K. S. (2000). *The developing person through childhood and adolescence* (5th ed.). New York: Worth.

Berger, K. S., & Thompson, R. A. (1995). *The developing person through childhood and adolescence* (4th ed.). New York: Worth.

Berk, L. E., & Winsler, A. (1995). *Scaffolding children's learning: Vygotsky and early childhood education.* Washington, DC: National Association for the Education of Young Children.

Billman, J., & Sherman, J. (1996). *Observation and participation in early childhood settings.* Needham Heights, MA: Allyn & Bacon.

Birren, F. (1972). *Color psychology and color therapy.* New York: University Books.

Birren, F. (1978). *Color and human response.* New York: Van Nostrand Reinhold.

Bishop, A., Yopp, R. H., & Yopp, H. K. (2000). *Ready for reading: A handbook for parents of preschoolers.* Boston: Allyn & Bacon.

Bloom, L. (1998). Language acquisition in its developmental context. In W. Damon (Ed.), *Handbook of child psychology* (5th ed.) (Vol. 2, pp. 309–370). New York: Wiley.

Boehm, A. E. (1992). Glossary of assessment terms. In L. R. Williams & D. P. Fromberg (Eds.), *Encyclopedia of early childhood education* (pp. 218–293). New York: Garland.

Boehm, A. E., & Weinberg, R. A. (1997). *The classroom observer: Developing observation skills in early childhood settings* (3rd ed.). New York: Teachers College Press.

Borg, W. R., & Gall, M. D. (1989). *Educational research: An introduction* (5th ed.). White Plains, NY: Longman.

Boutte, G. (1999). *Multicultural education: Raising consciousness.* Belmont, CA: Wadsworth.

Brause, R. S., & Mayher, J. S. (1991). Collecting and analyzing classroom data in theory and in practice. In R. S. Brause & J. S. Mayher (Eds.), *Search and re-search: What the inquiring teacher needs to know* (pp. 131–156). Bristol, PA: Falmer Press.

Brazelton, T. B. (1992). *Touchpoints: Your child's emotional and behavioral development.* Reading, MA: Perseus.

Brazelton, T. B., & Greenspan, S. I. (2000). *The irreducible needs of children.* Cambridge, MA: Perseus.

Bredekamp, S. (1992). What is "developmentally appropriate" and why is it important? *Journal of Physical Education, Recreation, and Dance, 63,* 31–32.

Bredekamp, S., & Copple, C. (Eds.). (1997). *Developmentally appropriate practice in early childhood programs* (rev. ed.). Washington, DC: National Association for the Education of Young Children.

Bredekamp. S., & Rosegrant, T. (1992). Reaching potentials: Introduction. In S. Bredekamp & T. Rosegrant (Eds.), *Reaching potentials: Appropriate curriculum and assessment for young children* (Vol. I, pp. 2–8). Washington, DC: National Association for the Education of Young Children.

Bredekamp, S., & Shepard, L. (1998). Assessing young children's learning and development. In R. Brandt (Ed.), *Assessing student learning: New rules, new realities.* Arlington, VA: Educational Research Service.

Brett, A., Moore, R., & Provenzo, E. Jr. (1993). *The complete playground book.* Syracuse, NY: Syracuse University Press.

Bronson, M. B. (2000). Recognizing and supporting the development of self-regulation in young children. *Young Children, 55,* 32–37.

Brown, J. R., & Dunn, J. (1996). Continuities in emotion understanding from three to six years. *Child Development, 67,* 789–802.

Brown, K. W., Cozby, P. C., Kee, D. W., & Worden, P. E. (1999). *Research methods in human development* (2nd ed.). Mountain View, CA: Mayfield.

Buell, L. H. (1984). *Understanding the refugee Vietnamese.* San Diego: Los Amigos Research Associates.

Burton, A. W. (1992). The development of movement skills. *Early Report, 19,* 3–4.

Burts, D. C., Hart, C. H., Charlesworth, R., Fleege, P. O., Mosley, J., & Thomasson, R. H. (1992). Observed activities and stress behaviors of children in developmentally appropriate and inappropriate kindergarten classrooms. *Early Childhood Research Quarterly, 7,* 1–17.

Bussey, K. (1999). Children's categorization and evaluation of different types of lies and truths. *Child Development, 70,* 1338–1347.

Calkins, L. (1994). *The art of teaching writing* (new ed.). Portsmouth, NH: Heinemann.

Calkins, L., with Bellino, L. (1997). *Raising lifelong learners: A parent's guide.* Reading, MA: Addison-Wesley.

Carlo, G., Koller, S., Eisenberg, N., DaSilva, M., & Frohlich, C. B. (1996). A cross-national study on the relations among prosocial moral reasoning, gender role orientations, and prosocial behaviors. *Developmental Psychology, 32,* 231–240.

Carlson, K., & Cunningham, J. L. (1990). Effect of pencil diameter on the graphomotor skill of preschoolers. *Early Childhood Research Quarterly, 5,* 279–293.

Center Management Staff. (1990, September/October). Design: Keep the kids in mind. *Center Management, 10,* 12, 14–15.

Chi, M. H. T. (1978). Knowledge structures and memory development. In R. S. Siegler (Ed.), *Children's thinking: What develops?* (pp. 73–96). Hillsdale, NJ: Erlbaum.

Coie, J. D., & Dodge, K. A. (1998). Aggression and antisocial behavior. In W. Damon (Ed.), *Handbook of child psychology* (5th ed.) (Vol. 3, pp. 779–862). New York: Wiley.

Colby, B. (1990). *Color and light: Influences and impact.* Glendale, CA: Author.

Coopersmith, S. (1967). *The antecedents of self-esteem.* San Francisco: Freeman.

Corbin, C. B. (1980). *A textbook of motor development.* Dubuque, IA: Wm. C. Brown.

Cozby, P. C. (1997). *Methods in behavioral research* (6th ed.). Mountain View, CA: Mayfield.

Cratty, B. J. (1986). *Perceptual and motor development in infants and children* (3rd ed.). Upper Saddle River, NJ: Merrill/Prentice Hall.

Crosswhite, L. (1995). *A guide to a shared reading experience.* Jacksonville, IL: Permabound.

Csikszentmihalyi, M. (1996). *Creativity: Flow and the psychology of discovery and invention.* New York: HarperCollins.

Cutting, A. L., & Dunn, J. (1999). Theory of mind, emotion understanding, language, and family background: Individual differences and interrelations. *Child Development, 70,* 853–865.

Dahl, R. (1998). *The BFG.* Harmondsworth, UK: Puffin Books.

Davis, G. A., & Rimm, S. B. (1998). *Education of the gifted and talented* (4th ed.). Upper Saddle River, NJ: Merrill/Prentice Hall.

DeLoache, J. S., Miller, K. F., & Pierroutsakos, S. L. (1998). Reasoning and problem solving. In W. Damon (Ed.), *Handbook of child psychology* (5th ed.) (Vol. 2, pp. 801–850). New York: Wiley.

DeLong, A. J., Tegano, D. W., Moran, J. D. III, Brickey, J., Morrow, D., & Houser, T. L. (1991, July/August). Effects of spatial scale on cognitive play in preschool children. *ASID Report,* pp. 8–9.

Derman-Sparks, L. (1994). Empowering children to create a caring culture in a world of differences. *Childhood Education, 70,* 66–71.

Derman-Sparks, L. (1999). Markers of multicultural/antibias education. *Young Children, 54,* 43–46.

Derman-Sparks, L., & A.B.C. Task Force (1989). *Antibias curriculum: Tools for empowering young children.* Washington, DC: National Association for the Education of Young Children.

Diffily, D., & Fleege, P. O. (1992). *Portfolio assessment: Practical training in evaluating the progress of kindergarten and primary grade children in individualized portfolio formats.* Houston, TX: Texas Association for the Education of Young Children. (ERIC Document Reproduction Services no. ED 354082.)

Diffily, D., & Fleege, P. O. (1993). *Sociodramatic play: Assessment through portfolio.* Fort Worth, TX: Alice Carlson Applied Learning Center. (ERIC Document Reproduction Service no. ED 354079.)

Dixon, G. T., & Chalmer, F. G. (1990). The expressive arts in education. *Childhood Education, 67,* 12–17.

Dooley, D. (1990). *Social research methods* (2nd ed.) . Upper Saddle River, NJ: Merrill/Prentice Hall.

Dunn, J., Brown, J. R., & Maguire, M. (1995). The development of children's moral sensibility: Individual differences and emotional understanding. *Developmental Psychology, 31,* 649–659.

Duro-Test (1988). *A guide for simulating natural light in interior environments to maximize the quality of working life.* Fairfield, NJ: Author.

Eccles, J. S., Wigfield, A., Harold, R. D., & Blumenfeld, P. (1993). Age and gender differences in children's self- and task perceptions during elementary school. *Child Development, 64,* 830–847.

Edelman, M. W. (1992, May). Letter to my sons. *Parents,* 98–102.

Edelman, M. W. (1999). *Lanterns: A memoir of mentors.* Boston: Beacon Press.

Edwards, C., Gandini, L., & Forman, G. (Eds.). (1993). *The hundred languages of children: The Reggio Emilia approach to early childhood education.* Norwood, NJ: Ablex.

Eisenberg, N., & Fabes, R. A. Prosocial development. In W. Damon (Ed.), *Handbook of child psychology* (5th ed.) (Vol. 3, pp. 701–778). New York: Wiley.

Eisenberg, N., Guthrie, I. K., Murphy, B. C., Shepard, S. A., Cumberland, A., & Carlo, G. (1999). Consistency and development of prosocial dispositions: A longitudinal study. *Child Development, 70,* 1360–1372.

Eisner, E. (1998). *The enlightened eye: Qualitative inquiry and the enhancement of educational practice.* Upper Saddle River, NJ: Merrill/Prentice Hall.

Elkind, D. (1994). *Ties that stress: The new family imbalance.* Cambridge, MA: Harvard University Press.

Elkind, D. (1998). *Reinventing childhood: Raising and educating children in a changing world.* Rosemont, NJ: Modern Learning Press.

Elkind, D. (2001). *The hurried child* (3rd ed.). Cambridge, MA: Perseus.

Engle, B. S. (1995). *Considering children's art: Why and how to value their works.* Washington, DC: National Association for the Education of Young Children.

Fabes, R., & Martin, C. L. (2000). *Exploring child development: Transactions and transformations.* Boston: Allyn & Bacon.

Feeney, S., Christensen, D., & Moravcik, E. (2001). *Who am I in the lives of young children?: An introduction to teaching young children* (6th ed.). Upper Saddle River, NJ: Merrill/Prentice Hall.

Feeney, S., & Kipnis, K. (1992). *Code of ethical conduct & statement of commitment*. Washington, DC: National Association for the Education of Young Children.

Feldman, D. H. (1980). *Beyond universals in cognitive development*. Norwood, NJ: Ablex.

Feldman, D. H. (1999). The development of creativity. In R. J. Sternberg (Ed.), *Handbook of creativity* (pp. 169–186). Cambridge, UK: Cambridge University Press.

Fisher, S. (1995). The child and the learning environment. *Early Childhood News, 7*, 4–37.

Flavell, J. H., Green, F. L., Flavell, E. R., & Grossman, J. B. (1997). The development of children's knowledge about inner speech. *Child Development, 68*, 39–47.

Flavell, J. H., Green, F. L., Flavell, E. R., & Lin, N. T. (1999). Development of children's knowledge about unconsciousness. *Child Development, 70*, 396–412.

Flavell, J. H., & Miller, P. H. (1998). Social cognition. In W. Damon (Ed.), *Handbook of child psychology* (5th ed.) (Vol. 2, pp. 851–898). New York: Wiley.

Flavell, J. H., Miller, P. H., & Miller, S. A. (1993). *Cognitive development* (3rd ed.). Upper Saddle River, NJ: Merrill/Prentice Hall.

Follmi, O. (1989, December). Journey to knowledge. *Life*, 109–116.

Folmer, K. (2000, January 10). Brighter in the daylight. *LA Times*, Orange County section, B1, B4.

Framer, J. F. (1994). Defining competence as readiness to learn. In S. G. Goffin & D. E. Day (Eds.), *New perspectives in early childhood teacher education: Bringing practitioners into the debate* (pp. 29–36). New York: Teachers College Press.

Fredette, B. W. (1994). Use of visuals in schools. In D. M. Moore & F. M. Dwyer (Eds.), *Visual literacy: A spectrum of visual learning* (pp. 235–256). Englewood Cliffs, NJ: Education Technology Publications.

Freeman, Y., & Freeman, D. (1991). Portfolio assessment: An exciting view. *Bilingual Education Office Outreach, 2*, 7.

Frost, J. L. (1992). *Play and playscapes*. New York: Delmar.

Gallahue, D. L. & Cleland, F. (2002). *Developmental physical education for today's children* (3rd ed.). Champaign, IL: Human Kinetics.

Gallahue, D. L., & Ozmun, J. C. (1998). *Understanding motor development: Infants, children, adolescents, adults* (4th ed.). New York: McGraw-Hill.

Gardner, H. (1980). *Artful scribbles: The significance of children's drawings*. New York: Basic Books.

Gardner, H. (1999). *The disciplined mind: What all students should understand*. New York: Simon & Schuster.

Gaustad, J. (1996). Assessment and evaluation in the multiage classroom. *OSSC Bulletin, 39*, 28–41. (ERIC Document Reproduction Service no. ED 392149.)

Geary, D. C. (1994). *Children's mathematical development*. Washington, DC: American Psychological Association.

Genishi, C., McCarrier, A., & Nussbaum, N. R. (1988). Research currents: Dialogue as a context for teaching and learning. *Language Arts, 65*, 182–191.

Getty Center for Education in the Arts. (1985). *Beyond creativity: The place for art in America's schools*. Los Angeles: J. Paul Getty Trust.

Ginsburg, H. P., Klein, A., & Starkey, P. (1998). The development of children's mathematical thinking: Connecting research with practice. In W. Damon (Ed.), *Handbook of child psychology* (5th ed.) (Vol. 4, pp. 401–476). New York: Wiley.

Goleman, D. (1995). *Emotional intelligence*. New York: Bantam.

Golinkoff, R. M., Hirsh-Pasek, K., Bailey, L. M., & Wenger, N. R. (1992). Young children and adults use lexical principles to learn new nouns. *Developmental Psychology, 28*, 99–108.

Gonzalez-Mena, J. (1997). *Multicultural issues in child care* (2nd ed.). Mountain View, CA: Mayfield.

Gordon, A. M., & Williams Browne, K. (2000). *Beginnings and beyond* (4th ed.). Albany, NY: Delmar.

Grangaard, E. (1993). *Effects of color and light on selected elementary students*. (Doctoral dissertation). Las Vegas: University of Nevada–Las Vegas. (ERIC Document Reproduction Service no. ED. 383445.)

Greenman, J. (1988). *Caring spaces, learning places: Children's environments that work.* Redmond, WA: Exchange Press.

Greenman, J. (1993). It ain't easy being green. *Child Care Information Exchange, 91,* 36–40.

Greenman, J. (1998). *Places for childhoods: Making quality happen in the real world.* Redmond, WA: Exchange Press.

Hamid, N. P., & Newport, A. G. (1989). Colour of reading material and performance decrement. *Perceptual and Motor Skills, 74,* 689–690.

Harms, T., & Clifford, R. M. (1989). *Family day care rating scale.* New York: Teachers College Press.

Harms, T., Clifford, R. M., & Cryer, D. (1998). *Early childhood environment rating scale* (rev. ed.). New York: Teachers College Press.

Harms, T., Cryer, D., & Clifford R. M. (1990). *Infant/toddler environment rating scale.* New York: Teachers College Press.

Harms, T., Jacobs, E. V., & White, D. R. (1996). *School-age environment rating scale.* New York: Teachers College Press.

Harter, S. (1998). The development of self-representations. In W. Damon (Ed.), *Handbook of child psychology* (5th ed.) (Vol. 3, pp. 553–617). New York: Wiley.

Hartup, W. W. (1992). Peer relations in early and middle childhood. In V. B. Van Hasselt & M. Hersen (Eds.), *Handbook of social development: A lifespan perspective* (pp. 257–281). New York: Plenum.

Hathaway, W. E. (1982, September). *Lights, window, color: Elements of the school environment.* Paper presented at the Council of Educational Facility Planners 59th annual conference, Columbus, OH.

Hathaway, W. E. (1995). Effects of school lighting on physical development and school performance. *Journal of Educational Research, 88,* 228–241.

Hathaway, W. E., Hargreaves, J. A., Thompson, G. W., & Novitsky, D. (1992). *A study into the effects of light on children of elementary school age—a case of daylight robbery.* (Unpublished paper.) Edmonton, Alberta, Canada: Planning and Information Services Division.

Healy, J. M. (1999). *Endangered minds: Why children don't think—and what we can do about it.* New York: Touchstone.

Heidemann, S., & Hewitt, D. (1992). *Pathways to play.* St. Paul, MN: Redleaf Press.

Helm, J. H., Beneke, S., & Steinheimer, K. (1998). *Windows on learning: Documenting young children's work.* New York: Teachers College Press.

Hendrick, J. (1998). *Total learning: Developmental curriculum for the young child* (5th ed.). Upper Saddle River, NJ: Merrill/Prentice Hall.

Hendrick, J. (2001). *The whole child: Developmental education for the early years* (7th ed.). Upper Saddle River, NJ: Merrill/Prentice Hall.

Henniger, M. L. (1994a). Enriching the outdoor play experience. *Childhood Education, 70,* 87–90.

Henniger, M. L. (1994b). Planning for outdoor play. *Young Children, 49,* 10–15.

Herberholz, B., & Hanson, L. (1995). *Early childhood art* (5th ed.). Dubuque, IA: Wm. C. Brown.

High/Scope Educational Research Foundation. (1992). *Teacher's manual of the COR.* Ypsilanti, MI: High/Scope Press.

Hintze, J. M., & Shapiro, E. S. (1995). Best practices in the systematic observations of classroom behavior. In A. Thomas & J. Grimes (Eds.), *Best practices in school psychology—III* (pp. 651–660). Washington, DC: National Association of School Psychologists.

Hirsch, E. S. (Ed.). (1996). *The block book* (3rd. ed.). Washington, DC: National Association for the Education of Young Children.

Hohmann, M, & Weikart, D. P. (1995). *Educating young children: Active learning practices for preschool and child care programs.* Ypsilanti, MI: High/Scope Press.

Hopkins, D. (1993). *A teacher's guide to classroom research* (2nd ed.). Bristol, PA: Open University Press.

Husén T., & Postlethwaite, T. N. (Eds.) (1994). *International encyclopedia of education* (Vol. 8, pp. 4923–4930). New York: Elsevier Science.

Jablon, J. R., Dombro, A. L., & Dichtelmiller, M. L. (1999). *The power of observation.* Washington, DC: Teaching Strategies.

Jalongo, M. R., & Stamp, L. N. (1997). *The arts in children's lives: Aesthetic education in early childhood.* Boston: Allyn & Bacon.

Jenkins, J. M., & Astington, J. W. (2000). Theory of mind and social behavior: Causal models tested in a longitudinal study. *Merrill-Palmer Quarterly, 46*(2), 203–220.

Johnson, H., Brady, S. J., & Larson, E. (1996). A microcomputer-based system to facilitate direct observation data collection and assessment in inclusive settings. *Journal of Computing in Childhood Education, 7*, 253–269.

Kagan, J., & Gall, S. (Eds.). (1998). *The Gale encyclopedia of childhood & adolescence.* Detroit: Gale Research.

Kalverboer, A. F., Hopkins, B., & Geuze, R. (Eds.). (1993). *Motor development in early and later childhood: Longitudinal approaches.* New York: Press Syndicate of the University of Cambridge.

Kapel, D. E., Gifford, C. S., & Kapel, M. B. (1991). *American educators' encyclopedia.* New York: Greenwood Press.

Katz, L. G., & McClellan, D. E. (1997). *Fostering children's social competence: The teacher's role.* Washington, DC: National Association for the Education of Young Children.

Kerlinger, F. N., & Lee, H. B. (2000). *Foundations of behavioral research* (4th ed.). Fort Worth, TX: Harcourt Brace.

Kettman, S. (1994). *Family-friendly childcare.* Waco, TX: WRS Publishing.

Kochanska, G., Murray, K., & Coy, K. C. (1999). Inhibitory control as a contributor to conscience in childhood: From toddler to early school age. *Child Development, 68*, 263–277.

Kochanska, G., Padavich, D. L., & Koenig, A. (1996). Children's narratives about hypothetical moral dilemmas and objective measures of their conscience: Mutual relations and socialization antecedents. *Child Development, 67*, 1420–1436.

Koster, J. B. (2001). *Growing artists: Teaching art to young children* (2nd ed.). Albany, NY: Delmar.

Kreutzer, M. A., Leonard, C., & Flavell, J. H. (1975). An interview study of children's knowledge about memory. *Monographs of the Society for Research in Child Development, 40*(1, serial no. 159).

Kritchevsky, S., Prescott, E., with Walling, L. (1977). *Planning environments for young children: Physical space.* Washington, DC: National Association for the Education of Young Children.

Küller, R., & Lindsten, C. (1992). Health and behavior of children in classrooms with and without windows. *Journal of Environmental Psychology, 12*, 305–317.

Ladd, G. W., Birch, S. H., & Buhs, E. S. (1999). Children's social and scholastic lives in kindergarten: Related spheres of influence? *Child Development, 70*, 1373–1400.

Ladd, G. W., & Coleman, C. C. (1993). Young children's peer relationships: Forms, features, and functions. In B. Spodek (Ed.), *Handbook of research on the education of young children* (pp. 57–76). New York: Macmillan.

Ladd, G. W., Kochenderfer, B. J., & Coleman, C. C. (1996). Friendship quality as a predictor of young children's early school adjustment. *Child Development, 67*, 1103–1118.

Lawler, S. D. (1991). *Parent-teacher conferencing in early childhood education.* Washington, DC: National Education Association of the United States.

Leavitt, R. L., & Eheart, B. K. (1991). Assessment in early childhood programs. *Young Children, 46*, 4–9.

Lee, K., & Cameron, C. A. (2000). Extracting truthful information from lies: Emergence of the expression-representation distinction. *Merrill-Palmer Quarterly, 46*(1), 1–20.

Leppo, M. L., Davis, D., & Crim, B. (2000, Spring). The basics of exercising the mind and body. *Childhood Education*, 142–147.

Liberman, J. (1991). *Light medicine of the future.* Sante Fe, NM: Bear.

Linderman, M. G. (1997). *Art in the elementary school* (5th ed.). Madison, WI: Brown & Benchmark.

Lindholm, G. (1995). Schoolyards: The significance of place properties to outdoor activities in schools. *Environment and Behavior, 27*, 259–293.

Lobel, T. E., & Menashri, J. (1993). Relations of conceptions of gender-role transgressions and gender constancy to gender-typed preferences. *Developmental Psychology, 29*, 150–155.

Lovett, S. B., & Flavell, J. H. (1990). Understanding and remembering: Children's knowledge about the differential effects of strategy and task variables on comprehension and memorization. *Child Development, 61*, 1842–1858.

Lowenfeld, V., & Brittain, W. L. (1987). *Creative and mental growth* (8th ed.). New York: Macmillan.

Maccoby, E. E. (1980). *Social development.* New York: Harcourt Brace Jovanovich.

Maccoby, E. E. (1990). Gender and relationships: A developmental account. *American Psychologist, 45,* 513–520.

Maccoby, E. E. (1992). The role of parents in the socialization of children: An historical overview. *Developmental Psychology, 28,* 1006–1017.

Maccoby, E. E. (1998). *The two sexes: Growing up apart, coming together.* Cambridge, MA: Belknap Press.

MacDonald, S. (1996). *The portfolio and its use: A road map for assessment.* Little Rock, AK: Southern Early Childhood Association.

Mahnke, F. H. (1996). *Color, environment, and human response.* New York: Van Nostrand Reinhold.

Mann, J., Ten Have, T., Plunkett, J. W., & Meisels, S. J. (1991). Time sampling: A methodological critique. *Child Development, 62,* 227–241.

Marshall, N. L., Robeson, W. W., & Keefe, N. (1999). Gender equity in early childhood education. *Young Children, 54,* 9–13.

Martin, A. (1994). Deepening teacher competence through skills of observation. In S. G. Goffin & D. E. Day (Eds.), *New perspectives in early childhood teacher education: Bringing practitioners into the debate* (pp. 95–108). New York: Teachers College Press.

Maslow, A. H. (1970). *Motivation and personality* (2nd ed.). New York: Harper & Row.

Mayesky, M. (1998). *Creative activities for young children* (6th ed.). Albany, NY: Delmar.

McAfee, O., & Leong, D. (1997). *Assessing and guiding young children's development and learning* (2nd ed.). Needham Heights, MA: Allyn & Bacon.

McCormick, E. J., & Ilgen, D. (1980). *Industrial psychology.* Upper Saddle River, NJ: Merrill/Prentice Hall.

McCutcheon, G. (1981). On the interpretation of classroom observations. *Educational Researcher, 10,* 5–10.

McKernan, J. (1991). *Curriculum action research.* New York: St. Martin's Press.

Measell, J. R., Ablow, J. C., Cowan, P. A., & Cowan, C. P. (1998). Assessing young children's views of their academic, social and emotional lives: An evaluation of the self-perception scales of the Berkeley Puppet Interview. *Child Development, 69,* 1556–1576.

Medinnus, G. (1976). *Child study and observation guide.* New York: Wiley.

Mertens, D. M. (1998). *Research methods in education and psychology: Integrating diversity with quantitative and qualitative approaches.* Thousand Oaks, CA: Sage.

Milburn, S., & Gotthoffer, D. (2000). *Quick guide to the Internet for child development.* Needham Heights, MA: Allyn & Bacon.

Mindes, G., Ireton, H., & Mardell-Czudnowski, C. (1996). *Assessing young children.* Albany, NY: Delmar.

Moore, R. C., Goltsman, S. M., & Iacofano, D. S. (Eds.). (1992). *Play for all guidelines: Planning, design, and management of outdoor play setting for all children* (2nd ed.). Berkeley, CA: Communications.

NAEYC. (2000). National Association for the Education of Young Children. Retrieved November 15, 2000, from http://www.naeyc.org.

National Academy of Early Childhood Programs. (1991a). *Accreditation criteria & procedures of the National Academy of Early Childhood Programs* (rev. ed.). Washington, DC: National Association for the Education of Young Children.

National Academy of Early Childhood Programs. (1991b). *Guide to accreditation* (rev. ed). Washington, DC: National Association for the Education of Young Children.

National Association for the Education of Young Children and the National Association of Early Childhood Specialists in State Departments of Education. (1991). Guidelines for appropriate curriculum content and assessment in programs serving children age 3 through 8, a joint position statement. *Young Children, 46,* 21–38.

National Task Force on Day Care Interior Design. (1992). *Design of the times: Day care.* Seattle, WA: Dan B. Spinelli.

Nilsen, B. A. (1997). *Week by week: Plans for observing and recording young children*. Albany, NY: Delmar.

Page, R. M., Frey, J., Talbert, R., & Falk, C. (1992). Children's feelings of loneliness and social dissatisfaction: Relationship to measures of physical fitness and activity. *Journal of Teaching in Physical Education, 11*, 211–219.

Papa-Lewis, R., & Cornell, C. (1987). Selecting the best lighting for your school facility. *School Business Affairs, 53*, 32–35.

Papalia, D. E., Olds, S. W., & Feldman, R. D. (1999). *A child's world: Infancy through adolescence* (8th ed.). Burr Ridge, IL: WCB/McGraw-Hill.

Parten, M. B. (1932). Social participation among preschool children. *Journal of Abnormal and Social Psychology, 27*, 243–269.

Paton, S. (1995). *Cry, the beloved country*. New York: Scribner.

Payne, V. G., & Isaacs, L. D. (1999). *Human motor development: A lifespan approach* (4th ed.). Mountain View, CA: Mayfield.

Pellegrini, A. D. (1996). *Observing children in their natural worlds: A methodological primer*. Mahwah, NJ: Erlbaum.

Petrakos, H., & Howe, N. (1996). The influences of the physical design of the dramatic play center on children's play. *Early Childhood Research Quarterly, 11*, 63–77.

Phinney, J. S. (1982). Observing children: Ideas for teachers. *Young Children, 37*, 16–24.

Pipher, M. (1996). *The shelter of each other: Rebuilding our families*. New York: Ballantine Books.

Poest, C. A., Williams, J. R., Witt, D. D., & Atwood, M. (1990). Challenge me to move: Large muscle development in young children. *Young Children, 45*, 4–9.

Poysner, L. R. (1983). *An examination of the classroom physical environment*. Unpublished research paper. Indiana University, South Bend.

Presbury, J. H., Benson, A. J., & Torrance, E. P. (1997). Creativity. In G. G. Bear, L. M. Minke, & A. Thomas (Eds.), *Children's needs III: Development, problems and alternatives* (pp. 449–467). Bethesda, MD: National Association of School Psychologists.

Pressley, M., & Schneider, W. (1997). *Introduction to memory development during childhood and adolescence*. Mahwah, NJ: Erlbaum.

Rhodes, L., & Nathenson-Mejia, S. (1992). Anecdotal records: A powerful tool for ongoing literacy assessment. *Reading Teacher, 45*, 502–509.

Rockwell, R. E., Andre, L. C., & Hawley, M. K. (1996). *Parents and teachers as partners: Issues and challenges*. Orlando, FL: Harcourt Brace.

Rody, M. (1995). A visit to Reggio Emilia. *Early Childhood News, 7*, 14–16.

Rogoff, B. (1998). Cognition as a collaborative process. In W. Damon (Ed.), *Handbook of child psychology* (5th ed.) (Vol. 2, pp. 679–744). New York: Wiley.

Rothbart, M. K., & Bates, J. E. (1998). Temperament. In W. Damon (Ed.), *Handbook of child psychology* (5th ed.) (Vol. 3, pp. 105–176). New York: Wiley.

Rubin, K. H., Bukowski, W., & Parker, J. G. (1998). Peer interactions, relationships, and groups. In W. Damon (Ed.), *Handbook of child psychology* (5th ed.) (Vol. 3, pp. 619–700). New York: Wiley.

Ruble, D. N., & Martin, C. L. (1998). Gender development. In W. Damon (Ed.), *Handbook of child psychology* (5th ed.) (Vol. 3, pp. 933–1016). New York: Wiley.

Rudd, A. (1978). What to look for in classroom lighting. *American School and University, 51*, 45, 48.

Ruffman, T. (1999). Children's understanding of logical inconsistency. *Child Development, 70*, 872–886.

Russ, S. W. (1996). Development of creative processes in children. In M. A. Runco (Ed.), *Creativity from childhood through adulthood: The developmental issues* (pp. 31–42). San Francisco: Jossey-Bass.

Rylant, C. (1992). *When I was young in the mountains*. New York: Dutton Children's Books.

Santrock, J. W. (2001). *Child development* (9th ed.). Burr Ridge, IL: McGraw-Hill.

Scherer, M. (1996). On our changing family values: A conversation with David Elkind. *Educational Leadership, 53*, 4–9.

Schirrmacher, R. (1998). *Art and creative development for young children* (3rd ed.). Albany, NY: Delmar.

Schneider, W., & Bjorklund, D. R. (1998). Memory. In W. Damon (Ed.), *Handbook of child psychology* (5th ed.) (Vol. 2, pp. 467–521). New York: Wiley.

Schneider, W., & Pressley, M. (1997). *Memory development between two and twenty* (2nd ed.). Mahwah, NJ: Erlbaum.

Schreiber, M. E. (1996). Lighting alternatives: Considerations for child care centers. *Young Children, 51,* 11–13.

Senda, M. (1992). *Design of children's play environments.* New York: McGraw-Hill.

Serbin, L. A., Powlishta, K. K., & Gulko, J. (1993). The development of sex typing in middle childhood. *Monographs of the Society for Research in Child Development, 53*(2, serial no. 232).

Shaffer, D. R. (1999). *Developmental psychology: Childhood and adolescence* (5th ed.). Pacific Grove, CA: Brooks/Cole.

Sharpe, D. T. (1974). *The psychology of color and design.* Chicago: Nelson-Hall.

Shores, E. F., & Grace, C. (1998). *The portfolio book: A step-by-step guide for teachers.* Beltsville, MD: Gryphon House.

Siegler, R. S. (2000). The rebirth of children's learning. *Child Development, 71,* 26–35.

Silverman, I. W., & Ragusa, D. M. (1990). Child and maternal correlates of impulse control in 24-month-old children. *Genetic, Social, and General Psychology Monographs, 116,* 435–473.

Smith, L., Kuhs, T. M., & Ryan, J. M. (1993). *Assessment of student learning in early childhood education.* Columbia, SC: South Carolina Center for Excellence in the Assessment of Student Learning. (ERIC Document Reproduction Service no. ED 358163.)

Sovik, N. (1993). Development of children's writing performance: Some educational implications. In A. F. Kalverboer, B. Hopkins, & R. Geuze (Eds.), *Motor development in early and later childhood: Longitudinal approaches* (pp. 229–246). New York: Cambridge University Press.

Stallings, J. A., & Mohlmar, G. G. (1990). Observation techniques. In H. J. Walberg & G. D. Haertel (Eds.), *The international encyclopedia of educational evaluation* (pp. 639–643). Elmsford, NY: Pergamon.

Stipek, D., Feiler, R., Daniels, D., & Milburn, S. (1995). Effects of differential instructional approaches on young children's achievement and motivation. *Child Development, 66,* 209–223.

Stoddart, T., & Turiel, E. (1985). Children's concepts of cross-gender activities. *Child Development, 56,* 1241–1252.

Stormshak, E. A., Bierman, K. L., Bruschi, D., Dodge, K. A., Coie, J. D., & the Conduct Problems Prevention Research Group. (1999). The relation between behavior problems and peer preference in different classroom contexts. *Child Development, 70,* 169–182.

Sylwester, R. (1995). *A celebration of neurons: An educator's guide to the human brain.* Alexandria, VA: Association for Supervision and Curriculum Development.

Tegano, D. W., Moran, J. D. III, DeLong, A. J., Brickey, J., & Ramassini, K. K. (1996). Designing classroom spaces: Making the most of time. *Early Childhood Education Journal, 23,* 135–141.

Theemes, T. (1999). *Let's go outside! Designing the early childhood playground.* Ypsilanti, MI: High/Scope.

Torrice, A. F., & Logrippo, R. (1989). *In my room.* New York: Ballantine.

Tull, C. Q. (1994). Preserving commitment to teaching and learning. In S. G. Goffin, & D. E. Day (Eds.), *New perspectives in early childhood teacher education: Bringing practitioners into the debate* (pp. 108–119). New York: Teachers College Press.

Venolia, C. (1988). *Healing environments.* Berkeley, CA: Celestial Arts.

Vergeront, J. (1987). *Places and spaces for preschool and primary (indoors).* Washington, DC: National Association for the Education of Young Children.

Vygotsky, L. S. (1987). *Thinking and speech.* N. Minick (Trans.). New York: Plenum.

Waber, B. (1999). *An anteater named Arthur.* Topeka, KS: Econo-Clad Books.

Walter, M. B. (1996). *The beneficial use of color and light in child care environments.* Unpublished thesis, International Association of Color Consultants. San Diego, CA.

Wasserman, S. (1991). Serious play in the classroom: How messing around can win you the Nobel Prize. *Childhood Education, 68*(3), 133–139.

Wellman, H. M., & Hickling, A. K. (1994). The mind's "I": Children's conception of the mind as an active agent. *Child Development, 65,* 1564–1580.

Wellman, H. M., Hollander, M., & Schult, C. A. (1996). Young children's understanding of thought bubbles and thoughts. *Child Development, 67,* 768–788.

Werner, E. E., & Smith, R. S. (1982). *Vulnerable but invincible: A study of resilient children.* New York: McGraw-Hill.

Wheeler, P., & Haertel, G. D. (1993). *Resource handbook on performance assessment and measurement.* Berkeley, CA: Owl Press.

White, C. S., & Coleman, M. (2000). *Early childhood education: Building a philosophy of teaching.* Upper Saddle River, NJ: Merrill/Prentice Hall.

Willis, S., & Mann, L. (2000). *Differentiating instruction: Finding manageable ways to meet individual needs* (excerpt). Association for Supervision and Curriculum Development. Retrieved April 15, 2001, from http://www.ascd.org/readingroom/cupdate/2000/1win.html.

Witt, J., Heffer, R., & Pheiffer, J. (1990). Structured rating scales: A review of self-report and informant rating processes, procedures, and issues. In C. R. Reynolds & R. W. Kamphaus (Eds.), *Handbook of psychological and educational assessment of children: Personality, behavior, and context* (pp. 364–394). New York: Guilford.

Wohlfarth, K. (1981). *The effects of color/light changes on severely handicapped children* (Unpublished paper.) Alberta, Canada: University of Edmonton, Alberta Education.

Wolfgang, C. H., & Wolfgang, M. E. (1992). *School for young children: Developmentally appropriate practices.* Boston: Allyn & Bacon.

Yizhong, Z. (1984). Effects of color rendering properties of light sources on visual acuity. *Acta Psychologic Sinica, 16,* 193–203.

York, S. (1991). *Roots and wings: Affirming culture in early childhood programs.* St. Paul, MN: Redleaf Press.

Zahn-Waxler, C., & Smith, K. D. (1992). The development of prosocial behavior. In V. B. Van Hasselt & M. Hersen (Eds.), *Handbook of social development: A lifespan perspective* (pp. 229–256). New York: Plenum.

Index

ABC narrative event sampling, 201–221
  applications, 216–218
  description, 203–204
  guidelines for, 205–207
  preschool example, 207–211
  primary grade example, 211–216
  purpose, 205
Aggression, 63–65, 374
Anecdotal records, 135–157
  applications, 151–153
  description, 136–138
  guidelines for, 140–141
  preschool example, 144–147
  primary grade example, 147–150
  purpose, 138–140
  reasons for, 150–151
Authentic assessment, 12–13
Axioms, 36

Block play
  preschool growth indicators of, 74, 374
  time sampling and, 291–292, 299–301
Body growth
  preschool years, 34
  primary grade years, 78
Brain development, 34–35

Category system, 261, 263
Checklists, 159–179
  applications, 172–173
  description, 160–161
  guidelines for, 163–165
  preschool example, 165–169
  primary grade example, 169–172
  purpose, 161–163

Child portfolios, 224–235
  children's storage choices, 232–234
  description, 225–226
  guidelines for, 234–235
  teacher's storage choices, 226–232
Classification
  preschool years, 53–54, 372
  primary grade years, 92–93, 373
Code of Ethical Conduct, 10. *See also* Ethical conduct in early childhood education.
Cognitive development
  preschool years, 44–58, 372–373
  primary grade years, 85–95, 373
Concurrent time-sampling technique, 280
Conference form, 236
Conferences. *See* Parent conferences
Creative development
  preschool years, 67–74, 374–375
  primary grade years, 104–109, 375
Creativity, 67, 68, 106, 374, 375

Delayed time-sampling technique, 280
Descriptors, 181
Developmentally appropriate practice, 8–9
Differentiated instruction, 12
Documentation, for parent conferences, 240–241
Drawing, 72, 108, 374, 375

Environment. *See* Physical environment

Error of central tendency, 187
Ethical conduct, in early childhood education, 9–10, 14–15, 31, 75, 110, 133, 157, 176, 198, 221, 252, 271, 303, 327, 361, 371
Events, 256. *See also* ABC narrative event sampling; Tally event sampling; Time sampling.

Fast mapping, 47
Fears, 62–63, 64, 374
Fine motor skills
  preschool years, 36, 40–44, 372
  primary grade years, 81–82, 83, 372
Full-spectrum lighting, 340–341

Gender identity, 60
Graphic rating scale, 181
Gross motor skills
  preschool years, 36, 37–40, 372
  primary grade years, 79–81, 82, 372
Growth indicators
  adult-child relationships, 60, 373–374
  aggression, 65, 374
  block play, 74, 374–375
  classification, 54, 93, 372, 373
  creativity, 68, 106, 374, 375
  drawing, 72, 108, 374, 375
  fears, 64, 374
  fine motor development, 41, 83, 372
  gross motor development, 37–39, 82, 372
  impulse control, 66, 374
  language, 48, 88, 372, 373
  logical thought, 90, 373

memory, 58, 95, 373
metacognition, 91, 373
moral reasoning, 100, 374
number development, 56, 94, 373
peer relationships, 60, 102, 373–374
play, 63, 99, 374
prosocial behavior, 100, 374
reasoning, 50, 372
representational abilities, 46, 86, 372, 373
self-concept, 61, 98, 374
self-esteem, 98, 374
seriation, 55, 373
social cognition, 52, 372
Guidelines
ABC narrative event sampling, 205–207
anecdotal records, 140–141
checklists, 163–165
child portfolios, 234–235
designing and using observational instruments, 306
observation, 23–25
parent conferences, 241–243
rating scales, 185–186
running records, 115, 117–121
tally event sampling instruments, 260, 271–272
time sampling, 281, 283–286, 298–299

Halo effect, 173, 195–196
Hostile aggression, 64

Impulse control, 65–67, 374
Individual Family Service Plan (IFSP), 224
Individualized Education Plan (IEP), 224
Indoor environments, 330–332
lighting, 339–341
room arrangement, 332–339
visual appeal, 341–346
Instrumental aggression, 64
Inter-rater reliability, 261, 311, 313–315

Journalistic approach, 137

Language
preschool years, 47–50, 372

primary grade years, 86–89, 373
Logical thought, 89–91, 373

Memory
preschool years, 56–58, 373
primary grade years, 94–95, 373
Metacognition, 91–92, 373
Mind, theory of, 51
Moral reasoning, 98, 100–101, 374
Motor development
preschool years, 35–36
primary grade years, 78, 83–85

Narrative event sampling. See ABC narrative event sampling
Number development
preschool years, 55–56, 373
primary grade years, 92–93, 94, 373
Numerical rating scale, 180

Observational categories, 309–310
Observational questions, formulating, 306–308
Observer bias, 195–196
Organizations, professional, 7–8
Outdoor environments, 347
design factors, 348–349
developmental benefits, 347–348
materials and equipment selection, 350–353
teacher's role, 350

Parent conferences, 235–252
applications, 243–247
evaluation of, 250
facilitating, 238–239
guidelines for, 241–243
practice activities, 248–249
preparation and content, 235–238
supporting documentation, 240–241
videotapes and, 243
Peer relationships

preschool years, 58–59, 60, 373–374
primary grade years, 101–102
Physical development
preschool years, 34–44, 372
primary grade years, 78–85, 372
Physical environment, 329–330
indoor, 330–346
observing, 353–359
outdoor, 347–353
Pilot testing, 311
Play
preschool years, 61–62, 63, 374
primary grade years, 97, 99, 374
Portfolios, 18. See also Child portfolios
Preschool years
ABC narrative event sampling, 207–211
anecdotal records, 144–147
checklists, 165–169
cognitive development, 44–58, 372–373
creative development, 67–74, 374–375
physical development, 34–44, 372
psychosocial development, 58–67, 373–374
rating scales, 186–190
running records, 122–126
tally event sampling, 260–270
time sampling, 286, 288–292
Primary grade years
ABC narrative event sampling, 211–216
anecdotal records, 147–150
checklists, 169–172
cognitive development, 85–95, 373
creative development, 104–109, 375
physical development, 78–85, 372
psychosocial development, 96–104, 374
rating scales, 190–194
running records, 126–128
tally event sampling, 270–271, 273
time sampling, 292–299

behavior
school years, 59
primary grade years, 98,
100–101, 374
Proximal development. *See*
Zone of proximal
development
Psychosocial development
preschool years, 58–67,
373–374
primary grade years, 96–104,
374

Qualitative data, 114. *See also*
ABC Narrative event
sampling; Anecdotal
records; Checklists; Rating
scales; Running records.
Quantitative data. *See* Tally
event sampling; Time
sampling

Rating scales, 179–198
applications, 194–196
description, 180–184
guidelines for, 185–186
preschool example,
186–190
primary grade example,
190–194
purpose, 185
Reasoning
moral, 98, 100–101, 374
preschool years, 50–51, 372
Recall memory, 56

Recognition memory, 56
Records. *See* Anecdotal records;
Running records
Relationships. *See* Adult-child
relationships; Peer
relationships; Prosocial
behavior
Reliability, inter-rater, 261, 311,
313–315
Representational abilities
preschool years, 45–46, 372
primary grade years, 85,
86, 373
Representative sample, 203
Running records, 113–133
applications, 129
description, 114
guidelines for, 115, 117–121
preschool example, 122–126
primary grade example,
126–128
purpose, 115, 116–117

Sampling, 202–203. *See also* ABC
narrative event sampling;
Tally event sampling; Time
sampling
Self-concept
preschool years, 59–61, 374
primary grade years, 96–97,
98, 374
Self-esteem, 96–97, 98, 374
Seriation, 54–55, 373
Sign system, 261, 263
Social cognition, 51–53, 372

Specimen records. *See* Running
records
Stress management, 103–104
Subjectivity, 25–29
Supporting documentation, for
parent conferences,
240–241

Tally event sampling,
255–277
applications, 273–274
description, 256–259
guidelines for, 260–261
preschool example, 260–270
primary grade example,
270–271, 273
purpose, 259
Theory of mind, 51
Three-dimensional materials,
357
Time sampling, 279–303
applications, 299
description, 280–281, 282
guidelines for, 299–301
preschool example, 286,
288–292
primary grade example,
292–299
purpose, 281

Videotapes, for parent
conferences, 243

Zone of proximal development,
47, 49, 66, 87, 100, 151